Long Journey to Justice

Critical Human Rights

Scott Straus & Tyrell Haberkorn, Series Editors; Steve J. Stern, Editor Emeritus

Books in the series Critical Human Rights emphasize research that opens new ways to think about and understand human rights. The series values in particular empirically grounded and intellectually open research that eschews simplified accounts of human rights events and processes.

Long Journey to Justice

El Salvador, the United States, and Struggles against Empire

Molly Todd

The University of Wisconsin Press

The human rights theme is not a humanitarian issue today but rather a political one.

—J. R., San José Las Flores, Chalatenango

It was quite a difficult time in our country due to the repression by the government. . . .
Sister cities were seen as more than an attempt for economic support; they were for political
support. . . . The U.S. invested a million dollars a day in financing this war. Therefore, the sister
cities were made up of North American citizens in order to pressure their government into not
continuing to invest in the killing of the Salvadoran people. The other objective was to denounce
all of the human rights violations that the Salvadoran government had been committing . . .
against civilians just because they lived in conflict zones. Therefore, the sister cities played an
important strategic role in the entire process of repopulation. . . . Now [after the war] the sister
cities no longer exist for the purpose of repopulation but rather for the strengthening of the social
organization in the rural zone and the development of the communities. In this manner, they
[continue] the struggle but on a different level. . . . They are able to support in strategic ways.
And I believe that it will continue being a very important relationship to maintain.

—Isabel Hernández, cofounder, Christian Committee for the Displaced of El Salvador

If Trump's message is poison, the antidote is sistering. Instead of building walls, we build bridges,
learn to walk in each other's shoes. We've done it for thirty years. It is as relevant now as it was then.

—Dennis Chinoy, Bangor-Carasque Sister City Project

Contents

Illustrations

Peace pins. (Photo by the author)

Preface

The Past in the Present

n one of my early memories, I am in a crowd of people flowing down the Summit Avenue hill toward the Capitol building in St. Paul, Minnesota. My mother marches beside me and although she does not carry a sign, she wears her favorite jean jacket, a canvas of pins proclaiming peace: *Women Against Military Madness*; *Freeze Nuclear Weapons*; *Minnesota Women's Peace Camp*; *Not Our Children, Not Their Children*; *Civil Disobedience Is Civil Defense*. I stick close enough to her, except for one frightening moment when my red superball jolts out of my control on the bridge over Interstate 94. I bound after it and manage to clinch its rubberiness in my hand just as it finds a space between parapets. To this day I can still feel the mix of relief and dread: What would have happened if I had not stopped that red orb, if it had continued on its path between concrete barriers to bomb down an innocent person below?

The same sentiments inspired my mother's presence at that protest march in downtown St. Paul. Her fears, however, centered not on a child's toy but on man's weapons of war. More specifically she was concerned about the actions of the new US president, a screen actor-turned-politician named Ronald Reagan, who restarted production of neutron bombs; sent lethal military aid to Central American dictators; declared the so-called War on Drugs, leading to the mass incarceration of African American men; and cut social programs for Vietnam veterans, single mothers, and others who found themselves in hard times.

I did not fully understand any of this at the time. In fact, sometimes I perceived a kind of fun with it all. One pin Mom wore depicted a bottle of ketchup alongside Reagan's cartoonish mug. NUTRITION QUIZ read the pin, "Which one is the vegetable?" (a play on how his administration's deregulation frenzy reached into the public school system). And a little book that floated around our house featured a colorful cover and stories about a hundred monkeys working together to build peace.

But that book, *The Hundredth Monkey* by Ken Keyes Jr., also warned of nuclear warfare—a message that echoed through the "duck and cover" nuclear strike drills I survived at Randolph Heights Elementary School. And it bled into the moments when our grainy black-and-white television featured Reagan's visage and voice alongside images from war-torn areas of the world—the same moments when Mom launched from her chair and fled the living room, exclaiming, "I just can't *stand* it!"

Even if I did not understand the nuances, I sensed something was wrong. Really wrong.

Fast forward a couple of decades to another memory. I am a doctoral student in history at the University of Wisconsin–Madison. While tracing the backstory of the Madison–Arcatao Sister City Project—one of the organizations that figures prominently in this book—I discover an open letter to the president of El Salvador, Alfredo Cristiani, published on October 19, 1992, in the Salvadoran news outlet *Co-Latino*. The authors of the letter, "civic leaders in the United States," express "serious concern" about the Cristiani administration's "grave delays in complying with the Peace Accords" that brought the country's civil war to an end nine months earlier. The authors call attention to human rights violations and, particularly, the resurgence of "death-squad style killings." They urge Cristiani to follow through with provisions outlined in the Accords, including the dismantling of the Immediate Reaction Infantry Battalions responsible for massacres in the 1980s, the completion of a land transfer program, and the promotion of national reconciliation processes. The authors close by reaffirming their "commitment to accompany our Sister Cities in El Salvador" and promising to continue pressuring the US Congress and President George Bush to end all military aid.

Among the signees of this letter is Steve J. Stern, professor of history and one of my principal mentors at the university. Stern's name, in fact, appears on many of the documents I uncover during my research—alongside Florencia Mallon, Stern's historian colleague and life partner, as well as Al McCoy, Thomas McCormick, and other prominent scholars. Among the documents are letters to elected officials, published editorials, petitions, programs for teach-ins, and posters and fliers for public lectures. Finding each of these documents delights me; every time I say, "I *know* that person—and here she is in the historical record!" Over time and taken as a whole, this process of discovery has a profound impact on me; I see how highly respected scholars apply their critical analyses beyond the classroom and the so-called ivory tower. I see how historical thinking can—and should—influence our understanding of and response to contemporary issues.

It was Stern who told me about the Madison–Arcatao Sister City Project (MASCP) shortly after I arrived at the university. "This is a story that needs to be written," he said. Aware of my previous work on Central America, which included a master's thesis and a stint as a research assistant at the National Security Archive in Washington, DC, Stern introduced me to Barbara Alvarado, Marc Rosenthal, Ian Davies, and other core members of MASCP. I would go on to work closely with these local activists, organizing files in their office, taking notes at meetings, accompanying and interpreting delegations and tours, and helping with holiday fairs, panel discussions, and other events. And I would come to count these individuals and others as my colleagues and friends.

The MASCP crew also introduced me to Rosa Rivera, Nicolás Rivera, Milton Monge, and others in Arcatao, which brings me to another, more recent memory. It is November 2015, and I am seated on a bed next to Rosa Rivera. Our backs press against the cool cinderblock wall of her bedroom, and our eyes fix on a tiny television screen where her own grainy likeness speaks to us of historic memory.

I am in El Salvador as part of an international delegation; our objective is to observe a public referendum process (Consulta Popular). This is a momentous occasion, for it is the first time that Salvadoran communities have employed this Municipal Code in the postwar period. This is one of the many positive outcomes of years of struggle by popular and politico-military forces in the country; each group fought in its own way to challenge authoritarianism and foment more democratic and egalitarian practices. These public referenda—the results of which are legally binding—offer evidence that such struggles can bring significant change. In this particular case, the town council of Arcatao organized the referendum to determine whether corporations should be able to prospect and mine for gold in municipal territory. The international observer delegation, co-coordinated by US–El Salvador Sister Cities and the Association for the Development of El Salvador (CRIPDES)—two organizations at the heart of this book—was to lend additional legitimacy to the process.

My participation in this delegation is part of my research for this book. Although I have reviewed reams of documentation about Sister Cities delegations in the 1980s and 1990s, and have interpreted for delegates at many events since 1999, I have never fully experienced a delegation—a key tool in the Sister Cities repertoire. Now, I travel alongside journalists, social workers, educators, and students from Germany, France, Canada, and the United States, learning from Salvadoran activists about the toxic legacies of mining in their communities; how people are organizing at local and international levels in resistance to mining companies and their projects; and ongoing lawsuits involving the Salvadoran State and the multinational corporations of Commerce Group, Pacific Rim, and Oceana Gold (based in the United States, Canada, and Australia, respectively). As I learn more about how gold links El Salvador to other nations and corporations around the globe, I am also observing the dynamics of the delegation, interviewing participants and co-coordinators about their own observations and motivations, and drawing parallels with the historic delegations I knew so well through the archival record.

The result of the referendum in Arcatao was striking: of the 1,027 ballots submitted by registered voters in this remote rural municipality, 1,023 said "no" to mining. In other words, 99 percent of those who voted registered opposition to metallic mining in their municipality. Three earlier referenda in neighboring municipalities produced similar landslides: in late 2014 San José Las Flores and San Isidro Labrador registered 99 percent and 98.74 percent in opposition, respectively, and 99.25 percent of voters in Nueva Trinidad formalized that municipality's opposition in early 2015. These referenda fed into broader efforts, ultimately contributing to the Salvadoran Legislative Assembly's decision to turn a temporary moratorium on mining into permanent law. In March 2017, El Salvador became the first country in the world to ban metallic mining.

That Arcatao's vote—or any of these referenda and associated grassroots efforts—would play a role in prompting a national law was unknown to any of us in November 2015. But sitting with Rosa Rivera in her house, with the day cooling into night, I am struck by the many interconnections between past, present, and future. Activists at the forefront of the environmental and anti-mining movements in El Salvador frame their struggle in terms of future generations. By this point, toxic runoff from the San Sebastian mine has already poisoned pigs, chickens, and fish in the Lempa River watershed. This has significantly hampered or outright ruined traditional rural livelihoods, and pushed people—especially youth—onto migrant trails. Calling attention to the multigenerational consequences, activists sport T-shirts and posters declaring "¡No a la minería, sí a la vida!" (No to mining, yes to life!) and "El agua vale más que oro" (Water is more precious than gold). As they play it forward, they draw from past experiences and the victories of previous generations. Local activists and international allies acknowledge that the anti-mining struggle would not exist as it does without the country's long history of collective struggle, social movements, and networking with international solidarity groups. The very existence of the public referendum process is a testament to earlier rounds of collective struggle.

My hostess, Rosa Rivera, has played an important role in these struggles. During the 1980s, she helped thousands of Salvadorans escape from the military's scorched-earth operations, cross the international border into Honduras, and find refuge in United Nations–supported camps. Later, she helped many of these same people return to El Salvador to begin rebuilding their homes, communities, and selves. In the late 1980s and 1990s she was indispensable to a center for war orphans in Arcatao, the *directiva* (grassroots town council), and other community organizations that addressed needs and contributed to broader democratization pushes. She and her compatriots volunteered for these initiatives in the hope that their children would someday have access to education, opportunities to rise out of poverty, to have a voice in government affairs.

Rivera continues her work to this day. In the early 2000s, she helped found another initiative, the Surviving Historic Memory Committee (Comité de Memoria Histórica Sobreviviente). The objectives of this committee include gathering testimonies from war survivors, pressing for accountability for violations of human rights, facilitating the exhumation of clandestine graves and the Christian reburial of their loved ones' remains in a new sanctuary built for this purpose; and the creation of a museum. As Rivera explained to a group of students and faculty at an International Seminar on Historic Memory in September 2019, all of these projects revolve around the "recovery of historic memory so that the new generations know how difficult it was, so that together we can work toward a better present and future."

The film we are watching in Rivera's home is one of the newest tools of the Historic Memory Committee. Aptly titled *The Past Is Not History* (*El pasado no es historia*), the film is the work of the talented young British filmmaker Richard Duffy in collaboration with Arcatao's Memory Committee and the historian Jenny Pearce. It highlights the work of the committee to rescue their community memory and transmit it to the next generations. By knowing and understanding this history of collective struggle, sacrifice, and resilience, Rivera and her committee mates contend, youth will take up the banner of civic engagement, and run with it into the future.

Although I am of the same generation as Rivera and others from the Comité, I have been inspired into action by their work. In 2014 I attended my first national meeting of the US–El Salvador Sister Cities network, where I proposed to the board of directors and attendees a Sister Cities Historic Memory Project to parallel and build on the efforts of Salvadorans in Arcatao and other rural communities. The group enthusiastically agreed, and we began working to (1) collect and preserve historic materials and memories relating to Salvadoran refugee experiences, the rural repopulation movement in El Salvador, and the transnational Sister Cities human rights work from the late 1970s through the 1990s; (2) facilitate opportunities for former refugees, grassroots activists, and others to engage with those materials and to contribute their own stories and archives to the historic record; and (3) introduce these "hidden histories" into official historical narratives in El Salvador, the United States, and beyond.

At the time of this writing in mid-2020, we have collected approximately forty-five banker-sized boxes of historic documentation, videos, and other historic materials; digitized more than 6,600 original photographs from refugee camps and repopulated zones; used these historic materials in interactive exhibits, workshops, classrooms, and other events in El Salvador and the United States; facilitated the transfer of several other collections to university archives; and supported Salvadoran nongovernmental organizations in their preservation and access efforts. This amazing transnational archive is what gives life to this book.

The archive and the Sister Cities Historic Memory Project has helped me inform and inspire a new generation of US-based thinkers and doers. What began as case studies and "Archive Dives" in my Latin American history classes soon expanded to independent studies and internships, as students volunteered with Sister Cities, CRIPDES, and Arcatao's Surviving Historic Memory Committee. Pilot projects and courses in archival preservation and exhibit curation led to the creation of the Public History Lab at Montana State University. Students who have worked in the lab have gone on to attend Sister Cities workshops and national meetings, and to take on leadership roles in the organization.

In large part due to the efforts of two of these students, Jacey Anderson and Emma Folkerts, a fourth-year PhD student and a recent BA, respectively, the US–El Salvador Sister Cities network formally established the Historic Memory Working Group as part of its 2020 work plan. The group has a core membership of about twelve people, with many college students and early-career professionals. The group has been holding regular phone meetings, and planning and carrying out a variety of events—events that link past and present displacements, and highlight the intertwined histories of Salvadorans and US Americans. The Past Is Not History, indeed.

These are some of the seeds that have grown into this book. I have been inspired by many people, including Rosa Rivera, Steve Stern, and, of course, my mother, Marjorie Todd—average citizens whose profound beliefs in the promises of democracy, justice, and human and civil rights have prompted them into action. In ways small and large, they have worked to bring equality and justice to their local and global communities; to hold leaders accountable;

and to put into practice the ideals outlined in constitutions, conventions, and laws. They offer positive models of civic engagement through their behaviors as professionals, parents, partners, consumers, and community members. Together, they have expanded my understandings of the meanings and practices of solidarity, sister/brotherhood, and globalization.

These individuals also have helped me make sense of problems I began perceiving as a youngster. As I was growing up in the 1970s and 1980s, my hometown of St. Paul welcomed thousands of Russian Jews, Hmong, Khmer, Lao, Vietnamese, Central Americans, and Somali. As a student in the public school system, I had the opportunity to learn alongside many people from these distant places. And although I exchanged notes with Biriam and Pao, rode the bus with the Nguyen siblings, and skied with Mariquita, most locals and newcomers remained nameless to each other. The reasons for this were especially visible in the long, glassed, central corridor of Highland Park Junior High School. The eastern windows opened to Snelling Avenue and the school's sports fields. The western windows fishbowled the Special Education and English as a Second Language classrooms. As the mainstream kids passed from class to lunchroom and gym, we could not help but peer in on the differently dressed, mostly brown-skinned, foreign-language-speaking kids. This literal separation raised questions for me about the forces that contribute to human movements, my own immigrant roots, and the things we carry with us—and leave behind—when we cross borders.

My questions about the refugees and migrants in my midst intertwined with other questions: Why did so many Vietnam veterans frequent the drop-in centers and emergency shelters where my mom worked in the winter? Why did it always feel weird crossing into Frogtown when my parents took me, a white girl, to play at the house of my elementary school friend, Colanda Cooper, a Black girl? Why did street gangs target the teenage boys of my mom's American Indian friend, Cindy, who lived in southeast Minneapolis? And why, for goodness sake, couldn't Sister Rose Tillemans be a priest?

Arising from such questions, this book speaks to the systems and structures that erect borders, maintain difference and distance, and perpetuate poverty by allowing some to accumulate wealth, resources, and privileges while denying those same opportunities to others. Rather than examining the structures themselves, this book explores how an extraordinary network of ordinary people find ways to join together across boundaries to challenge injustice and thus create new ways of knowing and being with each other and in the world.

The voices and perspectives in these pages are not impartial; they are subjective. But I want to be clear: subjective does not mean fake. All sources arise from particular contexts, and the creators of those sources are influenced by the sociocultural, economic, and political realities of a specific place and time. The best historians acknowledge this "positionality"—that of the historical actors under study as well as their own. With this preface, then, I position myself in relation to the people who make up the network of US–El Salvador Sister Cities activists. My own background influenced my interest in grassroots movements, in activist challenges to militarism and authoritarianism. This helps explain why and how I have chosen to trace a history that until now has been excluded from dominant narratives.

I now share that history with you.

Abbreviations

ADC	Democratic Campesino Alliance
AFSC	American Friends Service Committee
ALCA	Free Trade Area of the Americas (ALCA)
ARENA	Alianza Republicana Nacional (National Republican Alliance)
BFA	Banco de Fomento Agrícola (Agricultural Development Bank)
CAFTA	Central American Free Trade Agreements
CALA	Community Action on Latin America
CARECEN	Central American Resource Center
CCR	Coordinadora de Comunidades y Repoblaciones de Chalatenango (Coordinator of Communities and Repopulations of Chalatenango), reorganized after the peace accords as Asociación de Comunidades para el Desarrollo de Chalatenango (Association of Communities for the Development of Chalatenango)
CCSCP	Columbus–Copapayo Sister City Project
CISPES	Committee in Solidarity with the People of El Salvador

CNR	Coordinadora Nacional de Repoblamientos (National Coordinator of Repopulations)
CORDES	Fundación para la Cooperación con Repobladores y Desplazados Salvadoreños (Foundation for Cooperation with Salvadoran Repopulators and Displaced), reorganized after the conflict as Fundación para la Cooperación y el Desarrollo Comunal de El Salvador (Foundation for Cooperation and Communal Development of El Salvador)
CRIPDES	Comité Cristiano Pro Desplazados de El Salvador (Christian Committee for the Displaced of El Salvador), reorganized after the peace accords as Asociación para el Desarrollo de El Salvador (Association for the Development of El Salvador)
ERP	Ejército Revolucionario del Pueblo (People's Revolutionary Army)
FMLN	Frente Farabundo Martí para la Liberación Nacional (Farabundo Martí National Liberation Front)
FPL	Fuerzas Populares de Liberación Nacional (Popular Liberation Forces)
FUAR	Frente Unido de Acción Revolucionaria (United Revolutionary Action Front)
MASCP	Madison–Arcatao Sister City Project
IOA	Interfaith Office on Accompaniment
ISD	Iniciativa Social Para la Democracia (Social Initiative for Democracy)
NAFTA	North American Free Trade Agreement
NEST	New El Salvador Today Foundation
SHARE	Salvadoran Humanitarian Aid, Research and Education Foundation

USAID	United States Agency for International Development
USESSC	US–El Salvador Sister Cities
WICOCA	Wisconsin Coordinating Council on Central America

Sister partnerships in chronological order, 1982–2003

1. San Antonio Los Ranchos, Chalatenango—Berkeley, CA
2. Arcatao, Chalatenango—Madison, WI
3. San José Las Flores, Chalatenango—Cambridge, MA
4. San Antonio El Barrio, Cuscátlan—Baltimore, MD
5. Teosinte, Chalatenango—Arlington, MA
6. Guarjila, Chalatenango—Placita, CA
7. Santa Marta, Cabañas—Takoma Park, MD
8. Ellacuría (Guancorita), Chalatenango—Detroit, MI
9. Ellacuría (Guancorita), Chalatenango—Los Angeles, CA
10. El Higueral, Chalatenango—Belmont, MA
11. Nueva Esperanza (El Tremedal), Chalatenango—Watertown, MA
12. Ellacuría (Guancorita), Chalatenango—Boise, ID
13. El Buen Pastor, San Salvador—Woodstock, NY
14. La Bermuda, Cuscatlán—Wichita, KS
15. Las Americas, Cuscatlán—Newton, KS
16. Copapayo, Cuscatlán—Delaware, DE
17. Las Anonas de Santa Cruz, San Vicente—Philadelphia, PA
18. Guarjila, Chalatenango—Bucks County, PA
19. Carasque, Chalatenango—Bangor, ME
20. Agua Caliente, Cuscatlán—Concord, NH
21. Copapayo, Cuscatlán—Columbus, OH

USESSC network. (Maps by Rachel V. Dunlap)

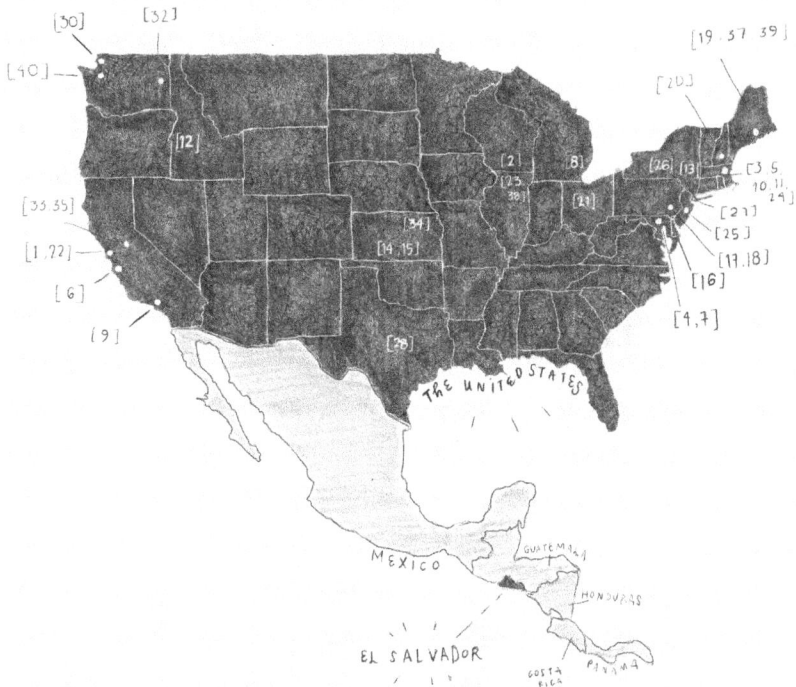

22. Las Anonas, San Vicente—San Francisco, CA
23. Cinquera, Cabañas—Chicago, IL
24. Nueva Trinidad, Chalatenango—Boston, MA
25. Los Amates/San Isidro, Chalatenango—New Jersey, NJ
26. El Charcón, La Libertad—Binghamton, NY
27. Tecoluca, San Vicente—New York, NY
28. Guajoyo, San Vicente—Austin, TX
30. Isla de Montecristo, San Vicente—Bellingham, WA
32. Ita Maura (La Escuelona), La Libertad—Spokane, WA
33. Rutilio Grande (El Jicarón), San Salvador—Davis, CA
34. El Papaturro, Cuscatlán—Lawrence and Manhattan, KS
35. San Bartolo, San Vicente—Sacramento, CA
37. CCR and CORDES, Chalatenango—Maine Organic Farmers and Gardeners, ME
38. Chilama, La Libertad—Crystal Lake, IL
39. Radio Sumpul (Guarjila), Chalatenango—WERU, ME
40. La Ceiba, Chalatenango—Seattle, WA

Not shown:
29. Santa Marta Mártires de Maryknoll, San Vicente—Houston, TX
31. El Porvenir, San Vicente—Wesleyan University, CT
36. Las Vegas, Chalatenango—Edgewood College, WI
41. Izotalillo, Chalatenango—Crested Butte, CO

Long Journey to Justice

Introduction

Grassroots Sistering and Politics

In May 1986, Mary Kay Baum, single mother and member of the Madison School Board, left Wisconsin and set off on a dangerous journey into the mountains of Chalatenango province to El Salvador. The tiny Central American country was in the midst of a brutal civil war pitting the Salvadoran government against the Farabundo Martí National Liberation Front (FMLN). Northern Chalatenango was a hot zone in this war, with the FMLN declaring it "liberated" territory and the Salvadoran armed forces struggling to oust the insurgents and regain control. Baum's purpose for going there was not revolutionary in a traditional sense; she had no intention of taking up arms for the FMLN. Nonetheless her voyage was indeed revolutionary: Baum was a citizen diplomat, purposefully operating outside official channels. Her compatriots, affiliated with the Madison Common Council and a coalition of El Salvador solidarity organizations, appointed her to deliver an important message to the residents of Arcatao, an isolated village tucked in a valley a few kilometers south of El Salvador's border with Honduras.

Under the cover of a grove of *sapote* trees, just beyond reach of military confrontations, Baum unrolled a sweat-dampened document and began to read aloud in Spanish to the dozens of peasants who had only moments earlier given her a heartfelt welcome. The citizens of Madison, she read, decried the exclusion of rural Salvadorans from basic health and education services, and condemned the Salvadoran military for wartime atrocities, including bombing and massacring civilians. Madisonians commended the citizens of Arcatao for responding to such violence through peaceful means, including "democratically elected town councils and cooperative projects" that sought to build a more equitable society. As unarmed civilians with legitimate demands for civil and human rights, the Arcataenses, as they called themselves, deserved Wisconsin's support.

The proclamation went further, its final lines carrying a powerful indictment: "The United States government is intimately involved in the conflict in El Salvador and our tax dollars are funding the war there."[1] According to this perspective, President Ronald Reagan's policy toward El Salvador had failed. An alternative approach was necessary: a more humane diplomacy based on mutual respect and self-determination. By declaring a Sister City relationship with Arcatao, Madisonians set out to model a new foreign policy for the United States.

For the Salvadorans listening, the proclamation came just in time. Government-supported counterinsurgency operations had recently swept through Chalatenango and neighboring areas. In a quest to flush out FMLN guerrillas and collaborators, troops razed dozens of hamlets, left 454 people dead or "disappeared," and forcefully displaced more than 2,600 people.[2] A survivor, Milton Monge, later described how helicopters disgorged hundreds of troops who "rounded up everyone they found" and forced them into the central plaza of Arcatao. There, soldiers tortured and murdered seven residents, interrogated scores more, and threatened the entire community with annihilation if they remained in Arcatao. Monge recalled the military commander using "a string of obscenities" as he ordered his prisoners to "make your peace . . . for soon we will kill you all."[3]

Coincidentally, a group of European journalists observed the initial occupation. A military helicopter quickly whisked them away, but these international witnesses publicized the news of the attack. Among the first to respond were Tracey Schear of New El Salvador Today (NEST), a California-based humanitarian aid foundation that had been supporting projects in Chalatenango since 1983, and Madison-based activists who had been working with Schear to establish a sister-city relationship with Arcatao. Mary Kay Baum joined Schear's emergency delegation, while Madisonians arranged publication of an open letter to the president of El Salvador, José Napoleón Duarte, in *El Mundo*, a Salvadoran daily. The letter, signed by state representatives, city council members, University of Wisconsin professors, and religious officials, announced Madison's adoption of Arcatao as its Sister City and demanded "an immediate end to attacks against Arcatao and other areas inhabited by civilians."[4]

This response was part of a widening web of Central America solidarity activism in the United States. In the 1970s and 1980s, citizens across the country established an estimated two thousand organizations to lend support to

Guatemalans, Hondurans, Nicaraguans, and Salvadorans who found themselves enmeshed in bloody conflicts. These "civil wars" (as many observers
called them) had deep local roots, many of which reached back to the region's
colonial era.[5] But these local tensions were exacerbated by the global context
of the cold war and, more specifically, the US government's efforts to maintain
hegemony in its "backyard" in the face of perceived incursions by the Soviets.[6]
As the US-inspired doctrine of national security spread, the governing elites of
the region deemed subversive any groups and persons advocating for reforms
to long-standing (and exclusionary) economic, political, and social structures.
According to one United Nations report, violent acts committed by state agents
during the 1980s "originated in a political ideology that had made synonymous
the concepts of political opponent, subversive and enemy. People who put
forth ideas contrary to official ideas, ran the risk of being eliminated as if they
were armed enemies on the battlefield."[7]

Such ideology brought chilling consequences. According to conservative
estimates, the conflicts in Guatemala, El Salvador, and Nicaragua resulted in
approximately 350 million dead, 3.7 million displaced, and countless thousands tortured, disappeared, wounded, and orphaned. The vast majority of
victims resided in rural areas. Official truth commissions in Guatemala and El
Salvador held government forces responsible for, respectively, 93 percent and
85 percent of extrajudicial killings, massacres, torture, and other violations.[8] If
we consider also the undeclared "dirty wars" elsewhere in the region, notably
Honduras and Panama, the tolls rise even higher.

The US government played a powerful role in supporting the region's conservative forces during their periods of conflict. Sometimes this occurred
covertly, as with the Nicaraguan Contras.[9] More often it occurred overtly
through military and economic aid packages mounting to billions of dollars.
Seeing the direct connections between US interventions and violations of rights,
tens of thousands of US citizens became involved in human rights and solidarity work. Through organizations large and small, and drawing on experiences
and lessons from the civil rights and other movements, they lent support to
Central American people affected by violence. Many of these groups adopted
strategies known as "witnessing" and "accompaniment," which, according to
theologian Robert McAfee Brown, entailed walking "alongside the victims—
not trying to strategize on their behalf, or propose our solutions for their
problems, or otherwise give them the benefit of our 'wisdom'—but simply
being there in acts of physical solidarity."[10] Physical accompaniment connected
with human rights response efforts, material aid, educational campaigns, and
congressional policy work to create a powerful web of moral, spiritual, material,
and political support.

Sistering was an especially successful accompaniment tactic. The concept of "sister cities" evolved in the early 1980s as a means of linking US Americans with "at risk" Central Americans—specifically Nicaraguan and Salvadoran activists who were working to defend democracy and human and civil rights in their countries.[11] Formal connections between citizens in the United States and Nicaragua began after the Sandinista National Liberation Front came to power in 1979, and as it became clear that US officials did not intend to offer the new revolutionary government fair play. In contrast, sistering connections between US and Salvadoran citizens developed during the height of the Salvadoran conflict as a means of offering additional legitimacy to the efforts of Salvadorans working for social and political change. At the heart of the sistering movement were civilians working parallel to and directly with the politico-military forces of the Farabundo Martí National Liberation Front (FMLN)—a coalition of insurgent forces that ultimately would achieve a "negotiated revolution" rather than a decisive military victory like their Nicaraguan contemporaries.

This book focuses on the sistering relationships that developed between Salvadoran and US citizens. Unlike the Nicaraguan case, these were grassroots connections born from war. These unique relationships played an important part in ending civil war in El Salvador and ushering in a more peaceful and democratic era. Because of this, and in light of the fact that many of the pairings that formed in the 1980s and early 1990s continue strong today, US–El Salvador Sister Cities offers many valuable lessons of relevance not only to history but also to our present.

The Madison-Arcatao Sister City Project (MASCP) was among the first enduring links between the United States and El Salvador. Arcataenses learned of Madison's declaration soon after the military commander issued his ultimatum to leave or die. Esperanza Ortega recalled hearing the news on the radio. "This announcement," she said, showed "those of us who lived in the conflict zone [that] the people of Madison had the spirit of brotherhood and the desire to support us."[12] "It was a source of great rejoicing," Agustín Menjívar explained, "to know we had the support of someone who identified with those of us who most suffered."[13] Arcatao was no longer alone; Wisconsin was watching.

Given the cold war context, United States and Salvadoran authorities responded less enthusiastically to such announcements. They aligned sistering, and accompaniment more generally, with subversion. More specifically, officials alleged that Sister Cities committees were front groups for the Salvadoran insurgents and had direct ties to the Soviet Union. Viewed from this perspective, sistering activists became military targets.

That authorities took such notice was, in fact, one of the objectives of sistering. Madison's "adoption" of Arcatao was a bold move, calculated to make waves. And it did. The project helped set the foundations for a new transnational sistering movement that, in the words of activist Juliana Barnard, served as "a direct challenge to the gunboat diplomacy, the carrot and the stick, the bombs and bullets, and the rigged elections. . . . We say there is another way, based on justice, mutual respect [and] self-determination. . . . Since we can't wait for our government to make the change, we will begin to do it ourselves."[14] By 1992, when the Salvadoran government and the FMLN finalized a peace agreement, bringing the country's military conflict to an end, the US–El Salvador Sister Cities (USESSC) network had expanded to include more than thirty city pairings; dozens of companion congregations, clinics, and schools; full-time staff in Salvadoran and US offices; and thousands of volunteers. These US and Salvadoran citizens used sistering as a springboard for transnational debates about the meanings of democracy, good government, rights, and citizenship.

Of course, the participants in this network did not invent the concept of sistering. The mid-twentieth century holds many examples of town twinning and municipal internationalism, including unification projects in western Europe after World War II and, in the American hemisphere, the People-to-People and Partners of the Americas programs. This book argues, however, that the Salvadoran sistering of the 1980s was different. Rather than emerge out of "official" government programs, these sistering relationships were grassroots endeavors, established and maintained by average and less privileged people from El Salvador and the United States—subsistence farmers, refugees, schoolteachers, nurses, housewives—who found common cause in countering the cold war perspective propagated by the elite sectors of both countries. These grassroots activists shared a deep commitment to radical and participatory democracy, liberty and justice, and human and civil rights. Moreover, they shared feelings of intense frustration with their national leaders who hailed the same democratic ideals in speeches but then behaved in distinctly antidemocratic ways. Moral outrage at this gap between rhetoric and reality motivated citizens to action, and sistering offered an outlet for both nonviolent protest and the modeling of alternatives. Sister Cities was designed to not only challenge the Salvadoran government's depopulation strategies and to protest US interventionist policies but to construct viable alternatives to exclusionary systems and imperial relations.

A New Model

This book introduces the concept of "grassroots sistering" and offers a social history of US–El Salvador Sister Cities as a lens through which to examine and better understand transnational solidary relations and human rights engagements in the late twentieth century. Surprisingly, scholars have not yet taken up the phenomenon of grassroots sistering, despite its significance and widespread practice. A few geographers, sociologists, and political scientists have explored town twinning, primarily in the post–World War II European context. These scholars have explained twinning as a commercial and technical phenomenon, or as a postwar strategy to reunify Europe and reduce tensions between the United States and the Soviet Union. Their studies emphasize the role of local governments and chambers of commerce, and pay special attention to economic development aspects. Similarly, studies on US government-sponsored programs abroad, such as Partners of the Americas and Sister Cities International from the Alliance for Progress years, typically approach sistering as part of the heroic narrative of US development assistance, a "cheerful subject."[15]

Even more surprising is the fact that scholars who study US Central America solidarity movements have glossed over grassroots sistering. Only a few authors mention sister cities—almost always in passing. Instead, they privilege a small number of groups with US bases in coastal megacities and the southwest, such as sanctuary and Witness for Peace. Such a narrow focus is in part due to the comparatively easy accessibility of documentation about these groups.[16]

In this book, I draw from private archives, oral histories, and publicly available materials to argue that grassroots sistering between Salvadorans and US Americans marked an entirely new model of transnational activism. I base this claim on three points that I develop in detail in the following chapters. First, the people who established and maintained these sistering relationships were ordinary citizens. Most authors to date have focused on what might be called "the human rights elite": representatives of human rights commissions of high-level international state-centered organizations, professionalized international non-state organizations, and groups based in urban South America. This book shifts our perspective, bringing into focus the work of voluntary "community councils."

Second, grassroots sistering was based on sustained people-to-people relationships—what participants called "permanent accompaniment." The founders of Sister Cities intended that the relationships endure for the foreseeable future, linking whole communities to one another across geographic and political borders. This stands in sharp contrast to the human rights accompaniment practices of other groups, including Peace Brigades International, Witness for Peace, and Fellowship of Reconciliation—organizations that sent (mostly) northerners to countries in the so-called Global South for temporary sojourns accompanying high-profile individuals whose actions in defense of human rights jeopardized their own safety. Although many US Americans who traveled to Central America with Sister Cities often did serve as "unarmed bodyguards," US–El Salvador Sister Cities was far more than this: it was a two-way street, a mutually beneficial relationship.[17]

Third, grassroots sistering blended political solidarity and human rights work. Many scholars treat these two arenas as mutually exclusive—a group engaged in either one or the other. In most instances, scholars present human rights work as "above politics," and solidarity activism as "more political."[18] Whereas human rights activists moved through official circles "self-consciously trumpeting a depoliticized politics of emergency" and pushing "moral claims," solidarity activists were radicals—"typically revolutionary anti-imperialists"— who refused to engage "with what they saw as establishment politicians in the epicenter of US imperialism."[19] This case study of the US–El Salvador Sister Cities network demonstrates that such a separation did not always hold true.

In developing these lines of argument, I draw inspiration from and expand on several emerging fields: interdisciplinary human rights history, the new solidarity studies, and transnational history. Although most scholars in human rights history—a field of study that expanded dramatically in the last decade— have tended to emphasize the European roots of human rights, recent work by Latin Americanists has begun to shift attention to "the activist workshop of the Americas, where much of the language of global human rights talk and practice was forged."[20] Historians, political scientists, and others have demonstrated the importance of local actors in specific contexts and the role of Latin Americans themselves in motivating and maintaining human rights movements and sentiments of solidarity among transnational activists.[21]

For all these advances, however, the current state of this interdisciplinary field remains narrow. Many scholars have focused on the 1970s as the "breakthrough" decade for global human rights politics, often supporting their claims with case studies from northern Europe, the United States, and Latin America's Southern Cone.[22] Influential studies by political scientists have emphasized how events in Chile and Argentina set in motion human rights "boomerangs," "spirals," and "justice cascades."[23] Repeated study of the same countries and groups has elevated certain players to a kind of human rights elite riding the apex of human rights activism. All that follows is shadowed, weak, and disappointing by comparison. In the words of Patrick Kelly, "Few countries could sound the alarm quite like the resonant 'sovereign emergencies' of Brazil, Chile, and Argentina."[24]

Following this line of thinking, activism relating to Central America in the 1980s is part of the postsurge era, with Sister Cities, sanctuary, and other endeavors relegated to "episodic" blips on the world's human rights radar.[25]

The supposed failure of these and other movements of the 1980s to capture global attention is linked to what many observers have characterized as the death of the international Left. As armed revolutions failed and "third ways" gave way to dictatorships and authoritarian democracies (tied to US power), "disenchanted warriors" turned to human rights as "a minimalist program for social change" or, as the historian and legal scholar Samuel Moyne termed it, "the last utopia."[26]

The Central American case study presented in this book contests such claims. The narrow focus on the 1970s, the "human rights elite," and Latin America's Southern Cone ignores an important reality: even as activists on the left mourned the fall of Peronism in Argentina and democratic socialism in Chile, and even as they watched with horror the rise to power of military dictatorships and bureaucratic authoritarians in those countries and elsewhere, they also tracked more hopeful events in other regions of the world, including the evolution of the Cuban Revolution, the expansion of the Black consciousness and antiapartheid movements in South Africa, and the rise to power of the Sandinista National Liberation Front in Nicaragua. The revolutionary movements in El Salvador and Guatemala inspired similar expectations that additional major change was just over the horizon. In short, if the 1970s was the "experimental" stage of human rights, with Latin America's Southern Cone as a main arena for "trial-and-error," as Patrick William Kelly argues, then 1980s Central America was where human rights–related activism gained its fullest expression.[27] Instead of representing the last gasp of the international Left, Central America solidarity activities around the world illustrate the Left's continued engagement within the rapidly shifting contexts of the late twentieth century.

This examination of grassroots sistering further presses the boundaries of human rights history by moving beyond the framework of individual defense. Most studies have focused on human rights activism as reactionary, defensive, and individualistic. That is, human rights workers reacted to violations of internationally recognized human rights by launching campaigns in defense of specific individuals. They sought the reappearance with life of "disappeared" sons, daughters, wives, and husbands, for example, and pressured officials to stop the torture of identified political prisoners. The narrow focus on individual bodily integrity came at a high cost, some scholars maintain—namely, ignoring the broader economic and social contexts that gave rise to abuses.[28]

The US–El Salvador Sister Cities network offers an example of how activists successfully blended individual and collective rights frameworks as well as both defensive and constructive methods. Network members certainly defended individuals who fell victim to abuse, but they also defended entire communities including Salvadoran refugees living in camps in Honduras and returning home to El Salvador, repopulators in rural villages, and the rural population at large. And while sistering advocates defended the physical bodily integrity of these communities—denouncing military incursions, bombings, and massacres, for example—they also promoted their economic, social, and political rights. Indeed, Sister Cities contributed to the much broader long-term goal of constructing a New Society. This meant not only overturning militarized authoritarianism in El Salvador but also raising radically democratic—and, from some perspectives, socialist—structures. Likewise, this meant opposing US imperial politics in El Salvador and around the world, and then developing new, mutually respectful ways of knowing each other and being together in the world.

This blended strategy offers an important revelation: human rights work and solidarity work were not always as separate as has been portrayed. Until recently, human rights history and solidarity studies typically fell into two distinct realms of scholarly literature; one explored human rights and humanitarian endeavors as neutral and apolitical, and the other highlighted the politically engaged—even radical—nature of solidarity activism. Within solidarity studies, further distinctions separated the anti-interventionists (who opposed US military involvement in foreign affairs) from true solidarity activists (who went a step further to support progressive reformist and revolutionary movements).[29] Such representations arose from the realities of the cold war and reflect some of the tensions and fissures within the Left in the late twentieth century.

The work of the Sister Cities network illustrates that this distinction is false: Grassroots sistering merged individual and collective rights frameworks, and employed both defensive and constructive tactics. Within any given space and time, sistering advocates engaged in multiple forms of human rights and solidarity activism.[30] From a bird's-eye perspective, the same thread of hope ran through these multiple forms. At a very basic level, sistering created a sense of connection and identification between people of different backgrounds and histories who, despite their differences, banded together in common cause. A sense of urgency often motivated people to begin working together, while a sense of hope maintained their engagement. Directed campaigns on local and international levels thus took on broader symbolism; securing a refugee's release from custody or ousting government soldiers from a repopulated village became evidence that the people "have the power to alter existing conditions."[31] Combining many small victories like this in the transnational sphere contributed, in turn, to the "imagining [of an] unbounded Americas," the belief that "the world could, in fact, be changed."[32] In this, sistering activists became part of a much wider and older web of thinkers who imagined a new and more integrated Americas. This web included Cuba's José Martí, who, while in exile in New York in the late nineteenth century, penned his now-famous essay "Nuestra América" ("Our America"); the Argentine anthropologist Néstor García Canclini, who popularized a new theorization of "hybridity"; and the award-winning Chicano scholar José David Saldívar, who remapped borders and explored "Trans-Americanity."[33]

The belief that a better world is possible—and the actions to bring such a world into being—brought grassroots sistering advocates into direct confrontation with the status quo. Sistering encouraged a critical analysis of specific government policies as well as broader political, economic, and social structures and systems. By reassessing standing traditions and practices, activists set the stage for the transformation of those very traditions and practices. In other words, they sought not just to critique and deconstruct but to redesign and construct new, viable alternatives. Whereas the status quo represented social atomization, exclusion, inequality, and injustice, the alternative experiments implemented by sistering activists were often utopian in their ideals. They emphasized a "new set of roles and responsibilities" based on unity, mutuality, collaboration, and equality.[34] In the same vein, sistering work intentionally countered long-standing traditions of hierarchy and centralized authority (and their parallel relations of domination and dependency) by adopting decentralized organizational models and promoting horizontalism and reciprocity.

In short, sistering was one of many *commons*. Historically, commons arose as a reaction to enclosures—the privatization and commodification of shared resources such as land and information. More recently commons have emerged in response to "new enclosures" including the "structural adjustment programs" promoted by the World Bank and the International Monetary Fund, along with the development of the "debt economy."[35] Over time, these enclosures have resulted in what the feminist political philosopher Silvia Federici referred to as "the disarticulation of the social body, through the imposition of different regimes producing an accumulation of 'differences' and hierarchies."[36] Commoners contest this atomization of society. They challenge the state/market duopoly by creating spaces focused on sustainable livelihoods, community integrity, and the "equitable distribution and responsible use" of material and cultural resources; and by "demand[ing] control over the decisions that most affect their lives, assert[ing] their capacity for self-government."[37] In contrast to the individuality and egotism of our modern market-driven society, the commons emphasizes interconnectivity. As a kind of voluntary association or intentional community based on principles of solidarity, reciprocity, and mutuality, commons require one to opt in, to adopt "the posture and attitude of working alongside, shoulder to shoulder."[38] In so doing, commoners invite us to think about, move through, and be in our world in a more holistic way, with an understanding that "we humans co-evolve with and co-produce each other. We do not exist in grand isolation from our fellow human beings and nature."[39]

The US–El Salvador Sister Cities network at the heart of this study offers an intriguing example of how ordinary folks in different parts of the world joined together to create a new kind of commons, a transnational fictive kin network, which, like the other past and present commons explored by David Bollier, Silke Helfrich, and others, was highly generative. Not only did this grassroots initiative "enable people to discover, innovate and negotiate new ways of doing things for themselves," it also connected people and resources in ways that stimulated a blending and reconstituting of citizenship and governance.[40]

To bring into focus the power and promise of this sistering commons, I rely on methods drawn from the emerging field of transnational historical studies. In contrast to the long-standing fields of international history and global history, transnational histories trouble, unsettle, and even disrupt conventional national narratives by intentionally "siting" history in multiple geographic locations and on multiple perspective-scales. Transnational historians examine and historicize the connections and disjunctures between spaces, geographies, and boundaries as a way of "unthinking the taken-for-granted," as historian Paul Kramer stated. By approaching history as multilayered process rather than event, transnational history positions the local(s) in the global(s), thus destabilizing national fixed-beginning/origin points.[41]

This transnational history of grassroots sistering places ordinary people in multiple sites at the center of inquiry. Rather than focus on political and economic elites or major international organizations, it focuses on average and less privileged people in El Salvador, Honduras, and the United States: subsistence farmers, refugees, schoolteachers, nurses, housewives, and others. This study also brings attention to less well-studied zones of activism, including El Salvador's northern Chalatenango province where a coalition of Left-leaning groups coalesced in the 1970s and early 1980s, transforming this frontier region—once dubbed "the forgotten land" (la tierra olvidada)—into the center stage of a globalized political conflict and the heart of the sistering movement.[42] Cities in the US midwestern states of Kansas, Ohio, and Wisconsin, as well as Maine, Massachusetts, New Jersey, and Philadelphia in the Northeast, also figure prominently in this book.

This study pays special attention to transnational activists—that is, people from El Salvador and the US whose organizing and mobilizing trajectories took them across international borders. Although US activists were important, providing material, moral, and political support to refugees in Honduran camps and repopulators in rural El Salvador, this story also reveals the critical roles played by politically committed Salvadorans who were displaced by violence. More specifically, it examines how members of the Salvadoran popular movement, displaced by state-led violence and living as internal and external refugees, helped shape El Salvador solidarity work in the United States.[43] These activists—who ranged from peasants and students to clandestine representatives of the Popular Liberation Forces (FPL)—helped inspire and motivate some two thousand US-based organizations representing a diverse range of interests, from the faith-based sanctuary movement to more politically engaged groups like the Committee in Solidarity with the People of El Salvador (CISPES).[44]

Researchers focusing on the conflict era in El Salvador have not yet seriously considered transnational actors. This is surprising in light of the fact that El Salvador is an exceedingly small country—just over twenty-one thousand square kilometers (about 8,108 sq. mi.), the size of the US state of New Jersey. A vehicle can travel between its northern and southern borders in around three hours with decent roads and weather, and from west to east in just over five hours. When violence intensified in the 1970s, El Salvador was home to about six million people; the conflict ultimately displaced approximately two million—more than one-quarter of the country's citizens. Hundreds of thousands remained internally displaced, while hundreds of thousands more traveled across international borders and, in host countries around the world, they established new political, social, and affective networks. At the same time, tens of thousands of foreigners went to El Salvador—some to lend assistance to health, education, and relief efforts headed by civil and religious groups, others to collaborate directly with the insurgent forces. With a conservative estimate of cross-border movement and activism reaching well over one million people, this is a phenomenon that merits attention.

South American case studies offer inspiration and comparative insights into cross-border human rights and solidarity activism. Innumerable books and articles about Brazil, Argentina, Chile, and Paraguay have led to a deeper understanding of the work of professionalized organizations such as Argentina's Madres de Plaza de Mayo, Chile's Vicaría de la Solidaridad, and Amnesty International, as well as human rights commissions within state-centered organizations such as the United Nations and the Organization of American States. A host of other studies reveals the layered nature of organizing at local and international levels, the complex power dynamics of cross-border relationships, and the unique challenges and opportunities experienced by people exiled from these countries during the region's military dictatorships. In addition, we have learned that solidarity need not always entail clear and intentional structures and orchestrations; it also can involve multiple loose collections of people coming together for a while and then drifting apart, sometimes reconverging in a later moment. Especially pertinent are the conclusions drawn by a new cohort of solidarity scholars who are moving beyond conventional North–South narratives to showcase the south-to-north and south-south dynamics of solidarity activism. In so doing, they hone in on unique contributions of Latin American agents, varied meanings of local agency in Latin America, and the distinct dynamics in the Global South.[45]

Even if El Salvador lags far behind its southern neighbors as far as published studies, there is no question that international solidarity was just as important a component in Salvadoran progressive and revolutionary movements. A few foundations have been laid. For example, some foreigners—*internacionalistas*—have published books about their experiences working directly with the FMLN. Some of these publications, like the popular book *Witness to War* by Dr. Charles Clements, appeared during the war years, helping humanize the FMLN and condemn the Salvadoran military for its attacks on villages populated by civilians, field hospitals, and other sites protected under the Geneva Convention.[46] In the wake of the war, as new Salvadoran and world contexts took shape, a genre of war memoirs appeared, offering additional examples of transnational engagements by Mexicans, Europeans, and US Americans, among others.[47] More recently, publications have begun to move beyond pure memoir, with scholars—some of whom were directly involved in the events—offering more nuanced and historicized analyses of the FMLN's "accumulation of forces."[48] As we learn more about how the five factions of the FMLN recruited and mobilized civilian collaborators as well as combatants, we are opening new windows onto the relations that developed among Salvadorans and between Salvadorans and their international allies. Recent work by Eudald Cortina Orero, Oscar Martínez Peñate, Andrea Oñate-Madrazo, and others illustrates how, as the different politico-military forces came together and formed the FMLN in 1980, they consolidated and formalized efforts vis-à-vis international audiences, sending representatives abroad to work with diverse audiences, including high-level government officials (through "parallel diplomacy" channels) as well as solidarity organizations and the broader publics (through their own alternative broadcast and press agencies).[49] There is much we still have to learn, of course, but all indicators point to the fact that the FMLN—and the Popular Liberation Forces (FPL) in particular—were "masters . . . of building transnational solidarity networks," converting solidarity into "just another actor in the war," as Van Gosse, a noted historian of the US Left, put it.[50]

In fact, Gosse—a scholar as well as a participant in the Central America solidarity movements himself—called attention to the "North American Front" of the Salvadoran revolutionary struggle well before the end of the conflict. More specifically, he highlighted the importance of politically active Salvadoran

exiles to the development of "a highly structured and tightly integrated movement in the United States."[51] A new generation of scholarship now is building
on Gosse's early interventions, further exploring the key roles that Salvadoran
and Nicaraguan exiles played in the development of the US Central America
solidarity movements, and encouraging us to think critically about US Central
America solidarity and global grassroots relations more broadly.[52]

This study contributes to these discussions by bringing together and, as
much as possible, placing on equal ground the Salvadoran and US American
transnational activists, and revealing the new communities they created in the
US–El Salvador Sister Cities network. Rather than draw distinct boundaries
between north/south or First World/Third World, or emphasize the "issue
campaigns" of large-scale institutions, this case study presents a new model: a
transnational fictive kin network that disrupted conventional understandings
and practices of citizenship, nationalism, and globalism during the latter years
of the cold war and the first years of the postwar era.

Empire, Solidarity, and Human Rights

Even as I seek to place activists from the north and south on
equal ground, I approach the sistering movement—and, by extension, solidary
relations more generally—as a kind of "contact zone."[53] In her seminal text
Imperial Eyes, the literary theorist Mary Louise Pratt defined a contact zone as
"the space of colonial encounters, the space in which peoples geographically
and historically separated come into contact with each other and establish
ongoing relations, usually involving conditions of coercion, radical inequality,
and intractable conflict." Like Pratt, I am interested in spaces of overlap and
relations between people, the "spatial and temporal copresence of subjects previously separated by geographic and historical disjunctures, and whose trajectories intersect."[54] Whereas Pratt focused on Northern Europeans and "their
colonial subjects" in Africa and South America during the eighteenth and
early nineteenth centuries, I focus on relations between the people of two
independent nations—the United States and El Salvador—a full two centuries later. Although El Salvador and most of its Latin American and Caribbean
neighbors gained independence from their European colonizers during the
nineteenth century, they have since struggled under the weight of "the Colossus of the North," the United States of America.[55]

This book moves beyond simple heroic narratives of solidarity as a kind of
unified march toward a utopian commons, to highlight the intimate ties between empire and solidarity, and to reveal the less romantic side of transnational

activism. I draw inspiration from several political scientists who have explored how, despite even the best of intentions, human rights work and its associated humanitarian aid are "deeply enmeshed in politics."[56] In exposing the very political nature of the supposedly apolitical United Nations High Commissioner for Refugees (UNHCR), for example, Michael Barnett shows how humanitarianism encompasses elements of both emancipation and domination, and thus has the capacity to empower and disempower at the same time.[57] Fiona Terry and Sarah Kenyon Lischer illustrate similar themes for nongovernmental organizations; they argue that Médecins sans Frontières and other agencies involved in the provision of humanitarian aid can and do unwittingly prolong conflicts and exacerbate suffering, thereby contradicting their own principles and objectives.[58] Several others have shed light on the broader contexts contributing to increasingly blurred lines between "classicist" principles of humanitarian action on the one hand and politics and market economics on the other.[59] And scholars from other disciplines have begun to further broaden those contexts by intentionally connecting the fields of humanitarianism and imperial histories. As Robert Skinner and Alan Lester point out, "It is not a simple matter of resemblance—how contemporary humanitarian action appears to echo the patterns and ambitions of earlier imperial 'projects'—but that the two phenomena are ultimately bound together in a series of mutually constituting histories, in which the ideas and practices associated with imperial politics and administration have both been shaped by and have in themselves informed developing notions of humanitarianism."[60]

It is for this very reason that many Latin American activists on the left resisted taking up the human rights banner in the 1970s and 1980s. Latin Americans' concerns about "the imperialistic nature of human rights politics," as the historian Patrick William Kelly explains, related to "the ways in which only certain spectacles of violence drew the gaze of Western activists and defined which peoples in faraway lands were deserving of empathy." Moreover, westerners rarely responded to "the plight of the poor, or genocides . . . for those would require a reckoning not only with the legacies of Euro-American colonialism and the white racial hierarchy, but also with the growing inequalities of the late twentieth century's neoliberal world order."[61]

And here we begin to see additional layers of the politics of human rights and solidarity activism. The multiple forms of activism that exist at any given time often rub against each other, painfully revealing the "fault lines" that hide just beneath the surface—the disconsonant attitudes and behaviors based in each group's unique culture, geography, and sociopolitical experience.[62] Lesley Gill details precisely these kinds of disjunctures that arose during a Colombia/US solidarity campaign against the Coca-Cola corporation. The campaign, she argues, emphasizes "the difficulty of synchronizing diverse activist agendas in the context of unequal power relations" and exposes the ways in which "solidarity and fragmentation are . . . part of the same process."[63]

In a similar fashion, the US–El Salvador Sister Cities network examined in these pages illustrates how relations of solidarity between US and Latin American actors are intriguingly paradoxical. Northerners who join in solidarity with an Other from the so-called Global South are typically aware of the histories of marginalization wrought by colonial/imperial relations, and much of their work aims to counter such histories. To break down borders and boundaries between people and nations, for example, they often strive to build a unified "we" and emphasize similarities rather than differences. To invert paternalistic relations, they distinguish their work from traditional altruistic charity and highlight how, rather than impose their own visions, they respond to calls from the south and take the lead from their southern partners.

Yet, even as sistering advocates seek to subvert unequal power relations, their solidarism is defined by those very asymmetries. The following pages explore, for example, how sentiments of sympathy and charity often initiate and undergird solidarity work, and how, to build support at home, northern solidarists often portray their southern partners in caricature, as helpless victims in desperate need of succor. Such "pornography of poverty," however, can encourage the belief that "problems can only be solved by Northern charity."[64] As the political geographer Sara Koopman puts it, "The good helper role is part of the imperialism that we carry within."[65]

In fact, the US–El Salvador Sister Cities case study illustrates that much of what makes US/Latin America relations of solidarity actually function is the privileged positions that US participants occupy vis-à-vis Latin Americans. This is visible in campaigns that draw attention to US foreign policy, during which United States citizens draw on their "privileged social locations to gain political access to elected representatives and claim authority to challenge the US government."[66] It is perhaps even more obvious in accompaniment campaigns, a strategy that figures prominently in this book. Accompaniment entails "privileged foreign bodies" literally living alongside human rights and popular movement activists of the so-called Third World. They serve as "unarmed bodyguards," their presence "a compelling and visible reminder to those using violence that it will not go unnoticed."[67] The concept of visibility is key here; observers around the world have noted with regard to accompaniment that government and police forces accord higher degrees of respect to "the outsider, especially those with white skin."[68] In the context of US/Latin America accompaniment and solidarity projects, then, "staking out one's own agency as an imperial citizen" entails employing "white privilege" and engaging (consciously or not) with racial, ethnic, and class inequalities as well as uneven geopolitical power relations.[69]

Moreover, although solidarity groups contest marginalization, they suffer from their own forms of exclusion. Like all social movements, Sister Cities is to a great extent about "essentializing—claiming fixed, shared, and enduring identities that may differ significantly from people's daily experiences and beliefs."[70] To facilitate communication with outsiders, sistering leaders simplify complex realities; they "select from among a wide array of information according to particular news values and ideological frames, crystallizing and condensing these images into major themes, and, at times, relaying images that can be so partial as to be downright deceptive."[71] For instance, the public narratives of northern sistering activists often feature victim testimonies, tortured bodies, and martyr stories. Although these can be useful as "propaganda bombs," they also can be counterproductive: such strategic framing "establishe[s] a culture of suffering," which constrains southern participants' abilities to act.[72] Some northern voices also are silenced as one essentialized movement identity takes precedence over others.[73] Moreover, as Judith Adler Hellman argues for the Zapatistas' transnational network, solidarists' representations often leave potential sympathizers "in a very weak position to understand and analyze the events as they unfold."[74] A failure to link solidarity campaigns to parallel domestic issues (e.g., poverty, conflictive race relations) further limits a movement's reach. In short, the essentializing strategies adopted by solidarists can unintentionally reify uneven power relations between northern and southern participants, and alienate potential partners. In short, this book examines empire and human rights/solidarity as two sides of the same coin.

The very existence of this book is a testament to these asymmetries. More to the point, uneven relations of power and privilege undergird this entire research project—a fact made exceedingly clear in the documentary evidence. As I describe in the preface, at the heart of this study is a series of "hidden archives" of the late cold war era—that is, personal collections (and recollections) that individuals have guarded carefully through the years. These materials are critically important for our understanding of transnational activism during war and its aftermath—and particularly the roles played by Salvadorans. Many of the Salvadoran protagonists were, at best, marginally literate when sistering began and their circumstances demanded that they pay attention to surviving rather than to methodically documenting their movement-building efforts for future use by researchers. In some cases, caches of important documents were destroyed—voluntarily by protagonists for security reasons, or by military operations that purposely targeted sites holding local and regional records. Although today the country is ostensibly at peace, its tenuous democracy dictates (understandably, perhaps) that more attention and funding go to controlling street gangs than to organizing pallets of files in the National Archive. And while libraries, museums, and nongovernmental organizations are working to preserve, grow, and make more accessible their collections relating to human rights, the popular and revolutionary movements, the peace process, and postwar reforms, these archives rarely contain materials about the transnational networks of Salvadoran rural activists.

At the same time, dozens of Sister Cities activists across the United States—in Wisconsin, Kansas, Massachusetts, New Jersey, Ohio, Texas, and elsewhere—have created and maintained their own personal archives. An enormous amount of documentation has been tucked away; records of sistering committees in Wisconsin, New Jersey, and Ohio alone fill a storage locker, an attic, and some twenty-two linear feet of archival shelf space. The documents within each collection are predominantly in English, produced by northern participants for a US audience. Typed and computer-generated materials abound, along with telegrams, telexes, and faxes, mostly focusing on the inner workings of the US-based sistering committees. Also present—although much fewer and farther between—are items produced by Salvadoran activists, including project proposals, photos, posters, drawings, audio recordings, and letters. Many of these letters are handwritten by newly literate hands, folded into tiny squares, and shipped through the postal service. These are precious materials; they have been unfolded and refolded by their recipients so often that light now passes through the paper's creases.

Comparable collections simply do not exist in El Salvador. The Salvadoran communities that have paired with towns in the United States do not have boxes, let alone storage sheds, of documentation about their work. There are many underlying explanations for the different patterns of recording, accumulation, and preservation of materials, but one point bears emphasizing here. As Michael Ring, a former Sister Cities staff person, eloquently explained, the Salvadoran villages that formed the southern hub of this transnational network "are first and foremost organized communities part of CRIPDES [the Christian Committee for the Displaced of El Salvador] and a historic social revolutionary struggle for liberation, justice and dignity in [El Salvador] and ONE thing they do is participate in sistering as one tactic in their overall work. Sistering committees in the US, on the other hand, only exist to 'sister' in response to this much broader struggle that their sister communities are part of."[75] Largely for this reason the north dominates the sistering network's historical record. While we all benefit from this record, we also must recognize its limitations and biases.

This book could not have been written even a few years ago. Although Van Gosse has long encouraged his colleagues in the Central America solidarity movement to be open about the politics of solidarity and particularly the role played by Salvadorans, Nicaraguans, and Guatemalans, most US activists have been reticent to discuss such details. When I first began researching the transnational relations forged by Salvadoran refugees, the peace accords were only about a half-decade old. Salvadoran and US citizens continued to rely on the same tropes that had dominated their wartime communiqués and publications, emphasizing victimhood, humanitarianism, FMLN heroism, and utopian dreams. Developed over many years, these essentialized narratives had proven safe; they intentionally evaded frictions and other aspects of internal politics. One US citizen who had been living in El Salvador since the early 1980s and who had worked closely with Salvadoran refugees in Honduras, simply refused to meet with me, fearing, as I later learned, that I intended to reveal "political secrets." Although this was an extreme stance, it illustrates how political concerns prevented transnational activists from sharing certain histories with people they deemed outsiders. In addition, most activists did not fully trust the peace process; even into the first years of the new millennium, they continued an uneasy wait-and-see approach. Would peace hold, or would the nation return to open war? With such questions constantly on the mind, it is no wonder that most people chose to hold their cards very close.

Yet time passes and contexts change. El Salvador's peace has held, even as "everyday violence" rises. The FMLN has proven its mettle as an official political party, its candidates elected to offices across the country, including mayorships, the Legislative Assembly, and the presidency. Yet the Left no longer idealizes "el Frente"; like any political party, the FMLN suffers from internal tensions, with leaders frequently splintering into new wings then reconverging again. The party's dirty laundry airs in the public media, and followers are more open with their critiques of the party's shortcomings.[76] At the same time, in the wake of the cold war, US foreign policy has shifted attention away from Central America and toward fields in the Middle East, and neoliberal reforms have brought new challenges for average citizens of both El Salvador and the United States.

These new contexts affect peoples' willingness to discuss the past. In the late 1990s, for example, one Wisconsin-based solidarist chose not to reveal that during the Salvadoran civil war, he had crossed into FMLN-held territory in Chalatenango without the requisite permission from the Salvadoran High Command. By 2015 he openly described his ventures and the political motivations behind them. Whereas earlier he explained sistering as a tool to provide humanitarian aid, in later years he drew direct lines between US-based sistering advocates and the Salvadoran Popular Liberation Forces (FPL), and even went so far as to declare US-based sistering advocates to be part of the Salvadoran revolutionary movement.[77] I saw similar trends among activists in both countries. It must be noted, too, that many of the network's founders and most stalwart supporters are aging; a number of them have died in recent years. This reality brings a new urgency to peoples' stories. In El Salvador, many repopulated communities have established Historic Memory Committees to "rescatar la historia" (rescue history). As Rosa Rivera of Arcatao explained, those who lived through the war have a moral duty to record and pass on their truths to El Salvador's new generations—not only to avoid repeating the traumas of war ("Never Again!") but also to recognize, honor, and build upon the gains achieved through struggle, including the freedom of association with international partners.[78] In short, Rivera, the Wisconsin activist, and many others in El Salvador and the United States believe in the past and present political importance of sistering, and they wish to see the legacy of their work continue. They want their stories recorded; they seek permanent homes for their personal archives and historical ephemera.

This book is, in large part, a result of these new contexts. It builds on two decades of inquiry into the experiences of refugees from El Salvador's rural communities, and an equally long-standing connection to the US–El Salvador Sister Cities network through scholarly investigation, engaged research, and advocacy (see preface). The professional and personal relationships that evolved over time have facilitated unprecedented access to the personal records and memories of network activists. This historical data offers insights into the forms and functions of grassroots sistering; it also opens a truly unique window onto an intense period of transformation for the United States, El Salvador, and the world.

The book moves in a general chronological order as it traces the transnational work of Salvadoran and US activists. Chapter 1 uncovers the roots of the US–El Salvador Sister Cities movement. It illustrates how sistering emerged out of the 1960s to early 1980s radical Left in the United States and El Salvador, and how border-crossing activists from both countries worked together to build a coherent transnational political solidarity movement, which posed formidable challenges to authoritarian and imperial practices.

Chapter 2 explores a key strategy in this transnational movement's oppositional repertoire: "popular education." More specifically it examines human rights–themed delegations of US citizens to El Salvador and tours of Salvadorans in the US as consciousness-raising tools. Carefully crafted by Salvadoran and US sistering activists, these people-to-people exchanges were a powerful means to mobilize US citizens and to lend international legitimacy to El Salvador's rural repopulation movement.

The third and fourth chapters bridge the eras of conflict and peace. Most studies draw a hard dividing line at 1992, when negotiators from the FMLN and Salvadoran government finalized a peace agreement. The grassroots point of view of this study reveals, however, that 1992 was not the watershed that it has been portrayed to be. Chapter 3 traces how sistering activists presaged the end of military hostilities in El Salvador and helped define the nation's transition to peace. These pages emphasize how Salvadoran activists, accompanied by their international allies, redefined political relations for the postwar era. Whereas chapter 3 focuses on military and political relations, chapter 4 turns attention to how activists reframed social and economic relations. The chapter traces struggles over agricultural issues and social services to reveal deep competition between two different visions of the postwar world.

Together these chapters illustrate how grassroots sistering crossed literal and figurative borders, bringing activists from El Salvador and the United States together in a common struggle to build a more just and equitable world. "Another world is possible," declared left-leaning participants from around the globe who came together in the World Social Forum and other late twentieth-century events. Sister Cities activists took concerted actions to make that alternative world a reality. This book traces the early history of that work of mutual accompaniment, as US and Salvadoran activists traveled "shoulder to shoulder . . . down the long road toward peace based on justice, and social, political and economic democracy."[79]

1

Radical Roots

Conquering Our Rights

In the wee hours of the morning on October 10, 1987, Salvadorans began gathering at the gates of the Mesa Grande refugee camp, situated on a vast plain outside the town of San Marcos de Ocotepeque, in southwestern Honduras. As the sunlight strengthened, more than four thousand anxious women, men, and children loaded their belongings—plastic sheeting, straw sleeping mats, cooking pots, chickens—onto flatbed trucks, then boarded brightly painted buses. At around 6 a.m. the caravan of 110 vehicles began slowly snaking down from the mesa, through San Marcos, and toward the border with El Salvador. After years of living as refugees in the militarily cordoned camp—prohibited from seeking employment, interacting with local Hondurans, even moving between subcamps without an official pass and accompaniment—the Salvadorans were going home.

The people who boarded the buses that day were among the more than two million Salvadorans displaced by the civil war. More specifically, these refugees had escaped the state's "scorched earth" sweeps and associated massacres, such as those at the Sumpul and Lempa Rivers and in rural villages like Copapayo and La Cayetana. They had survived days and months of hiding in caves, ravines, and man-made underground holes (*tatús*), and the arduous cross-country flights known as *guindas*. They had witnessed the deaths of parents, children, spouses, and other loved ones. And they had weathered harsh years as refugees in a foreign country.

Displacement inevitably brought suffering in many forms. But contrary to popular representations of refugees, the Salvadorans' separation from home did not mean complete detachment. In fact, like displaced people elsewhere, many Salvadorans continued to mobilize and act with an eye toward a better future. Similar to the Communities of Population in Resistance of Guatemala, community associations of Sudanese and Somali immigrants in the United States, and Palestinians everywhere, Salvadorans displaced by the conflict in their country did what they could to maintain a sense of normalcy, securing food and shelter, protecting their families, and educating their children. To better guide them through difficult times, they assigned individuals to oversee the various tasks necessary for their group's survival, developed leadership structures, and elected representatives to *directivas*, or community councils. Through news media, clandestine information networks, and communications with international aid and solidarity workers, displaced Salvadorans remained informed about and involved with events occurring at home and abroad. And they framed many of their activities in the context of providing support (*dando un aporte*) for the revolutionary transformation of Salvadoran society from a military-oligarchy dictatorship to a participatory democracy.

There is perhaps no clearer sign of their commitment to building a New El Salvador than the grassroots mass repopulation movement.[1] As observers in the early 1980s reported, the displacement of Salvadoran civilians was "a result of a military policy of depopulating the countryside. The objective, in the words of one military official, is 'to take away the water from the fish,' regardless of the human and material cost. The fish are the guerrillas and the water the rural civilians."[2] Beginning in 1985, however, displaced Salvadorans joined together to directly challenge this policy of depopulation. First, internally displaced people began trickling back to villages in northeastern Chalatenango in a series of "silent repopulations."[3] Soon thereafter, groups of internally and externally displaced people were carrying out high-profile, large-scale repopulations in rural Chalatenango, Cabañas, Cuscatlán, and other departments (an administrative unit similar to US states). By mid-1988 more than thirty repopulations had occurred.[4] They continued in subsequent years so that, by the time representatives of the Salvadoran government and FMLN insurgent forces negotiated an end to the conflict in early 1992, most of the refugee camps were already closed.

The repopulators (*repobladores*) framed their return home as a component of the larger national liberation struggle, as a means to "defy the government and military to conquer our rights."[5] The first order of business was to make the Salvadoran government recognize and honor "the right that we have to return to and stay in our places of origin."[6] They would then "struggle to achieve peace . . . by planting our crops on our lands and demanding that our lives be respected."[7] By resettling abandoned villages, regaining their lives as farmers, and continuing to develop their communal structures and organizations, they would "forge democracy from the inside," compel the government to seek a negotiated solution to the conflict, and "participate in the construction of our future."[8]

The caravan that left the Mesa Grande refugee camp on October 10, 1987, marked a new stage in the grassroots repopulation movement. In addition to being the first mass return of Salvadorans from refuge sites in the exterior, it also was the largest repopulation to date. The goal was to send several hundred families each to five different villages: Santa Marta in Cabañas department, Copapayo in Cuscatlán, and San Antonio Los Ranchos, Las Vueltas, and Arcatao in Chalatenango. But the refugees involved in the first Mesa Grande repopulation knew that intentions and reality rarely lined up in wartime; their undertaking was extremely dangerous, the outcome entirely uncertain. Salvadoran government officials already had spent ten months refusing the refugees' right to return on their own terms; it was not until 9:30, the night before their scheduled departure from the camp, that the Salvadoran vice minister for the Interior relented. And although "cheers and applause" greeted the first refugees to step off the buses at the Honduras–El Salvador border station the next morning, neither the international press nor the religious and human rights representatives could erase the presence of the US Embassy officials or Salvadoran Army troops bearing M16s.[9] Nor could they ease the strain of the required interview by Salvadoran immigration officials, with its odd questionnaire that many believed was "designed to provide a base of information on each refugee, his/her family and political leanings [in order to] target specific individuals or families for surveillance."[10] In the back of the refugees' minds were the stories of their compatriots who had returned home only to be arrested and tortured, assassinated, or "disappeared." Just five weeks earlier, in fact, the Air Force of El Salvador had bombed and strafed Santa Marta—one of the planned repopulation sites—injuring six people and killing a man who had returned from Mesa Grande in 1985.[11]

It was the looming threat of state-sponsored terror that motivated displaced Salvadorans to insist on collective return rather than the individual voluntary repatriations promoted by the office of the United Nations High Commissioner for Refugees (UNHCR). It also inspired their marshalling of international religious peoples, solidarity activists, and human rights workers to accompany them. Hundreds of internationals physically accompanied this return from Mesa Grande, providing, in the words of one US-based organization, "moral and political support and protection to the refugees of Mesa Grande through their presence alongside them and in face-to-face meetings with military, political and religious leaders in Honduras and El Salvador."[12]

Despite harassment at the border and military checkpoints, along with lengthy delays and a general sense of insecurity, the Salvadorans succeeded in

Retornos from Mesa Grande. *Top*: "It Is Our Right to Return to El Salvador." Salvadoran refugees await the start of the fourth mass return from the Mesa Grande camp in Honduras. *Bottom*: Salvadorans leave Mesa Grande, starting their dangerous but hopeful journey home to El Salvador. (photos © Harvey Finkle, used with permission)

returning to the designated sites, where they began rebuilding communities from the ashes of war. Echoing the sentiments of the repopulators, a US-based support group called the return from Mesa Grande "a victory." As the group explained in a lengthy report, "The refugees asserted themselves as active agents in the struggle to claim their rights as Salvadoran nationals and noncombatants in a civil war." When combined with the other grassroots repopulations occurring around the same time, the return from Mesa Grande "represents a larger triumph as well," a complete "altering [of] the landscape of the decade-long war." In short, the report concluded, "Communities of refugees returning to their villages in conflictive zones may well represent a peace initiative in itself."[13]

The story of the Salvadoran rural repopulation movement is an unconventional narrative of the cold war era. It is unconventional in the sense that, rather than centering on US or Salvadoran government officials or the insurgent forces of the FMLN, it highlights the agency of poor people from the so-called Global South. It defies conventional representations of refugees as "bare life," as stateless wards of international agencies, as passive victims of events beyond their understanding or control.[14] It tells of human beings who strategically access and mobilize resources across borders—in defiance of government policies and in pursuit of higher goals.

Yet this unconventional narrative cannot be told—or its significance fully understood—without its broader historical context: the power struggle between the United States and the Soviet Union known in US shorthand as "the Cold War." When Ronald Reagan took office as president of the United States in January 1981, he adopted a decidedly callous attitude toward Central America. For Reagan and his conservative supporters, Jimmy Carter's "soft" foreign policy had produced chaos in the isthmus: the fall of the Somoza dynasty in Nicaragua and the rise of the Sandinistas' "reign of terror" offered proof that Cuba and the Soviet Union were on a crusade "to install communism by force throughout the hemisphere." El Salvador was the new front line in this bold exportation effort. "What we see in El Salvador," President Reagan warned in a 1984 televised speech, "is an attempt to destabilize the entire region and eventually move chaos and anarchy toward the American border." With communism "at our doorstep," it was time to roll back the Red Tide, Reagan railed. The United States had a "legal right" to counter Soviet subversion in "our hemisphere," to protect "our way of life." But we also had "a moral duty" to come to the aid of our "peace-loving friends depending on our help." In El Salvador, for example, "it would be profoundly immoral" to ignore the "yearning for democracy" and leave that tiny, resource-poor nation "to slowly bleed to death." The United States would "get the job done," Reagan promised, with "strong-willed diplomacy" and sustained security assistance to friendly regimes and "freedom fighters" in Central America.[15]

Through El Salvador's war years (1980–92), the United States provided over $6 billion in aid—the bulk of it during the Reagan administration.[16] Many Salvadorans and international observers believe that had the United States not intervened, the conflict would have been much shorter and far less bloody. Instead, US aid heightened the levels of violence—and resistance. Many people from rural villages reported how, in the wake of state terror campaigns, they felt compelled to take action in defense of their families and communities— and against the Salvadoran state and its US backers.[17] Reagan's militarized response to troubles in the isthmus also contributed to a "reinvigoration of the Left" in the United States. As the longtime activist Marc Rosenthal explained, although Reagan's election marked the start of a terrible administration, it was also a "great moment" in that it spurred "political agitation and in a very real way."[18] Hundreds of grassroots groups focused on Central America emerged during the Reagan administration. Among them was US–El Salvador Sister Cities.

This chapter examines the deep roots of the Sister Cities network. It argues that although in many ways grassroots sistering—and US-based Central America solidarity work more generally—continued in the shoes of its New Left predecessors, it also took the struggle for radical democracy to new heights. The people who established the first sistering relationships in the early and mid-1980s initiated a new design of transnational activism—one that intimately intertwined with national liberation struggles occurring around the world as well as the emerging globalization of human rights activism. Key to the new design was that it was inspired by El Salvador's war-displaced as part of their struggle to return home to reclaim their rights as citizens and to rebuild their communities and transform their country into a just and equitable nation, a New El Salvador.

Empire and Dissent

Ronald Reagan was not the first US president to express an "almost paranoid concern" with foreign incursions into "our backyard."[19] In 1823 President James Monroe marked a new era of US foreign policy by declaring the American hemisphere off-limits to European powers; any attempt by a European nation to oppress or control the newly independent American nations would be considered "the manifestation of an unfriendly disposition toward the United States" and very "dangerous to our peace and safety."[20]

President Theodore Roosevelt offered a corollary to the Monroe Doctrine in 1904, promising that the United States would mobilize as "an international police power" in the Western Hemisphere to address "flagrant cases" of "chronic wrongdoing" or "impotence which results in a general loosening of the ties of civilized society."[21]

Such policies enabled the US government to apply direct pressure on its counterparts across the Americas. The first half of the twentieth century saw long-term US occupations in Nicaragua, Haiti, the Dominican Republic, and Cuba, and short-term interventions, invasions, and other direct shows of force in these countries along with Mexico, Uruguay, Panama, and across the Central American isthmus.[22] But, as the historian Alan Knight points out, this kind of direct involvement "incurs costs, in terms of both blood and treasure, and runs counter to American [sic] values of democracy and self-determination."[23] And so, the United States has often applied pressures through more indirect channels, spreading its own authority and "shaping the activities of its fellow American states to its own interests" not solely through military force but also through "economic, political, and cultural dominance."[24]

With the onset of cold war, these two forms of US empire—informal and formal—became tightly interwoven as the United States and its regional allies worked to counter Soviet expansionism. Using the looming threat of communist subversion as a rationale, US government agencies sought to quell any leftist movement in the region. On the military front, they invaded the Dominican Republic, Grenada, and Panama; attempted (with some success) to assassinate Leftist leaders throughout the region; promoted military coups in Guatemala, Brazil, and Chile; built new military bases and intelligence networks in Honduras, El Salvador, and the Southern Cone; and trained, equipped, and advised paramilitary organizations and regular armed forces in "counterinsurgency" and "counterterror" tactics. In addition to these overt and covert military actions, US government agencies applied pressures in the economic and political spheres. These ranged from employing blockades and sanctions to isolate "rebel" nations (e.g., Cuba), to sponsoring "demonstration elections," to devising and carrying out "civic action" programs to "win hearts and minds."[25]

Although US involvement spanned from the Southern Cone to Mexico, the small nation of El Salvador carried a particularly large weight in the "Empire's Workshop."[26] In the first four years of John F. Kennedy's Alliance for Progress, El Salvador received far more attention than its neighbors; according to the historian Walter LaFeber, some $63 million in aid converted the country into "the pride of the Alliance."[27] Support continued with some fits and starts through the Nixon and Carter years, and skyrocketed again under

Reagan in the 1980s. Although much of the assistance had direct military aims, funds also supported political and economic objectives through civic action programs, elections, land reform, and economic development initiatives. As the historian Greg Grandin stated, "El Salvador became Washington's most ambitious nation-building project since South Vietnam."[28]

Latin American nations and citizens were not simply passive recipients of all that the US government offered, of course. Many resisted US influences in a variety of ways, from Augusto Sandino's years-long effort to oust the US marines from Nicaragua, to Juan José Arévalo's fable, *The Shark and the Sardines*, which critiqued the crooked methods used by international powerhouses like the United States to take advantage of Guatemala and other nations.[29]

Other Latin Americans willingly engaged with the United States—although they did not necessarily adopt a "tow-the-line" attitude. Many of the region's business and political elites "became acutely aware of the utility of great power involvement and intervention, which they might creatively exploit," explained Knight. "A kind of geopolitical 'tail-wagging-the-dog' developed, as embattled Latin American leaders . . . angled for US support and even intervention."[30] This certainly was true in El Salvador. For instance, although politicians passed a number of the reform laws encouraged by the Alliance, the few that were implemented tended to benefit only the elite and, so, the "power and wealth of the oligarchs burgeoned with the Alliance."[31] Thus, following the anthropologist Adán Quan's lead, we must see foreign assistance as a social process, a series of negotiations that, despite uneven power dynamics, provides local actors opportunities to appropriate new resources, which they then can adapt to their own needs and realities.[32]

If Salvadoran elites could find ways to benefit from relationships with the US government, the majority of Salvadorans could not. Commercial export agriculture had dominated the country for more than a century, enriching a small number of families while impoverishing the rest. By the 1970s the disparities were highly evident in infrastructure development. El Salvador's export-heavy departments held more than 70 percent of the country's paved roads, along with the best access to electricity, potable water, education, and health care services. Departments with marginal effect on export markets, in contrast, ranked the highest levels of illiteracy and lowest access to services—as low as 2 percent in some areas.[33] Disparities were also clear in land distribution, as Elizabeth Wood has pointed out: "Farms of more than 200 hectares constituted less than 0.5% of all farms, but they held over one-third of the land; while half of the farms were smaller than 1 hectare but together comprised just 4% of the land." The landless population, moreover, had surpassed 51 percent—a nightmare for this agrarian society.[34]

Even within this broader context, it is important to acknowledge that rural Salvadorans, like marginalized people everywhere, adeptly built alternative livelihoods outside the bounds of the "official" economy. Recent research has begun to bring into focus the world's many alternatives, including gift economies, collective forms of subsistence and solidarity, and transnational exchange networks. Some of these alternative livelihoods are deeply rooted in precapitalist local histories and traditions. Others emerged alongside capitalism, functioning parallel to and at times overlapping with market relations. Still others appeared in direct resistance to what many academics and activists refer to as the "enclosure of the commons" that has undermined noncapitalist lifeways and modes of survival and sociality since the agrarian revolution.[35]

Just as marginalized sectors of Salvadoran society creatively engaged noncapitalist modes of livelihood in the twentieth century, they also joined together in myriad ways to confront an entrenched oligarchy and its military allies. Peasants, laborers, progressive Catholics, leftist intellectuals, and others formed mutual-aid societies, cooperatives, unions, and political parties to press for reforms in laws governing minimum wage, worker conditions, land tenure, access to agricultural credit, education, and other aspects of political and economic life. To further strengthen their voice, they joined in cross-sector coalitions, often linked to armed insurgent groups, to carry out nationwide marches, demonstrations, and strikes at schools, factories, and plantations. By 1980 the Popular Revolutionary Bloc (Bloque Popular Revolucionario) emerged as the largest of these mass coalitions, with some sixty thousand affiliates. Founded by peasants, educators, and students aligned with the Popular Liberation Forces (Fuerzas Populares de Liberación), the Bloc combined high-profile actions like the occupation of government ministries, embassies, and the national cathedral, with astute propaganda and organizational skill to challenge the authoritarian regime.[36]

Although such actions did produce some limited results, including salary increases at several plantations, efforts for wider reforms failed. An agrarian reform plan promoted by President Arturo Molina in the mid-1970s, for example, prompted such a backlash from plantation owners and business elites that Molina abandoned the plan. But the stillbirth of the Agrarian Transformation contributed to a growing realization: as the martyred Jesuit philosopher Ignacio Ellacuría put it in a 1976 editorial, "Certainly we can't expect any profoundly structural change in a Government that has the oligarchy as its principal ally." Combined with election fraud, increasing surveillance and arrests, and other repressive acts, this abrogation of state duty to promote the interests of the majority of its citizens served as a call to action for many of those citizens. "Reason lives on," Ellacuría promised. "The collective consciousness has advanced" and Salvadorans would further strengthen it as they worked together to bring change. "It is still the time to promote popular and peasant organizations," he wrote, and "to remind the Government that it does not have . . . the least right to repress people who are demanding what the Government itself has said is absolutely right and inalienable."[37]

Ellacuría and his colleagues, along with Salvadoran laborers, peasants, educators, and others, would continue to press for reforms through the late 1970s and 1980s, even in the face of rising levels of repression. In addition to targeting specific leaders of the popular movement organizations, state forces carried out large-scale maneuvers—for example, opening fire into crowds of demonstrators, raiding and occupying the National University, and massacring hundreds of peasants in rural "clean-up sweeps."

The intransigence of the Salvadoran regime propelled many on the left to consider the viability of armed revolt. In the early 1960s and continuing through the 1970s, predominantly urban activists—students, Catholics, and members of the Salvadoran Communist Party—began forming militant organizations. Although sectarian differences plagued relations between these groups, particularly on issues relating to political policies and strategies, insurgents across the spectrum operated on the shared belief that it was necessary to liberate the people and nation of El Salvador, which meant toppling the tyrannical military-oligarchic regime and replacing it with a "popular revolutionary government"; and reforming the nation's political, economic, and social structures to ensure the inclusion of previously marginalized sectors. By 1980 five of these politico-military organizations had begun to work around some of their differences, enabling their formal alliance in the Farabundo Martí National Liberation Front (FMLN). The FMLN would go on to wage war against the Salvadoran government and its US allies until 1992, when the two sides signed a peace accord and the FMLN transformed into a political party.

Arguably the largest and most influential of the organizations that made up the FMLN coalition was the Popular Liberation Forces (FPL). With origins in both the Salvadoran Communist Party and a politically active generation of university students, the FPL approached revolution in El Salvador as a prolonged popular war (*guerra popular prolongada*); through a concerted combination of military and political work, the FPL intended to gradually wear down the authoritarian regime and its US allies. Key to this strategy was engaging not only the radicalized urban middle classes but also labor movements and the poor peasantry. With the help of several astute organizers, the FPL became a key influence in the predominantly rural Chalatenango province, building close alliances with members of the Union of Rural Workers, the radical Catholic Church, and Popular Revolutionary Bloc affiliates based in this isolated area.[38]

The close relationship between the FPL cadres and rural residents of Chalatenango in particular is evident in the Local Popular Governments, through which residents in rural areas elected leaders, organized work committees and agricultural collectives, and coordinated services like education and health care. The Local Popular Governments began taking shape in FPL-controlled zones around 1982 and achieved their "highest level of development" in northern Chalatenango.[39] There, according to one FMLN source from the era, a "deep collaboration" (relación profunda) existed between the Popular Governments and the FPL. The true depth of this collaboration or, more to the point, the extent of insurgent direction of civilian organizing initiatives like these local governments is a matter of debate—and will continue to be until researchers gain unfettered access to documentation from the politico-military organizations that made up the FMLN coalition. Existing research suggests that the FMLN leadership imposed order and maintained tight control in some locales, while in other sites they served more of a guiding role. By the same token, some rural activists offer historical narratives tightly interwoven with the politico-military forces, while others tend toward more autonomous stories. No one narrative fits all experiences, of course, but we can say, in general terms, that without the military protection of the insurgent forces, the Local Popular Governments could not have functioned. At the same time, the local governments enabled the Popular Liberation Forces to promote a concrete alternative political project; they were, according to an FMLN source, "the foundation of the future democratic revolutionary government."[40]

Many people involved with El Salvador's left and center-left social and politico-military movements during the latter half of the twentieth century viewed la lucha (the struggle) in both national and international terms. They considered the country's legendary "fourteen families" (i.e., the oligarchy) and the US government as bedfellows, with US imperial pressures representing an extension of the Salvadoran elite's long history of internal colonialism.[41] As a result, popular mobilizations often linked national subjects like unequal distribution of land, inhumane labor conditions at factories and plantations, poverty, and facade democracy to international issues or, more specifically, US power. Each social movement and revolutionary organization had its own particular ideology and methodology, yet despite the differences they coincided on holding both Salvadoran and US elites accountable for the ills of society. Leftist intellectuals, for example, formed the United Revolutionary Action Front (Frente Unido de Acción Revolucionaria, FUAR) in 1961 to counter repression under President José María Lemus (1956–60) and to oppose deepening

US intervention in El Salvador. The Alliance for Progress, according to FUAR, represented "a new method of Yankee colonization," part of a US government plan to transform El Salvador into a US colony, a "second Puerto Rico."[42]

In a similar vein, the Federation of Rural Workers (Federación de Trabajadores del Campo) arose in the 1970s out of the "conditions of misery, starvation and exploitation that the field workers are forced into by the rich yankees and creoles [Salvadoran oligarchy]." The federation actively sought to change those conditions, publicly encouraging the struggle "against imperialism, the creole bourgeoisie and their puppet governments."[43] Likewise, the Revolutionary Coordinator of the Masses had a dual target: "To overthrow the reactionary military dictatorship of the oligarchy and Yankee imperialism."[44] Even the figurehead of El Salvador's Catholic Church joined the chorus. In a 1980 letter to President Jimmy Carter, the archbishop of El Salvador, Oscar Romero, argued that US military aid only enabled the country's security forces to use "even greater violence . . . in repressing the people" of El Salvador "who have been struggling because of their fundamental respect for human rights." Romero urged outgoing President Carter not only to "prohibit" further aid but also to "guarantee that your government will not intervene, directly or indirectly with military, economic or diplomatic pressure in determining the destiny of the Salvadoran people."[45]

If "Yankee imperialism" was a detriment, other international currents provided inspiration. Literary and cultural movements around the world influenced Salvadoran creative expressions through music, theater, poetry, and other forms. Similarly, inspired by the social doctrines of Vatican II and Medellín as well as liberation theology more generally, many Salvadorans broke from the conservative traditions of the Roman Catholic Church to adopt a "preferential option for the poor." Through a variety of projects, including peasant universities, literacy programming on the radio, and Bible study groups linked to Christian base communities, these Catholics worked closely with marginalized communities on political consciousness-raising and organizing initiatives as a means of challenging structures of exclusion.

The Salvadoran social movement organizations that mobilized between the 1960s and 1980s also found great inspiration in the Cuban and Nicaraguan Revolutions. In both of these countries, the United States had long backed repressive regimes. For many on the left, Fidel Castro's 26th of July Movement, which successfully toppled the dictatorship of Fulgencio Batista in Cuba in 1959, and the Sandinista National Liberation Front, which followed suit with the Somoza dynasty in Nicaragua in late 1979, symbolized the rewriting of power relations within the individual nations and between these nations and the United States. In early 1980, it appeared likely that El Salvador would be next in the revolutionary series. Despite increasing levels of repression, Salvadoran civil society continued demanding major reforms to the country's political and economic structures. Frustrations prompted general strikes, the occupation of government ministries, and public demonstrations such as a massive January protest march during which an estimated one hundred thousand people flowed through the streets of San Salvador to the National Palace and Cathedral. At the same time, armed organizations on the left stepped up their activities, occupying political party headquarters and foreign embassies, and confronting government security forces in city and countryside. When five of these groups united under the banner of the Farabundo Martí National Liberation Front, it appeared that "Final Victory"—and a further rewriting of regional power relations—was just around the corner.

Up north, meanwhile, a "movement of movements" in the United States struggled "to overturn existing structures of racial, gender, and economic privilege in favor of a radical vision of equality and democracy."[46] These movements on the left represented a range of different interests from labor, farming, and immigrants to students and free speech; to the rights of Black people, American Indians, Chicanos, and women, among others. They drew on and collaborated with dynamic political bands, from Grangers and Progressives, to Socialists, Farm Labor, and Democrats. They launched major challenges to the US status quo in the early and mid-twentieth century, sparking new legislation on a range of issues including direct primary elections, women's suffrage, labor rights, social security, consumer safety, regulations on corporations, and racial equality.

Even as they endeavored "to make life better on the home front," US leftists shared deep concerns about international affairs. Indeed, many critiques launched by the Left during the twentieth century intertwined national issues (internal colonialism) with international affairs (US imperial practices around the world). Midwestern socialists, for example, denounced World War I as "a tool of US capitalism and imperialism."[47] Some fifty years later, voices on the left condemned US intervention in Vietnam as "a significant part of the government's intensifying assertion of colonial rule within the US itself." Conversations among soldiers and veterans from working-class and poor backgrounds, many of them people of color, led to a growing awareness "about the similarities of the Vietnamese struggle for emancipation and self-determination and those then occurring among communities of color" in the United States. This, in turn, fed a variety of forms of "resistance within the military" and "confrontations with the draft."[48] In a similar vein, laborers like William Winpisinger of the International Association of Machinists denounced the US government's false bill of goods regarding military spending. "The arms budget has been viewed as a giant public works program to stimulate the economy and provide jobs and income," he wrote. "We now know the truth. Far from aiding prosperity, excessive arms spending weakens civilian industry and is a major cause of inflation and unemployment."[49] Activism around the war in Vietnam and the nuclear arms race represented more than a call to bring the troops home or for US and Soviet disarmament; it also represented a challenge to the cold war consensus and "the establishment."[50]

The Cuban Revolution offered great inspiration to leftists who sought to challenge the establishment. Many US citizens traveled to the island to witness firsthand the transformations happening there, and returned "stirred and impressed" by what they had seen.[51] Prominent African Americans and allies of the US civil rights movement joined the leadership ranks of the Fair Play for Cuba Committee; their protests against increasingly hostile and interventionist US policies toward Cuba were inspired in part by Fidel Castro's abolition of segregation in Cuba and his critiques of Jim Crow in the United States.[52] Radical scholars assessed the revolution "as a movement for freedom and an attempt to create a 'humane society,'" and student activists commended the "attempt to direct human history, to take hold of one's environment and shape it, to institutionalize better human values."[53] The Cuban Revolution was a "signal event" for the US Left in yet another way; it was "refreshingly new," activist Saul Landau recalled, as well as "bold and daring to stick its finger straight in Uncle Sam's eye."[54]

Although some argue that the impact of Cuban solidarity was limited, the underlying sentiments continued to inspire solidarity efforts elsewhere in Latin America.[55] Among those inspired was Arthur Lloyd, the Episcopal chaplain at the St. Francis House in Madison. In 1961 Lloyd had spent time in Brazil working alongside "companion churches," traveling, and learning about the lives of ordinary people in a society on the brink of upheaval. A few years later the Brazilian Armed Forces carried out a coup d'état, initiating a brutal military dictatorship that lasted until 1985. In the midst of that dictatorship, Presbyterians in campus ministry at Cornell University invited Lloyd and other representatives from the Universities of Wisconsin, Texas, and California to a meeting to determine how best to respond to feedback that they had been receiving from colleagues in Brazil for years: "Don't bring your students down here. Go back home and do your work at home." Out of the Cornell meeting came a plan to establish "little community campus organizations that would try to use the resources of the campus and the campus ministry connections to the churches . . . to develop educational programs around what was going on in Latin America and what was the US's involvement."[56]

On returning to Madison, Lloyd and the other Wisconsin representatives formed Community Action on Latin America (CALA). This campus organization promptly rose to national prominence by hosting two large conferences: the Non-Intervention in Chile founding conference in 1971 and, in 1974, the Conference on Repression and Development in Brazil and Latin America, which the historian James Green points to as the beginning of a "qualitatively different phase" in solidarity work with Latin America.[57] Indeed the 1960s and 1970s saw a rapid increase in the number of organizations dedicated to raising awareness about the currents of change flowing in Latin America as well as US policies in the region. These ranged from local groups like Madison's CALA and the Chicago Area Group on Latin America to national organizations like the North American Congress on Latin America, and the Latin American Working Group of the National Council of Churches.[58]

By the late 1970s and early 1980s, when Nicaragua, Guatemala, and El Salvador moved to center stage, these organizations took leading roles in the emerging Central America solidarity movement. In Madison, CALA affiliates helped to establish one of the country's first chapters of the Committee in Solidarity with the People of El Salvador (CISPES) in 1980. Likewise an active CALA member raised the idea of sanctuary in Madison. Drawing from biblical histories as well as more recent experiences with the underground railroad, civil rights movement, and conscientious objection during the US war in Vietnam, sanctuary offered a physical safe haven and legal assistance to undocumented Central Americans who were at risk of being detained by US immigration officials and subsequently deported to their home countries. In April 1983, with the support of some fifteen congregations, Madison's St. Francis House Episcopal Church became the first church in the area to declare itself a sanctuary for Central American refugees. Other Wisconsin faith centers followed and, in September 1986, Governor Anthony S. Earle proclaimed Wisconsin a Sanctuary State for refugees from Guatemala and El Salvador.[59] They joined more than three hundred other sites across the United States, and thousands of activists who "invoked and reinterpreted legal, cultural, and religious practices in new ways," forming what the anthropologist Susan Bibler Coutin termed a "culture of protest."[60]

Beyond sanctuary, hundreds of other groups formed across the country, ranging from local collectives of a handful of people to county- and state-wide organizations. They included student groups, faith-based initiatives, and organizations that specialized in medical aid. These were independent, not-for-profit organizations made up of average citizens from civil society: nurses and doctors, teachers and students, priests and nuns, a variety of other professionals, and homemakers. Thousands of people were involved. They were, for the most part, middle-class, white volunteers who donated time, money, materials, and skills to help staff offices and carry out projects. They brought with them a variety of backgrounds, experiences, and ideologies and, as a result, offered a wide range of skills and commitment levels.

The US–El Salvador Sister Cities network emerged out of and formed part of these fields of struggle. Each Salvadoran and US American group drew on rich local histories and resources particular to that site, and individual activists often participated in multiple efforts at the same time. And while sistering advocates participated in social movement organizing at the local levels, it was their shared frustrations with US empire that prompted them to come together in the early 1980s to forge a unique transnational copresence. Although the northern and southern participants in the sistering network came from such different backgrounds and contexts, they shared concerns about systems and structures of poverty and exclusion; political, economic, civil, and human rights; and the proper complementary roles of State and Citizen. Thus, as El Salvador became "a volcano in eruption" in the 1980s, many US activists rallied with the Salvadorans and their revolutionary cause.[61] Inspired by history and the promise of a better future, they organized and mobilized together against the "alienation characteristic of late capitalism" and toward community, fellowship, and solidarity.[62]

Repopulation, Accompaniment, and the Birth of Sistering

The year 1985 marked an important turning point in the Salvadoran conflict, as displaced people joined together to directly counter the government's policy of depopulation through the very public repopulation of villages they had been forced to abandon years earlier. Peace talks happened for the first time in 1984, and a new civilian president, José Napoleón Duarte, was elected late that same year after a campaign promising "national dialogue" and "democratization," among other things. In part to test Duarte's political opening and the related decline in scorched-earth campaigns, internally displaced people began trickling back home.

Some observers claim that this movement of displaced Salvadorans was the result of a directive from top FMLN leaders, yet the reality is more complicated, with myriad local-level nuances.[63] Many different people and organizations were involved with repopulations. Displaced Salvadorans nurtured their own organizations, including the Christian Committee for the Displaced of El Salvador (CRIPDES) and the National Coordinator of Repopulations (CNR), both of which were pro-FMLN. And El Salvador's Catholic and Lutheran churches along with a variety of national and international nongovernmental organizations and aid groups sponsored and otherwise supported repopulation projects between 1986 and 1992.

We still have much to learn about the relations between different participants, but there is no question that the repopulations could not have occurred the way they did without the motivation and support of the FMLN—and specifically the Popular Liberation Forces (FPL). Simply stated, relationships between civilian activists and FMLN factions influenced the timing of the repopulations, the selection of repopulation sites, and their subsequent development. For instance, in 1984 and 1985 hundreds of people emerged from hiding to carry out "silent repopulations" of Arcatao and other villages in northeastern Chalatenango.[64] This region was then under the control of the FPL, with Arcatao as the "de facto revolutionary capital," and the returns coincided with the strategic shift to smaller combat units.[65]

Similarly, activists associated with CRIPDES and CNR, particularly those in leadership positions, were aligned with the FPL, with many leaders shifting between work as armed combatants and civilian organizers. This helps explain why and how, by mid-1986, they began coordinating mass repopulations to Chalatenango and other zones of FPL influence—and why, despite their proven skills, they did not directly coordinate repopulations in areas dominated by other politico-military organizations. It does appear that the success of the early repopulations in FPL territory prompted affiliates of other politico-military organizations to organize their own repopulations, including Panchimilama, La Paz (Communist Party of El Salvador/Armed Forces of Liberation); Nuevo Gualcho, Usulután (Revolutionary Party of Central American Workers); and Meanguera, Morazán (People's Revolutionary Army). All of these certainly were part of the broader rural repopulation movement, but because they did not associate with the FPL, CRIPDES, CNR, or Sister Cities, they fall outside the scope of this study.[66]

It was, in large part, the October 1987 return of more than four thousand people from the Mesa Grande refugee camp in Honduras—described in the introduction to this chapter—that solidified FPL affiliates as the frontrunners of the repopulation movement. Over the next two years, CRIPDES and CNR, working closely with refugee committees at Mesa Grande and other allies, carried out six more mass returns from Mesa Grande, involving some fourteen thousand people.[67] By early 1991 CRIPDES and CNR had coordinated the repopulation of more than one hundred rural communities in eight of the country's fourteen departments.[68]

As population numbers increased in the different regions, CRIPDES-CNR affiliates created new committees to better coordinate their work. These soon consolidated into five major committees, each representing a distinct region

CRIPDES regions

1. Coordinadora de Comunidades y Repoblaciones de Chalatenango, CCR (Coordinator of Communities and Repopulations of Chalatenango)

2. Coordinadora para el Desarrollo Rural de San Vicente, CDR (Coordinator for Rural Development of San Vicente)

3. Promogestora de Repoblaciones Solidarias de los Departamentos de Cuscatlán-Cabañas, PROGRESO (Association for the Promotion and Advancement of Solidary Repopulations in Cuscatlán and Cabañas)

4. Comité de Desplazados y Marginados de La Libertad, CODESMA (Committee of the Displaced and Marginalized of La Libertad)

5. Unión de Comunidades y Repoblaciones del Norte de San Salvador y La Libertad, UCRES (Union of Communities and Repopulations of Northern San Salvador and La Libertad)

CRIPDES regions and committees. (Map by Rachel V. Dunlap)

of the country. Although each committee developed its own work plan that responded to unique local realities, committees coordinated on a national level through representatives elected to the CRIPDES National Board of Directors.

Even if we still have much to discover about relations between insurgents, displaced Salvadorans, and international solidarity groups, the currently accessible historical record is resoundingly clear about the critical importance of international support for the repopulation movement. Materials found in solidarity archives in the United States reveal that Salvadorans persistently lobbied US American audiences. Refugees in the camps of Honduras and other Central American nations wrote letters to *internacionales* requesting their moral and physical accompaniment in the camps and during their return home. From the repopulated communities, Salvadorans called for continued support: food aid, materials for shelter, protection from army operations, prayers for peace. Children and women created drawings and embroideries for international audiences, graphically depicting horrors of war, hopes for the future, and gratitude to international solidarity.[69] And allies in faith-based organizations in El Salvador issued a formal appeal to the "Religious Community of the United States" for "spiritual, moral and economic support" in the "search for peace." "We invite you to continue a permanent accompaniment," they wrote. "HELP US END THE WAR BEFORE THE WAR ENDS US."[70]

The calls from displaced Salvadorans and repopulators hit a chord in the United States. Some people responded out of a simple desire to help relieve suffering.[71] Many others were spurred into action not out of pity or charity but out of admiration; they celebrated the rural repopulations as a "movement of hope" that was bringing people home, rebuilding communities "from the ground up."[72] Visitors to the repopulated villages lauded them as "seeds of peace" offering "valuable lessons in faith and cooperative living" and "wonderful examples of grassroots democracy."[73] They were "so self-organized," Mary Kay Baum recalled, "creating their own schools . . . young people with an eighth grade education teaching third graders. . . . Just amazing."[74] Health professionals highlighted how grassroots health promoters and "medics make rounds to villages on a regular basis, thus delivering health care to people in rural areas who now receive medicines and preventive medical care for the first time."[75] Marc Rosenthal remembered visiting Arcatao and seeing "everyone coming out in the morning to sweep clean the streets together. Everyone ate in the *comedor* [communal café]. Collective life. Quite an experiment." It was, simply put, "an alternative world."[76]

We have seen similar sentiments arise in late 2018 and 2019 in response to caravans of Central American migrants arriving at the US border. Some observers interpret these caravans as a grassroots movement claiming the human rights to move across borders, to seek safety, and to create a dignified life. Some scholars have reconceptualized transborder migration from El Salvador to the United States as a movement of "civil disobedience" against the global apartheid of nation-states under capitalism.[77] Even for people who might not make such claims, the stories and hopes shared by migrants and their allies have inspired actions, from donations of labor and other resources to migrant support groups like No More Deaths, to human rights investigations and lobbying on Capitol Hill, to the formation of a new sanctuary movement.

In the 1980s, the Salvadoran repopulators' commitment to building a better world—in the midst of a bloody conflict in which the US government was intimately involved—also moved US citizens into action. Faith centers, student groups, and solidarity organizations collected donations of medical and educational materials, and raised funds for El Salvador's displaced by sponsoring events like bowl-a-thons, sock hops, and toga parties.[78]

By 1983 two California-based organizations had risen to positions as "solidarity brokers": the Salvadoran Humanitarian Aid, Research and Education Foundation (SHARE), and New El Salvador Today (NEST).[79] They served as funding channels for material aid and worked closely with community organizations across the United States to coordinate national information campaigns and delegations to El Salvador. Both SHARE and NEST had ties to the FPL. Both also laid the groundwork for long-term people-to-people relationships between Salvadoran and US communities. Whereas SHARE focused on connecting faith communities, NEST linked US Americans with the Local Popular Governments.[80]

The first formal sister-city relationship grew out of the work of NEST staff and repopulators at San Antonio los Ranchos, in northern Chalatenango department. The repopulators expressed the desire to establish "a close relationship" with a town in the United States whose "assistance and solidarity," they said, would "greatly help to resolve the most serious problems that we face at this time."[81] A few months later, on July 19, 1983, the city council of Berkeley, California, voted to adopt a resolution "Establishing a Sister City Affiliation with San Antonio Los Ranchos, El Salvador."[82] "The significance of this event cannot be underestimated," as NEST director Tracey Schear wrote of the city council resolution. "The sister-city program gives us, as citizens of Berkeley, the opportunity to assist the positive and concrete efforts of the people of San Antonio Los Ranchos as they build their society from the ashes of this war." That the US government was deeply implicated in the war was not lost on Schear or other supporters of the new sister-city affiliation. The economic and military aid that the US government provided the Salvadoran regime, Schear noted, "has resulted in the death of over 40,000 Salvadorans."[83] Karen Matthews of the *Berkeley Gazette* pointed out that the city council formalized the sister-city affiliation the very same week that "the state department certified the improvement of human rights in El Salvador and President Reagan appointed Henry Kissinger to head a new commission on Central America."[84]

The Berkeley–San Antonio Los Ranchos pairing became the model for subsequent pairings. To expand this model, NEST collaborated with "influential" leaders in communities around the United States "to develop a political plan for the passage of a sister city resolution by the local city council, that incorporates the broadest community participation."[85] The new sister cities would work, like Berkeley and Los Ranchos, "to build inter-cultural bonds of friendship and understanding, to provide a sustained source of economic, material and technical assistance to Salvadoran communities in distress, and to educate U.S. communities about the conditions and needs in El Salvador."[86] Over the next few years, NEST staff facilitated connections between repopulators in Arcatao and San José Las Flores—two villages just up the road from Los Ranchos—and activists in Madison, Wisconsin, and Cambridge, Massachusetts. After an initial period of exploration involving letters, proposals, and in-person meetings, the US activists took the sister-city resolution plan to their local leaders. Madison's Common Council passed a resolution establishing a sister city with Arcatao in April 1986 and, the following March, the Cambridge City Council "swiftly and unanimously" passed a similar resolution for San José Las Flores.[87]

Activists involved in these first three US sister cities would go on to help establish other sistering relationships and accompaniment projects. Paralleling the expansion of the repopulation movement in El Salvador and the growth of CRIPDES as the movement's representative organization, sistering committees in the United States increased from just three in mid-1987 to nine in November 1988, then from eleven to seventeen in 1991 alone.[88] During the same period, the SHARE Foundation expanded its sister parish program and CRIPDES broadened its sistering network to Canada, Germany, and Spain. By the time the peace accords went into effect in 1992, Salvadorans reported ninety-three sistering relationships—fifty-three of them with the United States.[89]

As the number of US-based sistering committees rose, leading activists perceived the need for more formal collaboration. Beginning in 1988, sistering advocates from around the country gathered annually to share successes and challenges, and to discuss collective goals and strategies. Out of the first national meeting in 1988 came the decision to form a national association to coordinate activities and facilitate communications among the US committees and with their Salvadoran partners; over the next several years, they established the National Center for US–El Salvador Sister Cities in New York, hired staff and recruited an advisory board, and acquired 501(c)3 nonprofit status. Paralleling their CRIPDES partners, they also began organizing on regional levels, appointing promoters for the Midwest, Northeast, and Mid-Atlantic, who facilitated meetings and training workshops in Boston, Chicago, and elsewhere on topics such as committee building and development, fundraising, and delegations. By 1992 the US–El Salvador Sister Cities network had established an office in San Salvador, staffed by two men, Guillermo Chacón, a Salvadoran who had been living in the United States, and Tim Lohrentz of Kansas.

If Salvadorans made the initial call to US citizens for accompaniment, Salvadorans also shepherded the work of sistering activists. CRIPDES affiliates maintained communication with SHARE, NEST, the National Center for Sister Cities, and individual sistering committees; beginning in October 1988, they also regularly hosted international sistering summits (*cumbres*). These two-day events served, among other things, to guide foreign sistering representatives, and to draw widespread media attention to the internationally supported repopulation movement.

Although US and Salvadoran teams collaborated to carry out the summits, the prominent Salvadoran leadership is evident in planning documents from the first summit. Sister Cities records include materials produced for the summit by CRIPDES and CNR staff as well as members of the directivas of repopulations. Far more prevalent, however, are materials from two Salvadorans living in the United States, José Artiga and Oscar Chacón. At the helm of a new organization, the Interfaith Office for Accompaniment, Artiga and Chacón contributed to the development and execution of the months-long summit work plan. In addition, they communicated regularly with sistering representatives and solidarity groups, convened a planning meeting of US Sister Cities in Washington, DC, and drafted and circulated the "Covenant of Solidarity" document that participants ultimately signed at the summit in San José Las Flores in October 1988.[90]

As materials from this first sistering summit suggest, US-based sistering work in general was due in large part to the work of Salvadoran refugees and exiles living in the United States. These activists—many of them affiliated with the Popular Liberation Forces and related mass organizations—had fled their homeland in the 1970s and early 1980s, only to take on new activist roles in their host country. They worked diligently to raise awareness among US citizens about the Salvadoran conflict, the role of the US government in that conflict, and the hope represented by the rural repopulation movement.[91] They also played a critical role in fostering connections between US solidarity activists, and guided the development of the US–El Salvador Sister Cities network.

José Artiga is one example of such a leader. Active with social movement organizations linked to the Popular Liberation Forces, Artiga fled El Salvador in 1980 after government soldiers murdered several of his friends and then threatened his own family. By October 1980, he was in Los Angeles, California, where he attended the founding convention of the Committee in Solidarity with the People of El Salvador (CISPES), an organization that quickly grew to thousands of members in dozens of chapters across the United States. A few months later Artiga relocated to San Francisco where, as executive director of the refugee support group Casa El Salvador, he "helped launch the sanctuary movement that helped refugees, denounced human rights violations, and called for a halt to U.S. intervention." Artiga was, in fact, one of the first sanctuary refugees in the Bay Area, and he used that unique position as a stage from which to draw attention to the plight of his compatriots. "Though there were thousands of refugees like myself with powerful stories to tell," he recalled, "many were afraid to share them publicly for fear of retribution. A few of us overcame our fear offering our personal testimonies with the hope that we could change hearts and minds to impact U.S. policies."[92]

Through sanctuary and grassroots organizations like Casa El Salvador, Artiga and other Salvadorans aligned with the Popular Liberation Forces began weaving together some of the first threads of what would quickly become a thick transnational web of solidarity. Over the years, Artiga added new strands to this web. He married Eileen Purcell, a US citizen and key player in both the Bay Area sanctuary movement and the SHARE Foundation. In 1986 they relocated to Washington, DC, where Purcell took over as executive director of SHARE and Artiga founded the Interfaith Office on Accompaniment (IOA), which he described as "an extension of the human rights work we did in San Francisco." The Office on Accompaniment went on to play a leading role in the coordination of delegations to El Salvador, with the first delegation taking Artiga, Purcell, and the Reverend Gustav "Gus" Schultz—a Bay Area friend, sanctuary movement supporter, and member of the SHARE board of directors—to accompany the 1986 repopulation of San José Las Flores. The following year, 1987, the Office and SHARE formalized a collaboration in the Going Home Interfaith Campaign in Support of Salvadoran Refugees Returning from Exile in Mesa Grande. "It was a tall order," Artiga recalled, "in the face of threats by the various governments and militaries and opposition of the UNHCR [United Nations High Commissioner for Refugees]."[93]

That very opposition, however, drove Artiga, the IOA, and Going Home organizers to mobilize mass political and moral support in the United States. To heighten the impact of media work, they recruited a "blue ribbon committee" of high-level religious leaders, many of whom were active in the sanctuary movement: archbishops, bishops, seminary presidents, theology professors, as well as directors of religious conferences and social action committees.[94] This, in turn, drew ordinary people to the campaign. Between 1987 and 1991, hundreds of US citizens participated in delegations jointly coordinated by the IOA, SHARE, Going Home, and allied organizations, including New El Salvador Today, the Wisconsin Coordinating Committee on Central America, and US–El Salvador Sister Cities. Delegates from the United States built connections with each other and with Salvadoran repopulation movement activists, and then "bombarded the press, the congress, and our congregations with what we learned," thus further raising the public profile of the rural repopulation movement.[95]

The Going Home campaign ultimately served as a powerful tool for supporting the rights of Salvadoran displaced and refugee groups and also for weaving together various solidarity threads into a dense web, which, in turn, developed and strengthened sistering relationships between US and Salvadoran citizens. At the center of this particular web of solidarity were Salvadoran exiles affiliated with the Popular Liberation Forces who, as part of their ongoing activism, intentionally cultivated connections between and among US-based solidarity activists and their organizations. Along with José Artiga, other Salvadoran activists prominent in the grassroots sistering movement included Guillermo "Grillo" Chacón, who was a catechist in El Salvador before fleeing to the United States, where he worked with the Central American Refugee Committee in San Francisco, the West Coast office of SHARE, the national steering committee of Going Home, and program coordinator for the Sister Cities national office. As noted earlier, Grillo Chacón returned to El Salvador in 1992 to work alongside Tim Lohrentz as coordinators of the new San Salvador office of US–El Salvador Sister Cities.[96] Chacón's brother, Oscar, worked with the American Friends Service Committee in Cambridge, Massachusetts, and served as the associate director and northeast regional coordinator of the IOA. Also in Cambridge, Mario Dávila, "a full time volunteer," represented the Comité El Salvador, worked with the American Friends Service Committee, and fostered the development of sistering committees in the northeast.[97] Saúl Solorzano was active with the Central American Resource Center (CARECEN) for years, "advocating for the rights of refugees in the United States and seeking support for the displaced communities in El Salvador." He later joined the Interfaith Office on Accompaniment team to help coordinate the Sister Cities Program.[98] Esther Chávez, a teacher, fled El Salvador in 1980 and settled in New Jersey, where she directed the Plainfield Center for Central American refugees for seven years. Chávez was a founding member of the New Jersey–Los Amates Sister City Project, and later worked for Sister Cities, first as the national coordinator and then as executive director of the National Center.[99]

These and many other Salvadorans were, as Dávila put it, "always active" with the Popular Liberation Forces (FPL), both in El Salvador and after relocating to the United States.[100] In fact, according to many Salvadoran and US American activists, the FPL leadership made a "deliberate decision" to work in the United States and to place representatives in strategic sites around the country.[101] According to Dávila, representatives typically stayed in one location for around eight months—long enough to get a sense for the situation on the ground, to make connections, figure out who they could trust, and, when possible, set up the foundations of an accompaniment or solidarity organization. In essence, they would assess whether such a group was possible in a given locale and, if so, start it up. After eight months or so, they would move on to a new locale and begin again.[102]

Thus, just as FPL leaders and representatives carefully worked with civilians on the ground in El Salvador, so too did they strategically engage different sectors of US society, from faith centers to radical leftists to more moderate groups. They encouraged different solidarity groups to take on particular roles, including organizing demonstrations, fund-raising, lobbying, and engaging in civil disobedience. Affiliates of the FPL, along with selected US citizen allies, coordinated these various groups and strategies through regular meetings. Near the end of every year, for example, representatives from all over the country met in Washington, DC. At these *nevadas*—so called because they were like "snow storms" of people descending on the city—they assessed their work during the previous year and set objectives for the coming year.[103] Similar meetings, often with high-level FPL leaders, occurred outside the United States as well. Through these assemblies, Salvadoran activists harmonized their own work; this allowed them, in turn, to orient US solidarity activists in a coordinated way. Over time, these efforts integrated US-based human rights and solidarity organizations into "a coherent political structure" that, according to one activist, was "refined over time to, as we said then, 'meet the needs' of the Salvadoran Revolution, and specifically the needs of the FPL."[104]

According to Dávila, one such refinement occurred during meetings in 1983. As internally displaced people began to gesture toward the resettlement of villages in Chalatenango, affiliates of the FPL devised the idea of accompaniment. What better way to do this than sistering? they thought. And so the concept of sister cities and sister parishes was born.[105]

Dávila's own trajectory offers one example of how these mobile FPL representatives in the United States helped lay the foundations for the US–El Salvador Sister Cities network. Dávila began his US-based work in Washington, DC, then relocated to a town in New Jersey. He found the conservative atmosphere there "difficult," however, and soon moved on to the more liberal Boston metropolitan area. After eight months in Cambridge, he opted to stay—in large part because he had married Sarah, an area resident. Dávila continued working from his Cambridge base, helping to launch sistering relationships between Cambridge and San José Las Flores, Belmont and El Higueral, and Arlington and Teosinte. In his role as builder of sistering relationships, Dávila attended meetings in DC; traveled to the Mesa Grande camp in Honduras, where he spoke with refugee leaders about returning, accompaniment, and sistering; coordinated delegations of US citizens to El Salvador; and facilitated the first national gathering of Sister Cities activists in 1988, among others.[106]

Thus, Dávila, Artiga, and a relatively small but very dynamic cohort of Salvadoran activists in the United States not only motivated the formation of new solidarity groups, from Casa El Salvador in San Francisco to the Interfaith Office on Accompaniment in DC, they also fostered cross-fertilization among key allies in organizations across the country, which directly contributed to the growth and strengthening of the sister cities network. Allies like Eileen Purcell and Gus Schultz of SHARE, for example, worked closely with Tracey Schear, Holly Grant, and Margi Clarke of New El Salvador Today; Eric Popkin and Tim Lohrentz of the Wisconsin Coordinating Committee on Central America; and members of sanctuary and sistering committees.[107] Many allies became active with multiple groups, further illustrating how cross-fertilization influenced the development of sistering connections. For example, Tim Lohrentz played an influential role in developing the Wisconsin Coordinating Committee's El Salvador Accompaniment Program, then spent a year in El Salvador strengthening the coordination between Sister Cities and other solidarity groups, before returning to his home state of Kansas, where he helped launch new sister-city projects with residents in Lawrence and Manhattan. One of his collaborators in Kansas was Barbara Schaibel, a SHARE supporter, who had spent a year in El Salvador accompanying a Lutheran bishop, Medardo Gómez, and his family in the wake of death threats. Ron Morgan of Philadelphia, who also provided accompaniment for Bishop Gómez, worked with SHARE and the Going Home campaign while helping start the Philadelphia–Las Anonas sistering relationship. And Joy Aruguete from Madison moved from being very active in the local sanctuary community to participating in NEST-coordinated delegations, staffing the Madison-Arcatao Sister City Project office, and serving as Midwest coordinator for the IOA.[108]

Together with their Salvadoran partners, these US citizens worked to bring into the world a new kind of transnational social movement: that of grassroots sistering. The grassroots angle of this movement is important to emphasize in light of the fact that activists associated with the US–El Salvador Sister Cities network were not the first to formulate the concept of sistering. Although a number of countries gained experience with "municipal internationalism" in the early and mid-twentieth century, it was not until the close of World War II that sistering emerged as "an organised phenomenon."[109] Western Europe became one of the cornerstones of "town twinning," with programs supported by a variety of organizations and patronized in varying degrees by government authorities, many of whom viewed them as potent instruments for constructing a unified postwar Europe.[110] In a similar vein, the US government established a number of programs to gain "broadscale public appeal" as part of "the new 'sweetness and light' phase of the Cold War."[111] These included Dwight D. Eisenhower's People-to-People Program, out of which Sister Cities International emerged, and John F. Kennedy's Partners of the Americas program under the federal Alliance for Progress.[112] Many pairings of US and Latin American cities emerged out of this context but, importantly, the chosen locales tended to already "enjoy friendly relations with the United States."[113] For instance, Wisconsin's governor John Reynolds launched the Wisconsin–Nicaragua Partners of the Americas (WNPA) program in 1964, which linked cities in Wisconsin to cities in Nicaragua and focused primarily on providing technological assistance in the fields of health care, education, agriculture, and rural development. Closely aligned with Kennedy's Alliance for Progress and the State Department's Agency for International Development, Reynolds and WNPA's executive board lauded Anastasio Somoza Debayle's Nicaragua as a "bastion of Western democracy and freedom." The sister state relationship promoted by WNPA, claimed Reynolds, was the perfect way "to directly demonstrate our support, and at the same time counter-attack hostile infiltrations."[114]

The sistering that emerged in the 1980s was qualitatively different; rather than "function[ing] as obedient servants of U.S. foreign policy," these were grassroots endeavors fueled by discontent with US foreign policy in Central America, as well as hope in the alternative projects then under development in the region.[115] The Wisconsin Coordinating Council on Nicaragua, for example, formed in 1984 out of frustration with the WNPA program—specifically the executive board's unwillingness to give the revolutionary Sandinista government fair play.[116] Although the Coordinating Council engaged in many different initiatives, it became especially noted for its sistering work, with its promotion of the Wisconsin–Nicaragua sister-state relationship, its role as regional coordinator of US–Nicaragua sister city activities, and its inauguration in 1986 of the annual US–Nicaragua Friendship Conference. According to its founders, the Coordinating Council's work was driven by the same democratic principles that inspired the US American Revolution: "they are concretely demonstrated in the ability of our people to challenge the 'established authorities' in Washington and to invent literally thousands of creative alternatives to war."[117]

At the same time that the Coordinating Council was redefining Wisconsin's sistering work in Nicaragua, the Wisconsin Interfaith Committee on Central America (WICCOA), along with SHARE, NEST, and other organizations, was establishing sistering connections with Salvadoran communities. These transnational sistering relationships "played an important strategic role" on local, national, and international levels. According to Isabel Hernández, cofounder of the Christian Committee for the Displaced of El Salvador, sistering activists pursued multiple objectives, including supporting the repopulations and "denounc[ing] all of the human rights violations that the Salvadoran government had been committing through the army against civilians just because they lived in conflict zones." Sistering activists also placed "pressure [on] the United States, which was the principal financial backer of the war in El Salvador . . . into not continuing to invest in the killing of the Salvadoran people." In short, Hernández concluded, the sister city connections were "more than an attempt for economic support; they were for political support."[118]

The Politics of Sistering

The US–El Salvador Sister Cities network involved a variety of people in different locations in several countries, pursuing multiple objectives. This approach enabled many successes, but it also brought significant challenges for the movement's leadership. Among the most salient issues were questions of leadership and authority: To what extent was the sistering movement directed by US Americans? By Salvadorans? By the Popular Liberation Forces and the FMLN? Who was "in the know" at any given moment? These questions were closely tied to ideological concerns, including the activists' varying commitments to the international left, revolutionary movements in Central America and elsewhere, anti-interventionism in the United States, and faith-based morals. Sistering proponents frequently debated these layers of commitment, trying to determine the extent to which they were incompatible with each other or went hand in hand. In a similar vein, they debated the appropriate methods for their work: should Sister Cities activists provide humanitarian aid, or engage in political advocacy, or employ acts of civil disobedience? Did one form of activism outweigh the others? Sister Cities was not alone in addressing these issues. The same kinds of questions and concerns spread across the entirety of the US-based Central America solidarity movements.[119]

A few examples of moments when tensions rose to the surface can help illustrate the layered nature of grassroots sistering. For some individual activists, it was by "random chance" that they became involved with one group rather than another. Margi Clarke, founder of NEST, recalled how one of her friends became involved with an FPL-linked group in Los Angeles. Her friend was bored and wanted to do something, so she offered to volunteer at El Rescate not due to any specific ideology but because it was closest to her mother's house.[120] In other cases, however, the decision to engage was deeply ideological, as Diane Greene, another activist, found in 1984 when she promoted NEST as a fund-raising channel to the five Los Angeles area chapters of the Committee in Solidarity with the People of El Salvador (CISPES), and the Pasadena chapter moved to block the proposal. "The people involved," Greene explained in a memo to her colleagues at NEST, "are known to be members of LRS, the

League for Revolutionary Struggle, a Maoist group." As the different chapters debated how to proceed, questions arose regarding NEST's leftist credentials, including whether or not the FMLN officially had endorsed the organization.[121] The historical record suggests that, in the end, although a couple of chapters maintained loose connections with NEST in later years, the Los Angeles–area CISPES as an organization rejected Greene's proposal based on the ideological commitments of its members.

Similar political concerns played a key role in the formation of the Madison, Wisconsin, sistering committee. Marc Rosenthal explained that the Madison CISPES chapter was "the first piece" of the El Salvador solidarity movement in Wisconsin and was, along with the national CISPES organization, a "hierarchical" and "sophisticated" leftist political movement that was "very specifically there as a support for the FMLN." Some leftists were "not very comfortable" working with CISPES, however, and instead worked with Community Action on Latin America (CALA), a "more socially democratic group." Initially, CISPES and CALA activists worked together to form the sistering relationship with Arcatao. But tensions prevailed. People in CALA "wanted more say about sistering. They didn't understand that those decisions were being made largely in El Salvador, that what we're doing is to a huge degree being determined by [leftist leaders in] El Salvador." Tensions came to a head during a CALA-sponsored delegation. At the time, the Madison–Arcatao sistering project was still in its infancy, functioning as "a subcommittee of CALA." The delegation brought to the surface the political "turmoil," as Rosenthal put it, with leaders and their differing visions butting heads. "All of a sudden people on the delegation are pointing at each other and saying 'He's a CIA agent!' And the other saying, 'He's a CIA agent!'" Rosenthal recalled. "Things got . . . really bad." But the experience had an "upshot": representatives of the Popular Liberation Forces who were involved with the sistering project "basically said to the people who are about to organize this, 'Get it out of CALA. This is too important. CALA cannot be the force that's going to be grounding the sistering project. Get it out of CALA, create your own organization. And that's what happened." In the wake of the "disastrous" delegation, with guidance from Salvadoran activists, the Madison–Arcatao Sister City Project (MASCP) took shape as an independent organization.[122]

Salvadoran activists affiliated with the Popular Liberation Forces also were key to the evolution of the US–El Salvador Sister Cities national organization. Since 1983 NEST had fomented and coordinated sister cities projects across the United States. In 1988, however, pressures rose for Sister Cities to break from NEST. Salvadorans were among those who pressed for this transition. Records indicate that this was a strategic move to create deeper and more direct alliances with Salvadoran activists in both the United States and El Salvador, which, in turn, would enable Sister Cities network activists to adopt a more politicized stance—something that NEST was reticent to do. Before the formation of the National Center for US–El Salvador Sister Cities in New York City, for example, Oscar Chacón encouraged sister cities activists in the Cambridge area to work directly with the IOA rather than with NEST. Such an alliance "should have been from the beginning," he argued. Not only did Salvadorans direct the IOA—José Artiga served as the organization's executive director in the Washington, DC, headquarters, and Chacón himself headed up the Cambridge/Boston field office—but the IOA placed "clear priority . . . on human rights" in El Salvador, and particularly the rights "of those who, historically, have been repressed the most: the rural population." Given such "advantages" over NEST, Chacón concluded that it was a "no brainer" for Sister Cities activists to work directly with the Office on Accompaniment.[123]

The explicit backing of rural human rights claims also meant allying in a more overt way with the left-leaning popular movement in El Salvador. Although this had been an undercurrent of sistering from the start, Salvadorans now asked US-based activists to unequivocally declare their support. At a meeting in Washington, DC, in late 1988, Monsignor Ricardo Urioste, visiting from El Salvador, along with an American Friends Service Committee representative (likely either Chacón or Dávila), urged more than one hundred sistering activists to "broaden" their work to include "civil disobedience and other direct actions" against the state terror then pervading the small Central American country and against the US military aid to the Salvadoran government that enabled such terror. They couched this request within the context of Salvadoran leftist activism. "The popular movement," they explained, "has never been as clear and determined to challenge the military. It is understood that if U.S. military aid ceased, the popular movements would win." Direct action by US citizens would help promote such an outcome.[124]

Many core activists within the US–El Salvador Sister Cities network supported a shift toward more overt political advocacy. In the wake of Urioste's call for direct action, for example, some Cambridge-area activists urged their committee to "be bolder, take offensive," and "become more explicit" in their work. Indicative of the political bent, their suggested actions included the need to "talk about what [the] FMLN means to people in countryside," and "support [the] right of [the] FMLN to be [a] legitimate party to [a] negotiated settlement."[125] Even Holly Grant, the NEST employee who headed the National Center for US–El Salvador Sister Cities in its first years, agreed with such suggestions. She explained that as the levels of repression increased in El Salvador, "it has become necessary for Sister Cities to denounce [the] politics of [the]

Salvadoran military and gov[ernmen]t." But "NEST is a humanitarian foundation," making it "complicated for NEST to also coordinate human rights
[and] political work." In short, Grant concluded, "NEST needs to maintain
distance."[126]

Not everyone agreed with the separation or the pressure to engage in direct
action campaigns. Notes from a November 1988 planning meeting of the Cambridge committee reveal deep tensions around these issues. Three of the four
small discussion groups were "leery of direct action." Participants expressed
many worries, including "Concern about losing [the] humanitarian and person-to-person appeal of [the] Project." Broadening their action repertoires to
include overt political action and civil disobedience, they argued, went against
the fundamental goals of their sistering relationship with San José Las Flores;
doing so would "weaken [the] character of local organizing" and "make it harder
to go into schools, etc." In short, overtly political action would "alienate people"
and make it impossible to "maintain our broad base."[127] David Grosser, who
staffed the Cambridge project for years, recalled similar discussions at the 1988
national gathering of Sister Cities representatives.[128]

Despite the reticence of some US-based Sister Cities affiliates, lead activists
ultimately moved the network in the direction of independence. Some people
left the network as a result of this transition, but those who remained were convinced that the organizational break with NEST would allow them more flexibility in accompanying their Salvadoran partners through the new contexts
arising in the latter half of the 1980s.

These examples offer insight into the tensions surrounding the leadership, politics, and methods of grassroots sistering. Such tensions never faded.
Yet, remarkably, sistering continued to operate successfully on multiple levels.
Marc Rosenthal explained that "a hallmark" of sistering work was "that we
were always wearing two hats, we were always actually doing two different
things." One layer of solidarity work "was straight-up humanitarian," he continued. "There was a humanitarian need, it was a human need. There were
people living desperate lives . . . and there was a real need to address this situation." Another layer of solidarity work recognized that these civilians "were a
critical component of the social movement and part of a revolutionary strategy
that included military strategy."[129] Margi Clarke of NEST similarly pointed
out the dual nature of sistering work. It was "not just moral" like some faith
groups, she said. It was also political, blending anti-war language and political
solidarity.[130]

Even if the Salvadoran and US American activists involved in the sistering network were "part of a revolutionary strategy," they were not combatants,
nor were they pawns of the FMLN or some international communist agenda.

Activists repeatedly underscored this point, defending themselves and their transnational relationships as legitimate and fully legal within national and international frameworks. It was toward this end that they often employed the language of human rights. Repopulators, for example, insisted on their rights as humans, civilians, and citizens of El Salvador. As the first group of refugees to return from Mesa Grande explained in a letter to President Duarte: "It is our legitimate right as Salvadorans to return to our country [and] the government you represent is morally obligated to provide us a satisfactory answer to our desire to return."[131] When Duarte indicated he would acquiesce if the returnees would settle in government-selected locations in the coastal lowlands, the refugees resisted, citing the Constitution of El Salvador and international laws that recognized citizens' rights to choose their domicile. In the repopulations, residents defended their right to remain in place, despite harassment by the state's armed forces. When describing incidents of harassment, Salvadorans nearly always distinguished the victim from the insurgent forces. They "tied her up against a Jocote tree and began torturing her," one such testimony went. Soldiers "were accusing her of being a guerrilla" but, the speaker went on to confirm, "the truth is, we aren't. . . . We were born here and live here and we are not guerrillas."[132]

Allies in the United States echoed these defenses. In Columbus, Ohio, sistering advocates explained that as long as their sisters and brothers in Copapayo "do not pick up arms against the government or act as a military garrison for the FMLN, they are not a military force and are not, under Geneva Conventions of War, legitimate targets."[133] In a similar vein, NEST staff members defined the "Local Popular Governments" in the repopulated zones as "a popular self-government body, autonomous from the FMLN . . . and any mass organizations, and is the concrete expression of the highest aspirations of the Salvadoran people to decide their own destiny."[134] Activists described other Salvadoran organizations, including the Christian Committee for the Displaced (CRIPDES) and the directivas in repopulated villages, in similar fashion, as civilian entities.

In describing their own work, US-based sistering activists highlighted that they engaged directly with civilians—not guerrillas—and that their goal was to help "defend the legitimate rights of the Salvadoran citizens [in the] repopulated communities."[135] They did so in part by closely monitoring the human rights situations in their sistered communities and activating their "emergency response networks" when violations occurred. On April 9, 1986, for example, Arcataenses released a communiqué denouncing a military attack on their village. Soldiers had tortured and murdered several residents, interrogated dozens of others, and threatened the entire community with annihilation if they remained in Arcatao. The frightened survivors called on the international community, "especially our sister city in Wisconsin, to help us survive this life-threatening situation and demand that President Duarte end these attacks and respect our right to live in peace in our places of origin."[136] In response, Wisconsin residents took action. Mary Kay Baum, for example, joined an emergency delegation to deliver humanitarian aid to "survivors of the ravaged town of Arcatao" and others affected by the Phoenix and Chávez Carreño military operations, and to document the "blatant and systematic violations of human rights resulting from such military maneuvers."[137]

Other incidents occasioned a similar response pattern, whereby Sister Cities affiliates emphasized the state's violations of the rights of the civilian repopulators. To really drive the point home, activists often focused on the "physical and psychological damage" that government operations caused for the most vulnerable groups, including pregnant women, children, and the elderly.[138] Press releases highlighted how children in the repopulations were dying because of the lack of medications, and testimonies revealed how soldiers targeted children, offering candy and other treats while "question[ing] them about the whereabouts of the wounded and what they do when confronted by guerrillas."[139] Activists from Ohio reported that children in Copapayo "are still trembling with fear" after a military strafing. Ann Chambers, who visited Copapayo shortly after the November 1989 attack, described how "a child of Copapayo drew a picture of the low-flying military helicopters that circle the village once a week. Below the helicopters, the child drew a house on fire." Chambers said, "I was horrified by the pictures . . . and then to realize this is the reality they live in."[140]

Such personalized stories made a compelling argument that human lives were at stake, and that the "humanitarian aid, financial assistance, [and] human rights intervention" offered by Sister Cities could make a real difference. In the words of a handwritten "pitch" from the Columbus–Copapayo Sister City Project: "It's a matter of life and death."[141] This human rights work also provided Sister Cities a kind of popular respectability, which was especially important as the network established itself in the mid-1980s. As the former staffer David Grosser explained, "Winning acceptance by lots of people and groups to our [political] right was a prerequisite to attaining sufficient influence to use the system in support of the Salvadoran communities."[142]

The human rights approach adopted by sistering activists also provided a framework for launching critiques of the Salvadoran government, US intervention, and imperialism more generally. In the context of egregious violations of internationally recognized human rights, leftist political demands became accessible to broader audiences. Thus, activists strategically combined the denunciation of human rights violations with bold critiques of world powers. During the 1986 emergency delegation to Arcatao, for example, Baum and her colleagues collected documentation confirming massive violations, and then used that material to ground a public denunciation of "the Salvadoran Armed Forces [which] made the depopulation of rural conflict areas one of their top priorities"; the government of President Duarte, which "shows little respect" for international law; and the Reagan administration's policy, which "has exacerbated the social and economic problems plaguing the country, and has adversely affected the majority of Salvadorans."[143] In a similar vein, activists in Columbus denounced the use of "U.S. built planes and helicopters" in the November 1989 attack on Copapayo that destroyed five homes and three boats, and left the children so "deeply affected."[144]

Other sistering activists delivered critiques and demands to leaders' doorsteps, as an angry Erik Breilid did in the wake of the attack on Arcatao. Breilid contacted Rep. Michael Barnes, chair of the Western Hemisphere Subcommittee, to denounce the "Salvadoran government forces [who] attacked our Sister City." Further, he demanded that Barnes "put as much pressure as you can on whoever you can" to "stop violations of medical neutrality, make the Salvadoran government observe the Geneva Conventions, especially Protocol 2, which their government ratified," and "let the civilians of Arcatao live in peace."[145] The Cambridge Sister City Committee addressed a similarly scathing letter to the people of Cambridge and to Senators Kerry and Kennedy in December 1989, after attacks on San José Las Flores. After listing the human consequences of the attacks, including threats of rape and murder, the beating of two residents, and damages to thirty homes, the childcare center, and subsistence crops, the letter declared, "These barbaric acts by the Salvadoran army should have been sufficient for all to call for an end to military funding to El Salvador months ago. We are angered that our tax dollars maintain an army that attacks its own citizens rather than defend them."[146]

This combination of human rights rhetoric and direct critique of governments was a hallmark of grassroots sistering activism and "a novel way" to do solidarity. "The novelty involved creative ways to circumvent the crippling constraints that the cold war put on our activity," Grosser explained. Whereas other solidarity groups "attracted the ultra-left," Sister Cities "allowed us to deliver a radical message about US imperialism through much more mainstream forms ('hey we're a humanitarian people to people project'). That then allowed us to focus attention on the realities of US policy thr[ough] the lens of what was happening on the ground" in the repopulated communities. "Gradually people in our home cities began to get to 'know' the people there and sympathize with their situations and trevails [sic]. That concern could then be channeled into more political opposition to US policy" as well as support for the social and politico-military movements underway in El Salvador.[147]

Thus, from the very beginning, people who coordinated the repopulation movement and associated sistering relationships used human rights to appeal to broad audiences while, at the same time, producing "hidden transcripts" that often were profoundly radical.[148] This helps to explain why not all sistering activists were aware of the integral role that affiliates of the Salvadoran Popular Liberation Forces (FPL) played in the movement. Grosser recalled that very few sister cities activists knew "the real relationship" between the repopulators, their representative organizations, and the FPL. Likewise, most were "in the dark about who was defining the priorities that guided our work and what their priorities were." Although a few activists gradually learned how integral FPL activists were to sistering and solidarity in general, "the majority of our activists did not," he said. "There were obvious security and political reasons for denying and obscuring this but it was true."[149] Michael Ring, who worked for years in the San Salvador Sister Cities office, explained that such secrecy happened "on purpose." In El Salvador "civilian organizing and the armed struggle were highly connected" and some US Americans knew this—including "folks organized in CISPES [who] were clearly aligned with the FMLN." But other efforts, Sister Cities among them, were intended "to widen the base to folks who were/might be uncomfortable with revolutionary violence."[150] To this day, many people are reluctant to discuss this "sensitive issue."[151] As José Artiga put it, "There are some things we don't talk about because it was clandestine."[152]

The archival record offers some hints about the construction of these hidden transcripts and hierarchies of knowledge. As NEST was establishing the first sister city link between Berkeley and San Antonio Los Ranchos, the activist Diane Greene prepared a background report on NEST for activists with the San Francisco chapter of the Committee in Solidarity with the People of El Salvador (CISPES) who "were interested in taking up NEST as our primary material aid channel." In presenting the report to a collaborator, Greene took care to explain that the report was not for use in "a general way but, instead, internally within the movement."[153] In a similar vein, after Saúl Solorzano began providing guidance to the Cambridge Sister City steering committee, one member implied his FPL affiliations when she inquired, "Who can know he is involved?"[154]

Former activists offer additional insights. Matt Nichols, who worked for years with NEST, recalled an early delegation to Copapayo during which Holly Grant, a sistering coordinator, carefully engaged with new activists from Columbus. Grant was particularly good at "working the line," Nichols said, between the delegates who "didn't get it" and those who already were "in the know." Although Grant and other sistering coordinators served as "go-betweens for peoples' political education" in the field, the deeper understanding of the relations between repopulators, Sister Cities, and the FPL that came with delegations could prove problematic for some people. Nichols recalled in particular a woman who had an anxiety attack when she learned that they were to have a brief late-night meeting with a small group of armed guerrillas. Another delegate, a man, did not want to participate in the meeting because he was committed to nonviolence. He was drawn in, however, when one of the combatants said, "I'm a priest, actually," and went on to explain how he had come to accompany the revolutionaries.[155] The following chapters detail the consciousness-raising work of delegations. For now, it is enough to know that some sistering activists took to sistering's hidden transcripts with little or no reservation, while others found it beyond their compass and consequently ended their involvement.

Although the "public transcripts" of sister cities activists emphasized the noncombatant nature of the rural repopulation and grassroots sistering movements, Salvadoran and US government officials labeled them "subversive," rendering participants no different than the armed cadres and, therefore, legitimate military targets. Indeed, Salvadoran authorities perceived the entire repopulation movement as an insurgent plan. Bold headlines on the front pages of national newspapers amplified this conviction: "Reds Intend to Use Repatriates" and "Armed Forces Uncover Communist Plan to Manipulate Repatriates."[156] According to Mario Dávila, this reaction was in large part due to simple geography: because the heart of the repopulation movement was in FPL-controlled zones in Chalatenango, officials saw them as part of the guerrilla threat. But officials also understood that vast numbers of the rural poor supported the FPL and the FMLN more broadly. For them, the distinction between civilian supporter and insurgent combatant was moot.

In light of this, Salvadoran repopulators were constantly at risk for harassment by state forces. The Christian Committee for the Displaced, along with regional and community organizations, produced literally thousands of pages detailing attacks against rural communities and their residents.[157] The most visible leaders, like Amadeo López and Manuel Cartagena, were at highest risk. Soldiers from the Fourth Brigade forcibly removed these two men from a United Nations vehicle in December 1988. Charged with being guerrillas, officials held them in custody—and tortured them—for a week. According to Sister Cities activists, the men's "only crime" was that they had led hundreds of refugees back to Chalatenango from Honduras a few months earlier. López, who served as the grassroots mayor of Berkeley's sister city of San Antonio Los

Ranchos, had "negotiated with the military to ensure the safe passage" of nine hundred refugees, "and since then the Army has resented his presence."[158]

In San Salvador, government forces targeted the entire leadership team of the CRIPDES. On April 19, 1989, soldiers stormed the organization's headquarters, arresting seventy people inside. After transporting the prisoners to the Treasury Police, soldiers proceeded to interrogate them. Over the course of a couple of days, officials released the majority of the captives; they held eleven people in custody for weeks, subjecting them to "intensive interrogations" and tortures, including "the hood" (*capucha*), food and water deprivation, and forced standing. One of the thirty-two people who regained freedom in a first wave of releases offered details on the torture of key leaders who remained behind: "He said he heard screams coming from the room where they were holding Innocente Orellana, that Isabel Hernández and Elizabeth Hernández were being beaten with rubber cords and rifle butts, and that Miguel Antonio Cruz was tied up, hanged from ropes, kicked, and then beaten again."[159] Several, including Miguel Mejía, remained political prisoners for six months, until "international pressure" prevailed "and crooked judges were paid a certain amount to release us one by one."[160] Such incidents made it clear that the Salvadoran government wanted to "decapitate" the rural repopulation movement "by killing all the leaders in the villages" and quashing CRIPDES "because it was a strong organization, for denouncing internationally and organizing displaced people."[161]

Salvadoran officials also turned attention to international activists, attempting to "limit accompaniment" during the 1980s and early 1990s. Sistering advocates whose names appeared on "lists of undesirables" were unable to acquire visas and other travel documentation. Customs officers confiscated countless humanitarian aid deliveries. Salvadoran military commanders denied delegations the safe conduct passes necessary to reach their intended destinations in rural areas. And immigration officials arrested and deported dozens of visitors.

US officials assisted in these endeavors, with federal and state agents targeting individual solidarity activists, many with connections to Sister Cities. Activists became subjects of Internal Revenue Service audits, interrogations by Federal Bureau of Investigation agents, and general surveillance by local "Red Squads." Their mail was tampered with, their phones tapped, their offices and homes raided. The scene "was very tense," recalled Rosenthal.[162]

The surveillance and harassment were part of a broader effort to stifle social activism. There is ample evidence that Reagan maneuvered to shut down the Central America solidarity movement. Covert public-private partnerships of the kind that gave rise to the Iran-Contra scandal, undercover surveillance projects like Operation Sojourner and the related arrest and trial of sanctuary

Send a telex, write a letter
To free

Miguel Mejia and Mirtala Lopez, spokespersons for CRIPDES and the re-populated communities

Isabel Hernandez and Inocente Orellana, executive committee members of CRIPDES and the CNR

Trinidad and Jorge Olmedo, mother and son, community organizers for the repopulated communities.

Leaders of the Displaced People of El Salvador

Urgent action poster, 1989. Sister Cities activists defend the lives of their partners at CRIPDES, arrested and tortured for their work with displaced people. (MASCP Records, USESSC Archive) workers like Stacy Merkt and John Fife, the highly publicized investigation into the Committee in Solidarity with the People of El Salvador (CISPES), and the curious work of the Office of Public Diplomacy are but a few examples.[163]

Sistering activists found themselves in the crosshairs of the Reagan administration's McCarthy-like approach. One undated State Department document summarized the rationale. Titled "Support Network for the FMLN/FDR," it drew direct links between the Communist Party of the Soviet Union, the Communist Party of El Salvador, and multiple organizations in the United States. Sharing center page with CISPES were NEST, SHARE, and Medical Aid to El Salvador (MAES)—three organizations that promoted sister city, sister parish, and sister health links between the United States and El Salvador. This document went even farther, identifying by name each organization's founders, executive director, board members, and notable "sponsors," with the latter list including priests, doctors, researchers with progressive think tanks, more than two dozen elected officials, and the Hollywood icon Martin Sheen.[164] Additional documentation from the US Embassy in El Salvador identified US–El Salvador Sister Cities directly as "a U.S.-based FMLN front group network."[165]

Federal and state agents subjected the individuals and organizations featured in the Department of State chart to deep scrutiny and harassment. In fact, within just a few months of incorporation, NEST board members already had begun discussing how to move forward in light of the "attacks on movement and relationship to NEST."[166] Shortly thereafter, in October 1984, the attorney general of the state of California launched an audit of NEST's activities.[167] Another campaign began in late 1986, spurred in part by a NEST fund-raising letter signed by Rep. John Conyers (D-MI). Elliot Abrams, then assistant secretary of state for Inter-American Affairs, severely chastised Conyers for lending his name to an organization that spread such "outrageous falsehoods" that were "designed to smear the Government of El Salvador and promote [its] violent overthrow." The letter, Abrams argued, was malicious, disingenuous, and, at base, "an insult to the thousands of Americans and Salvadorans trying to bring about change in El Salvador."[168]

Building on claims of NEST's "duplicitous fund-raising" tactics, congressional conservatives and researchers at right-wing think tanks began pressuring for a federal audit. A key justification for such an investigation was that the funds raised by NEST never made it to the Salvadoran people; instead, they went directly to the FMLN, characterized by the Council for Inter-American Security as "a terrorist organization backed by the intelligence agencies of the Soviet Union."[169] These ideas gained additional purchase during the June 1987 Iran-Contra hearings when Senator James McClure (R-ID) and Rep. William McCullom (R-Fl) named NEST and dozens of other solidarity organizations as likely violating their tax-exempt status by virtue of "the fact that a lot of the money that's been raised in the past . . . has indeed gone to purchase arms instead of humanitarian purposes."[170]

These hearings and other related debates from the period reveal a simple irony: whereas many conservatives upheld the legality of Reagan's support of both public and private funding to the Nicaraguan Contras, they painted the activities of NEST and other solidarity organizations as illegal, "in direct conflict with" and "undermin[ing] official U.S. policy" in El Salvador.[171] In fact, L. Francis Bouchey of the Council for Inter-American Security derided the IRS for being "politically discriminatory" in its granting of tax-exempt status to "organizations which channel aid to the communist guerrillas in El Salvador, while denying equal status to organizations sending aid to the anti-communist guerrillas in Nicaragua."[172] His claim was far from true; as the Iran-Contra hearings and subsequent investigations revealed, the IRS granted tax-exemption status to many "New Right 'humanitarian' organizations" including John Singlaub's Council for World Freedom. Yet the IRS submitted to the pressures of Bouchey and other conservatives and audited NEST's activities.[173]

Not in a Quiet Way

This chapter has outlined the development of grassroots sistering, a radical but nonviolent social movement to support transformational change in El Salvador. Activists in El Salvador and the United States drew from the lengthy leftist histories in their countries to organize and protest against exclusion, repression, and militarization. While they worked to halt unjust practices and tear down inequitable structures, they also modeled alternative relations based on equality and mutual respect.

Salvadorans with FPL connections were key to this transnational network. Although the revelations might raise the hackles of today's conservatives and be used as vindication by surviving Reaganites, political apologias are not my intention here. Rather, in this chapter I have uncovered some of the more hidden details about the inner workings of the Sister Cities network in order to problematize the narratives that continue to dominate analyses of the US–Central America solidarity movement and, indeed, much of the work on solidarity networks in general. The US–El Salvador Sister Cities case study illustrates that border-crossing activists from the so-called Global South— displaced people, refugees, exiles, and repopulators—were not simply "objects" of northern sympathy and succor. They were the designers, the groomers, the dreamers, and the doers.

Activists in the United States were a critical component of the Salvadoran politico-military and social movements strategies for national liberation. As Salvadoran civil society social movements and politico-military groups rose in reaction to injustices, including stolen elections, scorched-earth operations, and massacres, US Americans joined forces with them. Together, these activists challenged conservative leaders in both countries who argued that it was not only acceptable to slaughter peasants because they had ties to the guerrillas; it was a viable solution to ongoing problems.

An important motivating factor for many US Americans who joined Sister Cities and other solidarity efforts was the role of the US government in backing the Salvadoran government's terror campaigns. Because the US government was complicit with the scorched-earth policy "as long as it was quiet," solidarity activists "decided to accompany, but not in a quiet way."[174] As sistering advocates explained at the time, permanent accompaniment "represents a direct challenge to the U.S. government's policy of intervention. While the U.S. persists in bankrolling the Salvadoran government and military, and in directing military operations, this project is concerned with mobilizing . . . residents to work against that morally bankrupt policy, and with those Salvadorans organizing for change."[175] Put another way, one objective of US-based sistering activists was "to tweak Washington."[176]

The attempted suppression of US American activists indicates that they did, indeed, raise Washington's ire. Sistering represented a challenge to the US government's nation-building efforts in El Salvador—what several scholars have characterized as "one of the most costly and thorough interventions by the U.S. government in Latin America."[177] With their military and economic aid and strategic alliances with selected elites, Adan Quan explained, US officials "were challenging the old order" in El Salvador, attempting to usher in new "progressive" and "modern" policies and practices. One consequence was the creation of "a parallel Salvadoran state with its own agencies and a separate 'extraordinary' government budget in which large amounts of U.S. aid money were deposited."[178]

The Salvadoran and US American activists associated with the repopulation and sistering movements engaged in a similar process. But where state agents focused on military and market matters, leftist activists promoted a different nature of "progressive" goals: human rights, civil rights, and sustainable development.

2

Re-educating Empire

To Educate Is to Transform

In July 1983 a group of Salvadoran adults living in the Mesa Grande refugee camp in Honduras gathered to celebrate an important milestone; they had just completed a six-month literacy course through which they gained second-grade equivalency. To mark the moment, students penned their own songs and poems, many of which described the transformative possibilities of *alfabetización*, or literacy. Before the war, one group of graduates wrote, "we were / ignorant Peasants." Pedrina explained further by pointing to "those with power and the state who did nothing / to address illiteracy in El Salvador." The inaccessibility of education for the rural poor had dire consequences, wrote Cristóbal, another graduate: "that is why imperialism had us more oppressed." With the onset of war, however, things began to change. In the conflict zones of El Salvador and in refugee camps across Central America, campesinos took direct control of their education. At the Mesa Grande camp, Cristóbal explained, "we have the opportunity / to attend classes in order to discover the truth." With the new knowledge and skills gained through literacy, he continued, Salvadorans would finally "realize our dream / [and] escape from exploitation." From the perspective of Cristóbal, Pedrina, and the other graduates of this literacy course, education was an important contribution (*aporte*) to the struggle for justice and equality in El Salvador. Learning to read and write as refugees signified a way to "help with our contribution for our liberation."[1]

The adult literacy course at Mesa Grande was part of a broad system of "popular education" organized by Salvadoran activists. The system had roots in the local organizing initiatives of the 1970s, including consciousness-raising work in Christian base communities and the urban-rural networks forged between teachers, students, and campesinos. As early as 1982 rural Salvadorans, many of them living as mobile communities in zones under FMLN control, along with their compatriots in refugee camps abroad, had established popular education systems. Although classes were irregular, with meetings dependent on war-era security concerns, "education was part of the organizational development of the community and it grew stronger because it was considered one of the primary components of economic, social, and cultural growth."[2] According to a post–peace accords report by the Coordinator of Communities and Repopulations of Chalatenango, rebaptized after the conflict as the Association of Communities for the Development of Chalatenango (CCR): "Dialogue, the exchange of experience, the critique of reality, the discovery of the worth and problems of their communities, and, becoming conscious that they were transformative social agents, were always fundamental to Popular Education."[3]

In developing popular education in the refugee camps and rural countryside, Salvadorans drew from a much longer Latin American tradition. As the Brazilian educator Paulo Freire explained in his celebrated book *Pedagogy of the Oppressed*, popular education offered an alternative model for teaching and learning.[4] In contrast to traditional educational systems that typically relied on a "banking model" (whereby teacher-experts "make deposits" in their students), popular education focused on dialogue, with every participant in a given lesson drawing from their own lived experience to serve as an educator as well as a student. Through exchanges with each other, participants collectively produced new knowledge and new *conciencia* (sociopolitical consciousness), which they then directed into actions intended to change unjust systems and structures. That this education system marked an alternative to the conventional system is made clear in its designation as "popular." Whereas US culture typically uses "popular" in reference to popularity (e.g., a popular television show), Latin American cultures often use the term to denote the grassroots or community-based nature of something. From this perspective, then, popular education is of the people, for the people, and because of this, it stands apart from officialist educational systems.

Salvadorans drew from regional histories to develop their own popular education opportunities in churches, Christian base communities, unions, politico-military organizations, refugee camps, repopulated villages, and many other sites. As Equipo Maíz, a nongovernmental organization that has played a prominent role in developing popular education in the Salvadoran context, explained, whereas "the traditional education system transmits a vision of society (ideology) that supports the interests of the dominant classes," popular education in El Salvador "aims to have people become aware of problems, discover their causes, propose solutions, and commit themselves to those solutions."[5]

This approach to education inspired the Salvadorans' transnational network of allies, among them US–El Salvador Sister Cities. At the first US meeting in March 1988, representatives from the first six US sistering committees joined representatives from El Salvador in emphasizing the importance of education in their collaborative work. At the close of the Boston meeting, participants issued a statement expressing activists' commitment to "defend the legitimate rights of the Salvadoran citizens" living in repopulated communities "through relationships which build bonds of friendship [through which] the Sister Cities learn from as well as support the Salvadoran people in their search to end the war and bring social justice to their country." Statement co-signers pledged to "send at least twelve delegations in 1988 to accompany our sister communities in the rebuilding of their homes and in the creation of a new El Salvador." These delegations—"direct" and "personal experiences"—were critical to sistering work not only because they provided political and moral support to Salvadoran communities in need; they also helped US citizens "better understand the realities which our Salvadoran brothers and sisters live."[6]

Direct people-to-people exchanges were indispensable to US–El Salvador Sister Cities and the rural repopulation movement in El Salvador. Yet Sister Cities was neither the first nor the only solidarity network to employ the strategy in Central America. Indeed, dozens of activist groups with human rights concerns brought North Americans to Central America during the isthmus's revolutionary era. In the first few years of the 1980s, Witness for Peace began coordinating delegations to Nicaragua—often at a rate of four per month—with the "specific, concrete task [of] 'witnessing' and peacekeeping by a public, nonviolent presence in the war zones," and the Canada-based Peace Brigades International began accompanying human rights workers in Guatemala.[7] At the same time the Salvadoran Humanitarian Aid, Research, and Education Foundation (SHARE), New El Salvador Today (NEST), the Wisconsin Interfaith Committee on Central America, and other incubators for the US–El Salvador Sister Cities network began leading groups to El Salvador, sometimes on their own but increasingly in collaboration with each other. In the second half of the decade, Peace Brigades International expanded its work to El Salvador, joining many Sister Cities committees and other accompaniment organizations, including the Interfaith Office on Accompaniment and Voices on the Border. If in the early 1980s only a handful of intrepid northern activists traveled south, by the end of the decade delegations to Central America were routine, involving more than 230 organizations and tens of thousands of US citizens.[8]

Delegations were important to other groups as well, including US government agencies, news media outlets, and international organizations. In late 1980, for example, William Bowdler and William Rogers arrived to El Salvador as part of a diplomatic commission appointed by President Jimmy Carter to investigate the murder of four US church workers on the outskirts of the capital city. In a similar vein, in early 1982 the journalists Raymond Bonner and Alma Guillermoprieto along with a documentary photographer, Susan Meiselas, traveled to El Salvador to investigate what came to be known as the El Mozote massacre. The Americas Watch Committee sent teams to El Salvador to research human rights issues for its *Report on Human Rights in El Salvador*, released in January 1982, as well as the multiple supplements to that *Report*. These examples illustrate not only the broad interest in the investigation and reporting of human rights violations then occurring in El Salvador but also the fact that many people from the United States traveled to El Salvador in official capacities, fulfilling professional obligations.[9]

Delegations sponsored by sistering advocates and related solidarity groups also emphasized human rights, yet they were grassroots affairs. For the most part, they involved average citizens who took time off work to go to El Salvador and who paid their own travel expenses. These were citizen diplomats; although their delegations were legally sanctioned travel groups, they intentionally explored beyond typical authority channels. Even delegations that included elected officials or their aides purposefully pressed the boundaries of the official story.

In a similar vein, many Salvadorans "toured" the United States, visiting sister cities to speak, conduct workshops, and provide testimonies before a variety of audiences. Many of these visitors were representatives of the displaced and repopulated communities and the FMLN coalition forces. They also were unionists, health care workers, educators, and women's rights activists. Documentation from tours reveal their critical role in organizational outreach and public education.

To be sure, not all Salvadorans were temporary visitors to the United States. As noted in chapter 1, a number of activists with the Popular Liberation Forces (FPL) lived in the United States and worked closely with US activists, providing political analysis, guiding solidarity work, and transmitting a revolutionary *mística* or mystique.[10] These women and men also plugged into a network of organizations formed by Salvadorans who fled persecution in the 1970s and 1980s, gathering in cities like Los Angeles, San Francisco, Washington, DC, and New York City, where they continued their trajectories of activism.[11] In addition, many refugees associated with the sanctuary movement felt it imperative to share their testimonies "to create empathy, to spark a sense of urgency and obligation or responsibility that would motivate North Americans to take a stand against their own government on behalf of an 'other' with whom they were largely unfamiliar."[12]

Some scholars have acknowledged the impact that these people-to-people exchanges had on Central American social and revolutionary movements and the Central America solidarity movement in the United States. As the sociologist Christian Smith explains, in-country experiences introduced US travelers to the realities of poverty, injustice, and repression; raised "troubling challenges to people's political worldviews" and "moral sensibilities"; and "generat[ed] the basis of a massive, grassroots domestic opposition to the [Reagan] administration's Central America policy."[13] According to Van Gosse, the new critical perspectives born from delegations "continually refreshed the spirit and local base of solidarity." Interestingly, the US government banned its citizens from traveling to Cuba after 1963 precisely to avoid the potentially radicalizing consequences of people-to-people contact with Cuban revolutionaries and their civilian collaborators. That so many US citizens chose to travel to Central America during times of revolution and violent conflict, Gosse notes, is truly "a unique phenomenon in the cold war's history."[14]

More recent scholarship has pointed to these early solidarity delegations as the root of many of the new millennium's "voluntourism" programs. As the cold war ended and the Central American conflicts wound down during the 1990s, many solidarity organizations retooled for new postwar contexts. Witness for Peace, SHARE, and US–El Salvador Sister Cities, for example, continued their collaborations with Nicaraguans and Salvadorans, which "provided a structure" for later service initiatives and study-abroad programs catering to US citizens.[15] As one international development specialist concluded, the solidarity model of building long-term partnerships directly "contributed to the development of international service-learning programs."[16]

Despite such claims about the widespread practice and long-term impacts of delegations, the topic has received little critical attention. Most reviewers of today's service-learning programs either skim over or entirely ignore the historical roots of current programs.[17] Similarly, analyses of Central America solidarity offer only snippets of insight into the phenomenon through profiles of delegation-sponsoring organizations like Witness for Peace and Peace Brigades International.[18] William Westerman offers perhaps the lone exception to the trend; in a comparison of the early Central America solidarity delegations and later "pro-poor" tours, Westerman distinguishes the former as a type of revolutionary activism, which intended to undo structural injustices. Yet, although Westerman offers a quick nod to related issues, including US policy and human rights, he does not examine such issues in any detail.[19]

This chapter turns explicit attention to delegations and tours as cardinal tools of sistering during the years of the Salvadoran conflict. Internal documentation from key organizations along with memoirs and oral history interviews with leaders and participants reveal that sistering advocates developed highly organized delegation and tour systems with bidirectional objectives.[20] When viewed from north to south, these were humanitarian endeavors intimately connected to the human rights work of Salvadoran activists, and more specifically displaced people, refugees, and rural repopulators. When viewed south to north, these exchanges served as a unique form of public education, drawing from Latin American experiences with consciousness-raising initiatives through popular education and the liberation theology–inspired base communities. In short, delegations and tours were indispensable tools for raising critical political consciousness among US citizens and prompting deeper engagement with the movement in solidarity with the people of El Salvador.

The historical record of the sistering network's people-to-people exchanges also exposes some of the complexities of relations of solidarity. As transnational collaborations with bidirectional goals, sistering involved multiple activists from El Salvador and the United States. These activists shared many things in common, yet they came from profoundly different backgrounds and experiences, as described in chapter 1. These disparities introduced a significant amount of friction between southern and northern participants in the sistering network. Moreover, people came to the repopulation and sistering movements for diverse reasons and with a mix of motivations and goals. No amount of shared idealism and good intentions could completely unite such a diverse group and, indeed, sistering network affiliates sometimes openly collided.

Yet, as the anthropologist Lesley Gill states, "solidarity and fragmentation are . . . part of the same process."[21] This chapter builds on that idea with an examination of the complementary yet conflicting pieces of the US–El Salvador Sister Cities puzzle. It analyzes ways in which sister cities activists overlapped and diverged in their border-crossing and boundary-pushing work. Salvadorans and US Americans devised delegations of US citizens to El Salvador and US tours of Salvadoran citizens as a means of bringing international legitimacy to the grassroots rural repopulation movement and rewriting power relations both within El Salvador and between El Salvador and the United States. Leaders carefully crafted these events to challenge and to transform US participants, to push them beyond conventional humanitarian and charity relations, and thus into direct political engagement and solidarity activism. Yet because political, personal, and cultural tensions were never far from the surface, these exchanges were not always smooth. Both tensions and overlaps offer insight into the contentious meanings and practices of transnational solidarity.

The Power of Presence

Leaders of the sistering network were social change agents, and they encouraged others to adopt an activist approach that would translate into broad-scale pressures on US and Salvadoran officials to adopt more just and humane policies. An "essential" and "fundamental" step toward such grand change was public education.[22] Toward this end, sistering advocates carefully crafted consciousness-raising events for the US public. To appeal to the broadest possible audience, they often framed these events as humanitarian affairs. In delegation recruitment efforts, for example, US coordinators emphasized delegations as a means of providing succor to "communities in distress" in war-torn regions of El Salvador.[23] "Our purpose in visiting El Salvador," explained one announcement, "is to provide a supportive presence and humanitarian aid to those who have been injustly [sic] victimized by the war."[24] In a similar vein, Sister Cities tours featured Salvadorans who shared testimonies about scorched-earth operations, imprisonment and torture, and other atrocities. News coverage of these events portrayed the visitors as war survivors and human rights defenders who were "speaking up for victims"; some, like Mirtala López, received awards for their human rights work from entities as varied as Reebok and Houston's Rothko Chapel.[25] Even when activists framed people-to-people exchanges in terms of basic human rights—a literal "struggle for survival," "a matter of life and death"—the underlying blueprint was political advocacy.[26]

Like sistering relationships in general, delegations and tours had an explicit purpose of "strengthening international support and ligitmacy [sic] for the re-population sites in El Salvador as a means of acknowledging the rights of these civilians to continue to live and develop their communities as provided by the Geneva Accords."[27] They lent legitimacy in a number of ways. Delegations from the United States, for example, offered a measure of physical protection for Salvadoran activists associated with the repopulation movement. Refugees in Honduras had learned that the presence of internationals placed a check on Honduran and Salvadoran government officials and armed forces, thereby reducing both the number and severity of human rights violations. They applied this lived experience to the repopulation process. United States citizens supported the mass repatriations known as *returnos* by "stand[ing] alongside" the refugees, serving as "human shields" as they made the journey home.[28] After refugees resettled their villages, regular visits from northern citizens literally embodied the concept of permanent accompaniment, keeping the Salvadoran government on the defense.

The Reverend Gustav Schultz, a supporter of the SHARE Foundation and the Berkeley–San Antonio Los Ranchos Sister City, as well as a leader of a delegation during the first mass return from Mesa Grande in October 1987, believed it was critical for US citizens "to provide protection and accompaniment to the Salvadoran refugees in their move to repatriate and repopulate their homelands in community."[29] Their presence was necessary because, as the repopulation movement picked up speed, state forces and their paramilitary allies increasingly targeted displaced people and refugees who had voluntarily repatriated. Those affiliated with the Christian Committee for the Displaced (CRIPDES) and the National Coordinator of Repopulations (CNR) had been threatened, arbitrarily arrested, and imprisoned; the child-care center at Fé y Esperanza, an internally displaced-person camp in San Salvador, had been bombed; and the repopulated community of Santa Marta, Cabañas, was attacked by military airplanes and helicopters.[30] The presence of US citizens could help prevent such violations of human rights, thus defending the basic right to life of the repopulators.

Physical protection also entailed closely monitoring the human rights situation in the Salvadoran sistered communities and responding actively when abuses occurred. With information provided by the repopulators and other sources, CRIPDES produced regular reports and bulletins detailing the human rights violations and socioeconomic challenges faced by Salvadorans. Similar to the publications of the Pro-Peace Committee in Chile analyzed by Steve J. Stern, the CRIPDES human rights bulletins served as a kind of counterofficial "intelligence report," a means of "projecting an alternative reading of [the country's] reality into the public domain."[31] Bulletins also kept international solidarists apprised of the situation on the ground in El Salvador, priming them for action. Frequently, CRIPDES human-rights reports came with calls to action, including signing petitions, pressuring officials, and providing material and moral support.

Sister Cities, SHARE, NEST, and other sistering and accompaniment organizations in the United States promptly responded to the appeals. They used information from the CRIPDES reports and their sistered communities to guide their public education efforts in the United States, integrating congressional lobbying and postcard campaigns into their activities in response to requests from their Salvadoran partners, and launching nationwide actions like the 1989 "Stop the Invasion of Our Sister Cities" campaign.[32] On particularly urgent matters, such as the late 1988 abduction of Manuel Cartagena and Amadeus López, two leaders of the repopulation movement in San José Las Flores, some Cambridge-area activists sent telexes to the Salvadoran High Command and members of the US Congress demanding their release. They also informed and requested action by other organizations, including Amnesty International.[33]

Re-educating Empire

Following attacks on repopulated communities, US committees often sent emergency delegations to provide humanitarian aid, gather information on the incidents, and make inquiries with officials. Back in the United States, delegates used this information to prepare reports and issue public denunciations. After the Phoenix and Chávez Carreño counterinsurgency operations swept through Chalatenango and neighboring provinces in 1986, leaving dozens of razed hamlets, 444 dead and disappeared, and more than 2,600 displaced, Mary Kay Baum (from the recently established Madison–Arcatao Sister City Project) joined a NEST-coordinated "humanitarian emergency relief and fact-finding delegation."[34] The group traveled through the affected areas delivering food, medical supplies, and other basic essentials; meeting with victims of the military operations, government officials, and civil society leaders; and documenting the "blatant and systematic violations of human rights resulting from such military maneuvers."[35] Following their time in-country, delegates issued an eleven-page report that held both the Duarte and Reagan administrations "responsible for violation of the Geneva Conventions in regard to civilians in an armed conflict, and of the most basic human rights."[36] Similarly, in April 1987 Susan Freireich and Judy Somberg from Cambridge went on an emergency delegation to their sister city of San José Las Flores to investigate "another round of military harassment . . . which concluded in the capture of eleven civilians from the town." While there, the delegates collected information from witnesses about the arrests; met with Colonel Jesús Cáceres, the military commander in Chalatenango province; and scheduled an appointment with the case judge, believing that "he will be impressed by the fact that a North American delegation has traveled to investigate." The judge released the prisoners while the delegates were in-country, and Boston-area newspapers reported the victory.[37]

Another way that sistering activists helped protect and promote the legitimacy of repopulations was by challenging their officially imposed isolation. As chapter 1 explained, Salvadoran authorities perceived the repopulation movement as a strategy directly coordinated by the FMLN. Following this point of view, authorities treated repopulated communities as military targets, restricting travel to and from these sites; blocking deliveries of food, medicines, and other goods; occupying them for weeks on end; and physically punishing them. With such tactics, Salvadoran authorities—like authoritarian regimes elsewhere, past and present—sought to produce a "culture of fear" and to foment social isolation and fragmentation, thus weakening and rendering ineffectual any organized opposition.[38] In the context of extreme state control, direct human contact and solidary relationships became, in and of themselves, a marker of resistance. For the repopulated communities and the US–El Salvador Sister Cities network, such relationships were a badge of pride and a source of strength for their continuous work of physically and morally challenging the barriers imposed by officials. Chapter 3 examines in detail how sistering activists contested the isolation of the repopulated communities. For now it is enough to note that activists consistently pressured both Salvadoran and US officials to acknowledge and comply with the Salvadoran citizens' rights to move about freely; to receive humanitarian aid; to transport to their villages necessary resources, including food, medicines, and construction materials; and to express themselves.

If one objective of cross-border travels was for northern citizens to lend international legitimacy to the southern citizens' rights claims, an equally important goal was to educate northern audiences, as illustrated by workplans, itineraries, and promotional materials for delegations and tours. Announcements of upcoming delegations portrayed the trips to El Salvador as unmatched educational opportunities, promising that participants would *learn about* life in the country; they would *investigate, document*, and *seek answers* to important questions; and, like good students, they would *publicly share* their findings upon returning home.[39]

Sistering activists billed the US speaking tours of Salvadorans in similar ways. Work plans, brochures, and reports explained that the benefits from tours went beyond fund-raising; they were a way "to bring updated information . . . to cities in the United States" and to "help your community learn about El Salvador."[40] The bold heading of one tour poster asked the question "What is Really Happening in El Salvador?" The subsequent text promised that audience members would learn the answer from Ruth Navidad, a member of the CRIPDES board of directors and "one of many Salvadorian [sic] women who know the whole range of information about the war's effects on the civilian population."[41] A flier for a Madison event during Navidad's 1991 tour invited people to "find out about what repopulated communities like Arcatao are doing to rebuild and reshape El Salvador."[42]

The real power behind these public education events was the "direct people to people contact."[43] More to the point, Salvadorans brought with them to their encounters with US Americans the "objective of providing testimony" about the human rights situation on the ground in their communities.[44] In this they drew inspiration from a longer Latin American tradition of *testimonio*. Other scholars offer in-depth analyses of this genre, but two points are worth highlighting here. First, while a testimonio narrator offers a personal witness account of oppression, trauma, and resilience, their account also represents a larger, collective story. Second, testimonio is an important tool for consciousness-raising and action-orientation on domestic and international levels because new knowledge of inequities often inspires people to seek justice.[45]

Building Community

SAT. NOV 23 7:30

BY STUDENT of CARASQUE
EL SALVADOR

ST. JOHN'S
CATHOLIC CHURCH
YORK ST. BANGOR

Listen to Ruth Navidad

29 year old mother of two, teacher, and one
of 12 National Directors of CRIPDES -
The Christian Committee for the Displaced....

# of EL SALVADOR

TELL THE STORY of HER PEOPLE

SPONSORED BY...
PEACE IN CENTRAL AMERICA
FOR MORE OPPORTUNITIES TO MEET
WITH RUTH CALL **PICA** 947 4203

Poster announcing Ruth Navidad's tour stop in Bangor, Maine, 1991. (Arvidson Papers, USESSC Archive)

Salvadorans in the United States strategically tapped into these aspects when sharing their testimonial truths with US American audiences. While on tour, Salvadorans typically visited about ten cities, with dozens of events in each, from house parties to lectures in university halls. Itineraries were heavy with meetings with a wide range of organizations, including labor unions, faith communities, women's groups, cooperatives, high school and college classes, donors, journalists, elected officials, and, of course, Sister City committees.[46] At each of these meetings, Salvadorans shared their personal stories, framed within the broader context of *la lucha*, the struggle for justice in El Salvador. During his 1989 tour, for example, Julio Tobar, a community leader from Chalatenango, offered his eyewitness account of state-sponsored violence: the brutal death of his family members at the hands of Salvadoran government soldiers, attacks on his hometown and nearby villages, the capture and torture of neighbors and friends who worked to improve the lives of rural inhabitants, and his own imprisonment and torture. He explained how such violence forced him and thousands of others out of their homes and into the mountains, where they lived in hiding for years, and how he eventually arrived at the Calle Real camp on the outskirts of San Salvador. Tobar also described how he and his companions repopulated the village of San José Las Flores and continued to work on behalf of their communities, their hopes for lower prices on beans, and for dignified housing and health services.[47]

In a similar vein, Mirtala López framed her personal account as one example among many of "how the dignity of the Salvadoran people has been trampled and bloodied by . . . those who work against peace." In autobiographical statements disseminated around the United States in anticipation of her 1991 tour, López began with a description of growing up in grinding poverty in rural Las Vueltas, Chalatenango, then explained how and why peasants, women, workers, and others began to organize, forming social movements to contest the Salvadoran government's policies that were creating "a situation of utter misery in the households of El Salvador." López described the violence that engulfed the country and its personal effects, including the torture and murder of her father, an uncle, two younger brothers, and six other men by the National Guard, and the soldiers' subsequent threats that drove surviving family members out of their homes and into the hills. They spent more than two years constantly on the move "through thickets, pathways, beneath torrential rainstorms," and evading "the foot-soldiers and the Air Force's airplanes [that] were coming after us, firing at us, bombing, spraying machine gun fire, launching rockets." She explained how the conditions of life in the San José de la Montaña refuge in San Salvador prompted the formation of CRIPDES "to help those displaced people who wish to return to their places of origin" and to demand an end to repression and institute "respect for our rights." The latter half of López's account detailed her arrest and torture, alongside other colleagues from CRIPDES, as well as her subsequent release and ongoing harassment. Throughout her account, López contested the claims made by Salvadoran soldiers and government officials, and repeated by US government authorities, that she and her family members and colleagues were "Terrorists of the F.M.L.N." "In our country," she explained, "to strive after life and liberty is interpreted as belonging to the F.M.L.N. guerrilla, and under this pretext they've always attacked us." López also made clear that, like Tobar and many other rural Salvadorans, the violence she experienced at the hand of Salvadoran authorities only strengthened her resolve: "Each day I feel greater commitment to go on struggling alongside our people, trying to forge a more just and more gentle society for each and every Salvadoran. I am also striving after the truth. I will never forget that my father and seven brothers and sisters and many relatives and friends, and thousands of fellow patriots died for the sake of truth [and so] that there might be peace and real democracy founded on social justice for everyone." She would continue to follow in their footsteps, she promised, "firmly tackling whatever trial or tribulation the Army" set before her. López repeated many aspects of this autobiography during her tour in the United States, in public lectures, media interviews, and meetings with community groups and elected officials.[48]

Other Salvadorans offered similarly wrenching testimonies—both during their travels in the United States and for visitors to their communities in El Salvador. Although the speakers grounded their public testimonies in humanitarian philosophies and the language of international human rights, political realities infused their narratives. As William Westerman has pointed out, for Central American victims of state violence, "speaking itself was a political act, an act of denouncing the injustice."[49] Witness accounts allowed Salvadorans and their allies to hold up "an alternative mirror of reality," one that boldly revealed the untruths disseminated by the Salvadoran and US governments.[50]

The testimonial processes that were so central to tours and delegations were complexly political in another way as well; they required highly scripted performances by Salvadorans and US Americans playing "characters" based in uneven north-south power dynamics. In framing their work in this way, I do not mean that they were disingenuous. Rather, these activists were savvy, employing the same principles and techniques that professionals in the communications and education fields use in their public relations and media work. In order to be effective—to move "the audience to a new level of understanding or action"—Salvadorans followed a certain "aesthetic which was both conscious and well defined."[51] Part of that aesthetic relied on what Patricia Stuelke, an American Studies scholar, describes as "performances of virtuous, sacrificial Central American victimhood."[52] Yet Salvadorans affiliated with the repopulation movement went beyond victim narratives to present themselves as historical agents, participants in the struggle for justice. This required walking a fine line. Too much political analysis in a testimony might lead some audience members to perceive them as threatening. But with too little political analysis, speakers risked failing to mobilize audience members beyond sentiments of sympathy and acts of charity and into the realm of empathy, reciprocity, and solidarity. In short, effective testimony took practice.

If Salvadorans sometimes performed the role of victim, US Americans drew on their privileged positions as imperial citizens to perform what Victoria Henderson refers to as "proxy citizenship," which "hinges on the interposition of *corpus*, an individual (sub institutional) body through which claims to basic civil, political, and social rights can be actualized." Henderson contends, following the sociologist Saskia Sassen, that citizenship practices entail "the production of 'presence' by those without power." In the case of accompaniment, such "presence" refers to the "interposition of privileged foreign bodies that can influence the situation" along with the "(re)placement of local human rights defenders into the nation as rights-bearing citizens empowered to testify against impunity."[53] Viewed from this angle, Henderson continues, accompaniment is premised on divisions: more/less privileged, foreign/local, we/they. It is precisely these divisions that give accompaniment practices like delegations— and grassroots sistering—enduring power. As Henderson observes in the case of Guatemala, "accompaniment—to the extent it takes up the challenge to construct a 'we' based on the principle of democratic equivalence—can strategically, if incrementally, contest institutional and geopolitical boundaries and exclusions."[54] David Grosser put it this way: "Our political leverage rested . . . on our strategic location as residents of the US. Our government was funding the war and trying to control information about the imperial nature of the policy. They needed to keep the real war a secret from our fellow citizens. That we could expose the reality of that war to people who voted in the US and could potentially pressure the US Congress to cut funding for the war gave us our power."[55]

Pedagogy for the Privileged

To ensure that the right messages ultimately reached the US public, leaders of the sistering movement first needed to identify spokespersons and thus provide them with the appropriate foundations. Delegations offered a quick and hands-on way to do just that.

Delegations were carefully crafted learning environments designed to "widen the lens" through which US participants viewed the world.[56] More specifically, delegations took US citizens out of their comfort zones and introduced them to new localities and perspectives in ways that elicited not just empathy for poor and oppressed "Others," but admiration for their struggles, in the face of violence, to defend human rights and positively transform society. An engineered series of direct engagements with Salvadorans intentionally raised questions about mainstream representations of El Salvador (and the Global South more generally), and raised awareness about global structures that perpetuate inequality, injustice, and violence. At base, delegations sought to foment dissatisfaction with the status quo and then channel that new energy into radical democratic practices and political action to alter the status quo. In other words, delegations were training programs for social change agents.

In this sense delegations closely paralleled the Christian base communities and popular schools in El Salvador, both of which encouraged individual and community *concientización* (the raising of *conciencia*, or sociopolitical consciousness), with significant political implications. In addition to promoting basic skills like literacy and leadership, these systems helped marginalized Salvadorans to identify the injustices that surrounded them and empowered them to speak out and take action against those injustices. In the same way, the delegations that took US citizens to El Salvador and elsewhere in Central America promoted new knowledge and awareness about the structural inequalities that inspired the popular and revolutionary movements in the region, the local government's long record of abuses of power, and the support role played by the US government. Delegations also brought US Americans into a new consciousness about their own power and privilege as imperial citizens, which in turn empowered them to challenge injustices in new ways.

The internal records of sistering committees reveal the care with which organizers approached delegations, beginning with the planning phase. While advertising delegations as educational opportunities and humanitarian efforts, coordinators strategically recruited participants. They designed application forms to reveal important information about candidates' personalities, worldviews, and potential contributions to the group. For example, in response to a question regarding one applicant's reason for wanting to join the delegation, Margaret Topp wrote, "I hope to come away from this delegation with a (somehow) changed view of the world, of community, and of education and democracy."[57] This answer offered evidence that Topp already had some background on the repopulations, and that she was curious and willing to learn from the experience. Beyond students like Topp, delegation organizers sought high-profile participants, including members of Congress and their aides, priests and bishops, professors, and doctors. Many delegations intentionally revolved around the participation of such figures; not only did they attract US public attention to a delegation and its mission, but they also served as strategic leverage when dealing with Salvadoran government and military officials.[58]

Another aspect of delegation planning was to ensure that participants acquired all necessary travel documentation from the Salvadoran state. During the civil war, this was an arduous process that could take several months. To obtain a visa and a *salvoconducto* (military safe-conduct pass, required for travel in areas of the country deemed "conflictive") required myriad documents, including the requisite application forms, a valid passport, proof of citizenship, employment verification, police records, copies of plane tickets showing proof of return flight, and inventories of any humanitarian aid to be delivered.[59] The rules for visas and salvoconductos often changed without notice and "compliance is no assurance that passage will be guaranteed," yet obtaining these documents was a critical early step for every delegation.[60] Salvoconductos meant that a delegate's travel was legally sanctioned by the Salvadoran state. Completed salvoconductos in the archival records of sistering organizations indicate, too, that these documents were an important tool, framing their travels as humanitarian missions. Although copies of the actual applications for salvoconductos have yet to resurface in the archive, we do have access to coordinators' instructions to delegates as well as hundreds of letters of support submitted with applications. Curiously, the inscriptions on the salvoconductos often closely parallel the terminology used in these letters, from the description of the social position of delegation members ("city officials, religious leaders, health and education professionals") to their purpose in traveling ("a mission of goodwill . . . to make a humanitarian aid delivery.")[61] Such similarity indicates that delegation coordinators in the United States were strategic in their approach to acquiring Salvadoran documentation.

The deliberate nature of these earliest steps in delegation planning call to mind James Scott's "public transcript." According to Scott, the public transcript is the "open interaction between subordinates and those who dominate" or, put a slightly different way, "the public performance required of those subject to elaborate and systematic forms of social subordination."[62] Although US citizens involved in the sistering movement were not subject to the Salvadoran state in the same ways as Salvadoran citizens, they did have to play by that state's rules in order to enter the country. In order to receive that desired authorization, they shaped their "performance . . . to appeal to the expectations of the powerful."[63]

But as chapter 1 pointed out, where public transcripts exist, so too do private transcripts. According to Scott, the "hidden transcript" of subordinate groups involves discourse "that takes place 'offstage,' beyond direct observation by powerholders."[64] This transcript, inasmuch as it can be "read" by outsiders, can offer insight into the beliefs, cultures, and actions of the subordinates.

Internal records of sistering committees reveal that delegation coordinators began to write and rehearse private transcripts with their groups during a months-long pre-departure orientation. A series of two- and three-hour meetings addressed not just logistical matters such as health issues and what to pack; these meetings also served as the first phase of what Salvadoran activists referred to as *formación política* (political formation or training).

Orientations created a space for critical reflection about the situation in El Salvador and Central America more broadly as well as US connections to the region. They explored the roots of the Salvadoran crisis in the long history of alliances between the oligarchy and security forces. They examined the startling statistics of life in rural zones that resulted from these elite alliances: the deep poverty, high infant mortality, and lack of access to health care, education, and other services. They read accounts describing land struggles, labor strife, and the uniquely difficult experiences of women, refugees, and repopulators. They learned how different sectors of Salvadoran society began organizing in the 1960s and 1970s, taking their demands to government ministries, courts, and streets; how sectors allied with one another, giving rise to broad-scale popular movements; how state forces responded with electoral machinations and violence; and how repression prompted many to turn to armed rebellion.[65]

In their examinations of the FMLN, delegates viewed and discussed documentaries like *In the Name of the People*, which presented the FMLN as heroic freedom fighters struggling alongside the poor peasantry.[66] Reading lists offered additional favorable portrayals of the FMLN, the revolutionary struggle, and Salvadoran popular movements. Many lists recommended Jenny Pearce's *Promised Land: Peasant Rebellion in Chalatenango*, for example, along with Francisco Metzi's *The People's Remedy: The Struggle for Health Care in El Salvador's War of Liberation*, for their accounts of everyday life in FMLN-controlled zones.[67]

Such presentations offered an alternative to US mainstream representations of the Salvadoran conflict. Rather than solely view the war through a cold-war lens as the Reagan administration did, orientation materials underscored the internal roots of the Salvadoran conflict in structural inequalities. Rather than demonize "the enemy" as US officials and news media did, sistering delegation coordinators sought to humanize the Salvadorans who struggled to build better lives. As delegates' empathy intensified, so too did their antipathy toward groups that contributed to the perpetuation of inequalities.

Even as orientation materials offered substantive details about the local factors that contributed to the war, they also placed the Salvadoran crisis into broader contexts. More to the point, they revealed the negative consequences of historical and contemporary US policies in the region. Reading lists included dozens of sources critical of US political, economic, and military intervention in Latin American affairs, including *Open Veins of Latin America*, by Eduardo Galeano; *Trouble in Our Backyard*, edited by Martin Diskin; and *The American Connection: State Terror and Popular Resistance in El Salvador*, by Michael McClintock, a "detailed, meticulously documented account of the U.S. role in setting up El Salvador's repressive apparatus."[68]

To solidify lessons, coordinators facilitated discussions on questions like "What are the forces in El Salvador? What are their relative strengths? From whom do they get their support?"; "How is the role that Spain played in Central America different and how is it similar to the role the United States is playing now?"; and "Why does the U.S. give aid to El Salvador?"[69] Questions like these elicited exploration of the interrelationship between internal and external factors, moving delegates beyond the facile explanations offered in presidential speeches and media spots.

If the pre-departure orientation process encouraged participants to view events through an alternative lens, so too did it encourage them to act in certain ways. This was another component of the hidden transcript and critical to the success of delegations. So important was it, in fact, that coordinators developed multipage security guidelines that drove a significant portion of the orientation process.[70] "BE CONSCIOUS THAT WE ARE IN A WAR," one document warned. El Salvador is "a country with a history of systematic violations of human rights," where anyone could be targeted by paramilitary death squads, as evidenced by the 1980 assassinations of Archbishop Óscar Romero and four US churchwomen.[71] Because "lives are at stake, especially the lives of people who are committed to serving the poor and building a just world," all delegates had to commit to following "security measures," "rules," and "guiding principles of behavior."[72]

Documents outlined some common-sense rules (such as never travel alone) and guidelines for specific roles assigned to delegates: ensuring the functionality of water purifiers, taking sensitive pictures, watching luggage, interpreting, administering first aid, and coordinating deliveries of aid materials.[73] The majority of the rules also had political implications. At the top of the list was respect for hierarchy, or "internal security."[74] Simply put, participants must abide by the directions of the delegation coordinators and Salvadoran hosts "AT ALL TIMES even though we may not entirely understand them at the moment."[75] At issue here was the safety of the Salvadorans, all of whom were active in the popular and/or revolutionary movements; conspicuous engagement with international delegations only heightened the risks they faced. "We are in a setting in which a sophisticated counterinsurgency project is in full-swing [sic], attempting at all times to gather information, to discredit and sometimes repress our hosts and the people with whom we will be visiting," explained one document.[76] Because of this, another instructed, "We do not publicly discuss any of the conversations or visits that we have experienced nor do we speak openly about who we have seen, what we have seen, or where we are going."[77]

Indeed, delegates were to keep as low a profile as possible: "Don't do anything to draw attention to yourself."[78] Because the Salvadoran intelligence apparatus was "sometimes invisible to the inexperienced visitor and certainly outside our frame of reference," it was an absolute imperative to constantly "be alert to 'orejas' (ears = agents) . . . who will attempt to eavesdrop on conversations."[79] Guidelines advised delegates to "begin watching your conversation on the international flight" and, once in-country, be "kind and friendly" but guarded ("do not share anything of substance"), "assume all telephones and hotel rooms are tapped," and "be particularly careful" in taxis, buses, and restaurants.[80] When interacting with government and military officials, be "polite and correct at all times" but "don't be too friendly or joking; some have a sense of humor, but quite a few definitely do not."[81]

Such instructions were strategic; if a group maintained an unobtrusive demeanor, it had higher chances of being able to travel to their sister communities, deliver supplies, and carry out delegation objectives. During the war it was always unknown whether Salvadoran authorities would allow a delegation even to leave San Salvador, let alone spend several days in the repopulation zones. The government made no secret of its concerns about the political objectives of international visitors; this was well illustrated by the "Sworn Declaration" requiring signature on visa applications: "I declare under oath that during my visit to El Salvador, I will not participate in political activities, nor will I carry out actions that intervine [sic] in the internal affairs of the country."[82] Beyond this, Sister Cities records include many examples of officials prohibiting access to or limiting time in sistered communities. Military officials (like Chief of Military Intelligence Colonel Juan Orlando Zepeda) offered long "raps" warning delegates of the wily ways of the FMLN "communists [who] are specialists in manipulating."[83] Like Zepeda, who told delegates from Cambridge that their sister city San Antonio Los Ranchos "doesn't exist," officials repeatedly claimed that there were no civilians in the repopulated areas.[84] As the Chalatenango brigade commander put it, "Everyone in Arcatao was a subversive—even the chickens."[85]

Of course, the very raison d'être of sister cities ran counter to such blanket declarations and thus making it to the sistered communities was a crucial task for delegations. Once there, they collected direct evidence about civilian life in the repopulated villages. Here, too, security guidelines outlined proper documentation behaviors: "never" record the full names of people or locations, for example, or include any "details that would incriminate someone else if they fell into the wrong hands."[86] Although most documents advised against photographing soldiers or military complexes—"Don't even point your camera at them," warned one—some groups appointed a delegate as "photo shooter (for sensitive photos—e.g., military personnel)."[87] Whether with photography, note-taking, or audiovisual recording, delegates were well advised: "Be extremely careful."[88]

An especially intriguing aspect of the hidden transcript that developed was the use of coded language. Some guidelines explicitly instructed delegates to "develop your own, personal code" to add a layer of security to notes and journals.[89] In a similar vein, delegation coordinators and their emergency-response network allies in the United States established a veritable playbook of codes to facilitate discussion of sensitive issues over the phone when necessary. One such list included twenty-nine codes for organizations; specific Salvadoran and US religious, political, and military figures; locations on the delegation's planned route; and phrases such as "to have problems" and "we've been stopped."[90] Beyond that, delegation participants, as a group, designated code phrases, such as "It's so hot!" to indicate that the conversation was too loud and voices must be lowered.[91]

Collectively defined code phrases like these served a dual purpose. Not only did they direct immediate attention to problems that needed to be addressed, but they also were a way for delegates to police each other's behavior. Groups even rehearsed their "rap" in role plays during the final orientation meetings before traveling to El Salvador.[92] Coordinators from one delegation, for example, had participants act out a variety of tense scenarios, including being stopped at a military checkpoint, interacting with the military High Command, being harassed about cameras, and dealing with a "crank."[93]

Much like the Salvadorans scripting their testimonies while on tour in the United States, the entire pre-departure orientation process taught US Americans how to play particular roles while in El Salvador. Orientations encouraged them to shift perspective, to begin thinking and acting as political solidarists. At the same time, orientations trained them to dissimulate that role, instead presenting themselves as politically uninvolved charity workers. In addition to advising delegates on their characters and lines, coordinators provided instructions on costumes and props: "Dress up for the flight there" and, once in Central America, "dress conservatively" for "it's best not to look too 'hippie.'"[94] "Do not carry . . . any newspapers, books, magazines, or other material that would be considered leftist" one document commanded, but do always carry US passports and letters of introduction in case it was necessary at any point to apply imperial citizen pressures.[95]

If the pre-departure orientation process was the first phase of delegation participants' political training, time in El Salvador served as the second phase. Although each itinerary was "dependent on the particular situation in El Salvador and the schedules of particular people," a number of common patterns developed.[96] Over the years, sistering delegations visited the same locations to meet with community leaders, and delegates listened to similar testimonies about horrific violence, the hardships of exile, and the hope and resilience of the repopulation movement. When examined together, delegation itineraries reveal an intentional pedagogy: an orchestrated series of encounters with a variety of Salvadorans served to accentuate both the authenticity of grassroots voices and the impudent, even morally murky characters of state authorities. Experiences in El Salvador thus built on and deepened the lessons introduced at home during orientations.

Groups typically spent a total of four or five days in the capital city of San Salvador. From representatives of CRIPDES and the CNR, delegates learned about the history of the repopulation movement, its goals and objectives, and the many challenges faced by repopulated communities. At Calle Real, San José de la Montaña, and Fé y Esperanza, the US visitors heard testimonies from internally displaced Salvadorans. Intellectuals and opposition politicians critiqued the closed political system of El Salvador and outlined various proposals for reform. Members of peasant federations and trade unions explained how they organized together to press plantation owners, factory bosses, and other employers to increase wages, improve conditions, and stop abusing their workers. Staff and volunteers at nongovernmental agencies such as the Human Rights Commission of El Salvador, the Women's Association of El Salvador, and the Legal Aid office run by the archdiocese of San Salvador shared details about the dire human rights situation in the country and their own organizations' work on behalf of victims of violence, political prisoners, and the detained-disappeared.[97]

All together, these meetings taught delegates about the popular movement in El Salvador; grievances from multiple sectors of society had intertwined, giving rise to sweeping demands for reforms that would address long-standing political, social, and economic inequalities. Yet Salvadoran authorities, in league with the elite business class, repeatedly blocked major reforms, silenced citizen demands, and punished with violence any activity they deemed subversive. This grassroots perspective stood in stark contrast to official views, which delegates gleaned through meetings at Salvadoran government ministries, the high command of the armed forces, and the US Embassy.

If time in the capital city deepened empathy for the popular movement, several days in the *campo* (countryside) solidified the lessons and opened delegates further to the possibilities and even promise of revolution. In the campo, delegates witnessed in grim detail the poverty and suffering of life on the literal and figurative margins. Everywhere they heard testimonies from survivors of military sweeps, massacres, and the treacherous escape flights known as *guindas*.[98]

Eugene "Gus" Newport, the mayor of Berkeley, was among the first sistering advocates to publicize his travel to the repopulation zones of Chalatenango. In March 1985 he joined a two-week "fact-finding mission" sponsored by NEST.[99] Although the group was unable to make it to Berkeley's sister city of San Antonio Los Ranchos, Newport's annotated itinerary illustrated that he and his compatriots had ample opportunity to engage with rural Salvadorans.[100]

In a post-trip interview with a reporter from the *Berkeley Voice*, Newport reported that "everybody we talked to" near San Antonio los Ranchos "talked about having lost family who had been killed in bombing attacks, or at the hands of government soldiers, or chopped up with machetes."[101] Such horrific stories put into humble relief the US Americans' own difficulties with multihour hikes between villages, the extreme heat, and sleeping without beds.

The longer delegates spent in the campo the more they were able to also experience the "warmth, courage [and] community spirit of the inhabitants in these war zones."[102] In meetings with elected leaders of the Local Popular Governments and the directivas of the repopulations, visitors learned about the "history of the organizing in that region [and] how they became a government" as well as the existing "structure as to elections, production, education, health, [and the] judicial system."[103] They visited the "collective self-development projects," which included housing and agriculture programs; Christian base communities; support centers for war orphans and widows; and nutritional and educational programs for infants, youth, and adults.[104] Local health promoters led tours of medical and dental clinics, invited delegates' participation in public education workshops and needs-assessment surveys, and touted specialized programs such as one in Arcatao that integrated a mental health project into the grade-school curriculum as a means of helping children process their war experiences.[105] Such experiments in participatory democracy inspired delegates and offered them a deeper understanding of the revolutionary implications of rural organizing in a highly authoritarian and militarized society.

Although delegates primarily interacted with civilian repopulators in rural areas, it was also the norm for them to engage with FMLN representatives—although, in line with the hidden transcripts and hierarchies of knowledge described in chapter 1, such information did not always make it onto the public itineraries. Coordinators and hosts arranged meetings in Chalatenango with commanders of the Popular Liberation Forces (FPL), including "Jesús Rojas" and "María Chichilco," dynamic speakers who offered personalized versions of the birth of the FMLN coalition, its politico-military development, and its visions for the future. Foot soldiers and collaborators explained how grinding poverty, state-led violence, and the desire for something better had led them to *incorporarse* (incorporate themselves into the revolutionary effort).

These planned exchanges with FMLN combatants and civilian supporters were an important part of the pedagogy of sistering delegations; indeed, they were required events by 1989 or 1990, according to a US–El Salvador Sister Cities delegation planning manual.[106] They allowed US visitors to see the human faces behind revolutionary masks to better understand the conditions that drove some people to take up arms against their own government and inspired others, who would not bear arms, to collaborate in other ways. At the same time, for the FPL and the FMLN more broadly, presentations to Sister Cities delegations served as a kind of international public relations campaign; upon their return home, delegates could help spread favorable impressions of the FMLN insurgents and their struggle against authoritarianism and tyranny.[107]

Equally powerful, however, were unexpected encounters with the FMLN. Former delegates recalled in interviews how, on occasion, FMLN combatants would suddenly materialize in their sister communities, perhaps make a few purchases at a family's small store, then disappear; or how a group passed through town, greeting everyone they passed with a nod and a *salú*—an informal greeting ubiquitous in the campo. "The guerrillas were fed and received with open arms in these communities," said Michael Ring, a former Sister Cities staffer.[108] Others, like the Reverend Art Lloyd of Madison, remembered more intimate interactions. "They threw a party that night, the night before we left," he said. "That's one of the times when the guerrillas came into town. They came and joined the happy dance. There were guerrillas there with their arms on their shoulders, dancing up there."[109] Leah Iraheta, who led numerous delegations to El Salvador, recalled when the guerrillas sent their youngest recruits down to have a party; they used an old car battery to power a music player and danced to the music of Creedence Clearwater Revival. She likened this experience to the Latin American literary genre of magic realism. "It was surreal," she said. You could not really "get it," she said, unless you had been there yourself.[110]

Even when guerrillas were not physically present, US visitors sensed their import. Many repopulators affectionately referred to guerrilla combatants as *los compas*, a shortened form of *compañeros*, meaning companions or comrades, or *los muchachos*, the boys, the good kids who struggled on behalf of and alongside civilians, who helped them rebuild their communities and construct as "normal" a life as possible in the midst of war. And, indeed, the repopulations would not have existed where they did without FMLN sanction. These more informal observations substantiated information that the delegates had received about the FMLN during orientation meetings back home, thus further humanizing "the enemy." Rather than the "terrorists" portrayed by Salvadoran and US officials, delegates saw a rather motley crew of young and humble idealists, most of whom would rather dance to Creedence Clearwater Revival than study war maps.

If the experiences of delegations challenged mainstream characterizations of the FMLN, they also brought US citizens face-to-face with war for the first time—and the consequences of their own government's policies in the region. Graphic oral testimonies and tours through the countryside offered ample evidence of the devastation of scorched-earth tactics and the brutality of government soldiers. Many delegates, including Berkeley's mayor Gus Newport, directly experienced military attacks. As Newport later told reporters, he and his traveling companions first witnessed a "plane/rocket attack" and then, several days later, a "mortar attack, ground to ground."[111] Although they took cover and were spared, a rocket struck a nearby house. "There were eleven people inside," Newport reported, "eight children and three adults. They were all killed."[112]

Mary Kay Baum of Madison had a similar experience in May the following year. When touring a particularly devastated area, she recalled in a 2001 interview, "one of the scariest things happened." She explained:

> We were protected by—behind us and in front of us were FMLN soldiers. They were *very* young men, you know, teenagers. . . . We were walking along the side of a hill and it was burned out—that sort of scorched-earth policy, and that's what they were showing us. And the soldiers communicated with each other that there was a plane coming. I didn't hear or see anything yet. And they told us to scatter and to crouch down. There wasn't much cover there because, because it had been scorched. . . . We didn't know why they told us [to do this], but we did *exactly* what they said. They said to separate out and just be low, scrouch down. And then soon thereafter, we did see and hear a plane overhead. I saw the plane, I didn't hear it at first. And then the plane flew overhead and then, in the distance, under the plane, we saw puffs of smoke come up.

Here Baum paused. When she began to speak again, her cadence was slower and her voice cracked as she struggled to hold back tears. "And . . . and then the plane disappeared." She continued:

Re-educating Empire

After a little while, they gathered us together again and we walked around to a more protected area and they explained to us that we needed to separate because the US planes were equipped with heat sensors and they would exactly be looking for groups of people. And, so, for our own safety . . . that's why we separated. [They told us] that the smoke were bombs dropped. I remember asking if that was a guerrilla stronghold, or, you know, a fortress or something that the army was trying to bomb out, and they said, no, that was just a civilian area where just some small, like a hamlet would be.

Baum recalled that even as they were still processing what had happened, they continued the walking tour, examining "other buildings that were bombed out. . . . I suddenly felt just very light-headed and like I was going to faint." Up to this point in her story, Baum had managed to maintain her composure. But here, she began to cry openly, periodically wiping tears away from under her glasses.

One of those young boys . . . reached into his clothes and he pulled out this—it's like a hard cracker-like cookie. And he told me to eat that, because he could tell I was, that I needed something to eat. You know, we had had a big breakfast earlier, but the combination of things . . . And, uh, they just stayed with me. We were in a more wooded area. And sure enough I felt much better very soon and was able to keep on walking with them. But I felt their great caring and understanding. Probably everybody living up there certainly traverses those hills up and down all the time. But it was so caring on their part.[113]

Such events left Baum, Newport, and other US citizens profoundly moved. On one level, as illustrated by Baum's story, many delegates were humbled by the graciousness, generosity, and youthfulness of the FPL cadres and repopulators. On another level, they were troubled; what they heard, witnessed, and experienced in El Salvador crashed against their humanist moral standards and democratic ideals, and revealed alarming discrepancies between official pronouncements about the situation in El Salvador and the reality lived by most Salvadorans. The US government's complicity in the violence only magnified their indignation. From the perspective of the Salvadoran and US coordinators, such responses were a desired outcome of their delegation pedagogy; they wanted each delegation to serve as a sort of "triggering event" for participants, "provid[ing] the spark that converted new ideas about rights into sustained action." In line with anthropologist Winifred Tate's "paradigm of transformative witness," delegations revealed "how the experience of action in pursuit or defense of rights transforms those taking the action, moving them beyond their initial positions."[114] As former delegate-turned-coordinator Jeannie Berwick expressed in a 2013 interview, delegations to El Salvador were a truly "transformative experience" and people "came back on fire," motivated to take action.[115]

A Tangible Reality

Despite the painfully obvious alliance between the US and Salvadoran governments and militaries, Salvadorans associated with the repopulation and sistering movements distinguished between *el gobierno* (the government) and *el pueblo* (the people) of the United States. Although they had come to fear and despise the former, they still were able to embrace the latter. Because they perceived US citizens as having political clout, repopulators encouraged visits to El Salvador and offered celebratory welcomes to their allies from the north. Participants in delegations regularly remarked that their Salvadoran hosts were "warm and supportive" and "so happy to see somebody from North America."[116]

They also witnessed extreme suffering and, like visitors to other war-torn areas of Central America, often asked their hosts what they could do to help. The answer often shocked. Locals said "they didn't need help down there," recalled one coordinator of delegations to Nicaragua. "What we need you to do is go back to where you're from and educate and raise the issues, and make sure that people know what's happening down here and how U.S. policy affects us."[117] Mary Kay Baum received similar instructions from Salvadorans on each of her ten delegations there: "As I was leaving every single time," she said, "people told me, 'Now your real work begins when you get home.'"[118]

Sister Cities activists heeded these instructions by bringing lessons from El Salvador to the broader US public. Through post-delegation work, tours, and a variety of high-publicity events, they sought to construct a critical public. They designed events to challenge mainstream and official stances, highlight democratic contradictions, and encourage people toward more politically committed solidarity activism. This was a kind of "missionary in reverse," sistering advocate Art Lloyd explained, "where the object is to educate the US and develop a constituency that would support changes in policies."[119]

In fact, a founding objective of Sister City committees was "to inform and educate."[120] Toward this end, each group established Education and Outreach Committees "to develop and distribute organizational propaganda (educational materials)" and to promote educational events.[121] People-to-people exchanges were especially powerful tools, "giv[ing] the issue of El Salvador a human face" and making "the daily tragedy and hope of life in El Salvador a tangible reality for people in the United States."[122]

Yet there is another side to activists' goals with public education programs. Providing "reliable" information about El Salvador helped "counter Administration propaganda" and "demythologize words used as labels (communist, contras, etc.)."[123] Portraying "their reality," moreover, revealed "the devastating effects of U.S. aid on the civilian population." And, as NEST coordinators explained, "To know in a concrete and human way what this aid means . . . strengthens grassroots opposition to U.S. intervention."[124] When viewed from this perspective, public education on the home front was a sort of "agitational campaign."[125]

These events were, of course, very different from the educational experience of delegations. Whereas participants in delegations were prescreened and carefully selected, thus representing a known entity to some extent, there was no way to carry out similar assessments of the attendees at public events in the United States. One could get a general sense of the tenor of an audience and play to them accordingly, of course, but activists necessarily remained far less informed about the sociopolitical currents in the room. For this reason, these public presentations tended to be more circumscribed, even scripted.

This is not to say that public education campaigns in the United States had no teeth. In fact, most of them proved quite "agitational." One reason for this is they often integrated recently returned delegates. Press conferences offered a high-profile opportunity to share some of what they had learned in country, while it was still fresh—including the vast differences between Reagan's pronouncements about El Salvador and the reality lived by most Salvadorans. Kristi Hart, a homemaker from Potosi, Wisconsin, pointed out a series of such contradictions during her post-delegation press conference. After observing that "the Reagan administration has justified a continuation of aid based on the findings of the Salvadoran Human Rights Commission," she informed her audience that the Commission "is headed by a military officer" and that independent human rights monitors "have compiled detailed files of murders, disappearances and political prisoners which sharply contradict the government statistics." In a similar vein, Hart noted that despite Reagan's claim that the recent election of a civilian president (José Napoleón Duarte) represented "the birth of a free society," her delegation discovered "that democracy in El Salvador is no more than a mirage." She went on to describe the military's continued domination of society, repression of opposition parties, compulsory voting, intimidation of judges and juries, and generalized fear. "It seems clear to us," Hart concluded, "that our 500 million dollars a year are supporting a government that simply cannot be called a democracy."[126]

Sister Cities records reveal that such statements regularly made their way into local news media. This was especially true when delegates included prominent citizens like Gus Newport, whose visit to Chalatenango in 1985 garnered significant coverage. "Berkeley Mayor Eugene 'Gus' Newport cried openly as he discussed the fate of the peasants he visited in the Chalatenango region," began one account.[127] In an "exclusive interview" with a reporter from the *Berkeley Voice*, he described "lay[ing] out on the floor of a hut" while "under rocket attack," spending time "*counting.* These planes only carry eight rockets, and every time one would hit, we would deduct: how many were left?" The experience made Newport angry with the Reagan administration's "propaganda, which talks about the threat of Cuban and Soviet domination down there." Such fearmongering was just a "cover-up, to fool the American people," he charged. "They're saying they're fighting strictly guerrillas in those areas, but there's a large civilian population that's being killed on a daily basis." Although he was open about engaging with members of the FPL politico-military forces while in country, he explained that the people who were in the FPL's zones of control in Chalatenango—like the residents of Berkeley's sister city of San Antonio Los Ranchos—were there for a reason: "People look for an alternative. Either they're victims of attack or they can't make a living wage because the economy's so bad. I take into consideration that these people have been the victims of oppressive governments for so long that they're fighting for change . . . not necessarily to become Lenin-Marxists."[128] In this way, Newport used the local media to raise awareness about the violations of the repopulators' rights and to humanize the "opposition."

In order to get such messages to the broader public, media connections were important. Activists fostered close relationships with journalists, even recruited them to go on delegations so that they would produce favorable articles. As meeting notes from the Madison committee reveal, coordinators carefully tracked articles produced by invited journalists, assessing the extent to which they helped with project "projection." Committee members concluded that a *Wisconsin State Journal* story was "basically positive" yet registered their disappointment in a lengthy discussion. One delegation leader explained that they had strategically designed the itinerary with the "expectation that [the] article would focus on what we immersed journalists in." But the journalist presented an unbalanced account, with "too much on FMLN + not enough on civilians in communities." Despite this, ever conscious of the value of the press to their cause, they opted to respond with a "positive letter to the editor."[129]

Another key step taken in the wake of delegations was to follow up with members of Congress. Although it is difficult to measure the direct impact of these reports on US policy in general, the amount of written exchanges in Sister Cities records indicates that eyewitness reports from delegates did influence

Re-educating Empire

elected officials. A December 1989 mayor's letter to President George H. W. Bush and members of Congress calling for "a political-negotiated solution to the war and an end to all war related aid to El Salvador" offers just one of many examples.[130] Sister Cities delegates also provided testimony to city councils and Congressional committees both in person and through professional reports.[131] And, "in order to stimulate public discussion of U.S. policy in Central America" even further, Dick Williams, a Kansas sistering activist, ran for a seat on the US Senate.[132]

Sister Cities activists took their educational efforts beyond elected leaders to the general public through speaking engagements at schools, faith centers, and other community centers. Committee records are full of fliers announcing "send-off parties" for and "report-backs" from delegations, along with photographs, maps, and other materials from presentations. Sister Cities often collaborated with other solidarity groups in grand public education campaigns as well, including the yearly Central America Week, a national campaign "to update folks on a people-to-people basis on the current situation in Central America" and to "explore ways in which we can respond to the needs of the people of Central America."[133] Other coalition events included caravans and tours of Salvadoran and Central American refugees and visitors.

A particularly powerful format for presentations in the 1980s was the slideshow, which blended images from El Salvador, the speaker's personal anecdotes, and general educational information. According to Cambridge committee members, slideshow presentations in 1989 produced a strong "Cumulative effect" in the city. Van Hardy, a photographer who provided many of the committee's images, commented in particular about the impact of the slideshows in the schools; even if the "kids didn't really grasp [the] significance of [the] repopulation movement [they] did understand that $1.5 million/day for weapons was absurd."[134]

That sistering activists spent time speaking to school groups points to an important aspect of their public education campaigns in the United States: they pitched to a lowest common denominator. As noted earlier, coordinators of delegations were able to screen applicants, selecting only those who met certain standards of political awareness, curiosity, and flexibility. Activists who served as public speakers stateside did not have the same luxury. There was no way to know the backgrounds or political leanings of all the attendees at their presentations, whether children or adults. To reach the broadest possible spectrum of audience members, then, activists carefully scripted their presentations. In fact, the Sister Cities archive contains not only the carousels of slides from these slideshows but also many of the actual scripts that accompanied the images—some complete with stage notes and reminders such as "bring flashlight and glasses."[135]

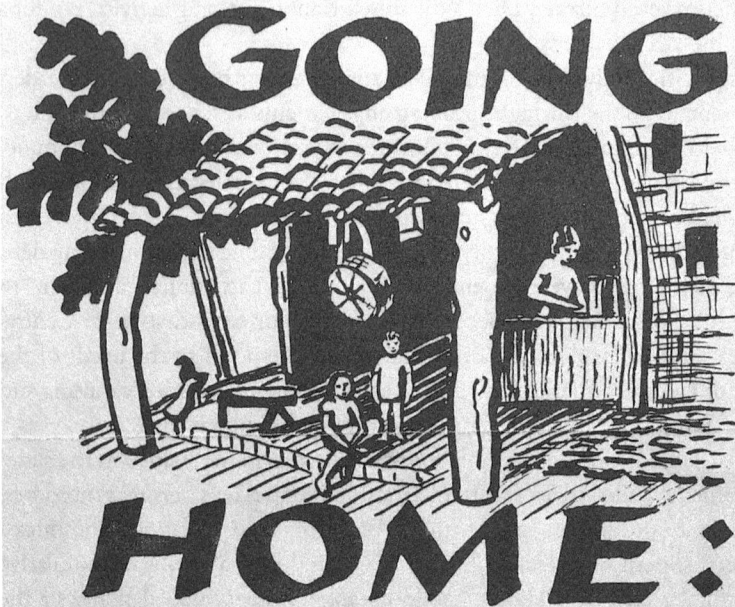

Poster announcing Tim Lohrentz's presentation in Wisconsin about the Going Home campaign, ca. 1991. (MASCP Records, USESSC Archive)

Although US American voices often dominate the historical record, Salvadorans offered an especially potent means of "agitating" the public. During the March 1987 Salvadorans for Peace with Justice Caravan, for example, fifteen Salvadorans, including several sanctuary refugees, traveled through the Upper Midwest to collect funds to support "the repopulation efforts of the displaced" and "to educate local communities about the current situation in El Salvador and the importance of stopping U.S. military aid."[136] Salvadorans in the United States used other high-profile actions to raise awareness, including numerous hunger strikes (such as the 1989 Fast for Peace and the 1990 Fast for Life). Activists associated with Sister Cities, SHARE, and other solidarity groups helped coordinate these events and accompanied the Salvadorans, sometimes joining in the fasts themselves or traveling with the fasting activists to Washington, DC, to lend support and offer their own eyewitness accounts from recent travels in El Salvador.[137]

Tours were another tool for Salvadorans to raise funds and political awareness among US audiences. As the presidents of Chalatenango's directivas explained, the people-to-people exchange that occurred during the tours "deepens the ties of sistering between our pueblos and helps one to know the reality in which our communities and people live."[138]

Materials from the tours illustrate that, like delegations, these were highly orchestrated affairs. They involved months of planning to address the logistics of visas, travel to regions across the United States, and event promotion. Planning materials from Julio Tobar's 1989 tour, for example, include a four-page checklist for setting up visits with potential donors, a "tour visit rap" sheet for volunteers making phone calls to invite people to events, guidelines for how to respond to "put-offs" such as "I don't have time" or "I don't know my schedule now," and records of a four-and-a-half-hour training workshop on tour fund-raising.[139]

In-country itineraries were intense, lasting anywhere between a week and a month; Salvadorans visited ten or more cities, met with a wide range of organizations, and gave multiple presentations. Each presentation followed a similar formula: the speaker shared personal experiences with state-sponsored violence, outlined the successes and challenges of community organizing in the repopulated communities, and made a "pitch" for project support.[140] Ruth Navidad told audiences how "they can help secure civil rights for her country's scattered refugees" and, like other Salvadorans, she and Guillermo Chacón also "urged Americans to press Congress to send money to El Salvador for reconstruction and education, not guns and bombs."[141] Sister Cities coordinators kept careful notes about the tours, assessing the speakers' performances as well as the responses of participants. The most successful tours brought in tens of thousands of dollars; the 1989 Leonardo Hidalgo tour, sponsored by NEST, projected raising $250,000 in six weeks.[142] But good tours always "attained the objectives of . . . public education (good press work and a wide variety of audiences)."[143]

Engaging with Salvadorans during tours, caravans, and other public events had a profound effect on many US citizens. According to Marc Rosenthal, these people-to-people exchanges were "*the* thing that was transformative" for the development of sistering and the Central America solidarity movement more broadly. "Instead of just being some distant image of somebody," he explained, "people were in our communities and they were talking about it." Personal contact with Salvadorans suddenly made the crisis in Central America "very real" for people in the United States and, for many, introduced Sister Cities as a "very legitimate humanitarian kind of thing."[144] For some, this meant simply attending fund-raising events and contributing to material aid drives. For example, a Madison resident, Prudence Barber, began her activism around Salvadoran issues because she shared a house with several refugees. She had learned Spanish as a Peace Corps volunteer in Colombia during the 1960s and, two decades later, as a property manager in the Jenifer Street neighborhood, she found herself providing housing to several Salvadorans. Friends in the sanctuary movement "brought them to my house, to stay at my house," she said, because they didn't speak English. The house became a new kind of community for Barber, "a lot of fun and very interesting." Soon thereafter, she found herself making fund-raising phone calls for the Madison–Arcatao Sister City Project, the first step in what became a decades-long affiliation with the group.[145]

Barber was just one of many US citizens prompted into action by the public education campaigns of Salvadoran and US American sistering activists. Face-to-face exchanges, eyewitness accounts, and photographs from El Salvador brought the issues home for US citizens. By deliberately highlighting the contrasts between the reality of life on the ground in the repopulated communities and the official narratives of the US and Salvadoran governments, these popular educators helped construct a critical public that, in turn, pressured for changes to US policies.

The Limits of Solidarity

The bulk of the analysis in this chapter has rested on the understanding that a high level of coordination and agreement existed within and between southern and northern partners in the sistering network. While it is true that participants reached significant levels of accord, these were still negotiated relationships between people with different backgrounds, experiences, and expectations. Thus, like all social movements, real tensions were endemic to Sister Cities.

Many of these tensions were "very personality driven."[146] In the repopulations, for example, some especially strong characters maintained positions of power for years on directivas and other committees, much to the frustration of other community members. Documentation from sistering committees in the United States offers glimpses of similar discontent, with an anonymous "request for no smoking at meetings," reports of conflicts that erupted into shouting matches, and internal assessments of potentially problematic delegates—including one who was "notoriously abrasive, very irritating, hard to deal with," and, if allowed to join the delegation, would be "the reason people would get shot."[147]

Other tensions related to local competitions. For example, the sistering committee in Belmont, Massachusetts, lost half of its members when it separated from the local sanctuary group, and complicated relations between San Francisco and Berkeley made it difficult to coordinate one of the 1991 tours.[148] Conflicts stemming from resource disparities between sistered and non-sistered communities in El Salvador ultimately prompted CRIPDES and affiliated organizations to attempt to "regionalize the impact" of sistering.[149] And insensitively handled invitations to tour the US contributed to "envy and dissention" within the repopulated communities in El Salvador.[150] Not all competitions were quite so heavy, however. When Madison contested Berkeley's status as the first Sister City, a national meeting report noted, "the question was settled in a friendly manner over a plate of chili and rice at dinner."[151]

The historical record also reveals tensions between southern and northern sistering partners. Some of these, too, were rather lighthearted, such as the surprise of US visitors when Salvadorans were unable to pronounce the name of their city. Stories still circulate about the man from San José Las Flores who greeted Cambridge delegates by saying, "Welcome to our brothers from Candracha!"[152] But more difficult situations arose as well, as revealed in communications about the logistics of financial support. As NEST, SHARE, Sister Cities, and CRIPDES formed sistering relationships, they also developed procedures for requesting funds and channeling financial support to the repopulated communities. Salvadorans who did not follow these norms elicited crusty comments from US Americans. When Arcatao sent a request for help covering the costs of the July 1990 festival to honor the town's patron saint, San Bartolomé, for instance, a NEST staffer sniffed to a Madison representative, "I'm not sure what expectations they have when they send these projects mid-year like this."[153]

As suggested by the Arcataenses' aberrant funding request, Salvadorans set their own norms and pushed against any US-formulated procedures they deemed too constrictive. This became especially clear when the directiva presidents from eight sistered communities presented NEST's executive director Tracey Schear with a "proposal about the use of economic aid that you so generously send us." At this point US funds arrived to El Salvador earmarked for specific projects. The insecurity of life in the repopulations, however, meant that local leaders needed to respond to "emergencies" as they came up, alongside the longer-term "global plans for community development." In light of this, the presidents proposed a new procedure for the administration of funds: "that this money be directed to a COMMUNITY FUND THAT WOULD BE ADMINISTERED BY THE COMMUNITY DIRECTIVA IN THE SISTER CITY ACCORDING TO THE NEEDS THAT ARE DEEMED PRIORITY FOR THE INHABITANTS AT THAT MOMENT."[154]

Although such incidents reveal some of the tensions that undergirded transnational sistering relationships, they also highlight the negotiated aspect of those relationships. Indeed, evidence from Sister Cities records indicates that the presidents' proposal received a favorable response. Most US committees subsequently deposited funds into a general sistering fund administered by the local directiva. In exchange, directiva members provided reports detailing how they spent those funds.

If resource management issues brought south-north tensions to the surface, so too did political tensions. These tensions existed on the ground in both El Salvador and the United States, as evidenced by the rocky relationships between the five politico-military groups that made up the FMLN coalition, and the similarly competitive relations between different US-based solidarity organizations. Within the US sistering sphere, activists sometimes directly addressed the issue. Records from sistering committees clearly note, for instance, the "global-in-local" political challenges of gaining citywide support for sistering. In the early stages of developing a sister cities relationship, activists in Belmont openly debated "how much effort to put into passing [an] official resolution" given that the local "political makeup [was] not solid," as the area's residents were "mainly conservatives and wealthy people."[155] These challenges were visible at the tail end of the development process as well, as in Berkeley, where two city council members voted against the resolution establishing a sister city relationship with San Antonio Los Ranchos. One of the dissenters, Leo Bach, explained his opposition as follows: "As sure as we're sitting here you're going to read in tomorrow's papers that the city of Berkeley supports guerrillas in El Salvador."[156]

These overt divisions directly tied to the broader cold war context and, more specifically, conflicting interpretations of the causes of conflict in Central America—including the role of the US government—and the possible solutions. The extreme polarization fed the hidden transcripts and knowledge hierarchies discussed in chapter 1 and earlier in this chapter. As previously noted, tensions underwrote meetings between sistering and solidarity activists in Los Angeles, contributed to the birth of the Madison–Arcatao Sister City Project, and prompted some people to leave the Sister Cities network when it broke from NEST.

Internal tensions like these also played into north-south relations. A June 1987 delegation reveals how tensions could boil over when activists were not in full accord in the field. Designed by CRIPDES-CNR and coordinated in the United States by NEST, this delegation was to be a grand affair involving "a large and visible delivery of humanitarian aid," a celebration marking the one-year anniversary of the repopulation of San José Las Flores, and a ceremony to formalize the new Cambridge-Las Flores Sister Cities Project.[157] The staff at NEST recruited twenty-one people from across the United States, with fourteen of those from Cambridge.[158] To amplify the delegation's voice, coordinators oversaw the collection of dozens of letters for Salvadoran officials from US city council members, senators, and representatives, and arranged for an open letter to President Duarte, signed by more than sixty-five people, to appear in *El Mundo* on the day the delegation arrived in El Salvador.[159]

Upon arrival, delegation members learned that the US group was only one part of a much bigger picture: CRIPDES-CNR had planned a massive caravan to the repopulations of Chalatenango, involving four buses carrying fifty internationals and one hundred Salvadorans as well as three trucks loaded with sacks of corn, beans, sugar, powdered milk, school supplies, blankets, clothes, and basic medicines.[160] When the caravan was detained at a military checkpoint near Chalatenango City, tensions flared between the Salvadoran and NEST coordinators about the best way to proceed. Whereas the Salvadoran team wanted to return immediately to San Salvador and take over the National Cathedral in protest, the US coordinators believed it made more sense to stay overnight in Chalatenango City, mobilize their Emergency Response Networks in the United States, and try to resolve the situation the next day. As one delegate recalled years later, "NEST staff really were trying to play this" carefully, to avoid confrontations, in part to preserve its working relations with church figures. But many of the Cambridge delegates disagreed with the NEST leadership, and pressed instead to accompany proposed sit-ins at the Cathedral and Ministry of Foreign Relations.[161] While delegates debated, caravan vehicles turned around and a CRIPDES representative instructed them to re-board the bus, saying "it was imperative that we all return to San Salvador immediately."[162] They did so and everyone traveled back to the capital, where tensions continued to simmer.

A new round of differences manifested the next day as the Salvadoran and US teams took distinct tacks in publicizing the government's obstruction of the caravan. The US delegates held a morning press conference in front of the US Embassy at which they firmly yet carefully framed the incident within a human rights context. The group's spokespeople, Nancy Ryan of Cambridge and Father Michael McFadden of Los Angeles, explained, "We were arbitrarily denied our right" to travel to San José Las Flores; the people of Las Flores were denied their "right to receive aid"; and CRIPDES-CNR "were denied their rights . . . to carry out their work for repopulation."[163] Later that same afternoon, CRIPDES affiliates adopted a much more confrontational stance during their own event in front of the US Embassy. They denounced by name the colonels and brigades responsible for stopping the caravan, "the North American Advisors who come to train more men for war," and the entire Salvadoran government of "assassins, repressors, corrupt thieves, and turncoats."[164] While CRIPDES statements declared that the "people are fed up with your demagoguery and your selling out to the interests of the U.S. Government," protesters gathered outside the embassy and set fire to a US flag.[165]

After three days of meetings and pressures, the group finally received authorization to travel to Las Flores on the condition that someone from the embassy be present, causing a new round of tensions. Cambridge delegates had met with David DeLoughy, deputy chief of mission at the embassy, who ultimately arranged permission for the group as well as embassy accompaniment. When Jim Wallace, the Cambridge team leader, approached his CNR collaborators to express "serious concerns about the prospect," the Salvadorans instructed Wallace to "proceed . . . even if the U.S. Embassy was playing a role" because "the most important thing was for the delegation to bring in the aid."[166]

The concerns of Wallace and others rested on "distrust" of the embassy officials. "They had been so nasty with us to begin with," recalled Wallace in a 2017 interview, "and not really provided the kind of support we wanted from them." Moreover, given the fact that US–El Salvador Sister Cities existed in large part to challenge US policies in El Salvador, many Cambridge delegates did not want embassy officials "to get another story out of all this."[167] So, as Nancy Ryan and Cathy Hoffman explained, Cambridge delegates strategized to isolate the embassy representative assigned to accompany them. According to Ryan, "He was kind of scary. He was clearly a kind of CIA dude-ish . . . keeping track of us." But "we just didn't want him talking. We didn't want

CRIPDES-CNR protest in front of the US Embassy, 1987. *Top*: Protestors preparing to burn the imperial flag. *Bottom*: "The Repopulation of San José Las Flores gains strength from the organization of the people." This CNR sign graces a graffiti-covered wall. (photos © Van Hardy, used with permission)

people talking to him, you know, we didn't want to reveal anything untoward—whatever that was. And so, so my job," Ryan said, "was just to talk insanely about nothing much, you know, and just keep him at bay."[168]

Records from this delegation reveal other layers of tension as well, specifically between NEST and Sister Cities activists. Aware that the Salvadorans planned to adopt an aggressive attitude at their embassy demonstration, for example, NEST coordinators banned delegates from participating or even attending—a directive that provoked "strong disagreement . . . on the part of team leaders and delegates themselves."[169] A post-delegation report prepared by NEST leveled thick critiques at the team leaders, in particular Jim Wallace of Cambridge and Father McFadden of Los Angeles, who exerted "too much responsibility . . . without enough control." Due to their "utilization of incorrect tactics," the report contended, the delegation "found itself taking an advocacy role in a context not appropriate for our [NEST's] character" as a humanitarian institution.[170] Although the report did not raise the point directly, it implied that the team leaders were largely to blame for their own deportation threat; the evening they returned to San Salvador from their visit to Las Flores, Dr. René García Araniva, the director of immigration, announced on television that the delegation had twenty-four hours to leave the country "or risk being deported as undesirables."[171] The following morning the front page headline of *El Mundo* read, "21 NORTH AMERICANS ORDERED TO LEAVE COUNTRY."[172]

Years later, Geoff Thale, one of the participants, still remembered this as being "an incredibly tense delegation," with the Cambridge group meriting special mention as "large and very committed," often adopting a "public confrontation role." The differing approaches of Cambridge, NEST, and other US contingents caused "a lot of internal struggles." For his part, Thale "took a small group and left." Rather than engage in the political wrestling, Thale followed through with his commitment to visit the Mesa Grand refugee camp in Honduras.[173]

But if tensions within the US group contributed to the challenges of this particular delegation, according to the NEST report the "problematic" CRIPDES-CNR leadership group also deserved some of the blame. "*Politically*, the CNR/CRIPDES have not demonstrated a sense of strategic overview to help inform delegation decisions and strategy in El Salvador," the report noted. More to the point, they did not respect "the need for separate/parallel activities" whereby some "entities confront and push the limits," while others "maintain a more institutional character and work to legitimize the efforts of the people." Because of this, the report concluded that "the delegation was brought into their own agenda for militant confrontation."[174]

In the end, although this June 1987 delegation was far more high profile than NEST coordinators had bargained for, it offers us a unique window onto some of the challenges of transnational solidarity work. As solidarity activists readily admit, tactical differences among people in separate organization are common. So even as these pages pay special attention to the concerns surrounding this particular delegation, tensions between CRIPDES, CNR, NEST, and Sister Cities activists were "relatively normative."[175] Yet these events offer insight into a moment of rapid expansion for both the repopulation and sistering movements, and they reveal how Salvadoran and US American activists negotiated different methods and strategies. Many US activists struggled over the meanings of solidarity, with some demanding a "humanitarian" (read: neutral or apolitical) approach and others insisting on direct political advocacy and civil disobedience. The way such tensions played out on the ground during this delegation foreshadowed the later debates about the formation of a Sister Cities organization independent of NEST.

Records from the US tours of Salvadorans provide additional nuance. More specifically, internal Sister Cities documentation reveals that, similar to the role that CRIPDES-CNR played with delegations in El Salvador, Salvadorans visiting the United States had "handlers": US Americans who carefully guided them during their time in-country, from hours of "orientations," particularly in the first days of their tour, to the management of their behavior and message.

Notes from one of Julio Tobar's first briefings, for example, reveal that his tour managers instructed him first about "who [he was] talking to" and then about how he should "lay [the] basis for [his] pitch." Tobar's orientation in Madison went farther, providing a thorough outline for his twenty- to thirty-minute talk, as follows: "(1) Thank you for being there, (2) Biography, (3) Why are they refugees? (4) Repopulations (how they started; achievements/advances, ex. of particular town, obstacles; (5) Peace: negotiations (ARENA); (6) International aid; (7) Project." In addition, his handlers in Madison instructed Tobar on how to behave ("elements of rap"), including "look at people" and "use personal examples."[176]

In some ways, such handling of Salvadoran representatives of the repopulation movement calls to mind the experiences of sanctuary refugees. As a number of social scientists revealed, the "strategic framing of the 'refugee identity'" by sanctuary activists and the "performing" of life stories by those refugees produced a paradox. Although these methods allowed Central American activists to reach very broad audiences in the United States, they also "constrained their ability to act in those settings and, by reifying the asymmetric power relations between North and Central Americans, limited the relationships that could be developed."[177] Debates about this framing led to significant tensions within and between individuals and groups involved in the sanctuary movement in the United States.

In other ways, however, interpersonal relations within the grassroots sistering network stand a world apart. In contrast to the unnamed sanctuary refugees who, out of very real concerns for their security, covered their faces with kerchiefs and identified themselves only by first names when performing in public, the Salvadorans who toured with Sister Cities and associated organizations had full names, life histories, and identities that went beyond those of *victim* or *refugee* to include *repopulator, community organizer, cooperative member, directiva president*, and *teacher*, among others. And although uneven power dynamics underwrote grassroots sistering at all levels, the accompaniment model adopted by grassroots sistering activists emphasized the ideals of horizontalism and shared authority. That Salvadorans took center stage in educational campaigns—not as nameless victims but as real people—distinguishes grassroots sistering from many other forms of Central America solidarity activism of the period, and illustrates another way that sistering advocates blended human rights work and political advocacy. By encouraging Salvadorans and US Americans to share the director's chair in the theater of public opinion, sistering advocates modeled a viable alternative to traditional imperial relations.

Expanding Frontiers

This chapter has examined delegations and tours as key tools in the Sister Cities repertoire. The direct people-to-people exchanges blended humanitarian and political objectives. They provided protection and thus political space for Salvadoran grassroots activists while also providing US-based activists the training and resources necessary to become effective change agents themselves. Together, Salvadorans and US Americans carried out public education campaigns that included coverage to break the media silences in both countries regarding the actions of the Salvadoran State, the death squads, and the US government; meetings with state authorities to push for transparency and accountability; and engagements with community groups in the United States to spread eyewitness truths. In the context of what activists deemed a war against fascism, it was impossible to be neutral with their work. "There was no center," said Michael Ring.[178] In the words of J. R. from San José Las Flores, "The human rights theme is not a humanitarian issue today, but rather a political one."[179]

I also have outlined here some of the power asymmetries of sistering work. Northern and southern activists were differently positioned and empowered, and although the solidarity model adopted by US–El Salvador Sister Cities emphasized horizontalism, northern activists carried with them many privileges and related assumptions such as "I want to and I can help; it is my right to travel when and where I wish; it is my right to freely express my opinions; and state authorities have a duty to listen and respond to me." These beliefs are in large part what made grassroots sistering such a successful tactic. But this same imperial privilege has sidelined Salvadoran activists in many ways. This chapter has offered an initial corrective by highlighting how Salvadoran activists engaged with and in many cases designed and managed the *formación política* (political training) of the US public. In collaboration with US American Sister Cities activists, these Salvadorans facilitated face-to-face exchanges that made the reality of the US-backed war in El Salvador accessible to broad cross-sections of US society and revealed the United States as an important field of struggle. In order to end human rights abuses and foment progressive change in El Salvador, it was necessary for grassroots activism to target not only the Salvadoran government and military but also US public opinion. The public could, in turn, press the US government into reducing—or stopping— its funding of the Salvadoran state and armed forces. This modification of what political scientists call the boomerang pattern demonstrates that interactions between local and international activist circles move in both directions and represents "the global North as not just a source of political pressure, but rather a field of conflict" in itself.[180]

Personal contact with Salvadoran activists had special power to inspire US Americans and motivate them into actions small and large. In this way, despite the tensions endemic to sistering, activists in south and north forged a forceful co-presence. While occupying the same literal and figurative space, they educated each other. They became familiar with unique aspects of each other's worlds: *pupusas* (a sort of stuffed tortilla) and snow; war-zone security measures and hyperscheduled tour itineraries; revolutionary folks songs and those of Creedence Clearwater Revival. In so doing, they produced shared cultural codes and negotiated what Adán Quan refers to as "allowable Otherness."[181] They warmly engaged with each other as equals and as a kind of fictive kin— as *hermanas y hermanos*, sisters and brothers. At the same time, they held up certain representations of each other that reified power inequalities. Certain representations of Salvadorans (i.e., victims) enabled US citizens to exert power and to take action. Thus, Sister Cities advanced its objectives by constructing an "object of intervention" amenable to a critical US public.

This grassroots pattern mirrored the behavior of the US Agency for International Development (USAID) in El Salvador, as examined by Adán Quan. Even as USAID officials admired the Salvadorans they worked with "who sought to reform Salvadoran society," Quan notes, they portrayed Salvadorans in folklorized and essentialized ways, disparaging an "intractable Salvadoran character," for example, or interpreting Salvadoran development officials' decisions as reflective of "a Salvadoran trait, craftiness." Such portrayals "served to justify and depoliticize U.S. intervention," Quan explained; the nation-building reforms that US officials promoted in El Salvador "required a deficient society, along with the identification of a progressive managerial elite to carry out reforms. The construction of an autonomous and deficient sphere of Salvadoran culture also obscured the US government's imperial influence and links to the less attractive aspects of the war, such as funding a military guilty of numerous human rights abuses, discursively separating such links from the extensive U.S. investments." In short, the US government exerted power in El Salvador not only through economic and military aid but also "through a variety of mechanisms of representation."[182]

Salvadoran and US American activists also employed representations to exert power—ironically, to challenge the power of Salvadoran and US officials by holding up "an alternative mirror of reality," one that unmasked official untruths.[183] This strategic framing, along with the internal negotiations described here, illustrate that transnational activism is both a social process and a contact zone. Following Mary Louise Pratt, Adán Quan, Saskia Sassen, Nestor García Canclini, and others, it is useful to consider these spheres of transnational activism as a kind of frontier zone where local and foreign activists negotiate with each other "to reform nation-states under international standards of governance and economic policy, reshaping both local power structures and transnational ideals and programs."[184] Through delegations, tours, and public education campaigns during the war years, Sister Cities activists blurred the boundaries between the national and global, and created unique transborder zones of interaction that held tremendous transformative power. They continued expanding these frontier zones through the 1990s, demonstrating great flexibility and creativity in adjusting to new circumstances as the world around them changed—and as they contributed to that change.

Re-educating Empire

3

New Horizons

From War to Peace

When the armed forces of El Salvador began dismantling its military checkpoints across the country in early 1992, observers attributed the move to the peace accords signed the previous month in Mexico, the culmination of a long process of United Nations–mediated negotiations between the Salvadoran government and the FMLN opposition forces. In a similar vein, observers celebrated the first postwar elections in 1994 as "the elections of the century," confirmation that El Salvador had joined the international club of modern democracies.

Both of these events were important moments in El Salvador's recent history, illustrating the "noteworthy progress" made by Salvadoran leaders in securing peace and stability for their war-torn nation.[1] Yet most analyses of these moments and the broader transition of which they were part remain exclusively focused on the warring parties and high-profile mediators, including the United Nations and the United States. This chapter and the next move beyond the watershed approach, introducing a grassroots perspective on the transition from war to peace in El Salvador. When examined from the perspective of grassroots activists, the transition began much earlier and lasted much longer than has been acknowledged.

Tracing the actions and rhetoric of rural activists and their allies during the late 1980s and into the 1990s reveals how they took advantage of developments at local and global levels to create new spaces for citizen action. They continued to highlight human rights as the basic right to life, but they also grew more explicit in their demands on a range of political, civil, and economic rights, from the rights to organize collectively and to vote in free and fair elections, to the rights of access to land, credit, education, and health care. Through their mobilizations in these varied realms, activists chipped away at the authoritarian system in El Salvador and helped usher in a new era.

Whereas the following chapter focuses on socioeconomic issues, this chapter examines military and political aspects of the long transition. I argue that demilitarization—publicly recognized with the official dismantling of checkpoints in 1992—had actually begun years before, in large part a result of grassroots transnational activism. If activists contributed to the deconstruction of the old ways through their demilitarization campaigns, then they also helped construct new and democratic systems of political representation at local and national levels. In short, rural activists and their partners in the US–El Salvador Sister Cities network presaged the official end of military hostilities and helped define El Salvador's transition to peace.

Opening Political Spaces

The repopulation movement picked up pace in the late 1980s in the midst of a complex context. On the one hand, the levels of violence rose as the Salvadoran right, coalesced into the National Republican Alliance (ARENA) party, jockeyed for political position. As the March 1989 Salvadoran presidential elections drew near, US-based activists warned about the "volatile" and "deteriorating" conditions in El Salvador. During their final months in office, outgoing president José Napoleón Duarte and his Christian Democratic administration, unable to rout the FMLN, continued "losing their credibility" to the point that one exiled man announced the government "is about to collapse."[2] The ARENA party, backed by the conservative military clique known as La Tandona, stood ready to fill the void. The Tandona referred to El Salvador's Military Academy class of 1966—an especially large cohort that marked the supposed modernization and professionalization of the Armed Forces of El Salvador. Tandona members, with close ties to the country's traditional elite, gained such powerful influence in the country's affairs that researchers with the US Congressional Arms Control and Foreign Policy Caucus cited them as one of the "barriers to reform" in 1990.[3]

That the ARENA party, supported by the Tandona and other conservative forces, maneuvered for control in El Salvador was deeply concerning for members of the grassroots sistering network. According to Michael Ring, former staff person in the El Salvador Sister Cities office, many people believed "there was no possibility of a real peace negotiation" with José Napoleón Duarte and his Christian Democratic party "because he did not represent any significant political force in the conflict. He was a pure US puppet." Instead, ARENA "was the force that had to agree to peace terms in order for them to hold." But because ARENA "represented the Salvadoran elite in all its brutality," the road to peace would be anything but smooth.[4] At meetings in mid-1988, Cambridge sistering committee members worried that the Tandona "has developed a higher level of power" and that leaders "are advocating for an all-out war." Notes from a July meeting include an especially frightening premonition: "ARENA supports a 'democracy' like that in Chile"—a reference to the military dictatorship headed by General Augusto Pinochet (1973–90). "So," the notes continue on to explain, "ARENA and La Tandona will launch an offensive to wipe out the opposition—including the repopulations."[5]

One leader of Chalatenango's grassroots Coordinator of Communities and Repopulations (CCR) predicted that the situation would worsen if ARENA's Alfredo Cristiani assumed office. In an April 1989 interview with Cambridge sistering representatives, he explained that because ARENA "is the party of the death squads . . . we consider that the situation will be more difficult for the repopulators in the entire country because we have seen the violence of these first few months of the year. In comparison with the events of the year before, the statistics of the number of disappearances, assassinations and captures has multiplied." As if that wasn't enough, he said, "They have told us that if ARENA won, that they were going to kill us all."[6]

To a great extent, this foreshadowing proved correct. Cristiani emerged victorious and even before he formally donned the sash of his new office, the situation unraveled further. "The recent alarming increase in repression," Cinny Poppen of Cambridge reported in May 1989, "seems to indicate that 'Total Warfare,' the program espoused by one contingent of the military establishment [La Tandona] is prevailing."[7] Death squads resurfaced and security forces stepped up the repression of popular movement organizations. A human rights report from the previous month listed dozens of incidents in which repopulators were "violently abducted," disappeared, threatened with massacres, and otherwise "treated very harshly." "The goal of the military seems to be to make life so miserable that people will leave," the report noted. Although determined to stay, repopulators feared "that the army will start burning houses and killing people in a continuation of the harassment."[8]

Violence increased further after Cristiani took office. "Only 70 days after the ARENA government took power," a CRIPDES human rights report from July 1989 noted, "the systematic violation of human rights has escalated." The thirteen-page report detailed hundreds of abuses, including illegal detentions and torture, military operations, and the occupations of repopulated communities and individual homes. The following month CRIPDES expanded its report to twenty-three pages as "the wave of repression continues reaching ever-higher levels."[9] Despite the violence, Salvadoran activists like Manuel Cartagena from San José Las Flores considered Cristiani's election "as primarily a defeat for the U.S., a repudiation of the Christian Democrat experiment."[10] Thirty years later, Michael Ring put it this way: "In an ironic way, ARENA's rise to formal power set the stage for the possibility of real negotiations by pulling the mask off the façade of a 'centrist' government."[11]

Yet, even in the midst of crisis, new political developments offered some hope. At the regional level, Central American leaders, encouraged by their counterparts around the world, engaged in formal talks seeking solutions to the hostilities then wracking El Salvador, Guatemala, and Nicaragua. Efforts of the Contadora Group between 1983 and 1986 gave way to the Esquipulas Process of 1986 and 1987, resulting in what became known popularly as the Central American Peace Plan. Although the August 1987 agreement set guidelines for national reconciliation primarily in terms of electoral politics, democratization, and disarmament, it also pledged "to attend, as a matter of urgency, to the flows of refugees and displaced persons caused by the crisis in the region, providing them with protection and assistance, particularly in the areas of health, education, work and safety, and to facilitate their repatriation, resettlement or relocation."[12] The subsequent International Conference on Central American Refugees (CIREFCA) focused exclusively on the problems of refugees, returnees, and displaced persons.[13]

Although displaced Salvadorans were excluded from these high-level regional talks, many did participate in the National Debate for Peace in El Salvador, launched in June 1988 by Monseñor Arturo Rivera y Damas, archbishop of San Salvador. More than sixty organizations joined in this public debate with the aim of finding "basic points of agreement that could assist the government, armed forces, political parties as well as the opposition alliance . . . to bring an end to the war." Over the course of several months, through a series of surveys and discussions, participants explored the causes of the Salvadoran conflict, analyzed the strengths and weaknesses of previous attempts to resolve it, assessed the progress of the 1987 Central American Peace Plan, and offered alternative solutions to the national crisis. The Final Document of the National Debate for Peace, released on September 4, 1988, emphasized that in light of the complex roots of war, there could be no simple fix; rather, the situation required a "political solution through negotiation-dialogue" and the implementation of a series of reforms that would "reorient the economic policy to satisfy the basic needs and development of the majority"; construct a political system "that guarantees pluralistic participation with the parties oriented to meet the needs of the majority"; and promote social programs in housing, education, health, and other critical areas.[14]

On the heels of the National Debate, another important local-level political development occurred; the FMLN issued multiple formal peace proposals.[15] At the time ARENA officials refused to engage, but repopulators saw it "as a hope" and sistering activists in the United States concluded "the peace process and/or negotiation framework [of the FMLN] are very likely to be used in the future."[16]

By the close of 1989, it became impossible for Salvadoran officials to continue seeking a military solution to the conflict. If the FMLN had proven its strength by pressing government forces into a stalemate by the mid-1980s, their Final Offensive of November 1989 helped tip the balance in favor of a negotiated political resolution. The offensive, planned by the FMLN's high command for the better part of a year, brought the war to the capital city of San Salvador for the first time, and although it did not precipitate the hoped-for mass uprising to topple the authoritarian regime once and for all, it did confirm the staying power of the FMLN forces. In addition, President Cristiani and ARENA's response to the offensive—which included the high-profile massacre of Jesuit intellectuals at the University of Central America—put the Salvadoran government into the international hot seat. One outcome of the offensive, then, was to bring Salvadoran officials to the negotiating table.

A spate of major changes on the global stage also encouraged the warring factions toward dialogue. Between 1989 and 1991, the cold war drew to a close as communist governments collapsed across Europe. In the United States, fears of a Soviet-inspired communist invasion of the Americas subsided as relations thawed between US and Soviet/Russian leaders, elections in Nicaragua in 1990 ousted the revolutionary Sandinista National Liberation Front, effectively ending the Nicaraguan Revolution, and US president George H. W. Bush heralded the start of "a new world order" while vowing to "achieve another victory, a victory over tyranny and savage aggression" in the oil-rich Middle East.[17] In light of such changes, Cristiani could no longer expect El Salvador's erstwhile US benefactors to continue their relatively unrestrained support for the war against the FMLN. Similarly, the Salvadoran revolutionaries lost a key ally when the Sandinistas left office in neighboring Nicaragua, and Cuban revolutionaries urged the FMLN to resolve the war through negotiation.

Thus influenced by both external and internal factors, the Cristiani administration and the FMLN General Command engaged in a series of United Nations–mediated peace talks between 1990 and 1992. Via fits and starts, they forged agreements on human rights (Human Rights Accord, July 1990), democratic constitutional reforms (Mexico Accord, April 1991), a cease fire, and other topics.[18] The process culminated in the signing of the final Peace Accords in January 1992, officially bringing the Salvadoran conflict to an end.

Affiliates and allies of the rural repopulation movement evolved with these changing contexts. Rural repopulators continued to denounce the military's occupation of their villages and other abuses. Sister Cities committees in the United States followed suit, employing their emergency response networks to defend their Salvadoran partners' human rights. But rural activists also engaged in public fora such as the National Debate for Peace in El Salvador, modeling civic debate and designing alternative paths forward. CRIPDES-CNR played leadership roles in the National Consultation of Aid Institutions and Organizations of Refugee, Returned, and Displaced Populations of El Salvador (Concertación Nacional de Instituciones de Apoyo y Organismos de la Población Refugiada, Retornada y Desplazada de El Salvador), which, in turn, formed part of the Permanent Committee of the National Debate for Peace (Comité Permanente del Debate Nacional por la Paz). On their own and as part of the Consultation, they took action to ensure that any negotiation processes and national reconstruction planning took into account the unique needs of rural people. As negotiations commenced, CRIPDES joined with twelve other Salvadoran popular movement organizations to form the Interinstitutional Coordinating Committee (Coordinadora Interinstitucional) "to propose structural changes in the state appuratus [sic] which may resolve the country's problems."[19] In the context of this collaboration, activists launched the New Initiative for Popular Self-Development to construct "an alternative socioeconomic development model, based on self-government and democracy."[20]

Their allies in the United States followed suit, pressing Salvadoran officials to pursue a political solution to the war. When the FMLN issued a peace proposal in January 1989, for example, the Cambridge sistering committee activated its local rapid response network "to obtain signatures and titles of key figures for an appeal letter" to Salvadoran officials.[21] Within a matter of days, the Cambridge group and sistering activists around the United States and Canada had collected more than 450 signatures for the letter urging then-president Duarte and the Armed Forces of El Salvador to "support a political negotiated solution to the conflict, specifically, support the FMLN peace proposal of January 23, 1989."[22]

Like their Salvadoran partners, Sister Cities activists joined with other US groups to strengthen the campaign against the war. Among the most prominent of the US allies was the Agenda for Peace in El Salvador, established by activists with experience in NEST, CISPES, and other solidarity groups. The Agenda for Peace served "as a liaison between grassroots organizations and Congress" in support of "a negotiated solution in El Salvador and a 'NO AID' position regarding US aid to the Salvadoran government."[23]

In short, through the late 1980s and early 1990s, Salvadoran and US activists collaborated to define the transition out of war and into a new era of peace. A closer look at the transnational campaign to counter the forced isolation of the repopulated villages in Chalatenango illustrates how these activists forged new spaces for citizen action well before the FMLN and Salvadoran government reached their accord.

Breaking the Blockade

In mid-1991 an El Salvador staff person for Sister Cities, Tim Lohrentz, observed that repopulators "have won enough space so that they can now participate in the economic and political processes of the country." At the same time, he promised, they "are not leaving behind the struggle for basic civil and human rights."[24] Indeed, the struggle for basic rights remained central to activist efforts as long as "the same antidemocratic attitudes and the same counterinsurgency objectives rule."[25] The alternative models represented by the repopulations and the CRIPDES-affiliated communities would be successful over the long-term only if the old, unjust structures fell. Toward this end, Salvadoran activists and their Sister Cities allies turned attention to ending the enforced isolation of the repopulations of Chalatenango.

As earlier chapters explained, Salvadoran authorities treated the repopulations as military targets, with levels of harassment increasing significantly in the late 1980s as more refugees and internally displaced people returned to resettle once-abandoned villages. As the grassroots repopulation movement grew, security forces became ever more severe in enforcing isolation on the rural villages, by denying state documentation to returnees, for example, and impeding the movement of people and materials to and from the communities. Although Salvadoran officials justified the isolationist actions within the context of national security concerns, campesinos on the receiving end viewed things in a different light. From their perspective, the isolation imposed on them by Salvadoran "insecurity forces" was a violation of their human rights—broadly defined to include basic physical integrity as well as economic, social, and political rights. And, so, Salvadoran activists turned the "military blockade" into a major rallying point. They worked with international allies first to "get around" the system and ultimately to "break" it. Their work offers a powerful example of how grassroots sistering blended human rights and political advocacy. More specifically, the campaigns against isolation show how activists strategically deployed humanitarian aid to serve broader purposes.

CRIPDES and Sister Cities continued their strategies of public denunciation, emphasizing not only the harmful consequences but also the illegality of the Salvadoran officials' practices of forced isolation. Repopulators regularly reported on the confiscation and destruction of food, medicine, educational materials, and other items intended for delivery to the newly resettled villages. When Jack Mills, an aide to David Scondras, a Boston City Council member, visited Guancorita (later rebaptized Ellacuría after Ignacio Ellacuría, one of the six Jesuit priests murdered by state forces in November 1989) with a US–El Salvador Sister Cities delegation in March 1990, he found that "the military embargoed tin needed to rebuild houses in Guancorita and even made it difficult for the residents to bring in bread. They need permission from the military to receive shipment of any kind of goods."[26] Ron Myers of Columbus, Ohio, reported that "the military searches every person attempting to enter [our sister city of] Copapayo to prevent food or medical supplies from reaching the people. This blockade has increased disease rates and malnutrition. . . . We would hope that their rights guaranteed under international law will be respected by military forces during this violent civil war."[27] Through the early 1990s, reports, paid ads, and other communications followed a similar pattern.

Activists developed strategies and campaigns to publicize and push back against the military blockade. The National Coordinator of Repopulations (CNR), for example, intentionally used the group's summits to challenge the blockade. Internal documents from the first summit—which occurred in the wake of the Esquipulas II agreement and celebrated the one-year anniversary of the first mass return of refugees from the Mesa Grande camp in Honduras—reveal that for months leading up to the 1988 summit, the Salvadoran and US leadership teams collected letters and resolutions of support from city councils, boards of supervisors, and "prominent people" from Madison, Buffalo, San Francisco, Cambridge, and elsewhere in the United States.[28] Publicized as the summit dates drew near, these proclamations went beyond congratulating the CNR on the hard-won achievements of repopulation; they condemned Salvadoran security forces for continuing to isolate the resettled communities and demanded that the government recognize the right of the repopulators to access supplies in their rural villages.[29] "[We are] aware of a deliberate government and military policy to prevent the entry of food and medicines into these communities," began one open letter to President Duarte, signed by civic and religious leaders from sister cities in the United States and published in Salvadoran newspapers. "The denial of food, the violation of medical neutrality, the refusal to issue proper documentation and the severe restrictions placed on access to these communities by national and international Church and humanitarian aid representatives," the letter continued, "contravene the

Geneva Conventions and Protocols as well as the spirit of Esquipulas II, of which you are a signatory."[30]

An explicit "congressional strategy" emerged as well, with members of Sister Cities delegations acquiring letters of introduction and support from their elected officials, as well as bishops and priests. Delegates used these letters as leverage when Salvadoran officials denied safe-conduct passes for rural travel or when they stopped the delegation at a checkpoint in El Salvador. Sometimes, a formal letterhead, gold seal, or other trapping of official office was enough to break the barrier. At other times, delegates or their emergency contacts at home put in calls to letter writers, who then exerted what pressure they could to allow the US visitors to continue their travel.[31]

Having congressional representatives or their aides as delegates proved to be an even more powerful tool. Delegation coordinators brought on board high-profile civic and religious leaders who could help facilitate entry into El Salvador and, more specifically, the rural areas where sistered communities were. The Cambridge sistering committee found that Paul Davis, an aide to Rep. Joseph P. Kennedy III (D-MA), played a critical role during the 1988 summit delegation, for example. Along with Cambridge, the Madison committee established "an incredible record for getting people in" to El Salvador during the late 1980s and early 1990s. "We never once failed to get into Chalatenango," Marc Rosenthal explained, "in part because of very *very* strong connections that we had in Milwaukee with Archbishop Rembert Weakland and Congressman Jim Moody [who] were two of our biggest allies. Then there was . . . John Fischer who was the head of the Wisconsin Council of Churches. These were really instrumental people in terms of our ability to get into El Salvador. Very influential people." Rosenthal emphasized, moreover, that "those connections didn't just happen. I mean, we worked for a long time to make those, and we used that in order to get in."[32]

Sister Cities activists also planned for direct confrontations with officials. Delegation preparation materials reveal that by January 1989 the New El Salvador Today Foundation (NEST) had established policies for its delegations to follow in case of confrontation. Later that year, Sister Cities coordinators warned potential delegates to the second sistering summit that they "should be prepared to play a confrontational role in El Salvador re[garding] blacklisting, visa denials, deportation, [and] military permission denials."[33] And in mid-1990, just a few weeks after the Salvadoran government and FMLN signed the Human Rights Accord in San José, Costa Rica, Wisconsin-based coordinators began recruiting volunteers for a delegation with an explicit objective of testing Salvadoran officials' willingness to comply with the new agreement. After explaining that the July 1990 accord "gave free access to the repopulations of

El Salvador without 'special permission,'" a letter to delegation candidates cautioned that "there is potential for the Salvadoran military to still ask for a safe-conduct pass [*salvoconducto*] to travel to Chalatenango; however, the delegation will ignore this and follow the July accord. They hope this decision will aid in the 'demilitarization' of El Salvador."[34]

As the activists expected, Salvadoran officials did not faithfully implement the accords; among other breaches, military commanders continued to demand that visitors obtain salvoconductos before traveling to rural areas. As Kathryn Wysockey reported to supporters of the Madison–Arcatao Sister City Project following her visit to El Salvador in early 1991, "We experienced enormous difficulty in securing a safe-conduct pass from the Salvadoran Military High Command. This was required of us before we could pass into the conflictive region of Chalatenango to visit the repopulations."[35] Wysockey and her compatriots put pressure on military officials and ultimately obtained the necessary permission to continue their journey. Reports like the ones that Wysockey's delegation issued from the Salvadoran field—highlighting the Salvadoran government's broken promises—drew attention from a wide range of international observers, including representatives of the United Nations Observer Mission in El Salvador. The reports often centered on humanitarian aid issues; the international visitors had critical health and wellness materials to deliver to the civilians in the conflicted zone, but Salvadoran officials would not allow this. Without powdered milk, vitamins, and medications, activists argued, children, pregnant women, and the elderly suffered unnecessarily from malnutrition and preventable diseases. Although Wysockey and other allies framed their arguments around humanitarian aid issues, their reports were, at base, tools for political change. In the hands of US legislators and UN representatives, the power of those tools multiplied.

In light of this, Salvadoran officials grew increasingly concerned about the activities of international visitors, as illustrated by higher levels of harassment and intimidation. When Salvadoran soldiers murdered Michaël de Witte, a Belgian doctor assisting the wounded in the conflict zones, in February 1987, many activists interpreted it as an act of intimidation against internationals involved in accompaniment projects—a sense that only intensified in subsequent months as Salvadoran authorities directly targeted sistering activists from the United States. In June, officials denied entry to a Cambridge-based delegation on the grounds that its members, most of whom were medical professionals, intended to support the FMLN. In August, officials demanded that members of another delegation leave the country. At the time of the first CNR summit in October, Salvadoran authorities denied entry to Nancy Ryan, a sistering activist and executive director of the Commission on the Status of

Women in the City of Cambridge, despite the fact that she had a valid visa, obtained by Representative Kennedy on her behalf. Exclusions only picked up pace in the wake of the 1988 sistering summit, with Salvadoran officials denying entry or safe-conduct passes to numerous representatives from Cambridge alone: Susan Freireich in December 1988, James Wallace in March 1989, Paul Davis in April 1989, and, in 1991, an entire delegation.

Activists denounced these exclusions as a government campaign intended to fortify the isolation of repopulated communities. At the close of the 1991 sistering summit, for example, activists condemned the military's "persistence in keeping our communities isolated by prohibiting free access to these regions to national and international solidarity delegations, the press and accredited diplomats in El Salvador." They went on to charge the ARENA government with politicizing humanitarian aid by "carr[ying] out a disinformation and defamation campaign through all means possible against national and international humanitarian institutions, churches and solidarity organizations, accusing them of being fronts of the [FMLN], and putting in danger the development of our work and the lives of those that pertain to these organizations." In sum, they concluded, the exclusions, military checkpoints, and barring deliveries constituted a "blockade," which violated the repopulators' "human rights even after the human rights accords were signed in Costa Rica on July 26, 1990."[36]

In conjunction with these denunciations, sistering activists vowed to "break the blockade."[37] Sister Cities records reveal how a transnational campaign began to coalesce around this goal in 1988. As one component of the campaign, activists in the United States stepped up the frequency of delegations, with at least one group traveling to El Salvador every month.[38] As another component, US American activists boldly contested Salvadoran officials who placed obstacles in their way.

Two high-profile challenges occurred in late 1988 and early 1989, when Salvadoran authorities denied entry to two members of the Cambridge Sister Cities committee. In October 1988, Nancy Ryan arrived at El Salvador's Comalapa International Airport, only to find that her name was on a list of persons prohibited from entering the country. She had anticipated difficulties in the wake of the previous June's conflicted anniversary delegation to San José Las Flores (see ch. 2). Authorities charged that Ryan had "played a key role" in the CRIPDES demonstration in front of the US Embassy on the afternoon of June 20.[39] One embassy staffer, Daniel Russell, even claimed to have a videotape proving "that Ryan was involved with the flag burning."[40] The charges were "absolutely false," delegate Jim Wallace explained; officials launched them simply "as a way to besmirch our entire image."[41] Ryan doggedly contested the charges during the next year, ultimately receiving confirmation from the US

Ambassador's office that "the confusion" had been resolved.[42] That the Salvadoran Consulate issued her a valid visa for her October 1988 travels offered additional evidence that the problem had been solved.

Ryan brought all of this to the attention of the officials who detained her at the Comalapa airport in October. None of the other members of the delegation were detained; as they continued on their way, Ryan remained in the airport pressing Salvadoran and US officials to allow her entry. Despite her efforts, echoed in the United States by members of the Sister Cities Emergency Response Network, authorities refused her appeal and advised her to leave the country. As night fell and concerns rose about her remaining alone in the airport overnight, she returned to Massachusetts to continue her inquiry.

A few months later, Jim Wallace, another Cambridge resident and a team leader of the June 1987 anniversary delegation, took the airport-based inquiry strategy to new levels. Like Ryan, Wallace had received a visa for his February 1989 travels to El Salvador, and he demanded an explanation when Salvadoran authorities detained him upon his arrival at the Comalapa airport. With the Salvadorans unable or unwilling to provide a reason for his exclusion, Wallace contacted the US Embassy. In a 2017 interview, he recalled telling them, "You know, there's something weird going on here. I need to find out what it is and I'll stay here until I find out."[43] Notes from the files of Judy Somberg, one of the Cambridge committee members who headed up the delegations working group, reveal that although faced with threats of deportation and even arrest, Wallace insisted on "waiting to get [a] written statement of charges."[44]

He waited six days in the airport, continuing all the while to seek information through diplomatic channels. Meanwhile, Wallace's wife, Julia, and colleagues in the Cambridge sistering committee involved Representative Kennedy as well as Senators John Kerry and Joseph Moakley, and the US–El Salvador Sister Cities network launched a "national campaign to get him in" to El Salvador.[45] What ultimately may have caused the tides of information to turn in Wallace's favor, however, was his decision to go on a hunger strike. As he recalled in 2017, "At the time there was some kind of hunger strike that was going on among Salvadorans" in the United States.

> So I told them, "I'll join in your hunger strike while I'm here." So *that* word got out . . . And then, you know, the authorities were worried that, you know, I was going to pass out, be taken away in an ambulance. They said . . . "Don't make such a scene about all this." [Eventually] the guy from the embassy did show up and he brought a copy of the communication from the [Salvadoran] military to immigration saying, "The following people have brought supplies to the *delincuentes terroristas*—or

whatever—on this occasion and they're not to be allowed to come back in the country."[46]

Wallace's name was number seventeen on that exclusion list, accompanied by the names of nearly all the members of a June 1988 medical delegation, which, according to the Salvadoran High Command, had "shared supplies with guerrilla elements."[47] "At that point," Wallace chuckled, "I said, 'Okay, I'll go back home. I won't push you any further.'"[48]

Although Wallace did not make it into the country that time, his Compalapa-based investigation got what he and his fellow activists needed: proof of the existence of a blacklist. With this new evidence of the government campaign, Wallace, Ryan, and Susan Freireich, another Cambridge resident and Sister Cities activist who had been excluded, continued "working with various authorities to try to get" the exclusion situation "cleaned up."[49] Cambridge sistering committee records contain dozens of letters and notes from meetings with elected officials and their staff. Kennedy and his aide Paul Davis even secured a meeting with the Salvadoran ambassador to the United States, Ernesto Rivas-Gallont. Although the ambassador agreed that "it's unfair to grant visa[s], knowing ahead of time that people will be denied entry," he was unable to help because "it's a military, not political matter." Kennedy also met with the US ambassador to El Salvador, William Walker, "who played dumb."[50]

Even as they continued to work diplomatic channels, activists had other actions on the docket, including making the matter more public through media coverage. Wallace, Ryan, and others "made noise" in the local and national press about the exclusion of US citizens by Salvadoran immigration authorities in addition to the collusion of US officials in the process. The crux of Nancy Ryan's lengthy report on her October 1988 exclusion, which she made available to journalists, was the role that US officials played in the decision-making process. In her report, Ryan noted that a Salvadoran immigration agent dialed the phone number of the US Embassy "without looking it up," and described Consul General Nick Ricciuti's "refusal" to help her. "I was convinced," she wrote, "that he could reach the proper officials or get the needed permission to allow me into the country if he chose to do so." Ryan's report made the case that her name had in fact been "placed on a list of persons prohibited from entering El Salvador by staff members of the US Embassy in El Salvador."[51]

The *Boston Globe* quoted liberally from Ryan's report in a front-section story highlighting the "increasing complicity between US officials and police and military officers in Central America in harassing, intimidating and, in some cases, endangering US citizens who travel to Central America to protest US policies in the region." The story's author, Ross Gelbspan, included the voices of other affected citizens as well as Representative Kennedy, who stated, "It is especially troubling to think that American officials may be contributing names of US citizens to a Salvadoran blacklist." Gelbspan juxtaposed such comments with the Department of State's "flat denial" of the charges.[52] Beyond this coverage in the daily *Boston Globe*, Cambridge sistering activists' experiences appeared in the weekly *Boston Globe Magazine*, national publications including the *Progressive*, and grassroots outlets such as *Ciudades Hermanas*, the newsletter of the Cambridge–El Salvador Sister Cities Project. At the same time, activists in other cities in the United States and El Salvador produced similar stories in a wide range of news media.

Like their Salvadoran partners at CRIPDES, US-based activists were also willing, when necessary, to "abandon diplomatic route[s]" and take to the streets to raise awareness of their cause. Toward this end the Cambridge committee began to plan a national protest.[53] "If it becomes clear that steps toward resolution are not happening," wrote Wallace to his contact in Kennedy's office, he and his colleagues would "make a much more public protest about this treatment and the policy it apparently represents, on the part of both the Salvadoran authorities and our own State Department." Citizens across the United States had been adversely affected by these policies of exclusion, he continued, "and we are determined to address the breadth of the problem, in whatever way possible."[54]

Although accessible Sister Cities records hold no evidence that activists ever carried out that particular protest, it is clear that the intention was there. The Cambridge group raised the specter of a national mobilization for the same reasons that they used Comalapa airport-based investigations and diplomatic pressures: to publicize and challenge the "blacklist" and, by extension, the military blockade of the repopulations. As Wallace pondered in spring 1989, perhaps the Cambridge exclusion cases "would prompt change."[55]

As activists investigated, lobbied, and promoted media campaigns in the United States and El Salvador, they repeatedly tested official boundaries. A 1991 delegation featuring Congressman Jim Moody from Milwaukee offers us particularly clear illustrations of the contentiousness of the transnational campaign to break the blockade on rural repopulations and the strategic mobilization of humanitarian aid toward broader sociopolitical goals. Sistering activists began planning the delegation following the 1990 Human Rights Accord, signed in July in San José, Costa Rica, by FMLN and Salvadoran government representatives. "The strategic need was to break the military blockade," Marc Rosenthal later recalled, but "every single time we got in it was really, really, really hard and there was always this big, like, confrontation thing, step by step with the embassy and the military and going in and having all this paperwork and, you know, 'Are you going to stop us?'"[56] With the new accord and continuing peace talks, Rosenthal and Wisconsin-based leaders of the accompaniment and sistering networks decided to try something different.

They organized an especially large delegation of religious leaders and health care workers to "attempt to deliver a large quantity of medical supplies" to Arcatao, Madison's sister city. Over several months, they amassed more than $10,000 worth of medical supplies for the community.[57] "We had thirteen crates," Rosenthal recalled, "I mean, big, big boxes of medical supplies."[58] They expected the worst, including the confiscation of the materials and the exclusion of delegates. And so they prepared.

Three people were central to their preparations: Archbishop Rembert Weakland of Milwaukee; US congressman Jim Moody from Wisconsin; and Arturo Rivera y Damas, archbishop of El Salvador. Weakland and Moody had supported sistering projects for years. Rivera y Damas recently had sent a priest to Arcatao, an act that symbolized the Catholic leadership's recognition that civilians inhabited the area—and a clear rejection of Salvadoran and US government claims that only "subversives" could be found in northern Chalatenango and other conflicted zones. Weakland officially assigned the Wisconsin delegation's medical supplies to Rivera y Damas who, in turn, assigned them to the newly posted priest in Arcatao. This church-based channel was a critical tool for the Wisconsin delegation, as it conferred official status, authenticated the humanitarian nature of the delivery, and confirmed the aid was destined for use by civilians in a repopulated zone.[59]

Congressman Moody provided another official channel. When Salvadoran military authorities denied the delegation's pre-departure request for a safe-conduct pass, Moody inquired about the reason. Madison committee records reveal that the head of the Joint Chiefs of Staff of the Armed Forces of El Salvador, Gilberto Rubio, responded first with the typical explanation. "It is not possible to provide safe conduct passes," he told Moody, "due to the military operations that are continuously being carried out in that zone; a situation that would put the visitors at high risk." But Rubio did not stop there; he continued on to explain the permanent exclusion of three delegates: Eric Popkin, Tim Lohrentz, and John Fischer. According to Rubio, Popkin "was declared by the government non grata to the interests of El Salvador" in 1988. Lohrentz joined Popkin on the exclusion list on November 2, 1989, when "days before the FMLN's terrorist attack, he was found in Chalatenango without permission, in open violation of our laws." And officials decided to exclude Fischer on May 23, 1990, when his "signature appeared on an open letter published in a national newspaper, accusing our President and our Armed Forces of attacks against communities of repopulators, an act which constitutes a clear intervention into the internal affairs of our country."[60]

Meanwhile, delegation coordinators, Popkin among them, prepared participants for confrontation. A two-day orientation just prior to travel emphasized the fact that "supplies will be difficult." They developed a phone tree of "hot contacts/personal contacts (call in emergency only)" and discussed possible "mobilizations" of the Emergency Response Network in case of problems. They debated the best strategy for getting through immigration and customs (e.g., present as individuals or as a group?) and role-played innumerable "what-if scenarios." Coordinators directed delegates to "cooperate but remember you're in control" as they moved through customs, and instructed the "Material Aid Carriers" to "Smile, Relax, Wait."[61]

They didn't have to wait long. Upon arrival to the Comalapa International Airport on July 23, the delegation "confronted significant resistance from the Salvadoran military and government." Officials continued to deny entry visas to Popkin, Lohrentz, and Fischer, and refused safe-conduct passes for travel to the repopulated zones. Most importantly, perhaps, they confiscated all thirteen supply crates. Delegation leaders and their support network in the United States made as much noise as possible. The records of the Madison–Arcatao Sister City Project and the Wisconsin Coordinating Council on Central America contain a flurry of press releases, letters, and other communications detailing the efforts of this "humanitarian delegation . . . to deliver desperately needed medical supplies" to conflicted areas "which receive assistance from Wisconsin churches and cities."[62]

But the delegates had another hand to play. According to Rosenthal, "We knew that [the boxes] would be confiscated," so they had planned for Congressman Moody to arrive on a subsequent flight and demand release of the materials.[63] When this played out as planned, Rosenthal recalled, "The US Department of State flipped out. Completely. We created a huge crisis. They sat him [Moody] down, told him 'You cannot go.' And he said, 'You can't stop me. I'm taking this to Arcatao.' Big stand off. He won. We won. We took all that material to Arcatao."[64]

This was a striking victory. As one press release announced, "We are only the second group to be allowed into this area of the dozens of humanitarian organizations who have attempted to visit it since early this spring."[65] Not only did the material-aid carriers recover their equipage; records show that Salvadoran military officials also provided entry visas and safe-conduct passes for the entire "Wisconsin delegation of religious nurses"—including Popkin, Lohrentz, and Fischer, the three individuals previously deemed personae non gratae.[66] Moreover, the delegation eased access to Chalatenango for a Salvadoran opposition politician, Deputy Sandoval, who, despite representing the Department of Chalatenango in the National Assembly, had been barred from traveling there to meet with his constituents. One delegation report described how officials, including the captain of the Fourth Brigade in Chalatenango, responded with "ire and frustration . . . at not being able to prevent Deputy Sandoval from entering the Department he represents."[67]

From the outset the organizers of this delegation intended to push the boundaries. As Rosenthal explained, "The idea was to no longer be finding ways to sneak around checkpoints. We would come up against them, challenge their legitimacy: 'You don't have the right to do this.'"[68] And in this instance the grassroots activists, in collaboration with a member of US Congress and high-ranking officials in the Catholic Church, were successful in physically defeating the military blockade.

With incident after incident, US and Salvadoran activists pushed against the boundaries erected by authorities. They drew from imperial privileges, humanitarian norms, and human rights agreements to justify their contentious actions. Over time, they counted some important successes with the delivery of aid and with reducing the isolation of the repopulations. Whereas in 1989, foreign visitors might wait ten days in country before receiving word from Salvadoran military commanders that their request for salvoconductos had been denied, by the 1991 sistering summit, the US and Salvadoran leadership team celebrated that a "high number of delegations arrived" without salvoconductos. Their campaign finally had torn down (*derrotó*) the blockade.[69]

The Right to Vote

If the transnational campaign to challenge imposed isolation illustrates the success that grassroots pressures could have on demilitarization and the deconstruction of authoritarian traditions, campaigns focused on political leadership and elections demonstrate the key role that grassroots activists played in constructing new spaces for democratic civic participation. A base objective of the repopulation movement was to "conquer" the rights associated with citizenship in a liberal democratic republic. Reoccupying once-abandoned territory was, in many ways, the easy part. Much harder was building the New El Salvador from the ground up, with few material resources, in the midst of war. Yet this is precisely what Salvadoran repopulators did with the leadership of their *directivas*, committees, grassroots mayors, cooperatives, and regional and national associations.

Drawing on their previous experiences with agricultural cooperatives, the Local Popular Governments in areas controlled by the Popular Forces of Liberation (FPL), and refugee camp governance, the repopulators established new grassroots structures of governance through which they modeled the participatory democracy they wished to see on a national level. In the latter half of the 1980s, the FPL and other FMLN factions had "dislodged" the central government from a significant percentage of national territory. Grassroots governance structures took root in precisely the regions where state government was "no longer able to function."[70] With the peace talks and formal accords that ended the conflict in 1992, however, tensions flared between the central government, eager to reestablish control in former conflict zones, and the new grassroots governments, equally eager to retain their hard-won power and influence. That the final agreements lacked specificity in terms of postwar political reforms only exacerbated tensions. Thus for the first half of the 1990s, repopulators confronted a host of new challenges relating to the legitimation and legal incorporation of their communities, structures, and leaders into the evolving postwar state.

The "municipal question" was among the earliest challenges, rearing an especially ugly head in Chalatenango department, the heart of the repopulation movement.[71] At issue was leadership of the municipalities and, more specifically, the role of what Tomasa Ruíz, the CRIPDES president, called the "mayors-in-exile." These were the mayors who nominally occupied the post but who "have not been living in these towns and were not elected by the people living there." With the signing of the peace accords, Ruíz remarked, "The mayors want to come marching into town and give orders."[72] Fearing new rounds of displacement should these mayors—most of them representatives of the old authoritarian system—resume their posts, the repopulators "made clear that the communities will not abandon the places where they are currently living."[73] Nor were they willing to abandon political control; in fact they insisted on negotiating power-sharing agreements with the mayors. "The position of the communities," Ruíz explained, "is that there should be an agreement between these in absentia mayors and the community on what powers the mayor will have."[74]

In meetings throughout 1992 and into 1993, local community leaders and their supporting organizations at the regional and national levels sought consensus and reconciliation (*concertación*).[75] The meetings bore fruit; by April 1993 the eight mayors in exile had returned to their posts, and most municipalities had established committees for reconstruction made up of directiva members and the mayors' appointments.[76] This was, in effect, the first step in formally legitimating left-leaning political bodies in the former territory of the Popular

Liberation Forces (FPL). During the conflict, the FPL and the other politico-military groups that made up the FMLN coalition established what some observers referred to as a "parallel state."[77] With the peace accords, the FMLN began the difficult transformation from insurgent coalition to legal political party. In the repopulations and other areas where the FMLN had dominated during the conflict, local leadership committees engaged in a similar process—often without due attention from the FMLN leadership, according to activists.[78]

The municipality of Arcatao offers one example of this contentious process. After local efforts failed to produce results, United Nations representatives were called in to mediate meetings between the mayor and the directiva. Only after a year of meetings did a pact occur—and then only with pressure from Boutros Boutros-Ghali, the UN Secretary-General, then in-country. Among the issues in debate were the locations of office space for the mayor and processes of decision-making. The mayor wanted to reclaim the old town hall, but directiva members said no; the building had been destroyed during the conflict, they explained, and community members had rebuilt it themselves. Instead, they offered the mayor a deal: she could use part of the new communal building for her office while "together we will build a new day care center" and once construction was done, "Then you can have city hall back."[79] Evidence suggests that the mayor accepted the offer, likely at the last minute and under pressure. The historical record indicates, moreover, that the mayor retained her residence in Chalatenango City, occupying her temporary office in Arcatao, the municipal seat, only on Mondays, Tuesdays, and Wednesdays, and that every two weeks she and her municipal council met with the directiva to make decisions regarding projects. At the first joint meeting, again with UN mediation, they established a Municipal Reconstruction Committee with the mayor, and three members each from the municipal council and directiva. Directiva members later reported that the mayor did not want them to be part of the committee, but the "UN pushed [so] she agreed."[80]

Repopulators elsewhere in Chalatenango encountered similar difficulties with the mayors-in-exile. "Most of the mayors still live in the city and travel to the municipal seat for one or two days per week," reported the CRIPDES Sistering Commission in April 1993, leading to "complain[ts] about the performance of the mayors" as well as "problems due to the absence of the mayors from the municipalities and negligence on their behalf."[81] Most problematic, however, was the returning mayors' refusal to recognize the community structures and, in some cases, their intentional efforts to hinder the work of local directivas and committees. In San José Las Flores, for example, the mayor launched "a gutter and street project" even though "the community identified other needs as more important." Moreover, according to the Coordinator of Repopulations and Communities of Chalatenango (CCR), the Las Flores mayor was "the ring-leader of the mayors in Chalatenango, trying to design campaigns that devalue the role of the community structures," leading to delays in the legal incorporation of directivas as community associations.[82] Along these same lines, mayors across Chalatenango balked at issuing identity documents to area inhabitants so that just ten weeks before the March 1994 elections, the directiva of Arcatao reported that between 60 and 70 percent of residents still lacked the documentation necessary to register to vote.[83] Mayors also impeded the transfer of housing and land titles to the repopulators by "organizing owners not to sell," an issue addressed in more detail in chapter 4.[84]

The repopulators mobilized on a number of levels to confront the obstinate officialist mayors. They sought consensus (*concertación*) through negotiations and when they felt they exhausted their options, they took to the streets to "demonstrate," as Arcatao's directiva promised to do at the end of 1993.[85] They also organized multiple pressure points. As mentioned earlier, they worked with UN mediators to convince mayors to acknowledge and collaborate with community leaders. In these efforts, they requested help from their allies in the Sister Cities network. In a December 1993 meeting with visitors from Madison, Arcatao directiva members asked them to pressure the mayor to issue personal identification cards and to facilitate land transfers, per the provisions of the Peace Accords, and the municipal judge to legally incorporate their communities as communal, cooperative associations. The Salvadorans also urged their northern partners to "focus on Senate and Congress" to put "pressure in E.S." Notes from the meeting indicate that Sister Cities activists targeted specific individuals and offices, including President Cristiani at the executive branch and authorities at various government agencies.[86] Sister City committees elsewhere in the United States received similar requests, and staff in El Salvador and the United States coordinated these efforts.[87]

These kinds of pressures paid off over time. Grassroots leaders in repopulated communities, backed by regional, national, and international supporters, negotiated new kinds of political relationships with the mayors-in-exile—relationships that constrained the old mayors' power while opening official spaces for the grassroots leaders to exert power. This was a contentious process with uneven results. In many sites, like Arcatao, problems persisted and "community relations remain[ed] fragile."[88] Nonetheless, grassroots leaders ultimately characterized it as a "triumph because the government has had to recognize us as a dual power structure."[89] These contributions to democratization at the local level in El Salvador not only brought a sense of pride; it also fed an increasing frustration with the FMLN, whose leaders, many rural repopulators felt, had forgotten about their civilian base of support at best or, at worst, sold out to neoliberal powers with the peace accords and the FMLN's transformation to a political party.

As these new political relationships formed in rural regions, repopulators in Chalatenango and elsewhere in the Salvadoran countryside began selecting candidates "to contest the mayorships" in the March 1994 elections.[90] Dubbed "the elections of the century," these were the first held under El Salvador's new Constitution (adopted in 1983) in which elections for president, vice president, all legislative assembly members, mayors, and city councils coincided—an event that would occur only every fifteen years.[91] Moreover, the peace accord–mandated institutional reforms had introduced a new elections oversight agency, the Supreme Elections Tribunal (Tribunal Supremo Electoral), along with a revised electoral code, which had gone into effect in January 1993.[92] Among other things, these reforms opened elections to opposition parties and coalitions, including the FMLN, which gained legal recognition as a political party after the last soldiers laid down their arms in December 1992.[93] Longtime leaders and leftist activists in the repopulated communities put forth their names as FMLN party candidates for mayors, national assembly deputies, and other offices.

These factors combined to produce high expectations across the board. A successful election, many observers contended, would mark the end of El Salvador's transition and the consolidation of peace, and thus prove that democracy had taken hold. With thousands of people coming from around the world to serve as official elections observers—the UN Observer Mission for El Salvador alone would field nine hundred observers on election day—the elections promised to be the most free and fair of the country's history.

Despite the high hopes, however, problems riddled the entire process, prompting one scholar and foreign policy advisor, William M. LeoGrande, to write a *New York Times* opinion piece titled "Salvador Election Follies."[94] To begin, he explained, although opposition parties of the left participated, it was not a level playing field in light of the FMLN's inexperience as a political party and its lack of resources to mount an effective campaign. In addition, the campaign took place in a context of escalating violence. In the months leading up to the elections, death squads resurfaced, murdering twenty-seven members of the opposition and threatening scores more to induce them to renounce their candidacies. When Joaquín Villalobos, an FMLN commander-turned-politician, publicly linked a prominent businessman, Orlando de Sola, to the death squad revival, government authorities arrested him on charges of slander.[95]

In rural El Salvador, too, a "climate of fear" resurfaced.[96] "We encountered peasants who are terrorized at the very prospect of elections," one sistering activist, Margaret "Gigi" Gruenke, reported to her representative, Jan Meyers (R-Kansas). "After the presidential election of 1989," she wrote, "soldiers were known to come to at least one town (Estanzuelas) to ask people if they knew who the fourteen who voted for the Democratic Convergence were." In spite of the high rhetoric of nominally peacetime El Salvador, the politically motivated assassinations and death-squad-style killings made it feel like nothing had changed. Moreover, Gruenke explained, "The vote isn't secret: you vote in the open with soldiers close by. The town tally is noted."[97] This was the reality on the ground, and it "kept hundreds of thousands from even daring to try to register and vote."[98]

Although the most common refrain about the upcoming elections was one of hope and promise, the escalation of violence dampened the mood. Even staff of the UN Observer Mission in El Salvador offered guarded comments on the increase of "politically motivated human rights abuses."[99] Sister Cities activists were more direct, identifying the violence as "part of a growing campaign of terror designed to prevent the FMLN and its supporters from participating in the nationwide elections scheduled for March 20."[100] Violence—and particularly the resurrection of the death squads, which should have been disbanded per the peace accord—"could unravel the fabric that is being woven," warned researchers at the Cambridge-based Hemisphere Initiatives research institute.[101]

Although violence played a key role in creating "confusion and disorder," so too did what Boutros-Ghali referred to as "massive" problems in the voter registration process.[102] The process was so "Slow, Arbitrary and Bureaucratic" that just three months before election day, only 200,000 of the 780,000 eligible citizens had received their voting cards, resulting in what Gruenke referred to as some "very frustrated Salvadorans."[103]

Rural activists confronted this problem head-on, working to ensure the implementation of the agreements relating to the reform of the electoral system and thus secure the rights of all Salvadorans to vote in a free and fair election. In practice this meant monitoring the new Supreme Electoral Tribunal and denouncing any irregularities. Documents from the period reveal that directivas, CRIPDES, CCR, and other organizations linked to the repopulations were highly critical of the performance of the Tribunal; it was at best ineffective and at worst breaking the law. They detailed how, through "problems and inertia," Tribunal members, "are marginalizing a great number of new voters."[104] They pointed out that the Tribunal repeatedly ignored the recommendations of national and international organizations, including the United Nations, and blamed "the deficiencies" not on "lack of time or technical or financial skills" but on "the lack of political will of the members of the Supreme Electoral Tribunal . . . who fundamentally obey the interests of their parties and not the needs required for strengthening the democratic process."[105] In sum, rural activists "denounce[d] the existence of an intent to commit electoral fraud on behalf of the Supreme Electoral Tribunal."[106]

By denouncing irregularities, activists pressed the Tribunal and related government offices to hold to the standards set forth in national law and international agreements. In other words, they framed their assessments within the rhetoric of rights. Marco Tulio Lima of the Social Initiative for Democracy (Iniciativa Social para la Democracia) stated that "the most serious problem is the exclusion of hundreds of thousands of citizens from the Elections Registry, which means that these people will not be able to exercise their rights to vote. This exclusion is not only a violation of the rights of citizens, but it also allows election results to be manipulated."[107]

The Social Initiative for Democracy constituted an important method that grassroots activists used to take matters into their own hands. A coalition of social movement organizations and human rights and development groups, including CRIPDES, the Initiative, formalized in 1993, vowed to "work for the full realization of the democratic process" and to "promote the widest participation of civil society in the process of reconstructing and strengthening the social fabric."[108] Affiliates carried out voter registration campaigns, including "emergency projects" to assist residents in former conflict zones in acquiring official identity documents, and civic education campaigns "so that citizens, particularly in the traditionally marginal sectors, can know and fulfill their rights and responsibilities."[109] The Promote and Strengthen Democracy project, for example, entailed two years of "national education campaigns for democracy with grassroots activities in 90 cities or villages in 12 departments." Phases of the project included To Know the Peace Accords Is to Know Your Rights; Participate in Town Meetings and Make Your Voice Heard; Voting Is A Right—Use It with Responsibility; Human Rights Are Right for Everybody; Participation in Society Is a Responsibility to Your Family and Country.[110]

Among the contributions of CRIPDES activists to the Social Initiative for Democracy was bringing on board its transnational sistering network, mobilizing activists in the United States, Canada, and beyond to lend support. Records illustrate how Salvadorans carefully guided this process. One document instructed US-based activists to lend "pressure for a new voter registration system and oversight of the Supreme Electoral Tribunal."[111] Another strategy paper divided duties among the different solidarity organizations, with Sister Cities, sister parish programs, the Committee in Solidarity with the People of El Salvador (CISPES), and other groups around the world assigned to specific "first priority" and "second priority" departments. This same document encouraged CISPES and European solidarity groups to establish sistering relationships with

Cover of CRIPDES civic education booklet, designed to inform repopulators about a new law regarding personal identity documentation, ca. 1992. (Arvidson Papers, USESSC Archive)

department-level committees of the FMLN, the FMLN-sponsored Farabundo Youth group, and the Mélida Anaya Montes women's organization.[112]

Sister Cities activists responded in a variety of ways, including developing a new Campaign for Democracy. Launched in January 1993, the campaign responded to the repopulators' needs relating to community organizing and sustainable development, through support for CRIPDES and Social Initiative civic education and electoral reform projects.[113] The National Center for US–El Salvador Sister Cities also sponsored and participated in national coalition campaigns, including the Transition to Democracy Campaign, National Advocacy Day, elections monitoring groups, and an international solidarity summit that took place at election time. Coalition partners included SHARE, the Agenda for Peace in El Salvador, the Center for Democracy in the Americas, CISPES, the National Debate for Peace in El Salvador, and the Central American Refugee Center (CARECEN), among others. Individual committees affiliated with US–El Salvador Sister Cities established local-level coalitions as well. Members of the Cambridge committee, for example, helped organize the Boston Coalition to Support the Peace Accords in January 1992.[114]

Salvadorans guided Sister Cities and solidarity coalitions to put "sustain[ed] pressure" on US and Salvadoran officials.[115] They continued to denounce violence through paid ads and letters to President Cristiani and other Salvadoran officials, and through "emergency alerts on human and civil rights."[116] And as CRIPDES carried out civic education campaigns in El Salvador, Sister Cities activists lobbied US policy makers "to support full implementation of the Salvadoran Peace Accords and to pursue policies that strengthen democratic participation and break with the past of electoral fraud and violence."[117] Among the new policies that Sister Cities and other solidarity organizations pressed was the conditioning of US aid on the Salvadoran government's compliance with the peace accords and the recommendations of the UN Truth Commission, in addition to the channeling of economic aid funds through nongovernmental organizations that worked most closely with the war-affected populations of El Salvador.[118] In addition, Sister Cities cosponsored a national campaign urging the incoming US president, William Jefferson Clinton, to "tell the truth" about El Salvador through "a full investigation into the US role in the war."[119]

Election day afforded the transnational activist network a highly public opportunity to press Salvadoran government compliance with the accords. A full year before the elections took place, Shelagh Flynn and Mike Prokosch, two supporters of accompaniment, observed, "We have a critical role to play in the 1994 Salvadoran elections." They explained, "By sending election observers and providing other kinds of support, we can limit right-wing terror, help level the electoral field, and give the opposition a fair shot at political power."[120] Delegations coordinated by Sister Cities and CISPES alone put more than two hundred US citizens on the ground in repopulated villages and other voting sites during the elections.[121] As official observers of the process, they publicized the continuing obstacles faced by Salvadoran citizens as they exerted their right to vote, including discrepancies in the voter registration lists and incidents of officials turning away voters at the polls.[122]

One of the more high-profile events involved Arcatao, Madison's sister city. Three days before election day, the Supreme Electoral Tribunal announced that despite being a municipal seat, Arcatao was "too small to get a polling place."[123] Instead, residents would need to travel to polls in Chalatenango City, an approximately four-hour drive from Arcatao. In rural El Salvador, where private vehicles were almost unheard of and public transportation was inconsistent and unaffordable for many, this meant, in effect, that "no one will go."[124]

According to the repopulators and their allies, this was precisely the point. "Arcatao has a population of 3,000 and is growing," explained Mary Kay Baum, coordinator of an election observation delegation to her sister city. "I don't consider that an insignificant number of people; there's something else going on there."[125] Baum and others believed that the Tribunal removed Arcatao from the polling site list because the residents there would likely vote for the FMLN candidates. From this point of view, to move polling to Chalatenango City made sense; those who left Arcatao during the war "now want to control it by voting in Chalatenango City for Arcatao's mayor and forcing Arcatao's real residents to travel a hard journey." Baum reported that one member of the Tribunal explained the decision to change the voting location simply by "call[ing] the citizens of Arcatao 'phantom residents'—as if they do not matter."[126]

Local leaders and sister cities activists rallied to reverse the Tribunal's last-minute decision and its political implications. Madison committee files reveal a flurry of activity from the US end of the network: press conferences and other media work; letters and faxes to and from US mayors, senators and representatives, and ambassadors in El Salvador and at the United Nations; faxes to Salvadoran officials, including members of the Supreme Electoral Tribunal; and paid ads in Salvadoran newspapers. Communications framed the situation as "a violation of the democratic rights of citizens of this region" and a threat that "flies in the face of the peace process."[127]

In Chalatenango, meanwhile, residents of Arcatao and three other communities that also had been denied polling rights announced that they would boycott the elections. All candidates from the communities withdrew from the official race, and local directivas planned to hold parallel elections, which they asked the United Nations to monitor.[128] As they prepared to hold their own elections, the directiva presidents denounced the "open violation of the Electoral Code" by the Tribunal and contested the portrayal of their communities as "ghost towns," pointing out that basic conditions for elections existed, including a sizable population, potable water, electricity, and telephones, and that the city halls and Ministry of Public Health offices were functioning. "We will not recognize any mayor that is elected in exile," the presidents concluded, "because it is illegal."[129]

Activists from Arcatao and Madison joined together in El Salvador to further press the point that Arcatao had the right to stand as a voting site in the Sunday elections. More than one thousand people from Chalatenango traveled to San Salvador, where they camped out for days in protest.[130] In a 2015 interview, Baum recalled having just arrived to Arcatao when the local leaders announced that "they needed people to go to San Salvador to protest at the hotel where the United Nations people were staying." Baum and her daughter, Dawn, complied; "we took a pick-up truck and went right back to the city to protest." They returned to Arcatao later that day and, the following day, a United Nations helicopter landed in town bearing UN officials who said voting would happen in Arcatao after all. Everyone was absolutely thrilled, Baum remembered. "The emotions!"[131]

That Arcatao ultimately served as one of the nation's polling sites—despite Salvadoran government officials' attempts to literally erase it from the political map—illustrates how transnational activists were able to work together to compel the Salvadoran government to comply with some of the agreements they had entered into with the FMLN and regional and international figures. In part due to the consistent work of grassroots activists, Salvadorans celebrated an elections process that, although not entirely free from violence, intimidation, or fraud, did "mark a partial step forward towards democracy," as the National Center for US–El Salvador Sister Cities reported to US affiliates.[132] Although the ARENA party retained the presidency, repopulators and their allies celebrated the victory of FMLN slates in a number of races. One Sister Cities staffer, Guillermo Chacón, reported from El Salvador that "the majority of our sister communities are in municipalities with new FMLN mayors" and town councils.[133] It was a remarkable achievement that an opposition party that was barely two years old won local races in fifteen municipalities and captured one-quarter of the seats in the National Assembly.[134] It left no doubt that the FMLN was the "leading opposition force in postwar El Salvador" and that many rural activists helped them reach that height.[135]

"Elections of the Century," 1994. *Top*: Traveling to San Salvador to protest to UN officials about the Supreme Electoral Tribunal's last-minute effort to strip Arcatao of its polling station. Mary Kay Baum's daughter, Dawn, then a sophomore at East High School in Madison, is seated at right. *Bottom*: People lining up at the Arcatao polling place on election morning. (Baum Papers, USESSC Archive)

Gaining New Ground

At the turn of the decade of the 1990s, the CORDES bulletin *Horizontes Nuevos* (New Horizons), designed largely for international solidarity audiences, tracked the challenges, successes, hopes, and goals of Salvadoran rural activists. Through interviews, stories, pictures, and statistics, the publication traced their experiences with repopulation, preparations for peace, development work, and civic participation. From the grassroots perspective of *Horizontes Nuevos*, progress (i.e., national transformation) was not an end point: it was a process.

Transformation at the international level was also a process, and as Sister Cities activists helped promote transformation on the ground in El Salvador, so too did they promote an alternative diplomacy. Again, a key principle of grassroots sistering was accompaniment, walking alongside each other in the struggle to create a better world. And while much of the energy of the US–El Salvador Sister Cities network flowed from north to south, it is important to note that it also moved from south to north. As activists in El Salvador and the United States came together through sistering, they created a kind of fictive kin network, intentionally constructing relationships based on mutuality. Put another way, Sister Cities activists encouraged horizontalism, "the flattening out of relations of power that promote equity and equality" not only within society as a whole but also within the activist network itself. As social movements scholars explained about the "new wave" of movements that emerged in Latin America in the early 2000s, "a central premise of horizontalism is a rejection of hierarchical relations of power."[136]

Toward this end, rather than mimic the top-down relations employed by many humanitarian and human rights organizations as well as the US government, US American activists with the Sister Cities network took time to listen to and learn from their Salvadoran partners. Sistering demanded, according to one group, "an openness to understand and connect with the economic, social and political context in which our sister communities live and to respond to their needs"—an approach that entailed "respect for our Salvadoran counterparts."[137] Lena Entin, who worked with US–El Salvador Sister Cities in the 1990s agreed. "A lot of what we're doing is learning how Salvadorans are organizing and being inspired by Salvadorans," she explained. "The Salvadorans recognize and we recognize that they have a very powerful social movement. . . . So there is a lot we can learn from them."[138]

Inspired by Salvadorans, US Americans often sought to emulate the Salvadorans' powerful organizing work and "to live out the objectives" of sistering in their home communities.[139] One background paper explained, "The spirit, courage, creativity and strength of Salvadoran community members also inspires us to renew our energy and faith in the efforts we all make for change in the United States. Sister Cities learn from the organizing models used by the Salvadoran communities, and apply variations to their own work. We also learn to analyze the problems of our own society and seek solutions that correspond to the reality and background of each situation."[140] In terms of organizational structures and operations as well, US committees emphasized horizontal relations and collaborative leadership rather than hierarchical relations.[141] Records reveal, for example, that some leaders referred to themselves as conveners of meetings rather than directors or presidents, that meeting-related duties such as facilitating and note-taking rotated among participants, and that most decision-making was by consensus. Such "openness to an inclusive process" was critical, for a "decision truly made by the whole community is more meaningful in its interpretation and application."[142]

Sistering activists in the United States sought to model inclusivity by building bridges at home. Like the CNR, CRIPDES, and CORDES in El Salvador, sistering advocates in the United States established alliances and, sometimes, close working relations with other organizations focused on Latin American issues. At the local level of Madison, for example, two groups that first promoted sistering, Medical Aid to Central America and Community Action on Latin America, debated the extent of their collaboration for years, with proposals ranging from a complete merger and adoption of a new name, to the former "staying independent but using the latter as fiscal sponsor and advisor."[143] The two ultimately shared office space just as, later, the independent Madison–Arcatao Sister City Project shared with the Wisconsin Coordinating Council on Central America, Wisconsin Witness for Peace, and the Colombia Support Network at different points.[144] Similar alliances and cross-organizational collaborations occurred across the Sister Cities map, with sistering and accompaniment groups sharing offices and other resources, producing joint publications, and co-coordinating events and campaigns with other activist groups.

Especially intriguing is that sistering advocates wanted to expand their base beyond white middle-class participants. At several meetings in the mid-1980s, Wisconsin sistering activists discussed establishing a budget line for "scholarships for underrepresented people—blacks, Indians, Hispanics," which would expand access to delegations.[145] In a similar vein, NEST planning materials from the same period pointed to the need to reach out to the Latino and Black populations in various cities in the context of expanding their work.[146] A 1985 proposal to the national convention of Committee in Solidarity with the People of El Salvador (CISPES) was even more insistent. Prepared by activists in Wisconsin with direct links to sistering, it urged solidarists to "expand [their] work from concentration on the U.S. war in Central America to include opposition to U.S. domestic policies which affect the material interests of working people, women, minorities, and other oppressed people in this country." By paying attention to domestic emergencies like "the poverty draft," social service cuts, plant closings, and physical attacks on minorities and abortion clinics, the proposal explained, solidarity organizations would "be more attractive to" the affected populations who had been left "angry and ready to hear an alternative point of view." In sum, "the oppressed of our own country" comprised "the social base" of a true solidarity movement; with their involvement, CISPES and its partners in solidarity work would "have a greater potential to educate people in our society" and, consequently, pose a stronger "ideological challenge to the imperialist war."[147]

Similar discussions about diversifying Sister Cities (in terms of both participation and issues) occurred at local and national levels. Solidifying a broader base proved to be a challenge, yet it remained an ideal toward which sistering activists continued to strive, with meeting minutes revealing repeated discussion and strategizing cycles. In this sense, too, we see how US Americans approached transformation (of both the network and US society more broadly) as an ongoing process.

Success points on "the long journey to justice" were far more visible in the particular Salvadoran context of the 1990s.[148] Activists marked those points, such as celebrating the dismantling of the military checkpoints and the election of leaders from repopulated communities. At the same time, they "continu[ed] to work in coalitions that formed around the elections to press for civil rights and resources." If activists viewed the 1992 peace accords as a tool in their ongoing organizing work, so too were the 1994 elections just one more step "in the ongoing battle to establish democracy in El Salvador."[149] In the words of CORDES sistering representative Enrique García, "Every day we are gaining new ground."[150]

4

🌿 This Promised Land

A Negotiated Revolution?

As the FMLN and the Salvadoran government finalized the peace accords in early 1992, observers around the world heralded the new peace. "Former Foes in El Salvador Cheer Signing of Peace Accord," announced one headline. "Never," Tim Golden reported in the *New York Times*, "has such a conflict ended with agreement to such sweeping reform." And Golden, along with journalists around the world, echoed Álvaro de Soto, the mediator for the United Nations, who claimed, "This is the closest that any process has ever come to a negotiated revolution." Tens of thousands of Salvadorans poured into the streets of the nation's capital of San Salvador. Notably, however, they celebrated at "rival block parties," with leftist FMLN supporters gathering in the Plaza Cívica, and the rightist ARENA party holding separate functions at Plaza Libertad. "Though separated by only 100 yards of pavement," Douglas Grant Mine of the Associated Press reported, "the two plazas were worlds apart. The figurative chasm underscored the magnitude of the task of reconciliation awaiting the country." The accords may have signaled some changes, but it certainly did not mean that all Salvadorans saw eye to eye.[1]

One of many concerns of rural repopulation movement activists was that during the years of talks that produced the 1992 accords, FMLN and government representatives bypassed most socioeconomic issues.[2] In fact, government representatives made it clear that economic issues were off-limits; the text of the peace accord openly acknowledged that "the general philosophy or orientation of the government's political economy . . . are not the objective of this Accord."[3] In lieu of using negotiations to devise new policies, government officials proposed to create a Forum for Economic and Social Consultation. The forum would involve "the egalitarian participation of government, labor, and business sectors, with the objective of reaching a series of broad accords aimed at the economic and social development of the country, benefiting all of its inhabitants," and would address issues such as labor relations, unemployment, conditions in the marginal communities created by mass flight from rural conflict zones, and "measures to alleviate the social costs associated with the structural adjustment program."[4] The government also promised to "make possible and promote the active participation" of the agricultural sector, but rural activists, drawing from their decades-long experiences of marginalization, doubted this would come to pass.[5]

Many participants and observers of the Salvadoran transition period argued that the negotiators' "pact" of silence on economic issues was necessary to push through key political reforms—including the reduction of the armed forces, the creation of a new civilian police force, and electoral changes that enabled the FMLN to participate in national leadership as a legal political party.[6] Critics debated who was most to blame for undercutting the transition out of armed conflict, with many pointing to the FMLN for "los[ing] its revolutionary edge [and] feebly oppos[ing] the neoliberal restructuring sponsored by the ARENA governments." Later critiques condemned the FMLN for having "mutated into a 'party-enterprise,' a combination political organization and corporation with major investments in various sectors of the Salvadoran economy . . . forming a new economic elite that is drifting away from the movement's 'original ideas.'"[7] Of course, "pacted transitions" and frustrations with them are nothing new. In Argentina, Brazil, Greece, Spain, and elsewhere, Steve J. Stern notes that outgoing regimes "impose[d] the fundamental rules of the game in the future." Yet, as Stern details for the case of Chile, such pacts always were limited and insecure precisely because the elites that established them had to contend with myriad pressures from civil society.[8]

In the Salvadoran case as well, activists put pressure on political elites not only to end the conflict but also to influence how the postconflict nation would function. Activists associated with the rural repopulation movement expressed unease with the government's agenda well before the signing of the peace accords, arguing that true peace would come only with the implementation of new policies "that guarantee the eradication of the root causes of the war."[9] As representatives from the Christian Committee for the Displaced of El Salvador (CRIPDES), the National Coordinator of Repopulations (CNR), and other organizations involved in the National Debate for Peace unanimously agreed in 1988, "the root cause" of the conflict in El Salvador "lies in the structural injustice, manifested in the unjust concentration of wealth, especially of land, but also industry and commerce into the hands of small social groups that reap huge profits. Thus material and spiritual production by the majority of the population becomes impossible. Structural injustice is maintained by institutionalized violence and repression, keeping the people in an inhuman state and denying their fundamental rights." National Debate participants also placed Salvadoran structures within global contexts. El Salvador's "capitalist, dependent agro-export model," for example, formed "part of an unjust structure of international commerce." In a similar vein, the economic crisis that brought the country to war was in large part due to the "imposition of economic measure[s] by international finance institutions," along with "the enormous interference" of the United States.[10]

As negotiators honed their final agreements in 1991, moderates and leftists, including activists with the rural repopulation movement, insisted that in order to address the root causes of the war, Salvadorans must surmount "the economic dependency and achieve self-government in ways "that benefit the great majorities in our country."[11] These were earnest exhortations that responded to issue gaps in the negotiation process and to concerns about the increasingly cozy relations between El Salvador's new "financial aristocracy" and international financial institutions.[12] From the perspective of rural repopulators and their allies, those relations signified a continuation of the *status quo ante* that put the entire peace process in jeopardy. As if confirming their fears, "a mere six days" after the peace agreements were finalized, the International Monetary Fund approved "a typical neoliberal economic stabilization and reform program" for El Salvador that, as former United Nations affiliates Álvaro de Soto and Graciana del Castillo put it, "prevented the government from complying with the financial requirements of the peace accord"—essentially "pull[ing] the rug out from under the peace accord."[13]

Thus even if the 1992 accords might offer "a new situation," it was clear to rural activists "that the attitudes of the oligarchy will still lead to social and economic confrontation." Sistering activists from Chalatenango predicted, "There will not be armed confrontation (that's the goal) but instead debate between the two visions of the world of national reconstruction."[14] This prediction proved accurate. Through the 1990s and into the new millennium, national and grassroots leaders and their respective allies repeatedly clashed over their "distinct projects"—what Salvador Orellana of CORDES defined as "the Government's neoliberal project" versus "the project of a democratic alternative."[15] This chapter traces these socioeconomic confrontations from the perspective of grassroots activists. Whereas chapter 3 explored how rural repopulators claimed political rights and redefined political relations during El Salvador's transition from war to peace, here I examine how they claimed economic rights and influenced the formation of new economic relations. As part of their expanding human rights work, they modeled alternative development practices, and pressed for rights to land, credit, and a dignified life as full citizens of El Salvador.

Looking Forward, Not Back

Whereas during the height of the war in the 1980s, rural activists often focused on "emergency and survival," as the decade of the 1990s dawned, they were able to more directly and consistently address a broader range of rights. "When we speak of rights," CRIPDES announced in its strategic plan for 1991, "we do so in a general sense; that is not only are we speaking of the right to return to our places of origin, but also of economic, social cultural, and political rights of every human being."[16] As the rural repopulation movement began to "diversify," transferring efforts "toward long-term and sustainable community development," each of their representative organizations adopted a specialization.[17] While CRIPDES served as the "trade union" of the displaced and repopulated communities, CORDES worked to "support their economic programs."[18]

The challenges were great: the government's long-standing lack of attention to rural development meant that "the repopulators self-govern everything" and "carry out projects in wartime."[19] Despite this, CORDES reported "great achievements" by mid-1991, with an expansion from thirty to ninety-nine affiliated communities and "positive" program results.[20] Their work, combined with that of CRIPDES, had brought significant and tangible improvements in standards of living to the repopulated zones, prompting new urban-rural migrations as well as continued mass returns from refugee camps in Costa Rica, Nicaragua, and Panama.[21] "The people in the repopulations," sistering network activists in the United States observed, "are a living symbol of hope and embody a future vision of El Salvador, one in which people participate in their government and have access to health care, education, food and housing."[22] In short, by the early 1990s, repopulations stood as "model communities" worthy of replicating on a national scale.[23]

In light of their successes, rural activists were dismayed by the National Reconstruction Plan, formally unveiled by the Salvadoran government alongside the peace accords in 1992. According to officials, the plan would improve conditions in former conflict zones; address the basic needs of the affected populations, particularly ex-combatants from both sides; and reconstruct damaged infrastructure. It promised, in sum, "a minimum platform of commitments aimed toward facilitating development to benefit all strata of the population."[24]

From a grassroots perspective, however, the government's plan fell short. Activists perceived it, in fact, as another means to perpetuate uneven power relations. As evidence they pointed out how officials had developed the plan behind closed doors; despite framing it within the context of peace and despite promises of inclusion, officials did not even attempt to "bring together the diverse sectors in the country" in a "genuine process of consensus-building."[25] The text of the January 16, 1992, peace accords made clear that the Salvadoran government had full control over the development and execution of the plan. The introduction to chapter 5, section 9 of the plan read, in part, "The Government of El Salvador will present to the FMLN . . . the National Reconstruction Plan that it has developed, with the objective of taking into account the recommendations and suggestions of the FMLN as well as the different sectors of national society."[26] The political scientist Elisabeth Wood argued that such provisions painted the FMLN into a "clearly secondary" position and illustrated that the government officials had "no intention of allowing beneficiaries to participate in formulating" the plan.[27]

The government's closed-door approach did not surprise many in light of the fact that officials rejected even acknowledging the existence of the repopulations and the nongovernmental organizations working in conflict zones. This intentional oversight continued and in many ways deepened through the negotiation period; anything else, officials believed, would "fortify the political power of the FMLN in the countryside."[28] For these reasons, sistering activists argued that what government representatives peddled to international donors as the National Development Plan, was not, in fact, *national*. As Gorka Gárate explained to the 1992 sistering summit attendees, the plan "is not the result of consensus politics."[29]

Even more problematic from the perspective of grassroots activists was the fact that the government's plan falsely detached economic development projects from the social and political spheres. In a joint statement on the National Reconstruction Plan, Salvadoran nongovernmental organizations drove home the extent of this disconnect with the government's own numbers. The estimated budget for national reconstruction allocated a total of only 4.14 percent of spending to land purchases and health, education, and community development programs, contrasted with 71 percent of spending allocated to infrastructure projects, including roads and electric energy.[30] Moreover, as Orellana explained, the bulk of spending emphasized the repair and expansion of "infrastructure created before the war." Such projects would, in essence, "serve a few wealthy families"—the same people who had had a stranglehold on the country's economy prior to the war. "Taking the electric power grid all the way out to sugarcane processors that haven't been on the power system before," for example, would do nothing for the majority of Salvadoran citizens; such "improvements" would simply increase "the productive capacity of those who already have a monopoly on the country's resources."[31]

In addition to perpetuating uneven power relations inside the country, the National Reconstruction Plan did nothing to upset the old pattern of Salvadoran subservience to foreign interests. In late 1988, participants in the National Debate for Peace in El Salvador had identified this subservience as a key factor in the Salvadoran conflict. In particular, they had pointed to "the enormous interference" of the United States, "exhaustion of the capitalist, dependent agroexport model as part of an unjust structure of international commerce," and the "imposition of economic measure[s] by international finance institutions."[32] Rural activists contended that the National Reconstruction Plan represented a continuation of these old patterns; from the point of view of Orellana and his CORDES associates, it was "essentially a counterinsurgency plan" that sought to "contain development within the parameters of the neoliberal model [that] the US government supports."[33] In an eerie repetition, the principle donor, the US Agency for International Development (USAID), channeled funds through Municipalities in Action, a war-era counterinsurgency program revived for this purpose. For rural people directly targeted by state terrorism during the 1980s, then, the government's National Reconstruction Plan and the associated neoliberal reforms amounted to nothing more than "actions of war in times of peace."[34]

The consequences of the government's neoliberal agenda were already obvious to rural Salvadorans by this point. Just three months into the ARENA administration of Alfredo Cristiani, in August 1989, CRIPDES reported that "severe and antipopular economic measures" had resulted in "an excessive rise in the cost of the basic food package, increased prices for public transportation, electricity, etc., aggravating hunger and misery."[35] Two years later CRIPDES affirmed "that the dispossessed masses are living our worst socioeconomic crisis."[36] Not only had "Cristiani's neoliberal economic program" caused "a steep rise in the cost of living," but the "policy of privatization" of businesses, land, and public services resulted in mass unemployment and landlessness, and even less access to education and health care for the country's poor.[37]

Because a neoliberal agenda underwrote the government's National Reconstruction Plan, activists associated with the rural repopulation movement concluded that the plan itself simply offered more of the same: "the rebuilding of the market for those with large amounts of capital, both within El Salvador and from outside" while "leaving aside" the rural population.[38] Rather than use the transition and postwar contexts to establish new norms, Salvadoran government and business elites revived old patterns. If one of the root "causes of the

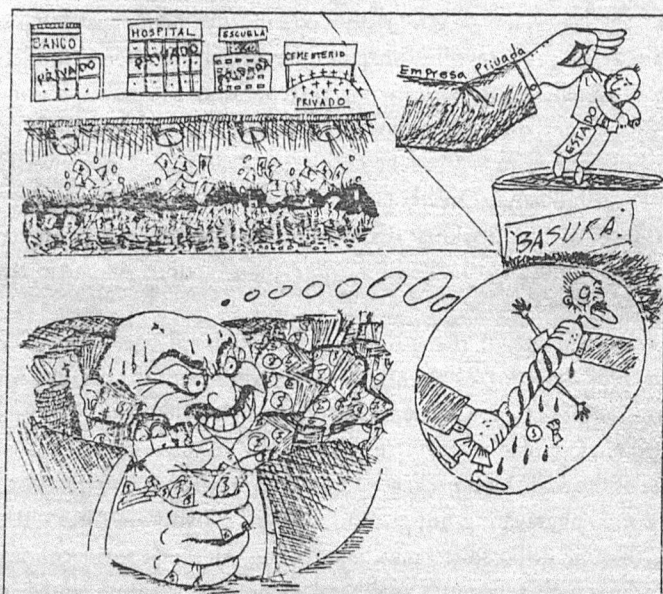

EL NEOLIBERALISMO PARA PRINCIPIANTES

Cover of *Neoliberalism for Beginners*, a popular education primer prepared by CRIPDES, ca. 2001. (CRIPDES Archive)

displacement problem" was the unequal distribution of resources, CRIPDES activists pointed out, then directly addressing this "internal debt" would help resolve the problem.[39] Instead, however, the government continued to pursue policies "at the expense of the majority of the population."[40] And rather than respecting "the local level organizational structures" of the repopulated communities and "their efforts to build self-management," thus empowering them as "active subjects in a development process," the government's "intent is to create beneficiaries."[41]

But rural activists remained intent on participating in debates and processes relating to national reconstruction. They drew from their experiences to develop the New Initiative for Popular Self-Development (hereafter New Initiative), "an alternative model of socioeconomic development, based on self-government and democracy."[42] The result of a coalition of nongovernmental organizations known as the Interinstitutional Coordinator (Coordinadora Interinstitucional), established in November 1990, the New Initiative centered on *desarrollo integral*, the integral or holistic development of Salvadoran communities "in cultural, social, economic, and political terms."[43] The CORDES bulletin *Horizontes Nuevos* (New Horizons) described how each project of the New Initiative involved a layering of goals, among them: fulfilling basic needs such as food, health, and education; community organization; "defense of Community rights vis-a-vis the State"; technical progress and training; and addressing the "ecological problem."[44]

The holistic approach of the New Initiative illustrates how, "from the perspective of the population affected by the war, we consider reconstruction to be more than just infrastructure." Tomasa Ruíz, the CRIPDES president, explained, "It includes the reconstruction of the lives of each person." Because so many Salvadorans, especially campesinos, "have been psychologically affected by the effects of the war," she said, "here there must be spiritual, physical, and economic reconstruction."[45] "Our position," agreed Orellana of CORDES, is that "the principal objective of national reconstruction is to rebuild the social fabric of our country. The reconstruction phase must begin to resolve the problems that caused the war, not just rebuild what previously existed."[46]

The New Initiative began to do just this in part by restructuring power relations. On one level the initiative intentionally "involv[ed] all those sectors that have been pushed out into the margins for decades." In contrast to the government's National Reconstruction Plan, then, Orellana pointed out, the New Initiative "belongs to the people [and] depends on people at the grassroots level." Rewriting power relations also entailed "breaking out of the traditional agricultural export mold" to prioritize agricultural production, animal husbandry, and processing of goods for internal consumption as well as export, and changing "the old financial structures" to facilitate broad access. In a similar vein, the New Initiative insisted that all capital investments, technology transfers, and other assistance were "appropriate" to the communities and nation of El Salvador. By placing "our own conditions" on foreign aid and investments, the New Initiative intended to establish foreign economic relations based on "cooperation" rather than "imposition."[47]

An important component of the New Initiative in terms of restructuring power relations was to bolster and expand the principles of collectivity and solidarity that had developed within the displaced and repopulated communities. Toward this end, coalition members worked together to "Break the barrier of community and 'our personal project,'" to promote the "radiation or impact of the project on neighboring communities."[48] It was at this moment that CRIPDES began outreach to a "new contingent" of rural communities that did not represent "repopulated communities formed in coordination with CRIPDES." As Ruíz said, "If we do not work with them, it would leave a great vacuum" because all rural communities in El Salvador "share similar interests and needs."[49] By collectively addressing those shared needs, rural residents not only would achieve new levels of self-sufficiency; they also would help break down "the system [that] up to now is paternalistic" and, in so doing, generate an "impact on the future of the nation."[50]

The New Initiative thus posed a fundamental challenge to the official National Reconstruction Plan. Whereas the government's plan meant *reconstruction*—"a return to where we were twenty years ago"—rural activists wanted something different. They wanted to "look to the future, toward development." Whereas the government's plan eschewed rural communities, the grassroots plan doubled efforts in that realm to "allow the people to become the subjects of their own development."[51] And whereas the government plan promoted individualism, the rural activists emphasized collectivity and communal approaches to challenges. As El Salvador transitioned out of conflict and into a new era in the last decade of the twentieth century, rural activists held fast to these ideals—even when the Salvadoran government and its allies tried to unravel them.

The Land Question

One component of the Salvadoran peace accords that had the capacity to begin addressing the unjust economic structures was the Land Transfer Program (Programa de Transferencia de Tierras). The cluster of provisions that made up the program stipulated a transfer of agricultural lands, credit, and technical assistance to beneficiaries of the stalled 1980 agrarian reform, as well as ex-combatants of both government and FMLN forces, and *tenedores*—a term that in general meant "landholders" but more specifically referred to the repopulators who had been using abandoned land for agricultural and community purposes.[52]

Rural repopulators viewed the Land Transfer Program as directly supporting their right to make a living off the land. Despite the program's promise, however, the reality of its implementation remained "uncertain," said CRIPDES president Ruíz, given staunch opposition from the "most wealthy and powerful."[53] Although assessments of the Land Transfer Program typically emphasize the roles played by the United Nations Observer Mission in El Salvador and the FMLN in pressing the Salvadoran government to meet its obligations to this program and the broader peace accords of which it was part, grassroots activism also was pivotal. Rural activists and their transnational allies assiduously pressed officials to fully implement all provisions of the Land Transfer Program. A closer look at this "long and contested road" of implementation illustrates the ongoing competition between the alternative and neoliberal models of development—and the precarious nature of peace in the 1990s.[54]

Rural activists approached the Land Transfer Program as a framework on which to build, a means of "asserting their rights to live on their lands in dignity and peace."[55] Individuals and their communities had much to gain. As internally displaced persons and refugees, they had argued for the right to return to what they referred to as their places of origin, and to plant crops and regain their lives. Through the repopulation movement, they physically conquered land, but the majority of them had no legal rights to that land; in essence, they were squatting on abandoned land. The Land Transfer Program offered a mechanism to gain legal title to agricultural land, along with credit to help rebuild productive capacities and attain a decent standard of living after decades of hardship. Although individuals certainly had much to gain, community leaders framed their work in terms of the broader, ongoing fight for justice. On one level, pressure on "the land question" contributed to "the overall struggle to realize full compliance with the Peace Accords." On another level, an earnestly implemented Land Transfer Program would enable campesinos "to fulfill the most basic and minimal requirements for a dignified life" and, in so doing, assure the "formation of new productive agents in the development of a more just society."[56]

The Salvadoran government, for its part, faced a formidable task. Officials started from zero with the Land Transfer Program; they had to establish new agencies, hire and train new personnel, and design and implement new policies and procedures. They worked with limited financial resources and an infrastructure compromised by war. Because the peace accords had left many terms of the program vaguely defined, officials had to make things up as they went: definitions of "beneficiary" and "productive agricultural lands," for example. Perhaps most challenging was the fact that El Salvador had no central land registry. Before any land could change hands through the Land Transfer Program, plots had to be legally registered, the terrain measured and surveyed, and the soil evaluated.[57] The legal landowners had to be involved in the process, but the war had displaced many of them and, in the majority of cases, their whereabouts and even identities were unknown. This made transfers especially complicated in repopulated areas where small subsistence parcels predominated, including Chalatenango and Morazán. According to one observer, the whole process was, simply put, "a nightmare."[58]

Although many people acknowledged the significant challenges with launching new programs in a country torn by war, critics became more vocal as time passed with little progress. Even the UN Secretary-General expressed "concern" regarding the "virtual paralysis" of the program.[59] Over two years into the program—and four months from the scheduled end date—less than 30 percent of titles had been transferred, prompting the first of several extensions.[60]

Whereas the Secretary-General and others often spoke in general terms about the process, rural activists and their allies were more direct, seeking to hold accountable specific agencies for putting the whole Land Transfer Program in jeopardy. They contended that the Land Bank and the Agricultural Development Bank employed "minuscule" teams that were "basically incapable [of] carrying out their assigned tasks in the stipulated time."[61] (Only two or three surveyors worked at any given time in the entire department of Chalatenango, for example, despite the fact that they had several hundred small parcels to survey and certify.[62]) The Liberty and Progress Institute subcontracted a number of its assigned tasks—including land titling—to other organizations, leading to a situation in which one group was unable to do its work until another completed its job.[63] And the agency responsible for certifying beneficiary status, the Government Office for Agricultural Affairs, arbitrarily excluded several hundred repopulators from the final beneficiary list. Chalatenango's campesinos were particularly hard hit; among those who did not appear on the list were 230 landholders in Guarjila, 130 in Arcatao, 125 in San Antonio Los Ranchos, 90 in Nueva Trinidad, 85 in San José Las Flores, 60 in Ellacuría, and 14 in Los Amates.[64]

The bottlenecks and inconsistencies were "much more than simple administrative errors," Mike Hoffman of SHARE reported in an update for US-based sistering and solidarity activists.[65] They represented "a politically motivated move to assure that the land transference not be carried out."[66] The end goal was to once again consolidate land ownership into the hands of a few wealthy families and force campesinos back into a position of subservient labor.

As evidence, Hoffman pointed to the fact that although many landowners initially had been receptive to selling their land to repopulators, they quickly "lost interest" due to the incessant delays on the part of government agencies. By 1994 a number of landowners already in the process of transferring their parcels had "lost hope in the possibility of getting their money and [thus] have withdrawn their offers." Some owners chose to "not even bother" going through Land Transfer Program channels; they began "demanding cash in hand" or simply "refusing to sell" to repopulators.[67]

In addition, the Land and Agrarian Development Banks delayed credits due, placed what many felt to be arbitrary ceilings on credits, or outright "denied that vital access" to repopulator beneficiaries.[68] Although activists held government offices responsible for the many problems, records from the era reveal rising tensions between campesino repopulators and FMLN cadres. Hoffman's updates document how ex-combatants received preferential treatment; by January 1995, 92 percent of ex-combatant beneficiaries had received their promised credits, compared to only about 10 percent of repopulator beneficiaries. Moreover, repopulators faced an eight thousand *colón* credit ceiling, compared to fifteen thousand for FMLN combatants.[69] Although many repopulators believed they received unfair treatment when compared with former FMLN combatants, many more Salvadorans received no direct benefits at all. A major critique of the National Reconstruction Plan was that it "concentrat[ed] exclusively [on] the rural population directly affected by the war." In terms of basic numbers, the plan addressed only 99 of 262 municipalities across the country, targeting fewer than 850,000 people in a population of more than five million.[70] Some considered such different levels of beneficiary status to be a divide-and-conquer strategy implemented by the Salvadoran government. Regardless of the officials' intentions or political ramifications, an important fact remained: the Salvadorans' capacity for subsistence was at risk.

As problems with the Land Transfer Program persisted, worries deepened. If the banks did not release the promised credits or funds arrived "too late for the normal cycle of agricultural production," the repopulators would find themselves in an even worse crisis.[71] Coming out of years of conflict, most campesinos had no "cushion to sustain themselves."[72] With no credit there would be no crops, "rais[ing] the specter of not being able to scrape out a subsistence for the coming year."[73] "The historical tendency is for the land to be re-sold at a point of crisis," activists warned, causing the land "to flow back to the hands of those who are land rich."[74] If this same pattern resumed postwar, they concluded, "the families will be assured the perpetuation of a state of absolute poverty."[75]

Activists drew direct connections between the credit delays and landowners "soured by the process" on the one hand, and land speculation on the other.[76]

As peace held and land values rose, prices soared especially high in areas in northeastern Chalatenango where repopulators had succeeded in developing a minimal level of infrastructure. Plans to reintroduce electrical power to these areas made the land even "more enticing."[77] The rise in value prompted some landowners to return to rural zones to reclaim their property, sometimes forcing repopulators out of houses and off land, despite rules in the peace accords stating that *tenedores* could not be displaced without first arranging another place for them to live.[78] In other cases, landowners began demanding rent from the repopulators, something they had not done since the start of the armed conflict.[79]

But the problems faced by repopulators were not solely due to the whims of the land market. According to rural activists, the Salvadoran government "exacerbated the situation by . . . facilitating the entrance of land speculators who, knowing the communities need to buy the land, have been able to purchase many tracts of land and raise the prices everywhere considerably."[80] The government's backdoor deals with these *coyotes* (land speculators) made massive tracts—in some cases one hundred manzanas or more—inaccessible to those who had repopulated and rebuilt the area during the previous half decade.[81] These sales were "done without consulting the land holders themselves" and involved "outsiders"—people "who neither are from nor have ever lived in the communities in question."[82]

Here again, economic and sociopolitical concerns merged, with political tensions influencing land sales well into the 1990s. Chalatenango-based activists frequently reported that many of the region's landowners were "recalcitrants" who "proclaim[ed] on principle they will never sell to their enemies"—that is, FMLN supporters—and promised to do whatever they could to dislodge the squatters.[83] Activists pointed out that the landowners' back-door deals often involved parcels located in the repopulations with the strongest community organizations, including Arcatao and San Antonio Los Ranchos. This, they felt, was part of an intentional plan to divide and conquer the residents of the repopulated zones. The subsequent arrival of comparatively wealthy outsiders, leaders feared, would damage the community cohesion that had developed through the cycle of exile and return. Concerns along these lines would drive the grassroots activists' actions and philosophies in the coming years.

An "almost complete overhaul" of Land Bank personnel in January 1995 deepened activists' perceptions of political machinations by the right.[84] Despite the Bank's recent improvements in efficiency prompted by pressures from external and internal groups, Salvadoran officials dismissed or transferred the director and some thirty staff members, who together held years of experience. Rural activists and their allies interpreted the staffing change as a move by the conservative hard liners (*línea dura*) of the reigning party, ARENA.[85] Whereas the outgoing director of the Land Bank, Jairo Merio, was a technician (*técnico*) associated with the party's more moderate faction, the new director, Fredy Portillo, was a politician (*político*) with deep roots in what many observers referred to alternately as the "Death Squad Group" or the "D'Aubuisson Group," after Roberto D'Aubuisson, one of the party's founders and a known force behind the wartime death squads. As the sociologist Oscar Martínez Peñate noted, the members of this faction of the ARENA party "have the common denominator of being fanatic, dogmatic, and reactionary." Moreover, because "the peace accords did not insist on the disarming or dissolution of the death squads," this group came to be "the most feared, both within the ARENA party as well as outside it."[86] With deep roots in El Salvador's traditional agricultural export sector, Portillo and his colleagues opposed land reform and, in contrast to the more moderate faction of the party represented by the likes of President Alfredo Cristiani, they were the "least interested in cowtowing [*sic*] to foreign interests and creating policies to please Capitol Hill."[87] Rural activists and Land Transfer Program beneficiaries thus interpreted the naming of Portillo's appointment at the Land Bank "as a means to halt the forward march of the land transference program itself and to frame an agrarian policy designed to preserve the interests of the largest landowners in El Salvador."[88]

All of this pointed to "more than just a bureaucratic question," as one activist put it.[89] A March 1995 report on the situation in El Salvador, likely prepared by SHARE's Mike Hoffman, expanded on this comment. "The real problem lies in the inability or unwillingness of the President to ensure that his subordinates carry out commitments that he has made," the report explained. Such ignorance or intransigence threatened not just the Land Transfer Program but the entire peace process. The lack of political will power "to operationalize the government's publicly stated commitments to implement the Peace Accords"—to comply with the very accords they had coauthored—illustrated just how deep the roots of structural injustice ran in El Salvador.[90]

In light of the "deliberate effort on the part of the government" to block the land transfer process, Salvadoran repopulators explained to their sistering allies in the United States, acquiring legal title to the land they had settled was "their only alternative for survival as a community." As members of the Nueva Trinidad directiva told visitors from the Boston area sistering committees, anything else "would mean the fragmentation of the organization they have worked so hard to achieve."[91] Because they could not trust the government to follow through on its obligations of its own accord, rural activists mobilized to oblige compliance. Rather than wait for the Salvadoran government to identify and locate landowners, for example, the repopulated communities in

northeast Chalatenango designated full-time work teams to track down registered landowners, help measure lands, negotiate the sale of lands, and begin the
paperwork process. San José Las Flores had six people working in this area in
1994, and nearby San Antonio Los Ranchos had four who, in the course of their
duties, traveled to areas scattered throughout the country, including Tejutla,
San Francisco Morazán, Apopa, San Salvador, Sonsonate, and Ahuachapán.[92]
These activists kept the pressure on so that "whatever velocity that the [Land
Transfer Program] has been able to muster," one report explained, "does not
have to do with the efforts of the Land Bank but rather the fact that the communities themselves have placed a tremendous amount of time and energy in
bringing about a resolution."[93]

Repopulators also launched a series of pressure campaigns as the initial
deadline for the Land Transfer Program neared. In September 1994, for example, campesino activists from at least eight of Chalatenango's repopulated
communities traveled to the Agricultural Development Bank (BFA) in San
Salvador to demand their promised credits. On Monday, September 26, two
hundred people from San Antonio Los Ranchos "arrive[d] en masse at the
office of the BFA to demand their rights." The next day, Tuesday, 110 people
from Arcatao did the same. On successive dates thereafter, repopulators from
Ellacuría, Las Vueltas, San José Las Flores, Carasque, Guarjila, and Los Calles
followed suit, heightening pressures on bank officials.[94] A few months later,
in December, CRIPDES cosponsored a four-day, nationwide Land and Peace
Accords Pilgrimage. From points across the country, caravans of campesinos
traveled on foot to San Salvador, calling for "the rights and revindications that
are just and necessary for peace." The long list of revindications included land,
respect for human rights, compliance with the Truth Commission's recommendations, effective reinsertion programs for ex-combatants, and compliance
with laws supporting the wounded and victims of war.[95] In March 1995, residents of San José Las Flores and other communities marched to Chalatenango
City, "where they rallied in front of the Land Bank and met with bank officials
to press for speedier payments and credits to work the land."[96]

Through these pressure campaigns, activists carved out new opportunities
to engage with government officials and influence their policies and procedures. As part of the Pilgrimage for Land and Peace, for example, several hundred people from the departments of Morazán, San Miguel, and Usulután
marched to the Legislative Assembly, where they presented a bill to reform
various articles of the Constitution regarding land ownership. Another group
from Chalatenango marched to la Casa Rosada, the nation's presidential palace,
where, accompanied by representatives from the UN Observer Mission and
the National Center for US–El Salvador Sister Cities, their representatives met

with a delegate from the office of the president, as well as the president of the Land Bank, the vice minister for Housing, and the secretary for National Reconstruction. Several hours later, negotiators emerged with an agreement that would speed the land transfer process via decentralization of decision-making; the channeling of additional resources to assist with the search for landowners, surveying, and other logistics; and monthly progress and evaluation meetings. In subsequent months, rural community leaders had an unprecedented number of meetings with officials at different government offices, including the Office for Agricultural Affairs, the Liberty and Progress Institute, the Agricultural Development Bank, the Secretary of the Interior, and others.[97]

Rural activists with CRIPDES and CORDES also mobilized their transnational sistering networks. Responding to requests from their Salvadoran partners, Sister Cities representatives in the United States launched a nationally coordinated Land for El Salvador campaign in 1994 to press for full compliance with the peace accords and the acceleration of land and credit transfers to beneficiaries in the repopulated villages. Tours of Salvadorans helped raise awareness among US citizens about the very human consequences of the postwar land struggles in El Salvador. Julio Tobar and Milagro Tobar, two of the original 120 repopulators of San José Las Flores and elected members of the Municipal Council, for example, toured in 1994 and 1995, respectively, and Guillermo Rivera of Cinquera visited in 1995 as well. To overlap with the visits of these and other representatives of the Salvadoran repopulation movement, local sistering committees organized vigils, city council resolutions, press conferences, letter writing and call campaigns, and other events, and sponsored paid ads in Salvadoran newspapers.[98]

In the months leading up to the original 1995 deadline for the Land Transfer Program, the National Center for US–El Salvador Sister Cities collaborated with other solidarity groups to plan a vigil in New York in December, a January press conference coinciding with the Sister Cities National Conference, a February congressional lobbying drive, a March delegation to El Salvador, and an April delegation to Washington, DC.[99] As part of these efforts, they disseminated guidelines and talking points for letters, telexes, faxes, and personal visits to specific "Advocacy Targets," including Land Bank officials Rafael Montalvo and Hugo González, Legislative Assembly president Gloria Salguero Gross, and Alexander Watson, Assistant Secretary of State for Inter-American Affairs at the US Department of State.[100] Even as they encouraged direct contact with such targets, campaign coordinators emphasized the need to work through elected congresspeople and senators. As an early 1995 information mailing explained, the Department of State and USAID are both "accountable to Congress, and less responsive to direct citizen advocacy, thus, U.S. citizens should direct advocacy requests to Congressional Representatives, asking them in turn to contact the State Department (and AID)."[101]

As suggested by this report, in response to their Salvadoran partners' requests, US-based activists also placed especially heavy pressure on the US Agency for International Development (USAID) "to get the land transfers moving."[102] As Nancy Ryan from Cambridge explained in a 1995 editorial, because USAID "is the largest single funder of the land transfer program," it "must intervene" and use "its financial clout and organizational know-how . . . to be a pro-active force for effectiveness."[103] Among the demands that Ryan and other US-based activists made of USAID officials were "to monitor the work of the Land Bank to eliminate bureaucracy and to improve efficiency"; to urge action by (and accountability of) Salvadoran authorities at the Land Bank and the Agricultural Development Bank on unresolved transfer, titling, and credit cases; to insist on more survey and technical assistance teams; to simplify the highly cumbersome title transfer process; to commit to tying future aid to completion of the land transfer; to pressure Salvadoran officials to renegotiate a realistic repayment plan for agrarian debt; and, not least, to "work with the campesino (farmer) groups themselves to resolve . . . outstanding issues."[104] USAID certainly felt the pressure; according to Antonio Álvarez of the FMLN's Land Commission, chief officials at the USAID office in El Salvador complained to him "that they were being deluged with letters from the United States asking that AID do whatever is possible to assure that the [program] is a success" and that "there be extra efforts made to assure that the Salvadoran institutions involved in the program be as agile and cooperative as possible."[105]

It is difficult to measure the precise impact of such lobbying on the Land Transfer Program, of course, but Sister Cities activists interpreted Álvarez's news as evidence that their efforts had a tangible effect. They saw adjustments in Salvadoran official policy in a similar light. In late 1994, for example, when Salvadoran officials "decided to make a complete overhaul of its transference program" to make it "much more efficient," as Hoffman put it, activists perceived this as "government acknowledgement," a direct response to grassroots critiques.[106] As Hoffman reported from El Salvador on the announcement of the overhaul, "Apparently the letters, and the pressure all-around has had its impact."[107] In a similar vein, Sister Cities activists considered the initial extension of the Land Transfer Program from April to December, 1995, as a result of "pressure from communities, popular organizations and solidarity." Jennifer Utech of Cambridge drew a direct link between the extension and a thirty-person Sister Cities delegation; in meetings with Salvadoran and US officials, Utech and her compatriots "cut through the fluff" of the officials' "statistics and slick summaries" with "information brought directly from our sister communities, impressing on the officials that we know what the real situation is and are monitoring it!"[108] "OUR PRESSURE IS PAYING OFF," a Cambridge flier for a Land Action Call-in Day declared shortly thereafter. "THE LAND TRANS-FER DEADLINE HAS BEEN EXTENDED! LET'S KEEP THE HEAT ON!"[109] The flier directed participants to call, fax, or write Alexander Watson, assistant secretary of state for Inter-American Affairs, to press him regarding full implementation of the peace accords, with special attention to land transfers.

Although adjustments and extensions were welcome, there were no assurances that these steps ultimately would lead to legal land titles for repopulators. "Without land to work and the assurance of a place to live," a Chalatenango sistering project report from late 1994 explained, "the communities cannot think of development."[110] In the words of another report, lacking clear title to land meant "living in a state of perpetual instability."[111] To address this land crisis—and as a work-around to sluggish government agencies and "organized political obstacles" presented by intransigent landowners—communities pooled their own resources and used their grassroots networks to speed land purchases.[112] In many of the "human settlements" excluded from the Land Transfer Program's land bank, for example, repopulators borrowed money from regional organizations such as CCR and CORDES, requested funds from their sister cities and other solidarity groups, and sold their own "hens and cows to scrape together enough to buy" a series of house lots (*solares*) scattered throughout the area.[113] Residents of El Higueral, for example, used funds from its sister city of Belmont, Massachusetts, to collectively purchase their first 150 manzanas, "small patches scattered about the outskirts of the village" where

"Defend the Peace Accords." Detail from flier for New York City event featuring the Salvadoran activist Marta Cerna Alfaro, sponsored by USESSC, SHARE, and area allies, 1992. (Arvidson Papers, USESSC Archive)

they had been "raising food and livestock." Teosinte applied funds from its sister city, Arlington, Massachusetts, toward a similar purchase.[114] Repopulators in Arcatao worked with Madison to purchase land in the town center, and their priest, a Spaniard, to purchase approximately 46.5 manzanas on the edge of the town.[115] Many other Chalatenango repopulations, including San Antonio Los Ranchos, Las Vueltas, Arcatao, Guarjila, Ignacio Ellacuria, and San José Las Flores were all "forced to buy their own land" in this way.[116]

Such purchases were no small feat. In fact, they are evidence of a deliberate strategy on the part of the rural activists, despite their small and patchwork nature. After each such sale went through, neighboring landowners often became more willing to sell, producing what Hoffman referred to as a "domino effect."[117]

In addition to myriad challenges associated with the government's handling of the Land Transfer Program, repopulators also faced the fact that wealthy landowning families who fled their rural farms during the war, typically politically conservative, often "refuse[d] to sell land to FMLN sympathizers" after the war. Classifying such landowners as "recalcitrants" at best or, worse, "local thugs," rural activists endeavored to wear them down.[118] In Guarjila, for example, the Santos family owned 280 manzanas. The patriarch, Pepe Santos, directed an offshoot of ARENA, and influential lawyers, teachers, and other professionals were members of the family network. At the close of the conflict in 1992, they declared "that they would not sell under any circumstances." As repopulators slowly extended their patchwork of individually and collectively owned plots through the town, however, Pepe Santos's "will began to crack." His first offer was an all-or-nothing deal, the entire property at ₡12,000 each. Later he offered smaller sections at ₡7,000 per manzana. Such an amount was "still beyond all possibility of the community" in 1995, yet local leaders continued "to transfer what is transferable."[119] In this way, residents of Guarjila and other repopulations increased legal control of territory for individual and communal uses and, in so doing, compelled landowners like Santos "to reflect and soften their otherwise rigid refusal to consider selling."[120]

With the collaboration of transnational allies, then, repopulators were able to make considerable progress even within the context of an essentially paralyzed Land Transfer Program. Repopulators in San José Las Flores succeeded in gaining 85 percent ownership of the community territory by early 1995—despite its supposed exclusion from the Land Transfer Program inventory. Similarly, repopulators in Nueva Trinidad and Arcatao had gained 70 and 60 percent ownership of their settlements, while Las Vueltas and San Antonio Los Ranchos were at 50 and 40 percent, respectively.[121] As activists monitoring the process observed at the time, the legal transfer of land to the repopulators—

in both collective and individual forms—was a watershed moment, carrying communities "across the psychological barrier, giving the residents in [each] town the sense that it is basically theirs and that is where they can dig in roots."[122]

Putting down roots meant being able to pursue longer-term development projects and, here too, the collaboration of the Sister Cities network is clear. Madison assisted the directiva of Arcatao with the purchase of buildings and equipment for various collectively run endeavors, including the café (*comedor*), bakery, and medical and dental clinics.[123] Funds from Madison and Spain went toward the construction of a new neighborhood (*colonia*) on the edge of town, where Arcataenses erected a church and dozens of houses that, in contrast to the temporary dwellings in which they had resided for years, sported walls of cement block and mortar as well as roofs of corrugated metal (*lámina*) and ceramic tile.[124] In Cinquera, Cabañas, repopulators rebuilt their church with assistance from a sister church in Kansas City, Missouri, and constructed a day care center with funds from their sister city of Chicago.[125] Las Anonas, San Vicente, received housing support throughout 1994 from the sister city committee in Philadelphia.[126] Similar projects occurred in repopulations across El Salvador, with villages making "enormous strides" in short time frames. Alice Vernier of Delaware observed in 1997 that housing in her sister city of Copapayo "had been vastly improved" since her previous visit in 1992, "with brick home construction and tile roofs [and a] new clinic and chapel had also been built. Each home now had its own water tap, outhouse, and would soon get electricity. These developments," Vernier concluded, "had made a major difference in the standard of living and the convenience of daily life."[127]

Many communities had postponed this type of development for years, "sacrific[ing] the funds that came earmarked for other projects" to ensure land purchases. El Higueral had done precisely this in order to protect subsistence farming projects already underway on occupied lands. Teosinte similarly diverted funds from at least three projects, including cattle raising, a pineapple plantation, and a day care center. And the Tremedal directiva reported years of "postponing their plans to build dignified housing, a community pharmacy, a stable for the livestock, and a system for processing animal feed until they knew with certainty where they would stay."[128]

As they purchased and gained legal title to land, repopulators turned attention beyond infrastructure projects to productive activities such as farming and small business ventures. In this realm, the Alternative Financial System, part of the New Initiative, played an important role. The system offered a rotational loan fund to which families and community groups could apply for support "for any kind of productive activity"—at just 12 percent interest (national banks then charged 18 percent interest to approved borrowers).[129] Within months of launching the program in Chalatenango in 1992, these loans supported the cultivation of more than 3,200 manzanas in twenty-three of the thirty-three municipalities, as well as cooperative business enterprises such as a "communal store that supplies all of the communal stores" in Cuscatlán and Cabañas, and a printing and silk-screening workshop (*taller de serigrafía*) run by women in Copapayo.[130] Through the Alternative Financial System communities also gained access to important technical and organizational development support. In Chalatenango, CORDES promoted the formation of Local Financial Committees, for example, and trained and advised community directivas in the management of loans.[131] In the departments of Cabañas and Cuscatlán, PROGRESO formed agrarian tech teams to assist with reforestation, the installation of irrigation systems, and the design and execution of pilot projects in organic agriculture; beekeeping; and dairy, poultry, hog, and fish farms.[132]

For rural activists, the alternative economic and development models were inseparable from the promotion of rights (*promoción de derechos*).[133] Economic, political, and social rights were all part of the same puzzle; the transition to peace would be unsuccessful without breaking down structures that perpetuated violence and building up new, more just structures. Thus, activists engaged in small and large ways to construct a commons—an alternative postconflict space where social and economic relations were more egalitarian. As they mobilized around land and related natural resources, communities also joined together to provide shelter, food, and other basic needs to orphans, widows, and people wounded by the conflict. They established programs to address the rights of women and girls. And rather than hire private companies to build concrete block houses and then sell the new houses on the open market, community leaders organized volunteer construction teams and then, via lotteries, granted the new buildings to people who put in labor.[134]

These alternative spaces were successful to a significant degree; although the levels of success were uneven across the country—and even within a particular community—many campesinos met their basic needs and also gained access to credit, technical support, training, and other resources, leading to improved capacities for making a living. As individuals, communities, and organizations, they purchased and acquired legal title to land, and invested in and developed what might be considered a diverse portfolio, mixing individual and collective land ownership and labor, and subsistence farming with small-scale commercial enterprises.

Pressures from multiple angles—long campaigns by community leaders, CRIPDES, CORDES, and other Salvadoran grassroots organizations, and their transnational networks, including Sister Cities—precipitated a series of small steps toward larger objectives. By September 1997 the Land Transfer Program, combined with completed phases of the 1980s land reform, had transferred 25.5 percent of the country's agricultural land, benefiting 23.6 percent of the total rural population of El Salvador, making it the second largest agrarian reform program implemented in Latin America.[135] And the rural repopulation movement had proven, in myriad ways, the viability of their alternative structures.

Promoting the Agricultural Sector

Even as rural Salvadorans celebrated new legal titles to the land they had physically conquered through the repopulation movement, other concerns surfaced. Chief among these concerns were debt and attacks on their communal principles, both of which activists directly linked to the neoliberal agenda forwarded by the governing ARENA party. As described earlier in this chapter, repopulators and many observers at the time interpreted the Salvadoran government's actions during the transition period, including the creation of the National Reconstruction Plan, within the framework of neoliberal economics that emphasized market-oriented reforms, including structural adjustment programs. These programs, encouraged by international financial institutions such as the World Bank, promoted liberalization of trade relations and increased foreign investment, along with privatization of state enterprises and deep cuts in spending on social programs. In contrast, the repopulators and their representative organizations promoted alternative systems—ones that depended on local rather than foreign resources and emphasized collective well-being over individual accumulation. As these two visions for the future of El Salvador rubbed against each other in the 1990s and into the new millennium, repopulators and their allies diligently defended the small gains they had achieved in their move toward a more equitable society. They backed the agrarian sectors that had benefited from the recent Land Transfer Program and worked to define new policies that would bring further benefits to the country's campesinos. In the neoliberal context of El Salvador's transition, however, some advances could prove to be a double-edged sword.

As the introduction to this chapter noted, government representatives ensured that the peace accords bypassed socioeconomic issues. They punted any discussion of the country's social and economic development instead to the proposed Social and Economic Forum, made up of delegates from the government, labor, and business sectors. Notably absent from the membership lists were the campesino-repopulators. Critics explained that Salvadoran officials rejected giving voice to any of the groups that had experience in former conflict zones, believing that to do so would "fortify the political power of the FMLN in the countryside."[136] Dismissing repopulations as "ghost towns" allowed officials to imagine the absence of organized opposition and, thus, more easily press forward with their own agenda.

Toward this end, during the first half of the 1990s, the Salvadoran government designed a new agrarian policy. The policy was part of a broader move, set in concert with international financial institutions, "to push a neoliberal model of economic adjustment."[137] The World Bank played an especially prominent role in this process through a number of loans, including the Agricultural Sector Reform and Investment Project (Proyecto de Reforma e Inversión Sectorial Agropecuaria), approved in 1994 for $56.5 million, and structural adjustment loans with recommended objectives that included "consolidate and restructure the agrarian debt" and "stimulate the land market."[138] Although the United States maintained a presence, providing economic aid and helping Salvadoran officials define priorities, the World Bank was paramount during this transition period, according to Salvadoran economist Alexander Segovia, "substituting for the role USAID had previously played in directing and supervising the Salvadoran economy in the 1980s."[139]

Like the government's National Reconstruction Plan, much of the new agrarian and economic policies developed behind closed doors, but the Salvadoran public had become increasingly attuned to the situation. When in early 1996 officials unveiled "a project for the partial forgiveness of the debt, accompanied by the 'privatization' of the remaining debt," many agriculturalists rose in protest against the new plan.[140] Repopulators helped lead the charge, spurred by deep concerns about debt. By that point, according to one account, the total debt had reached $400 million, with Land Transfer Program beneficiaries each owing an average of $2,224.[141] Two years earlier, activists with SHARE already had deemed the debt "essentially unpayable" for campesinos, a "dead weight on their shoulders."[142] Residents of the new Colonia Jesús Rojas in Arcatao, for example, shared with a Sister Cities delegation their "major concern" regarding repaying the money they had borrowed to purchase the neighborhood's sixty-six-plus manzanas. Because "people have only been able to survive on what they've cultivated," delegates reported, "there is very little extra to pay off the debt. If people cannot pay off the loans, the land will revert back to the bank."[143] Similar concerns, shared by campesinos in repopulated communities across rural El Salvador, prompted "growing fears that large-scale foreclosures would recreate the extreme concentration of land that gave rise to the war."[144]

Many communities, distrusting the government agencies and perhaps foreseeing these risks, made the conscious choice to *not* engage with state loan offices, instead "buying the land outright," often with help from Sister Cities, other solidarity groups, and remittances from Salvadorans who had found work

This Promised Land

abroad.[145] A report prepared by Boston area Sister Cities committees in late 1994 described how residents of Teosinte, after finagling for more than one year with a distant landowner and agents at the Land Bank, decided to forego their planned move to new territory and instead stay where they were and "try to . . . acquire more land in the immediate area." The report pointed out that residents "also decided that they were unwilling to take loans from the Land Bank to pay for these lands." The peace accords stipulated that land transfer beneficiaries had thirty years to repay their loan at 6 percent interest, but Teosinte's subsistence farmers "did not feel confident that they would ever have that much money at their disposal." This feeling deepened with the bank's inflated assessment of the land; whereas Land Bank officials assessed the land at ₡8,000 per manzana, locals estimated each manzana was worth ₡2,000. What good was a program for debt forgiveness if it only led to more debt? In the words of a member of the Teosinte directiva, "The Bank's programs won't help the campesino class. They will just make the rich richer." In this context, buying as much land as possible outright, as Teosinte and many other communities did, would help those communities "avoid the debt trap" to some extent.[146]

If the Salvadoran government's economic and agrarian policies produced a new debt trap, according to repopulators, they also represented a coordinated attack on the communal way of life that displaced campesinos had developed over the course of more than a decade. This, too, linked to the land question, because many repopulated communities had resettled lands as a group, collectively clearing and working agricultural plots and subsequently seeking collective title to the land. Recent Salvadoran law guaranteed the right to collective ownership of land. The 1980 Agrarian Reform Law (Decree 154, Article 1:3) provided for "private property within a communal framework" and stipulated the expropriation of landholdings in excess of five hundred hectares for conversion into agricultural cooperatives, and the 1992 Land Transfer Program included a form of land titling known as *pro indiviso*, through which "multiple beneficiaries signed a single title for a property large enough to provide each with the equivalent of approximately three hectares of good agricultural land."[147] This land titling concept came out of pressures by the FMLN, which had fomented collective organizing in the zones under its control "because it wanted to give the beneficiaries the option of deciding what form of production they adopted." With cooperatives and collective farming as legal possibilities, repopulators and other organized communities could continue to strengthen their communal principles. A well-developed sense of community, Salvadoran National Assembly Deputy Roberto Lorenzana explained in 1998, "would not only generate political strength but also lay the foundation for providing communal social services such as schools and healthcare."[148]

Although the pro indiviso concept was no panacea—according to one analyst, it was "fraught with problems"—it was a postconflict tool that repopulators and their allies could use to further press authorities on socioeconomic issues.[149] Armed with these legal tools, grassroots activists framed the Salvadoran government's restructuring efforts of the mid-1990s as a violation of the campesinos' rights. Several reforms, including Decrees 14, 698, 699, and 719, they argued, overtly discriminated against the campesinos who had benefited from the 1980 reform and the Land Transfer Program by placing rules and limits on cooperatives but not on other sectors; by offering benefits and breaks to individuals only (i.e., excluding cooperatives); and by providing higher discounts and subsidies to the owners of larger properties.[150] This was part of "a systematic attempt" to induce campesinos to sell, explained Pedro Juan Hernández, a Salvadoran economist associated with CRIPDES, "generating a process of selective reconcentration of land." Far from trying to reactivate the agrarian sector as purported, he continued, the government reforms "intend to favor the sale of land to people who will not put it to agricultural use" but who instead have other intentions including tourism and factory construction. This economic restructuring thus aimed toward "strengthening the financial sector, the commercial sector, and the service sector," while "displacing campesinos from their land" and "putting at risk the food security of the entire country."[151] That the government's reforms brought uneven benefits was more than evident in the numbers: between 1994 and 1997, the average growth rate of the financial sector was 14.6 percent, contrasted to less than 1 percent for the agricultural sector.[152] Such numbers linked to a major shift in the makeup of the Salvadoran business elite (from agricultural exporters to financiers) during the conflict as well as to a general postwar devaluation of agriculture.

As rural activists pressed the Salvadoran government to comply with the peace accords and fully implement the Land Transfer Program, they also took action against the reforms they considered disadvantageous and worked to influence the creation of policies more favorable to the campesino sector. Much of this work took place through the National Forum for the Defense and Recovery of the Agrarian Sector (Foro Nacional para la Defensa y Recuperación del Sector Agropecuario), a broad-based coalition formalized in 1995, which boasted forty-two member organizations by 1998. The Secretariat of Agrarian Affairs of the FMLN provided leadership, and CRIPDES and CORDES were key players in the Foro.[153]

According to a Foro strategy document, members countered the Salvadoran government's approach and methods by employing "a methodology of consultation and participation with the diverse Salvadoran agricultural sectors linked to peasant and cooperative organizations" to develop tactics and proposals for "rural development that have agricultural activities at their core, but that remain connected to the diverse aspects of the real world." This latter statement directly linked with the objectives of many of the member organizations, including CORDES, CRIPDES, and affiliated regional offices. In contrast to the Salvadoran government's National Reconstruction Plan and related economic policies, members of the Forum "have opted for the third way, which implies a commitment to these three components that are critical to development . . . gender equity, democracy, and sustainable economic growth."[154]

As part of their action orientation, the Foro focused on the debt issue, holding consultations with its member base to design possible solutions that would stimulate rather than condemn the nation's agriculturalists. They designed proposals, presented them to government entities, and loudly complained when officials ignored them. In March 1996, for example, Foro members presented the Legislative Assembly a draft law (*anteproyecto de ley*) titled "Agrarian Sector Reactivation Law" (Ley para la Reactivación del Sector Agropecuario). Nine months later, Foro leaders informed the UN Secretary-General's Special Representative to El Salvador, Álvaro de Soto, that although they had submitted the draft law before officials discussed what ultimately became Decrees 698 and 699, "the Legislative Assembly did not take the proposal under consideration, which translated into them not addressing the problem of the peasant woman head of household, the war wounded and disabled, seniors," and other critical populations.[155] The letter to de Soto went on to denounce their exclusion from the discussions on policy that directly affected them. Foro leaders decried that "the government of El Salvador has done nothing to comply" with agreements on debt relief "and far from it, it has refused to discuss this issue and others related to the Agrarian Policy that it is forwarding at this time."[156]

While activists pressured UN officials like de Soto, they also kept issues in the public eye within El Salvador. The Foro strategically used the media to make the "debt issue a matter of widespread public knowledge." According to the sociologist Lisa Kowalchuk, such sustained media work helped make debt cancellation a major issue during the 1997 election campaign season.[157] In addition, the Foro, on its own and in collaboration with other groups, organized marches and demonstrations to accompany the delivery of proposals to government offices. On the eve of presidential elections in March 1997, for example, an estimated forty thousand campesinos presented a proposal for total debt forgiveness. This was followed by at least four other demonstrations, including an especially large one in July, when activists presented a revised version of their debt-cancellation proposal. Along with the Foro, other groups, including the Democratic Campesino Alliance (ADC), ex-combatants, and former civil patrol members, organized their own petitions, marches, and land occupations.

"Total Forgiveness for Agrarian Debt!" Detail from CRIPDES *Communal Organization* civic education manual, ca. 1993. (CRIPDES Archive)

Although these various groups had contentious relationships—particularly the ADC and the Foro—their combined pressures magnified the issue and ultimately produced results.[158]

Through all these endeavors, rural activists associated with CRIPDES, CORDES, and their regional entities called upon their solidarity networks. Salvadorans informed their US-based Sister Cities allies about their main demands on the Salvadoran state, including complete forgiveness on land debt, "revision of the land tenure system," and the creation of "agricultural/ economic policies to reverse the trend to push peasants off the land." The US Americans responded, as they did with the Land Transfer Program, by exerting pressure on US and Salvadoran authorities. "Political Accompaniment," explained the Cambridge sistering committee, involved "lobbying our congressional representatives to put pressure on the U.S. Embassy and AID in El Salvador to support a new agricultural policy that gives poor peasants an opportunity to develop the land; and pressuring the Salvadoran government directly to insist that they implement a new agricultural policy that should be determined through negotiations with civil society."[159]

One example of high-level lobbying is a letter to President Bill Clinton on his visit to Central America in February 1999. The timing of this visit—three weeks before El Salvador's presidential election—was "no coincidence," according to US-based activists. Because the policies of Clinton and ARENA mirrored each other, activists presumed that Clinton planned to use his visit "to advocate 'Free Trade' and the global neoliberal economic model." Moreover, because activists on the left in El Salvador "must be very careful not to voice a strong anti-U.S. position, for fear that the public/electorate will be scared of the consequences of U.S. opposition to a local alternative government," the US-based activists had an important role to play: "WE MUST HOLD OUR PRESIDENT ACCOUNTABLE DURING HIS VISIT." Toward this end, Sister Cities and CISPES prepared a letter for the US president in which they made a series of explicit demands, among them that he express to Salvadoran and other leaders that "the US will work to guarantee that organized constituencies of civil society be brought into the policy making process around issues of economic development in the region." Specifically, they called for "the inclusion of organized small farmers and cooperatives in the planning of regional agrarian policies."[160]

Around this same time, US-based activists also launched a national campaign to pressure Armando Calderón Sol, the Salvadoran president, to allow debt-relief laws to move forward. The campaign stemmed from the opinion of Salvadoran activists involved with the agricultural Foro that such pressure was important in light of the fact that "the President's office and ARENA have continually argued against debt forgiveness, with great pressure from the county's bankers who oppose it vehemently."[161] Calderón Sol had made his opposition strikingly clear in late 1997 when the Special Law for the Extinction of Debts and the Reactivation of the Agricultural Sector came across his desk. The legislation promised to "improve the lives of more than half a million people" in El Salvador by erasing 100 percent of the first ₡500,000 (approximately $60,000) of all debts and accrued interest, and requiring repayment of only 7 percent of amounts owed above ₡500,000 (with a favorable refinancing option).[162] In light of its promise, the bill passed with multipartisan support in the Legislative Assembly. Calderón Sol vetoed it.

A little more than a year later, in early 1999, when the assembly passed a new "Law for the Rendering of Accounts and Compensation for Damages of the State in Favor of the Agricultural Sector," fears were high that Calderón Sol would again issue a veto.[163] As Calderón Sol, ARENA, and their backers wrangled with deputies in the Legislative Assembly and Salvadoran activists over the debt issue, Sister Cities activists rained faxes on the president's office. Many of these communications followed a model letter prepared by Barbara Alvarado of the Madison–Arcatao Sister City Project. "The agrarian sector is the home to over 50 percent of your people and provides food for all Salvadorans," Alvarado reminded Calderón Sol. "But in light of recent events," including war, violent storms, and economic crises, "much of their hard work as farmers has been lost." Alvarado continued, "Our brothers and sisters have told us how they desperately need support to have their debts, accrued through no fault of their own and in spite of their hard work, forgiven and access to credits granted so they can work their land." It was in this context, Alvarado concluded, that "we write to ask you to N O T veto the recently passed Law for the Rendering of Accounts and Compensation for Damages of the State in Favor of the Agricultural Sector."[164]

As Sister Cities activists mobilized around the issue of agrarian debt, they also included international financial institutions, and in particular the World Bank, among their advocacy targets. The first political accompaniment commitment listed on a Cambridge–San José Las Flores Sister City Project flier from early 1998, in fact, was "pressuring the World Bank to stop insisting that the Salvadoran government implement an economic plan which discourages development in the countryside."[165] Targeting the World Bank and other such entities responded again to the needs expressed by their Salvadoran partners. Minutes from the 1998 meeting of the US–El Salvador Sister Cities network in New York City offer insights into these exchanges. Salvadorans, via the agricultural Foro, "are increasingly clear that in spite of the awesome task it implies, the multilateral institutions are key players in this debate. They are also clear that it is the fundamental issue in terms of their future development." Based on the

Salvadorans' increasing attention to these financial institutions, participants in the meeting formalized the following advocacy objective regarding agrarian policy: "To hold the World Bank accountable for its role in the development of El Salvador's rural economic and social policy."[166]

Even their lobbying of US officials illustrates this approach. In the wake of the devastating Hurricane Mitch, which pummeled Central America in late October and early November 1998, international lenders organized a special meeting to discuss aid to the affected areas. Sister Cities joined other Central America solidarity groups to exert pressure on the US officials who would attend the talks. In a lengthy letter to the head of the US delegation, solidarity coalition leaders, including the USAID administrator Brian Atwood, boldly argued that any pledges of relief aid to arise from the meeting, "although extremely important for hurricane victims, will be rendered meaningless unless accompanied by complete and unconditional cancellation of these countries' foreign debts." The letter continued on to task the United States, "as the host of the meeting and the most influential player in making such decisions, [to] take the lead in urging cancellation of these debts." The letter went even further, warning against conditioning any aid on Central American pledges "to adhere to several additional years of strict structural adjustment policies," a reference to provisos attached to loans from the World Bank, the International Monetary Fund, the Inter-American Development Bank, and other agencies. "It is precisely these policies," the activists explained, "that were responsible for the decimation of these countries' social services and infrastructure before the hurricane hit." The letter concluded by echoing what Salvadoran rural activists had been saying for the better part of a decade: "Effective and sustainable reconstruction of the region is simply not possible within the context of increased austerity."[167] When Michael Ring, a US–El Salvador Sister Cities staffer, forwarded a copy of the Atwood letter to sistering committees in the United States, he also offered these two "immediate action" tasks: call elected officials urging "Mitch Reconstruction aid, debt forgiveness and relief from Structural Adjustment policies"; and call Jan Piercy at the World Bank to inquire about the Bank's plans on reconstruction.[168]

Between 1997 and 1999, a series of Legislative Assembly debates and votes, revised proposals, and policy adjustments made debt forgiveness a reality. Provisions included 100 percent debt relief for some sectors of Salvadoran society, including beneficiaries of the Land Transfer Program. As with the Land Transfer Program, US American and Salvadoran activists perceived the new laws to be a direct result of grassroots efforts. Celebrations began as early as January 1997 when CRIPDES obtained documentation of "an agreement between the Salvadoran government and USAID in which the government agrees to forgive the debt and AID agrees to finance this debt forgiveness." Although the agreement had not been formalized at that point and Salvadoran officials would, in any case, keep mum about it until after the March elections, Michael Ring of Sister Cities offered due credit. In a letter to sistering committees, he reported that the struggle carried out through the previous year by the communities through CRIPDES, the agricultural Foro, and solidarity "has paid off." Moreover, USAID's role in the expected solution "is in part due to our activities."[169] In a similar vein, when a new joint subcommission of the Legislative Assembly invited input from stakeholders regarding the debt situation in June 1997, El Salvador's rural activists celebrated this as a victory in their ongoing struggle to influence the agrarian policy-making process.[170] Two years later, in a December 1998 letter to Sister Cities committees, the tone of Ring's letter was even more celebratory, lauding the "historic victory of our Sister Cities communities and sister organizations CRIPDES and FORO AGROPECUARIO in gaining debt forgiveness of MILLIONS of dollars for HUNDREDS OF THOUSANDS of Salvadoran peasants. This unprecedented popular victory in Latin America, won in spite of powerful World Bank and in-country bank lobbying against it, has temporarily ensured that families throughout El Salvador will not lose lands won at great sacrifice!"[171]

Ring's point about the Salvadoran families' temporary security cannot be ignored. Nor can the fact that neither the provisions of the Land Transfer Program nor the debt-forgiveness laws implemented in El Salvador during the 1990s was a panacea; they were unevenly applied and excluded significant sectors of society, such as agricultural cooperatives and beneficiaries of the stalled 1980 Agrarian Reform. The incomplete nature of key postwar transitions compelled rural activists with CRIPDES, the agricultural Foro, and other groups to continue their struggles to remain in control of their land, to gain access to credit, and to participate in policy-making processes. Sister Cities activists, as always, accompanied these efforts.[172]

A great deal of the repopulators' efforts involved bypassing Salvadoran government programs even as activists pressed the government to comply with the accords and subsequent agreements and laws. Many opted to not wait for the Land Bank to complete its terrifically slow processing, instead setting up autonomous mechanisms of funding and development. There is no question that this was empowering in many ways and led to the acquisition of land and legal titles to it, along with access to credit. But the bypass mode also proved problematic. On a practical level, the work of directivas and regional organizations like the CCR and CORDES led to a series of discrete and typically unconnected projects. For example, with assistance from Sister Cities and other solidarity networks, community leaders established much-needed potable water systems in repopulated villages, yet those systems did not share common infrastructure. This led to structural and systemic challenges as well as resource-related tensions between communities at local and regional levels. On a more ideological level, over time the bypass mode reduced pressure on the Salvadoran state to comply with agreements and to provide constitutionally mandated services to rural communities. This, in turn, deepened the neoliberal tendrils in El Salvador, sluffed off state duties to nongovernmental organizations, and made it more difficult for activists and politicians on the left to block the ARENA government's plans to privatize services, including health care, education, and water.[173]

A Dignified Life

When defending their right to make a living off the land, Salvadoran repopulators often framed their arguments in economic terms. Yet their conception of this right was not exclusively economic; it was intimately connected to sociocultural concerns. The New Initiative made this connection clear; its holistic development (*desarrollo integral*) highlighted the multilayered nature of a dignified life. One layer entailed campesinos meeting their basic needs for food and shelter via legal access to land. Another layer involved building and sustaining healthy and strong rural communities through the provision of critical social services, including health care and education.

Activists associated with the rural repopulation movement perceived land and social services in the same way, as public goods to which they had rights, as citizens of El Salvador, per the national Constitution. They mobilized their networks to press Salvadoran officials to change the government's old patterns of marginalization and exclusion by providing public services as prescribed by law—and by acknowledging and collaborating with grassroots professionals in the process. By coordinating with grassroots leaders in education and health care, state agents would not only begin to right past wrongs; they would also comply with their constitutional duties. State and grassroots representatives had fundamentally different views about both the theory and the application of such services, however. This led to contentious negotiations between representatives of "officialist" and "popular" systems through the 1990s.

From the perspective of the rural activists, the Salvadoran state historically had failed to provide for its citizens, contributing to the inequities that ultimately led the country down the road to violent conflict. War exacerbated an already dire situation. As violence increased in the late 1970s and early 1980s, government entities, including the Ministries of Education and Health, pulled out of rural conflict zones. By late 1986, activists explained in an open letter to the US government, shared through international solidarity networks, the Salvadoran government had completely abandoned the people. "This year," they wrote, "the health budget was reduced to 145 million colones whilst the military budget was raised to 70 million colones, equivalent to 14 million U.S. dollars. Meanwhile military matters have been prioritized and nutrition and health ignored." The report's authors went on to cite grievous "official statistics" indicating that infant mortality rose sharply over the previous two years and that "malnutrition in children under 5 hit 74% in 1985." The authors framed this inattention as a violation of human rights, as indicated by the title given to their report: "Peace and Human Rights."[174]

The government's withdrawal from rural areas created a power vacuum. Campesinos and their allies moved to fill it. Some took it upon themselves to employ the traditional medicinal and herbalist practices of their elders, for example. A few who had attended school for a while taught others their letters and numbers. In territories under FMLN control, insurgents sponsored these endeavors, often providing the impetus for organizing services, along with resources and training for the volunteers. For example, by 1983 the Local Popular Governments, in collaboration with the Popular Liberation Forces (FPL), had created a grassroots health system in northeastern Chalatenango. According to José Antonio Mejía of Las Vueltas, men and women who had gained paramedic and nursing experience in FMLN field hospitals trained local health promoters (*promotores de salúd*) in preventive and curative care; these, in turn, "managed first aid kits and kept a register of patients, injuries, and illnesses in the community." The promotores, in short, used "popular medicine" to provide "simple cures, ensuring that each village at least had the basics."[175] In a similar vein, many Salvadorans living in camps for displaced persons and refugees had the opportunity to collaborate with international aid and solidarity workers, gaining new skills related to first aid, nutrition, prenatal and postnatal care, educational pedagogy, and other areas.

Leaders of the rural repopulation movement built on these experiences and integrated their transnational support networks as they established and formalized grassroots service systems in the repopulated communities. In Arcatao, for example, health promoters and directiva members requested and received significant support from Madison for its clinic, which for many years had provided the only health services to civilians in the surrounding areas. Records of Medical Aid to Central America (MACA), one of the incubators of the Madison sistering committee, illustrate repeated positive responses to proposals from Arcatao for cash assistance, medical supplies, and other materials. Madison also helped the clinic expand to meet new needs in preparation for the arrival of one thousand new residents with the first mass return from the Mesa Grande refugee camp in October 1987. The vast majority of this support arrived to the clinic in suitcases and boxes hauled by delegations.[176]

The Cambridge sistering committee supported similar initiatives in San José Las Flores. A June 1988 delegation of nurses, physicians, and health planners, for example, delivered medical supplies, provided clinical and didactic training for local health promoters, and assisted with a community health assessment. These professionals found in Las Flores "an organized community attempting to improve health conditions through the implementation of public health, preventive, and curative measures under extremely difficult circumstances."[177]

In their public communications, the Cambridge, Madison, and other sistering groups highlighted how popular health workers provided much-needed care in regions where the Salvadoran government and military intentionally targeted the civilian population. According to the 1988 Cambridge delegation, health promoters in Las Flores understood that the most pressing health problems in the village, including malnutrition and diarrheal morbidity, could be addressed relatively easily, but the Salvadoran military refused to allow delivery of necessary supplies, including powdered milk for the children and concrete for the construction of latrines. Such denial, delegates charged, "directly implicates the Salvadoran Armed Forces in the etiology of childhood malnutrition" and disease in the village. "The greatest concern raised by this study," they concluded, "is the past and ongoing conduct of the Armed Forces of El Salvador. Reports of [the military] blockade of shipments of food and medicine, and the restriction of access of health care personnel, raise serious questions regarding potential violation of the Geneva Conventions (to which the government of El Salvador is a signatory), that guarantees the right of civilian populations to receive medical care in times of war."[178]

Over time and with the support of their transnational sistering allies, rural Salvadorans established intricate self-governance systems with many committees dedicated to health care, education, and other social services. Activists referred to these as "popular" systems not solely because they stood in for absent state systems; these were programs of and by and for the people that addressed real needs. For these reasons, the popular systems gained high social legitimacy and produced concrete results.

The popular systems were highly successful. At refuge sites in and outside the country, observers reported that literacy levels rose remarkably in a very short time.[179] These levels continued to rise in the repopulated communities, with popular educators drawing from new resources, including regional networks and, after 1993, the national Educational Consultative Group of El Salvador (Concertación Educativa de El Salvador), which "provide[d] a forum for

Health promoters at the Martin Luther King Clinic, Arcatao, Chalatenango, mid-1989.
(photo by Marc Rosenthal, Rosenthal Papers, USESSC Archive)

unification" of popular educators across the country's fourteen departments.[180]
By the second decade of the new millennium, many mayors in the repopulated zones declared their municipalities "illiteracy free"—a feat grounded in
the repopulators' long history of popular education.[181]

Popular health programs proved similarly powerful. The anthropologist
Sandy Smith-Nonini, who examined El Salvador's popular health system in
detail, reported that the "popular system has been effective in reducing morbidity and educating peasant families on preventive health." In one repopulated community in Chalatenango, she tracked "consistent drops in incidents
of cases of diarrhea, malaria, conjunctivitis and skin infections during a period
when the clinic population was growing steadily." On a broader scale, Smith-
Nonini found that by 1989, vaccination coverage for diseases such as polio,
measles, and pertussis reached 85 percent in FMLN-controlled territory—
precisely where the popular health promoters worked—compared with only
58 percent coverage in government-held territory. The success of the popular
health care system was now visible in clinic and vaccination campaign records;
health professionals visiting from other countries also noted the difference.

According to Smith-Nonini, these foreign visitors "report that the *repopulated villages of former refugees in the ex-war zone seem to be healthier than peasants in government-controlled areas of Chalatenango.*"[182] These programs also received acknowledgment from the Pan American Health Organization (PAHO), which worked closely with Salvadoran officials during the transition period. In October 1992, during a series of negotiations between the state and popular health workers, a PAHO representative spoke enthusiastically about the popular system. Smith-Nonini, who was present, described how the representative "remarked to the group that the popular system had essentially put into practice what the ministry administrator had presented as theory. 'What is beautiful here is that we have [an application of the model]. We have a community base—the most difficult thing to achieve. . . . It's a great opportunity for the ministry!'"[183]

Grassroots activists agreed; they believed that the popular systems were viable alternative models, which could be replicated on a national scale. They already had experienced significant expansion, with continued success. What began on a small, local scale had expanded to regional levels as CRIPDES, in the latter half of the 1980s, introduced popular health and education programs to those rural communities that were not part of the repopulation movement, and formed regional coordinating bodies for health and education efforts.[184] In 1991, as peace talks proceeded, CRIPDES, CNR, and CORDES expanded to the national level with the inauguration of the Santa María Madre de los Pobres Medical Center. The Center expanded a one-room clinic that CRIPDES had begun operating in 1989 out of its San Salvador headquarters, offering additional support for the popular health workers in the repopulated communities. More specifically, the Center specialized in the treatment of "cases of illness that cannot be addressed in the communities."[185] The next step would be to duplicate these models in other rural communities and urban sites.

Activists promoted the popular systems as viable alternative models that promised to transform Salvadoran society. The popular systems offered more than basic public services: in the past, education and health care were available only for the wealthy, but now the popular systems began to address historic inequities and disparities. Activists pointed out that the Constitution of El Salvador obligated the Salvadoran government to provide certain public services; they justified their own actions within that context, as CRIPDES and colleagues did in a 1991 report on the opening of their new Medical Center in San Salvador. Citing the Constitution, the report declared that "the health of the inhabitants of the Republic is a public good" and that state agents "are obligated to oversee its preservation and recovery" and "to provide free care for sick people who lack resources, and to the broader population."[186] The state was not doing so, and the great needs of the people compelled grassroots groups and nongovernmental organizations into action.

The Medical Center and the entire system of popular services also modeled appropriate services—that is, programs that addressed the needs of a specific community of people based on their own lived reality. In essence, the popular systems provided poor citizens powerful tools for self-care. The capacity to defend themselves against abuse by employers or land agents, for example, rested on their ability to read and write. Good health likewise depended on their access to information and resources. For this reason, popular systems went beyond the superficial to address the true causes of poverty and disease: structural inequalities. Rather than solely focus on treatment of illnesses and rehabilitation after injury, the popular health care system emphasized "integral health" and the "whole person." Key to this approach was prevention. With information and resources—how and why to sterilize water for drinking, for example, or to use netting to protect sleeping spaces from disease-carrying mosquitoes—campesinos could significantly cut down or even eradicate many diseases, including dysentery, cholera, dengue fever, and chronic diarrhea.[187] When people were able to access and use new resources to care for themselves, activists contended, they became more productive citizens, better able to contribute to the greater good.

As health promoters, teachers, and other grassroots professionals formed and expanded the popular systems, they acted as "social change agents."[188] With their allies in the politico-military organizations of the FMLN, Salvadoran social movements, and transnational solidarity networks, they acted with an eye toward both present and future. "It is necessary to take steps to mitigate today's sufferings and set the foundations for a more prosperous future when peace arrives," explained CRIPDES-CNR upon the opening of the new medical clinic in 1991. The clinic did precisely this by offering "an alternative in health care," which, combined with other examples of "alternative socioeconomic models, [will] supersede the government's neoliberal model," "guarantee . . . human rights in El Salvador," and "effectively contribute to the construction of a new society."[189]

Had the FMLN coalition forces taken power of the state apparatus as their contemporaries did in Nicaragua, it is probable that they would have taken additional advantage of the opportunity to implement a version of the popular systems on a national level. But, as mentioned earlier in this chapter, the negotiated resolution to the Salvadoran conflict elided many socioeconomic aspects; the peace accords outlined how to dismantle repressive state forces and construct a new civilian police force, for example, but did not develop similar plans for education, health care, or other social services. In this context it is not surprising that government officials and grassroots activists held differing views of the popular systems. Whereas for grassroots activists and their allies and many observers at the time, popular systems represented an opportunity worthy of support and expansion, Salvadoran officials, steeped in years of ideological and military conflict, associated "popular" with "subversive." From this latter perspective, the popular systems represented a challenge to the state's political power and modernization efforts, both of which were closely connected to the Salvadoran private sector and, increasingly, international business elites. Because of this, throughout the transition period, state agents dismissed the popular professionals and their grassroots systems while working to reestablish government authority in rural areas through the Ministries of Health and Education, and other entities.

From the grassroots perspective, state agents worked to reinvigorate old structures of domination but with a new, neoliberal twist. The economic reforms promoted by the governing ARENA party led to the privatization of industries and services, activists pointed out. Although government officials and business elites argued that the free market would result in the best possible services, activists with CRIPDES and other organizations maintained that such services were "a right of the people" and that ARENA had violated that right by implementing programs through which services like health care were "converted into a commercial object, exclusive to those who have the economic resources to acquire it."[190]

Instead, grassroots activists promoted an alternative, holistic program of services through the popular systems. Yet given El Salvador's unique transition context, activists recognized a need for collaboration with the state. To gain access to necessary resources and ensure the longevity of services, popular teachers and health promoters needed to engage with government ministries. For this reason, they presented a variety of proposals to state entities that framed the popular systems as complementary to, rather than separate from, existing public programs. According to CRIPDES and colleagues, the objective of the new medical clinic, for example, was "not to replace state medical services, but rather to complement them, thereby seeking more efficient and effective attention for the poor people of El Salvador."[191] If the alternative models could not yet replace state programs, activists believed they could at least reform those programs.

Toward this end, Salvadoran activists and their transnational allies launched new struggles to have the state formally acknowledge and legally recognize the popular systems they had developed during the years of conflict and displacement. One of the "primary issues" facing Arcatao and other repopulated villages in northeastern Chalatenango in July 1995—three years after the peace accords— was the legalization of popular educators and teachers. A delegation from Madison reported that local activists were "trying to obtain from the Ministry of

Education certification to teach, and funding for their wages and support for the schools." At that time the schools received no support from the state; they operated with funds from Catholic dioceses, the Central American University, and nongovernmental organizations. Moreover, delegates explained, the Salvadoran Ministry of Education "is not recognizing the popular educators as teachers, but are [*sic*] recognizing the education that the students are receiving." According to popular teachers, students received a certificate of completion at the end of each grade; with that certification, when students transferred to a Ministry of Education school, they often advanced one or two grades. This offered ample evidence that the popular teachers were skilled instructors who prepared students well. Grassroots activists demanded that the Salvadoran state recognize them as such.[192]

The health promoters waged a parallel struggle. Similar to the process of negotiations between community directivas and the mayors in exile, popular health professionals sought "recognition and minimal salaries for the promoters"—in essence, a power-sharing agreement. But, as Smith-Nonini observed, such demands simply "were not on the ministry's agenda."[193] Officials from the Salvadoran Ministry of Health preferred a more Western, doctor-focused approach to health care, and as part of this program they began assigning doctors to rural regions. From the perspective of grassroots activists, however, this was an imposition—a return to prewar practices. By appointing outside doctors—without consulting community leaders—they intentionally sidelined popular health workers and fomented dependency, discord, and inequities among rural inhabitants. This, in turn, facilitated additional neoliberal reforms—to the detriment of the people and nation of El Salvador. Instead, health promoters insisted that the state recognize local practices and needs—as defined by locals themselves. It was critical, they argued, for insiders—popular health workers and community members—to take center stage in the postwar health system. Ultimately, medical doctors should be from the communities they served. Until that was possible, community members should have a say in deciding which doctors would serve them; these doctors would not replace local professionals but work alongside them.[194]

In short, grassroots activists presented their popular systems as a corrective to the old state systems. Whereas the Salvadoran government's education and health systems were centralized and paternalistic in nature, the popular systems engaged citizens in the planning, execution, and assessment stages, and emphasized the horizontal transfer of information, knowledge, and skills. By recognizing the viability of the alternative, integral approach represented by the popular systems, state representatives would begin to right past wrongs and help move the nation toward a more just and equitable future.

As with the Land Transfer Program and debt-forgiveness campaigns, popular professionals and their allies engaged with state officials in years of negotiation and, when necessary, took direct action to work around state obstructions. To compensate for the marginalization of popular health workers and teachers by the Ministries of Health and Education, for example, CRIPDES and other organizations drew on their alternative grassroots and transnational solidarity networks to coordinate professional development workshops.[195] At strategic moments in negotiations, activists and their allies raised their voices in public protests: paid denunciations in the news media, strikes, marches, demonstrations, and, in a uniquely audacious moment, blockading the government's mobile medical caravans.[196]

With time, Salvadoran activists associated with the rural repopulation movement contributed to the development of a kind of hybrid system of social services. These were neither a total imposition of the state nor a total grassroots victory but a bit of both. And while the activists' efforts had real impacts on local clinics and schools, so too did they influence national level negotiations and mobilizations. Building on the popular health professionals' struggles, Smith-Nonini explains, "advocacy for health reform bec[ame] the face of national resistance" by the early 2000s.[197] Responding to the government's push to privatize the health sector, community activists, grassroots organizations, and health care workers from around the country poured into the streets of San Salvador in a series of "White Marches" in late 2003—so called in recognition of the participants' choice to wear white "to show solidarity with the typically white-garbed medical profession and as a symbol of peace."[198] These actions—some involving an estimated two hundred thousand people—marked the largest public protests in the country since the early 1980s. Aimed in large part at supporting a legislative decree to prohibit privatization of health care in El Salvador, they were a kind of culmination of activist efforts dating back to 1992, when World Bank and International Monetary Fund loans to the Salvadoran government came with pressures to implement structural adjustment policies, including privatization of services. "Just as human rights advocacy articulated a resistance based on humanitarian narratives during the war, the White Marches demonstrated the potential power of solidarity around basic needs and the assertion of moral order as counterpoint to the politics of exclusion" for the postwar era.[199]

Negotiated Local Revolutions

The White Marches of 2003 attracted serious media coverage within and beyond El Salvador, with reporters often drawing parallels with the war era. Even those of us who did not live the war in person could feel the eerie similarities. I was living in El Salvador at the time, just down the street from the Sister Cities and CRIPDES offices. When President Francisco Flores (ARENA party) called out the military to quell the unrest, tanks appeared on the street in front of my apartment, and soldiers fired tear gas and rubber bullets into the crowds. Leslie Schuld, director of the Center for Exchange and Solidarity (CIS) and my former housemate, reported that "People wearing white were taken off the buses, searched, intimidated and threatened, in a style reminiscent of the violent era of the 1970s and '80s."[200] My doctor friend feared for his life as did my white-garbed colleagues and friends at Sister Cities and CRIPDES.

That the White Marches occurred as they did, and that observers like Schuld and me could draw such obvious connections between present and past struggles, was a testament to the decades of work by people who rarely made the news: rural activists associated with the repopulation movement. The repopulators had been organizing and mobilizing in defense of their own rights and in defense of their country since the early 1980s. They pressured political and military authorities to negotiate an end to the armed conflict, to comply with the peace accords and national and international laws, and to establish new and more just political and socioeconomic relations.

As this chapter and chapter 3 have shown, land, elections, and social services like education and health care were key points of contention in El Salvador's transition from war to peace. Each of these issues brought grassroots activists and their allies into direct engagement—and often conflict—with the state, as alternative development models wrestled with traditional models backed by powerful international capital. Activists argued that land, health, and education were public goods, rights accorded to Salvadoran citizens by the Constitution of El Salvador. However, successive ARENA administrations followed the direction of international financial institutions, cutting social programs, privatizing services, and launching World Bank–financed programs in rural areas. From the grassroots perspective, the Salvadoran Ministries of Education and Health intentionally used these externally funded-and-devised programs to displace the popular teachers and health promoters—that is, those rural community members who had served their compatriots throughout the years of war, exile, and repopulation. Rural activists engaged with the Salvadoran Ministries of Education and Health for more than a decade regarding the certification of popular teachers and health care workers, staffing and funding of rural offices, and appropriate decision-making processes.[201] This long struggle reveals important layers of the contest between the alternative and neoliberal models of development; it also uncovers the deep roots of the White Marches—and the long process of bringing about social change.

Conclusion

Unmasking Empire

On a sweltering morning in mid-July 2016, a caravan of flat-bed trucks and microbuses passed through northeastern Chalatenango en route to Arcatao. In village after village along the way, colorful banners marked the historic route. "Welcome to the repopulated and organized communities of Chalatenango," read the bright-green letters of one sign; another read, "Long live solidarity!" And yet another proclaimed, "For the right to live with dignity in our places of origin. Long live the organized communities of Chalatenango." In San José Las Flores—one of the first repopulated communities and also one of the first municipalities to activate a postwar public referendum process to formally declare their territory free from metallic mining—a sign encouraged, "Onward with the reform-oriented struggle [*lucha reivindicativa*] against death projects."

As the vehicles inched up the hill toward the center of Arcatao, they passed under yet another banner welcoming visitors "to the historic municipality of Arcatao where we work for organization, solidarity and sisterhood between pueblos." At the top of the hill, in the central plaza in front of the freshly painted sky-blue church, the drivers stopped, releasing their passengers: dozens upon dozens of Salvadorans, US Americans, and Canadians. Several hundred people greeted them with cheers, music, and more signs. Toddlers-in-arms waved hands of green, red, and yellow construction paper, while older children carried larger messages of peace and solidarity: "Thank you for your sisterhood [*herman-dad*]; Sharing makes you a human being; Do all the good you can for all the people you can; Combat racism not with racism but with solidarity; To give is to receive."

The crowd on the cobblestones moved in a fractal-like dance as people long separated recognized one another and came together in tight embraces; as one person led another to *mamá* or *tío* awaiting in the shade across the street; and as children and adults alike shrieked with delight in this very curious homecoming. Slowly, the whole mass, led by a troupe of young drummers, paraded around the town plaza to a stage in front of the city hall. There, José Alberto Avelar, the mayor of Arcatao (FMLN), formally commenced the two-day summit marking more than thirty years of international sistering and solidarity.

Much had changed in Arcatao and other repopulated villages since the birth of sistering in the early 1980s. With the end of the civil war in El Salvador, more people had returned to rural areas. They rebuilt houses, churches, and community centers; introduced electricity and running water; and started radio stations, eco-parks, and history museums. Centers for war orphans gave way to cybercafés; high school graduates became university graduates; once illiterate community leaders served as deputies in the Legislative Assembly; and CRIPDES founders served in the FMLN presidential administrations of Mauricio Funes (2009–14) and Salvador Sánchez Cerén (2014–19).

The US–El Salvador Sister Cities delegates to the 2016 summit had grown and evolved as well. The experiences of the 1980s fundamentally "changed the way we looked at Sister Cities," explained F. Joseph Sensenbrenner, a former mayor of Madison, Wisconsin (1983–89). Earlier sistering links were based on "logical" similarities in history and geography, along with shared economic and political ideologies of local business and political elites. The US–El Salvador relationships, in contrast, created a transnational political opposition movement.[1] While US presidents rallied against the "Red Threat," closely followed by other "terrorist" threats around the world, US activists on the left created grassroots organizations and allied with each other and with Salvadorans to challenge systems of exclusion, counterinsurgency, and imperialism. As US and Salvadoran authorities waved the banner of national security, solidarists hoisted an alternative security standard—one that went beyond weapons "to address the underlying political and economic structure." Put another way, US–El Salvador Sister Cities activists advocated for "real security" on a global scale: honest governments, freedom from repression and economic need, a communal ethos, and the citizens' "ability to impact world opinion and events."[2]

Participants in the July 2016 summit gathered not only to celebrate their many achievements; they also came to work. Over the course of two days, they engaged in a series of workshops and popular education-based activities to analyze the international realities of the moment and to comply with what Isabel Hernández, the CRIPDES cofounder, referred to as "our duty to establish a

Sistering and Solidarity Summit, Arcatao, 2016. *Top*: Locals welcoming delegates to the summit. *Bottom*: Representatives from Las Anonas and Philadelphia celebrate their many years of sistering. (photos by the author)

concrete plan for continuing our struggle together." We have advanced in many ways, Hernández continued, noting in particular the peace accords and the FMLN's political victories, both brought about with the help of sustained grassroots mobilizations. Yet, Hernández promised, "great challenges [*retos*] lie ahead."[3]

Many of the discussions at the summit revolved around four interconnected challenges. Perhaps the most dominant of these was the continuing interventionist politics of the United States. Participants critiqued the US government's role in what they referred to as "soft-coups" in the region, including Honduras, Venezuela, Argentina, Bolivia, and Ecuador. Underway in Brazil at the time of the summit was a concerted campaign, ultimately successful, to remove the leftist president Dilma Rousseff from office. This was part of a much longer pattern of disrespect of peoples' autonomy, said summit participants. It was important to stay alert; "if we don't take care" the same will happen here in El Salvador, one man warned. "The only place where there will be no coup d'état," quipped another, "is where there is no US Embassy."

A second challenge identified by summit attendees was the control of natural and human resources by transnational corporations (with close ties to the United States). Into this mix, they put free trade agreements including the North American and Central American Free Trade Agreements (NAFTA, CAFTA); free trade zones (*zonas francas*) with foreign-owned factories expanding across central El Salvador; "megaprojects" like the superhighways associated with Plan Puebla-Panamá (PPP); and Monsanto's dominance of seeds, fertilizers, and other agricultural tools. Especially heavy on activists' minds at the time of the summit was the mining company Oceana Gold and its $250 million claim against the government of El Salvador. Following Salvadoran officials' decision to not grant Oceana Gold a concession, company officials filed a grievance with the International Center for Settlement of Investment Disputes at the World Bank, citing lost potential profit. That company and others had been advancing their interests in El Salvador with proposals for "green mining" and promises of jobs, schools, and community development projects. At the same time, they hired thugs to harass activists leading the anti-mining movement, which led to death threats, attempted kidnappings, and between 2009 and 2011 a string of murders: Marcelo Rivera, Ramiro Rivera Gómez, Dora Alicia Recinos Sorto, and Juan Francisco Durán Ayala among them. These Cabañas-based activists were all involved in the fight against Oceana Gold's El Dorado mining project.[4]

One attendee of the 2016 celebrations, Santos of CRIPDES Sur, put it this way: no matter what corporate executives promise, "They don't have our interests in mind." Rural activists had been making this same argument since at least the late 1980s, when Salvadoran administrations began implementing reforms designed to attract international investment to the war-torn country. Time and experience had proven to people like Santos and others at the 2016 events that the neoliberal economic ideology driving the business elite's actions did not bring "a dignified life" to the majority of people; it brought only hunger and the destruction of communities. This marked a perpetuation of old patterns of violence—"It is not a declared war, but it is still a war."

Another concern shared by summit attendees was migration. This, too, was a continuation of old patterns. Rural activists and their allies are well aware that the gang violence driving people—especially youth—to flee El Salvador has roots in a previous generation of refugees. In the late 1970s and 1980s, hundreds of thousands of Salvadorans fled the conflict zones of El Salvador in search of refuge elsewhere. A small percentage of these people found themselves in Los Angeles, where they confronted a new kind of conflict zone, one that pitted different races and ethnicities against each other. Young Salvadorans banded together to better maneuver what was often a hostile host country; what began for many youth as a means of creating a sense of community, with time and circumstance shifted to defensive actions in the face of harassment from cliques of Mexican Americans and African Americans, which then led to more offensive and criminal behaviors. In the 1990s, the Clinton administration began rounding up these "gangbangers" and deporting them in record numbers. Deportees arrived to an unstable country that offered them few if any opportunities for security and advancement. Thus, the Mara Salvatrucha (MS-13) and 18th Street gangs became transnational criminal networks.

At the time of the summit in 2016, gang violence had reached phenomenal levels in El Salvador, spurring a new cycle of mass flight. Soon after the summit, in fact, Central American migrant caravans made world news, along with the Trump administration's confounding potpourri of immigration policy actions: "offshoring" border control through the militarization of Mexico; vows to cut aid to El Salvador and other countries sending people north; continued construction of a physical wall along the entirety of the Mexico–US border; refusal to admit asylum seekers into the United States but funneling them instead into open-air camps in Mexico to await hearings; increased workplace raids, followed by mass deportations; incarcerating immigrants on US soil, and forcibly separating children from their families; and banning US citizens from traveling to El Salvador. In that context, and in light of the dependence of many rural families—and, indeed, the nation of El Salvador—on remittances from loved ones living and working in the United States, activists expressed deep concerns about Trump's decision to "throw out all the migrants." This would, they argued, exacerbate an already difficult situation and only lead to more deaths. Human Rights Watch confirmed this argument in early 2020, in one of the first published studies tracing the direct connections between deportation and death. "As asylum and immigration policies tighten in the United States and dire security problems continue in El Salvador," the report concluded, "the US is repeatedly violating its obligations to protect Salvadorans from return to serious risk of harm."[5] From the perspective of rural activists, this, too, was an undeclared war. And just like the 1980s, the US Fugue State carried much of the responsibility.[6]

A fourth challenge identified by activists at the summit was environmental stewardship. The conflict—including the state's use of napalm and white phosphorous in counterinsurgency campaigns—had deeply damaged the country's ecosystems. Many repopulators had made significant progress in nursing their local environments to a healthier state through reforestation, soil remediation, watershed rehabilitation, organic farming, and other practices. At the same time, however, they noticed drastic changes in the climate: unusually high temperatures, droughts, unpredictable seasons, and superstorms complicated their stewardship efforts. In addition, communities in low-lying areas, including the coastal zones of La Libertad and along the lower Lempa River in San Vicente and Usulután, found themselves dealing with the horrific consequences of "agritoxins" (*agrotóxicos*). Massive sugarcane and cotton plantations dominate these regions, and landowners rely heavily on agrochemicals including glyphosate and paraquat, pesticides banned in many countries due to their toxicity to humans. These regions of El Salvador have seen a rapid increase in chronic kidney disease and other debilitating illnesses. According to recent epidemiological studies, renal failure has become the leading cause of hospital deaths, affecting not only field laborers but others who live in these areas.[7] Summit attendees noted that to solve the serious public health and environmental problems associated with agrotóxicos was a difficult chore, for it entailed confronting the "great powers"—national and transnational business elites.

From the point of view of Salvadoran activists, these four issues posed formidable obstacles to rural progress. According to one Salvadoran summit attendee, "The economic powers are suffocating us." Dennis Chinoy of the Bangor Sister Cities committee explained, "The same forces that subsidized repression thirty years ago in El Salvador are still alive today. As president, Donald Trump has managed to reach a whole class of economically disadvantaged people in the United States; he has rattled their cages, fed them a diet of distortion and distraction, encouraged them to resent and fear others, and to defend themselves against those others at all costs." Milton Monge, secretary for Sistering Relationships for the CCR and former FMLN mayor of Arcatao, declared, "The Empire still harasses us [*nos estorba*]. It's the same horse, different rider."

But if activists noted the circular nature of violence, they also identified another variation on a theme: the power of the people (*poder popular*). They knew from experience that collective organization and mobilization at local and transnational levels was, as Marc Rosenthal stated, a "strategy that worked." As this book has shown and the 2016 summit-goers highlighted, activists successfully defended the human rights of civilians who repopulated the conflict zones; they broke the isolation of the repopulated communities and contributed to the demilitarization of the country; and they helped bring about the negotiations that ultimately resulted in formal peace accords.

Not all was smooth, of course, and there were many moments of existential crisis. Rosenthal recalled one such turning point in the immediate wake of the peace accords. At that point, Lorena Martínez and others from CRIPDES met with US-based sistering activists in Miami. According to Marc Rosenthal, "We asked ourselves, Should we continue? Or are we done? The decision was made to continue; the struggle was not over, our work had not ended. We were still dealing with issues of the moment."

The historic record demonstrates that this transnational network did indeed carry on. Not content to simply bring about the peace accords, activists shifted their attention to pressing for "complete implementation of the Peace Accords" and "guaranteeing the advance of democratization."[8] Activists from south and north worked together to gain legal title to land and access to credit; have debts forgiven; improve the material conditions of rural communities through quality housing, potable water systems, and electrification; and meet other community needs through popular education and health care systems, and support programs for widows, orphans, war-wounded, seniors, and other special populations. They fomented new power dynamics on local and national levels through elections, sustainable development models, lobbying through coalitions like the Agricultural Foro, and campaigns for state recognition of directivas and popular professionals, including health promoters and educators.

The ability to refocus and retool along the way—in short, flexibility—was an important aspect of transnational sistering relationships and helps explain sistering's staying power. Rather than remain focused on a singular issue or methodology, activists in the Sister Cities network adapted their language and actions in relation with ever-changing contexts—always with an eye toward defending human and civil rights and "creat[ing] lasting change . . . for the generations to come."[9] If during the 1970s and 1980s they moved their bodies and raised their voices to contest the unjust policies of the Salvadoran government and its US backers, by the 1990s and 2000s they targeted the World

Bank, transnational corporations, and other global entities of "Neoliberalism and Capitalism," which, like plantation owners, soldiers, and foreign military advisors, thrived on "discrimination." Activists put it this way: "We must unmask them."[10]

As Krchnavek observed of the Salvadoran popular movement in 1994, grassroots activists needed to "keep changing and evolving in response to events. [They] held to their values without being rigid in their responses. There was, and is . . . a willingness to work with any situation that arises." The rural repopulators' engagement with state authorities illustrates this flexible approach; they recognized that "cooperation with the government does not necessarily lead to cooptation."[11] At the same time, they did not hesitate to bypass official institutions when necessary, thereby undermining old hierarchies and hegemonic forms of authority.

Of course, bypassing the state also proved problematic, as noted in chapter 4. Doing so resulted in infrastructural disconnects and intracommunity tensions. Communities with sistering relationships evolved into a comparatively privileged rural group, sometimes seeding envy and resentment in communities without direct foreign assistance. Moreover, while "outside assistance helps," lead activists had very real concerns about the "detrimental effects" of foreign aid, including "the creation of dependence."[12] As Smith-Nonini explained with reference to health care, "too much still depended on transnational efforts, with one or another humanitarian NGO or European agency filling in for a government that had long disregarded the welfare of most of its citizens."[13]

In fact, CRIPDES began raising flags of warning against *asistencialismo* (dependency) in the early 1990s, and waved those signals with increasing vigor through the rest of the decade. As the Salvadoran economy changed with the transition to peace, CRIPDES leaders found themselves spending more and more time bucking up the communal principles that had developed during war and displacement and thus defined the organized repopulations as an alternative to the status quo and models for the New El Salvador. "Since we are no longer suffering repression we faced during the war, we have lost some values," a CRIPDES report from 1995 observed. "It is as if we didn't realize that we are living a new dawn. . . . If we aren't careful we will lose the solidarity between ourselves, lose the Collective Experience and let ourselves be carried by egotist feelings of individualism." The report continued, "The new situation of the country shows us transformations at different levels of our society; for some, the peace accords have had an impact, and for others they have gained nothing." Because of the uneven benefits of peace, "there is deceit, tiredness, comfort, different interests, division, rumors, etc. that effect [*sic*] our work today.

There are communities that no longer want to coordinate with anyone else. . . . This won't lead us anywhere, because alone, it will be very difficult to achieve our demands." It was imperative, therefore, to "fight against the individualism" and "to agree to continue to be a part of a whole, to continue to be part of this community that continues to struggle for the full implementation of the accords to move out of the poverty and the backwardness and no one is going to solve their problems isolated from the rest."[14]

Here, too, we see the value of flexibility. CRIPDES and associated organizations analyzed the situation, then shifted approaches in response to that analysis. More specifically, they launched institutional restructuring processes and, among other new tactics, intentionally regionalized their work, reaching out to new rural communities and creating agricultural, educational, and health-related projects that benefited entire zones rather than specific towns. Meanwhile, US-based Sister Cities committees shifted support to the broad-based projects of CRIPDES regional offices and affiliated organizations, even as they continued to support their specific sistered communities. In this context, new regional sistering relationships began, including between community radio stations in both countries, as well as a unique three-point connection between CCR, CORDES, and the Maine Organic Farmers and Gardeners Association. Although these changes were not without challenges, they did ensure that CRIPDES and US–El Salvador Sister Cities continued to address current issues, gained legitimacy with new people and communities, and remained viable.

Activists also maintained a flexible mentality in the face of failure. Through the 1990s and into the 2000s, they carried out major campaigns—many of them lasting years—to no avail. For example, residents of Guarjila, along with their allies in CRIPDES and Sister Cities, fought to keep the Northern Longitudinal Highway (Carretera Longitudinal del Norte) away from the village. In spite of those efforts, officials built the highway straight through the center of the community, literally dividing it in two. As critics at the Central American University pointed out, the highway not only places "at risk the lives of hundreds of children and senior citizens, who must cross the lanes on a daily basis to go to school or to the health center"; it also "has contributed to divisions in the community and the disintegration of the social fabric that the people of Guarjila had constructed over the course of twenty years."[15] Many area residents argue that this was intentional on the part of authorities as a way to disrupt the historically well-organized and civically involved repopulated community. Other communities along the highway—many of which lacked histories of leftist activism—petitioned successfully for the route to bypass their towns.[16]

In a similar vein, Salvadorans in Guarjila and other repopulated communities, along with their US American allies, worked diligently to block the passage of the Central American Free Trade Agreement (CAFTA). Despite their efforts, the US government, five Central American countries, and the Dominican Republic ratified the agreement and, by 2006, began implementing its provisions. Yet, as Rose Spalding suggested—and this longitudinal study of rural activism and transnational solidarity networks supports—even though authorities went forward with the free trade agreement, it is likely that activists' critiques "played a role in the steady erosion of public enthusiasm for the measure." Nonetheless, even if the short-term impact was small, the medium- and long-term impacts may prove "more significant."[17]

In fact, Spalding's comments foreshadowed a major victory for Salvadoran activists and their transnational allies. After the disasters of CAFTA, the highway, and numerous other megaprojects, activists found themselves on their knees. But many stood up again, dusted themselves off, huddled up to strategize on the next play, and jumped back into the fray. Then, after a years-long transnational campaign headed by CRIPDES and the repopulated communities of Chalatenango and Cabañas, the Legislative Assembly of El Salvador voted in March 2017 to ban all metallic mining in El Salvador. It was the first country in the world to do so. And the activists celebrated this additional step in the long road toward a more just and equitable world.

Such transformation was a fundamental goal of sistering. With actions on both local and international levels, Salvadoran and US American activists strived to dismantle—or at the very least unmask—unjust structures while building new structures and relations based on equity and respect. They modeled democratic civic engagement, political diplomacy, and sustainable development, and framed their arguments within the contexts of democratic ideals within national and international laws and norms. They established new economic and political structures at a local level in El Salvador, including the Alternative Financial System and community directivas, while also creating alternative structures at an international level.

In this, Sister Cities was unique in comparison to other solidarity and human rights organizations operating at the same time. As a number of social scientists have pointed out, nongovernmental organizations proliferated in the 1980s and early 1990s. According to Margaret Keck and Kathryn Sikkink, the number of "international nongovernmental social change organizations" more than tripled between 1973 and 1993 (from 183 to 631), and nearly doubled between 1983 and 1993 (from 348 to 631).[18] Erin Beck found similar growth of the nongovernmental sector within Guatemala since the 1980s, particularly in the postconflict period as NGOs became favored channels for development

"Mining Contaminates My Country." Poster produced by CRIPDES-led National Roundtable Against Mining, urging support of a law banning metallic mining, ca. 2008. (photo by the author)

project funds.[19] As Beck, Keck, Sikkink, and others illustrate, many of these organizations brought attention to "new" actors and issues, including women, indigenous groups, the environment, and natural resources. Although these scholars might acknowledge that the organizations fed upon the cultural shifts taking place in the late twentieth and early twenty-first centuries—as well as changes prompted by revolutions in communications and transportation technologies together with the globalization of a human rights ethos—they continue to represent transnational activism as premised on a type of segregation of "First World" and "Third World" actors, with the former serving to "pry open space" for the latter.[20]

The "boomerang pattern" developed by Keck and Sikkink is among the most prominent examples of such a model. As they explain in their influential book *Activists beyond Borders*, "When channels between the state and its domestic actors are blocked," the boomerang model enables "domestic NGOs [to] bypass their state and directly search out international allies to try to bring pressure on their states from outside."[21] In explaining how such models work, scholars tend to focus on specific campaigns (e.g., torture, disappearance) and large-scale nongovernmental and intergovernmental institutions with international reach, including United Nations and Inter-American commissions on human rights, Amnesty International and Americas Watch, and domestic organizations funded by US and European foundations.

The model of sistering presented in this book illustrates that solidary relations are far more complex and dynamic than such a model allows. First, rather than reify institutional perspectives, this US–El Salvador Sister Cities case study emphasizes the historical value of a primarily volunteer-run grassroots citizen diplomacy network. As sistering activists themselves put it, their goal was not to build a "centralized" organization but to grow their transnational network, which they defined as a "coordinated relationship between a variety of organizations acting on the same issue" that shares a "general unity on political position."[22] An important aspect of the "coordinated relationship" was what scholars of Latin America today refer to as horizontalism. According to Richard Stahler-Sholk, Harry Vanden, and Marc Becker, this mode rose to prominence by the second decade of the twenty-first century as one of many challenges to neoliberal hegemony and the Washington consensus. "A central premise of horizontalism," they wrote, "is a rejection of hierarchical relations of power that are created and reproduced through vanguardism, political and economic elitism, and the goal of seizing rather than transforming state power." As an alternative, the movements examined by Stahler-Sholk and colleagues adopted a "non-vertical, not elitist, popular, horizontal essence."[23]

Some scholars have held up the Zapatistas of southern Mexico in particular as representative of this "new" model of activism. The Zapatistas rose into public view in 1996, as the governments of Mexico, the United States, and Canada formalized the North American Free Trade Agreement (NAFTA). Although the movement has symbolized many things to many people, including indigenous rights, human rights, and social justice, what matters here is that scholars have argued that the Zapatistas' work is substantively different from that of earlier social movements. According to Thomas Olesen, the Zapatistas "formulate social critique in a manner which is more profoundly democratic and global than that of most groups during the Cold War period" and "does not build on a distinction between the first, second, and third world." Olesen continues, pointing out that the relationships of solidarity that Zapatistas establish with "transnational activists is highly globalised in the sense that it is based on mutuality. In contrast, solidarity relationships in the Cold War period tended to have more of a one-way character in which there was clear distinction between providers and beneficiaries of solidarity."[24]

This Sister Cities case study makes clear that there was a precedent: events in Central America during the late 1970s and early 1980s gave rise to grassroots sistering relationships, which encompassed many of the convictions and practices that the Zapatistas and other activists on the left would embrace a decade and more later. The sistering relationships promoted by Salvadorans and US Americans—along with similar relations developed between US Americans and Nicaraguans during the Sandinista government and, to a lesser extent, Guatemalans affected by that country's civil war—connected people and the local, national, and global spheres through long-term mutual accompaniment, promotion of a wide range of human and civil rights, and grassroots civic engagement and political activism.

Critical to the development and maintenance of the transnational sistering connections examined in this book were the Salvadorans and US Americans who intentionally crossed international borders—in multiple directions. As chapters 2 and 3 presented, refugees, exiles, and participants in tours and delegations transferred news and information, material resources, and other forms of support between various sites in Central America and the United States. Over time, these direct people-to-people connections gave rise to a kind of fictive kin relationship and a transnational commons. As "sister citizens," they acted upon shared values, including self-determination, interdependence, mutual respect and understanding, peace, social justice, democracy, and human and civil rights.

Just as sistering involved physical movement in both directions, so too were the relationships mutually beneficial. There were, of course, drastic differences in terms of economic resources and social capital. Northern activists were, for the most part, well educated, white, and middle class, while southern activists were, by and large, poor rural farmers with comparatively less formal education. In light of these differences, it is true that sistering involved the north-to-south flow of a considerable amount of material aid. If we consider only this aspect, it would seem that sistering fits into the boomerang model. But the people involved with Sister Cities argue that sistering represents much, much more. The sentiments of reciprocity are clear in archival records of tours, delegations, phone calls, letters, and personal diaries. And they were powerfully obvious at the anniversary summit in 2016. Catie Johnston, a Texas native then serving as one of the San Salvador–based Sister Cities coordinators, pointed out, as she began one of the workshops: "We gringos learned from you to do this social analysis." Later, Marc Rosenthal teared up as he explained to his Salvadoran friends and colleagues: "You fed us both in El Salvador and in the United States. You inspired us to continue with struggles we have there. I am so grateful. I have learned so much from you." Another participant in the summit, Daniel Russell, agreed, saying "I look to you for answers. My involvement with you has changed my life. This is why you are called El Salvador," referring to the literal translation of *el salvador*: "the savior."

Of course, anniversary celebrations belie the very real tensions. As previous chapters have noted, activists often navigated rough waters. During the years of armed conflict, debates repeatedly surfaced regarding relations with the FMLN, for example, and the extent to which the network's "hidden transcripts" should be made public. Similarly, each organization established its own unique identity and way of doing things; at certain moments these organizational personalities clashed. As sistering relations continued to evolve through the 1990s, new frictions arose around finances, gender dynamics, and other issues.

But here, too, the activists' flexibility shows. Their shared focus on an idealistic—even utopian—vision for the future, helped them maneuver significant fault lines in their solidarity work. The ability of Salvadoran and US American sistering activists to successfully navigate tensions over the course of decades depended on the acknowledgment that each end of the network brought particular strengths and resources to the relationship, a critical awareness of the power differential between north and south, and a willingness to intentionally invert traditional power relations. They knew that in order to make progress toward their long-term objectives, they needed each other. In this, too, they were much like a family facing danger together. As Rosenthal expressed at the 2016 summit, "The same neoliberal structures and powers wreak the same damage in the United States and El Salvador."

That the Sister Cities network continues to exist to this day offers further evidence of its unique nature. Whereas the majority of Central America solidarity organizations folded by the mid-1990s, US–El Salvador Sister Cities continued to expand through the decade and into the new millennium. Today the network is somewhat thinner than it was at its height in the 1990s, but it still maintains a strong presence with seventeen active pairings, four paid full- and part-time staff people in El Salvador and the United States, hundreds of volunteers and interns, semiannual meetings, and regular international summits.

To be sure, with fewer people (many of them more gray-haired) than before, building a better world sometimes seems impossible in light of a continually evolving set of challenges. Such frustration was palpable at the 2016 summit, where many participants spoke as if the entire sistering movement was on the brink of collapse. Salvadorans in the repopulated communities were increasingly at odds with one another, with many feeling disillusioned—betrayed even—by the leftist leaders at both local and national levels. Disjunctures became more extreme between former commanders, rank and file combatants, and civilian supporters of the FMLN.[25] These political and economic tensions mirrored the organizational crisis within CRIPDES, fed by miscommunication, fiscal mismanagement, and sexism. The CRIPDES central office found itself shunned by the regional bases, and in factious discussions with the Sister Cities Board of Directors.

Activists lamented the continued breakdown of the Left in the United States too. As Daniel Russell explained to his Salvadoran counterparts at the summit, traditional organizing was in decline—the result of more than fifty years of strategic corporate and government actions. That many US Americans could not name their own hometown mayors illustrated the extent of their apathy. Moreover, Daniel continued, "We have no sense of community. The reality is that most of us don't even know our own neighbors." This, argued Rosenthal, has contributed to the rise of a new fascism, represented by the Trump administration. "And now," he continued, "here we are in this moment, confronting the same thing we confronted thirty years ago: projects that threaten our way of life."

Yet, Rosenthal, Russell, and other summit-goers decided that there would be no question but to carry on. In the words of Dennis Chinoy, another attendee, "If Trump's message is poison, the antidote is sistering. Instead of building walls, we build bridges, learn to walk in each other's shoes. We've done it for thirty years. It is as relevant now as it was then."

In more than three decades of walking shoulder to shoulder, this transnational activist network had accomplished much. Even if it did not entirely rewrite social and economic relations or completely halt "the neoliberal lion," as CRIPDES put it, this network kept socioeconomic issues and "real security" on state and international tables.[26] It succeeded in "reducing the most harmful impacts" of the militarism and neoliberalism of the late twentieth and early twenty-first centuries.[27] Even if many of the adjustments to official policies and practices were "a crude reflection of [activists'] demands," wrote Kowalchuk, "they stimulated further mobilization both because they were so dissatisfactory, and because they demonstrated that the movement had had some kind of impact."[28]

In other words, the victories as well as their imperfections motivated further activism, from the local-level struggles of popular professionals to national-level struggles like the anti-mining movement and the White Marches. From the grassroots point of view, the repopulation movement, with its communal principles and holistic approach to development, continued to serve as a model. Even in a new era marked by "austerity measures and structural adjustment imposed by foreign creditors," these organized communities forwarded a "vision for social and economic development . . . based on community self-sufficiency and grassroots empowerment." Applied at local levels over the long term, these efforts promised to reap rewards at local levels as well as at national and international levels. "Given the failures of neoliberalism and the decline of state socialism," US-based sistering advocates asserted, "these alternative solutions offer an exciting hope" for us all.[29]

Among the many points that became clear at the 2016 sistering and solidarity summit was that, from the perspective of these activists, progress is not an end point; it is a process. And, so, rather than throw up their hands at the daunting challenges, they shared a celebratory meal of *pupusas* and then rolled up their shirtsleeves and got back to work. They did as they had done for three decades: they learned from each other about the day's most pressing issues and committed themselves to organizing and mobilizing for change, and to living out the objectives of sistering by transforming the world into a place where peace, justice, and equality reigned.

Their efforts echo a maxim that Mary Kay Baum of Madison learned during her first journey to El Salvador in 1986: "Despair is a dishonor to the ones who have gone before us." Baum heard these words from a mother whose young son had just been killed by soldiers in US-provided helicopters. Even though military officials had warned her to stay away from Baum's delegation members, she sought them out and told them her story anyway. "I cannot be silent," she said, "for his death would have no meaning if I don't carry the message forward." This woman shows us "what hope really means," Baum recalled. "That even though she may not see change in her life," she was able to "imagine a better world and to make steps towards that for other people."[30]

Sistering activists continue to strive to emulate that mother and the tens of thousands of other Salvadorans with similar stories of tenacity in the face of pain and ongoing challenges. As CRIPDES leaders have argued for decades, "We are part of a bigger struggle."[31] And although *la lucha continua*—"the struggle continues," a popular saying in the repopulated communities—so too are the "interest and concern" kept alive by "the human contact and person-to-person bonds established through sistering relationships."[32] As Baum put it, echoing the young mother she met in El Salvador, on this long road toward peace with justice, "We don't have the luxury to give up."[33]

Acknowledgments

This book would not have been possible without the many people who provided me with access to their personal archives. I offer them the sincerest thanks for taking such good care of these historic materials, ensuring that they—and the valuable lessons they hold—will be accessible for generations to come: the late Pat Arvidson, Domitila Ayala, Mary Kay Baum, Beth Cagan, Steve Cagan, Harvey Finkle, Susan Freireich, Suzanne Geoghegan, Van Hardy, Frank Hollick, Lance Laver, Ann Legg, the late Art Lloyd, Sue Lloyd, Sally Milbury Steen, Rick Reinhard, Marc Rosenthal, Beth Salzberg, Barbara Schaibel, Judy Somberg, Jim Wallace, Dick and Diana Williams, and Carol Yourman.

I have also benefited from access to the archives of several institutions. Special thanks to Catie (Johnston) Mungía, Zulma Tobar, and Mario Guevara at the San Salvador Sister Cities office; CRIPDES associates Bernardo Belloso and Miriam Ayala; Daniel Stoner and Deacon Steve Wodzanowski at St. Joseph Parish in Seattle; and Katey Borland and Cassie Patterson at the Center for Folklore Studies at The Ohio State University, who provided virtual access to the Columbus-Copapayo Sister Cities collection. Staff at the Wisconsin Historical Society (WHS) have always been helpful, guiding me to the multiple interconnected collections with relevance to this study.

I have gained valuable insights into solidarity, sistering, and El Salvador through interviews and conversations with the above-listed people as well as the following: Barbara Alvarado, Mike Anastario, Jacey Anderson, José Artiga Escobar, Jeff Baker, Prudence Barber, Jeannie Berwick, Joanie Brooks, Esther Chávez, Erik Ching, Dennis Chinoy, Avi Chomsky, Margi Clarke, Jill Cornell, Ian Davies, Mario Dávila, Julie Derwinski, Elizabeth Dray, Jon Falk, Van Gosse, David Grosser, Cathy Hoffman, Leah Iraheta, Sandra Iverson, Carlos Lara Martínez, Jennifer Long, Katherine Kates, Jesse Kates-Chinoy, Héctor Lindo Fuentes, Tim Lohrentz, Willie Marquart, Lorena Martínez, Don McClain,

Sheila McShane, Milton and Norma Monge, Ellen Moodie, Betsey and Ron Morgan, Lauren Morse-Wendt, Carol Murray, Matt Nichols, Jenny Pearce, Héctor Perla Jr., Michael Ramos, Michael Ring, Hélida Rivera, Nicolás Rivera, Rosa Rivera, Lillie Rizack, Larry Rosenberg, Nancy Ryan, Eddie Salazar, Tracey Schear, Ronnie Schroeder, Leslie Schuld, Lotti Silber, Jessica Stites Mor, Steve Striffler, Marilee Sushoreba, and Geoff Thale. Many informal conversations with Salvadorans have also influenced this project over the years. I look forward to continuing these conversations and to starting new ones—especially with Salvadorans who helped foment organizing in the United States. Their perspectives are critical to the historical record—and our present reality; it's high time for US Americans to listen and learn.

Research assistants helped me sift through thousands of documents, photos, and transcripts. Thanks to Jacey Anderson, Rachel Dunlap, Morgan Craig, Emma Folkerts, Mac Gwinner, Grace Juhala, Elanor Nolan, and students in my spring 2018 Senior Capstone in History course.

Many talented people provided feedback along the way. Miranda Cady Hallet and Leigh Binford meticulously reviewed an earlier version of the manuscript for the University of Wisconsin Press. Portions of this text appeared in different form in the *Wisconsin Magazine of History* 101, no. 1 (Autumn 2017) and the *Journal of Civil and Human Rights* 3, no. 1 (Fall 2017), and I thank the editors and anonymous reviewers for their attention to detail. I also thank David Grosser, Michael Ring, Steve Stern, and participants in these workshops: International Solidarity Action Research Network (Toronto, 2019), Revising the Geography of Modern World Histories (York, UK, 2018), and Empire and Solidarity (New Orleans, 2010, 2011). The book is stronger because of their suggestions; all shortcomings are my own.

Generous funding from the following entities supported different phases of this project: a Public Engagement Fellowship from the Whiting Foundation (2018–19); and, at Montana State University, awards from the College of Letters and Science, Office of Research and Economic Development, Office of the Provost, the Center for Faculty Excellence, the Department of History and Philosophy, and International Programs.

Finally, I would like to thank my family for inspiration, encouragement, and support: Jeremy Ditto, who has treated me, his too-often-distracted partner, with patience and kindness; Tom Todd, my father, who instilled in me—among many things—a love of words; and Marge Todd, my mother, who showed me, through her words and deeds, the meanings of peace and justice. Margie did not live to see the completion of this project. I dedicate it to her memory because the histories in this book illustrate well what one of her 1980s-era pins proclaimed: Civil Disobedience Is Civil Defense.

Glossary

campesino/campesina	peasant, rural inhabitant who survives through a blend of subsistence farming, wage labor, migration, and other strategies
conciencia/concientización	sociopolitical consciousness/consciousness-raising
departamento	department, an administrative unit similar to a US state
directiva	community council
manzana	a unit of measurement common in Central America, with differing practices in each country as well as in urban and rural zones. In El Salvador, according to El Salvador's *Primer Censo Agropecuario* of 1950, 1 rural manzana is equal to approximately .7 hectares, 1.7 acres, 16 *tareas*, and 70 *áreas*.
promotores de salúd	health promoters, workers in the popular health system
salvoconducto/salvo	safe-conduct pass issued by the Salvadoran military to authorize travel in conflictive areas of the country

Notes

A Note on Archival Sources

Much of the material for this book comes from private archives, which poses certain citation challenges. When I accessed them, the collections were in varying levels of organization (or disarray, in some cases). Some have since been turned over to professional archives, and others are in the process of being deposited. The US–El Salvador Sister Cities archive, which I am building with the organization's board of directors and various committees, currently includes materials from Austin–Guajoyo, Cambridge–San José Las Flores, Wichita–La Bermuda, Madison–Arcatao, New Jersey–Los Amates, and the USESSC National Center. The archive is in two pieces, with part in Madison and the other part in my Bozeman office. The board of directors is assessing options and will decide where to place the materials for long-term preservation and public access. Some Sister Cities records are held at the following institutions (with some parts unprocessed as of this writing): the Center for Folklore Studies at The Ohio State University (Columbus–Copapayo); the Kenneth Spencer Research Library at the University of Kansas (Lawrence–El Papaturro); Binghamton University Special Collections (Binghamton–El Charcón); and the Wisconsin Historical Society (Berkeley–San Antonio Los Ranchos and others). Given this shifting archival landscape, I have done my best to cite according to standards of the historical profession. In the case of the Madison–Arcatao Sister City Project records, I have created some file titles but used original file titles when possible. For more up-to-date information, I invite inquiries.

Introduction

1. "A Resolution for the City of Madison to Establish A Sister-City Relationship with the City of Arcatao," March 7, 1986, Records of the Madison-Arcatao Sister City Project (hereafter MASCP Records), US–El Salvador Sister City Archive (hereafter USESSC Archive).

2. New El Salvador Today Foundation (hereafter NEST), "The Destruction of Rural Life in El Salvador," May 1986, File 10, Box 16, Center for Democracy in the

Americas Records, Wisconsin State Historical Society, Madison, WI (hereafter CDA Records).

3. Milton Monge quoted in Lippold, *Hope*.

4. "Carta abierta al Presidente José Napoleón Duarte," *El Mundo*, May 3, 1986, MASCP Records; Mary Kay Baum, interview with author, February 13, 2015, Middleton, WI. All translations from the Spanish are my own unless otherwise noted.

5. Many Salvadorans prefer the term "politico-military conflict" or simply "conflict" rather than "civil war" in light of the US intervention that sustained the Salvadoran government in its decade-plus struggle against the FMLN insurgent forces. I will use the war and conflict terms interchangeably for ease of reading.

6. I choose to not capitalize "cold war" as a means of distinguishing my discussion of the era from literature that focuses on the US–USSR contest. Because this study contributes to efforts to decenter cold war studies by shifting attention to non-state actors—particularly those in the so-called Global South—it makes sense to de-emphasize the state-centered perspective that resulted in the proper name designation of the Cold War.

7. Naciones Unidas—Comisión de la verdad para El Salvador, *Informe de la Comisión de la Verdad*, 58.

8. Comisión para el Esclarecimiento Histórico, "Memoria del Silencio"; Recovery of Historical Memory Project, *Guatemala: Never Again!*; Naciones Unidas—Comisión de la verdad para El Salvador, *Informe de la Comisión de la Verdad*; Smith, *Resisting Reagan*, 51; National Commissioner for the Protection of Human Rights in Honduras, *The Facts Speak for Themselves*; Catholic Institute for International Relations, *Right to Survive*.

9. Consider Byrne, *Iran-Contra*; Kornbluh and Byrne, *Iran-Contra Scandal*.

10. Robert McAfee Brown, "A Theological Reflection on Accompaniment," in "A Call to Accompaniment," edited by José Escobar and Lana Dalberg, ca. 1987, 2, MASCP Records.

11. The terms "America" and "American" are problematic in many ways, among which is their use as shorthand for the country name of the United States of America. In light of the fact that the United States is but one country among many in the Americas, I use America/American for general reference to multiple nations in the hemisphere, United States and US in reference to the country, and US American to refer to US citizens (paralleling the Spanish use of *estadounidense*, or "united-statesian"). For lack of a meaningful alternative, I use the term "Latin America" despite its equally problematic nature (emphasizing as it does the European traditions in the region to the detriment of African, indigenous, and other traditions).

12. US–El Salvador Sister Cities (hereafter USESSC), *Aquí estamos* (San Salvador: USESSC, 2011), 39.

13. MASCP 25th Anniversary Celebration, October 10, 2011, Madison, WI, recording and transcript in author's possession.

14. Juliana Barnard to Friends of USESSC, April 29, 1993, File 1988–1994 National Office, MASCP Records.

15. Zelinsky, "Twinning," 3. See also Lofland, "Consensus"; Clarke, "Town Twinning in Cold-War Britain"; Clarke, "In What Sense"; Vion, "Town Twinning in France";

Campbell, "Ideals." On US/USSR citizen diplomacy, see Grabill, *What Happens*; Warner and Shuman, *Citizen Diplomats*; Shuman, "Dateline"; Cremer, de Bruin, and Dupuis, "International Sister-Cities." On sistering components of Eisenhower and Kennedy administrations, see Allcock, "The First Alliance"; Leppert, "Eisenhower"; Bush, "Seattle"; Finch, "People to People"; Juergensmeyer, "Short History"; Osgood, *Total Cold War*.

16. Passing references to sister cities appear in Gosse, "'El Salvador Is Spanish for Vietnam,'" 318; and Binford, "Reply: Solidarity," 179–80. The few studies on grassroots sistering include Chilsen and Rampton, *Friends in Deed*; Moodie, "Untellable Stories" and "Inequality"; Seagle, "Figured Worlds"; Bush, "Seattle"; and Munkres, "Being 'Sisters.'" On "sister churches," see Bakker, *Sister Churches*.

17. Mahony and Eguren, *Unarmed Bodyguards*.

18. Kelly, *Sovereign Emergencies*, 206, 10.

19. Kelly, *Sovereign Emergencies*, 11, 206, 10, 189.

20. Kelly, "The 1973 Chilean Coup," 168. Some works that illustrate this Eurocentric interpretation include Hunt, *Inventing Human Rights*; and Moyn, *The Last Utopia*.

21. For examples of new work emphasizing local actors' interplay with global contexts, see the contributions to Stern and Straus, *Human Rights Paradox*; Stites Mor, *Human Rights*.

22. Moyn, *The Last Utopia*; Eckel and Moyn, *Breakthrough*; Schmidli, *State of Freedom*; Keys, *Reclaiming American Virtue*; Bradley, *The World Reimagined*; Kelly, *Sovereign Emergencies*.

23. Keck and Sikkink, *Activists*; Risse and Sikkink, "Socialization"; Sikkink, *Justice Cascade*.

24. Kelly, *Sovereign Emergencies*, 279.

25. Kelly, *Sovereign Emergencies*, 279.

26. Kelly, *Sovereign Emergencies*, 275; Moyn, *The Last Utopia*.

27. Kelly, *Sovereign Emergencies*, 244. My conceptualization of grassroots sistering also is informed by the following studies on historical roots, philosophies, motivations, and processes of solidarity: Smith, Chatfield, and Pagnucco, *Transnational Social Movements*; Giugni and Passy, *Political Altruism*; Guidry and Sawyer, "Contentious Pluralism"; Stjernø, *Solidarity in Europe*; Dussel, "From Fraternity to Solidarity"; Scholz, *Political Solidarity*; Stahler-Sholk, Vanden, and Becker, *Rethinking*.

28. Moyn, *Not Enough*; Kelly, *Sovereign Emergencies*.

29. Especially clear examples of such distinctions include Grossman, "Solidarity with Sandino"; Olesen, *International Zapatismo*; Kelly, "The 1973 Chilean Coup."

30. For additional insight into the coexistence of multiple forms of activism, consider Binford, "Reply: Solidarity"; Nelson, *Reckoning*; Olesen, *International Zapatismo*; Tarrow and McAdam, "Scale Shift"; and the work of Gosse.

31. Nepstad, *Convictions*, 11.

32. Gosse, "'The North American Front,'" 15; Nepstad, *Convictions*, 125.

33. Martí, "Nuestra América"; García Canclini, *Culturas híbridas*; Saldívar, *Trans-Americanity*.

34. Stites Mor, "Introduction," 7.

35. Federici, *Re-Enchanting the World*, 13.

36. Federici, *Re-Enchanting the World*, 16.

37. Bollier and Helfrich, *Wealth of the Commons*, xiii, xviii; Federici, *Re-enchanting the World*, 7.

38. Linebaugh, *Stop, Thief*, 15.

39. Bollier and Helfrich, *Wealth of the Commons*, xv.

40. Bollier and Helfrich, *Wealth of the Commons*, xviii.

41. I am grateful to Paul Kramer and colleagues at the February 2018 working conference Revising the Geography of Modern World Histories at the University of York, UK, for inspiration on this issue.

42. El Salvador's *Prensa Gráfica*, November 23, 1965, refers to the country's northern reaches as "tierra olvidada." For further discussion, see Todd, *Beyond Displacement*.

43. Although many scholars follow the strictures of international law and distinguish between internally displaced persons, refugees, and exiles or political asylees, I consider such distinctions to be false, predicated as they are on imagined or socially constructed differences in class, political ideology, and a value hierarchy of nations. That the United States and other wealthy and powerful nations historically have defined who is and who is not a refugee—through their leadership in the United Nations, for instance, and their heavy influence in global media and culture—should give us pause when applying such labels. In this study, then, I use the terms "refugee," "exile," and "displaced" interchangeably, deferring to the activists' own terms whenever possible.

44. Gosse, "'El Salvador Is Spanish for Vietnam,'" 318; C. Smith, *Resisting Reagan*, 387. For a partial list of groups across the United States, see Central America Resource Center, Directory of Central American Organizations, Austin, Texas, 1984.

45. A sampling of the literature on South America and solidarity includes the work of Patrick William Kelly and of James Green, listed in the bibliography, as well as Gill, "Limits"; Sattamini and Green, *A Mother's Cry*; Faulk, *In the Wake*; Adams, "What Is Solidarity Art?"; and Bruey, *Bread, Justice, and Liberty*. See also these special issues on solidarity: *Dialectical Anthropology* 32, no. 3 (2008); *Latin American Perspectives* 36, no. 6 (2009); and *NACLA Report on the Americas* 48, no. 1 (2016). On exiles, see especially Wright and Oñate, *Flight from Chile*; Markarian, *Left in Transformation*; Rollemberg, "Brazilian Exile"; Sznajder and Roniger, *Politics of Exile*; Roniger, Green, and Yankelevich, *Exile*. On the new solidarity studies, consider essays in Stites Mor, *Human Rights*; Stites Mor and Suescun Pozas, *Art of Solidarity*; special issue of *Journal of Iberian and Latin American Research* 20, no. 2 (2014); and the CALACS/ISARN Virtual Forum, "Beyond Borders: Refuge, Asylum and Solidarity," August 15–21, 2019.

46. Clements, *Witness to War*. See also the related Oscar-winning short documentary Shaffer, *Witness to War*. Other examples include the journal of Belgian physician Michaël De Witte, published after his death, as *Diario Sebastián*.

47. Ibarra Chávez outlines the role he and some of his compatriots played as "internacionalistas mexicanos" in *El Salvador*. The Venezuelan Henríquez Consalvi

describes his work as founder and operator of Radio Venceremos in *La terquedad*. Several US Americans have penned memoirs of their experiences bearing witness in El Salvador between the late 1970s and the early 1990s: Hutchinson, *When the Dog Ate Candles*; Corrigan, *El Salvador at a Crossroads*; Forché, *What You Have Heard*. The Salvadoran Maria Teresa Tula offers insight into her many years of human rights work, including while living in exile in the United States, in *Este es mi testimonio*. For a broad view of postwar memoirs and related publications, see Ching, *Stories*.

48. Eduardo Sancho (Fermán Cienfuegos) discussed the FMLN's "accumulation of forces" in his memoir, cited in Grenier, "Rise and Fall," 20–21.

49. On FMLN media work, see Cortina Orero, "Discurso"; Cortina Orero, "Redes militates y solidaridad"; and Perla, "Transnational Public Diplomacy." On parallel and insurgent diplomacies, see Martínez Peñate, "Diplomacia paralela"; and Oñate-Madrazo, "Insurgent Diplomacy." For longitudinal local/global insights, see Sprenkels, *After Insurgency*; and Silber, *Everyday Revolutionaries*.

50. Grenier, "Rise and Fall," 326; Gosse, "'The North American Front,'" 35.

51. Gosse, "'The North American Front'"; Gosse, "'El Salvador Is Spanish for Vietnam,'" 320.

52. See in particular the work of Héctor Perla Jr., listed in the bibliography, as well as Perla and Coutin, "Legacies"; Stoltz Chinchilla, Hamilton, and Loucky, "Sanctuary"; Todd, *Beyond Displacement*; Bassano, "Boomerang"; Stuelke, "Reparative Politics"; Todd, "Politics."

53. This project employs the term "solidarist" to signify a person who participates in solidarity-related activities, and "solidary" as an adjective relating to the sentiments of community interests and responsibilities shared by solidarists. Despite their obvious utility, these terms have not yet been integrated into solidarity studies and related fields.

54. Pratt, *Imperial Eyes*, 6–7; Pratt, "Arts of the Contact Zone."

55. For an early exploration of this relationship, see Hinman, "The Colossus of the North."

56. Weiss, "Principles," 20; Weiss, *Humanitarian Business*; Barnett and Weiss, *Humanitarianism*.

57. Barnett, "Humanitarianism"; *Empire of Humanity*.

58. Terry, *Condemned to Repeat?*; Lischer, *Dangerous Sanctuaries*. For a journalistic perspective, see Polman, *Crisis Caravan*. For another angle—how "refugee warriors" strategically manipulate humanitarian aid groups—consider Zolberg, Suhrke, and Aguayo, *Escape from Violence*; Stedman and Tanner, "Refugees as Resources in War"; Nyers, *Rethinking Refugees*, esp. ch. 5; Greenhill, *Weapons of Mass Migration*.

59. Weiss, "Principles," 20; Weiss, *Humanitarian Business*; Barnett and Weiss, *Humanitarianism*.

60. Skinner and Lester, "Humanitarianism," 731.

61. Kelly, *Sovereign Emergencies*, 12.

62. Olesen, "Globalising the Zapatistas," 263.

63. Gill, "Limits," 677, 668.

64. Plewes and Stuart, "The Pornography of Poverty," 24.

65. Koopman, "Imperialism Within," 300. For an examination of such processes in the Guatemalan context, see Todd, "Paradox."

66. Weber, *Visions*, 21.

67. Mahony and Eguren, *Unarmed Bodyguards*, 1.

68. Vincent Bulathsinghala, cited in Coy, "Cooperative Accompaniment," 98.

69. Gosse, "'The North American Front,'" 15. On white privilege in accompaniment, see Weber, *Visions*; Henderson, "Citizenship"; Coy, "Cooperative Accompaniment." On the problematic nature of the "currency of whiteness" in one US activist field, see Valencia, "Making of the White Middle-Class Radical."

70. Rubin, "Meanings," 125.

71. Tarrow and McAdam, "Scale Shift," 142.

72. Kelly, "The 1973 Chilean Coup," 181.

73. Green, "(Homo)Sexuality"; Weber, *Visions*.

74. Quoted in Tarrow and McAdam, "Scale Shift," 142. See also Hellman, "Real and Virtual Chiapas."

75. Michael Ring, email communication, January 26, 2020.

76. On FMLN internal tensions, see Montgomery, *Revolution*; Harnecker, *Con la mirada en alto*; Grenier, "Rise and Fall"; C. McClintock, *Revolutionary Movements*; Martínez Peñate, *Conflicto armado*. For insights into the Salvadoran right, consider Martínez Peñate, "ARENA."

77. Todd, "We Were Part."

78. Rosa Rivera, personal communication, November 8, 2015. See also Rosa Rivera, Jenny Pearce, and Richard Duffy, "La guerra civil contada por los campesinos," *El Faro*, November 30, 2015.

79. "Rebuilding Lives, Rebuilding Communities," Declaration from the US–El Salvador Sister Cities National Conference, January 26, 1992, File National Meetings and Encuentros, MASCP Records.

Chapter 1. Radical Roots

1. I examine the rural repopulation movement in detail in Todd, *Beyond Displacement*.

2. "The Policy of Rural Depopulation," in "A Call to Accompaniment," edited by José Escobar and Lana Dalberg, ca. 1987, 2, MASCP Records. See also Americas Watch, "Draining."

3. Schrading, *Movimiento*.

4. Central American Refugee Center (hereafter CARECEN), *Repopulation*, 71.

5. "Memoria del IV Cumbre de hermanamientos," ca. March 23, 1992, File Regional Reports: Jan–Mar '92, Box 6, Papers of Pat Arvidson, USESSC Archive (hereafter Arvidson Papers).

6. CRIPDES, Denuncia, ca. June 25, 1987, File 3-New El Salvador Today (NEST), Box 8, Records of the Center for the Democracy in the Americas (hereafter CDA Records), Wisconsin Historical Society, Madison (hereafter WHS).

7. Going Home Campaign, "Questions and Answers about the Mesa Grande Repatriation/Repopulation to El Salvador," August 23, 1982, CDA Records.

8. John Clifcorn, "Masivo retorno de salvadoreños," *Noticias Aliadas*, 27, no. 7 (March 1, 1990): 3; Norberto (pseudonym), interview by author, February 22, 2003, Chalatenango, El Salvador; and "Refugiado" in *Mesa Grande: Rescate cultural, Collection of writings of Salvadoran refugees at Mesa Grande (1982–1984)*, compiled by Gisela Ursula Heinrich, 1999, in author's possession (hereafter *Rescate cultural*).

9. CARECEN, *Repopulation*, 177–78; Compher and Morgan, *Going Home*, 52.

10. CARECEN, *Repopulation*, 179.

11. CARECEN, *Repopulation*, 147.

12. Going Home, Delegation announcement, September 24, 1987, File 23, Box 10, CDA Records.

13. CARECEN, *Repopulation*, 197, 201.

14. Agamben, *Homo Sacer*.

15. All quotations are from President Ronald Reagan's address to the Nation on United States Policy in Central America, May 9, 1984, http://www.reagan.utexas.edu/archives/speeches/1984/50984h.htm.

16. Quan, "Looking Glass," 280, 289n9.

17. See testimonies in Barba and Martínez, *Memoria*; Servicio Jesuita para el Desarrollo "Pedro Arrupe," *Tiempo de recordar*. See also Todd, *Beyond Displacement*.

18. Marc Rosenthal, "Reflections on Madison–Arcatao Sister City Project," presentation to MASCP members, June 30, 2010, recording and transcript in author's possession.

19. Knight, "U.S. Imperialism," 38–39.

20. President James Monroe, Annual Message to Congress, December 2, 1823, transcript, in *A Century of Lawmaking for a New Nation: U.S. Congressional Documents and Debates, 1774–1875*, 13–14, https://memory.loc.gov/cgi-bin/ampage?collId=llac&fileName=041/llac041.db&recNum=4.

21. Theodore Roosevelt, Annual Message to Congress, December 6, 1904, transcript, https://www.ourdocuments.gov/doc.php?flash=true&doc=56&page=transcript.

22. Classic studies on US interventions in Central America include Pearce, *Under the Eagle*; Chomsky, *Turning the Tide*; LaFeber, *Inevitable Revolutions*; and LeoGrande, *Our Own Backyard*. On Latin America more broadly, consider McPherson, *Intimate Ties*; McPherson, *A Short History*; and Rabe, *The Killing Zone*.

23. Knight, "U.S. Imperialism," 25.

24. Rosen, "Introduction," 2.

25. In addition to the sources listed earlier, on military and intelligence networks (legal and extralegal), see Michael McClintock, *American Connection*; *Los escuadrones*; Huggins, *Political Policing*; Dinges, *Condor Years*; Gill, *School of the Americas*; Menjívar and Rodríguez, *When States Kill*; McSherry, *Predatory States*. On assassination attempts, see U.S. Senate—Select Committee to Study Governmental Operations (Church Committee), "Alleged Assassination Plots Involving Foreign Leaders: An Interim Report," November 20, 1975, http://www.intelligence.senate.gov/sites/default/files/94465.pdf.

On demonstration elections and other forms of propaganda, see Herman and Chomsky, *Manufacturing Consent*.

26. Grandin, *Empire's Workshop*.

27. LaFeber, *Inevitable Revolutions*, 173.

28. Grandin, *Empire's Workshop*, 102. Aid was far more complicated than this overview suggests. On debates and negotiations, consider Arnson, *Crossroads*; LeoGrande, *Our Own Backyard*; and Quan, "Looking Glass." For a comparative approach on US investment, see Cynthia McClintock, *Revolutionary Movements*.

29. Arévalo, *Fábula del tiburón y las sardinas*; Grossman, "Solidarity with Sandino"; Kozel, Grossi, and Moroni, *Imaginario*.

30. Knight, "U.S. Imperialism," 31.

31. LaFeber, *Inevitable Revolutions*, 175. See also Brands, *Latin America's Cold War*; McPherson, *Intimate Ties*. For insights through the lens of education, see Lindo-Fuentes and Chink, *Moderninzing Minds*.

32. Quan, "Looking Glass."

33. Todd, *Beyond Displacement*, 17.

34. Wood, "Agrarian Reform," 144–45. See also Lindo-Fuentes, *Weak Foundations*; Browning, *El Salvador*; and Lauria-Santiago, *Agrarian Republic*. Central Americans typically use *manzanas* rather than hectares or acres. Two hundred hectares (494 acres) is the equivalent of about 286.2 manzanas.

35. On alternative transnational networks, consider Anastario, *Parcels*; and Tsing, *Mushroom*. On "the commons, consider Hardt and Negri, *Commonwealth*; Bollier and Helfrich, *Wealth of the Commons*; Linebaugh, *Stop, Thief*; Federici, *Re-Enchanting the World*.

36. Although some observers point to the Bloc as a creation of the FPL as part of the armed left's strategy to take power, recent research paints a more complex picture. See in particular Chávez, *Poets and Prophets*, 153, 160–61.

37. "A sus ordenes, mi capital," draft editorial, Centro de Documentación Virtual Ignacio Ellacuría, S.J., Universidad Centroamericana José Simeón Cañas, accessed July 14, 2020, http://www.uca.edu.sv/centro-documentacion-virtual/wp-content/up loads/2015/03/C12-c30-.pdf. On the failed agrarian reform, see Chávez, *Poets and Prophets*, 155–56; and Binford, *El Mozote Massacre*, 291–92n11.

38. On the FPL and the popular movements in Chalatenango, see Pearce, *Promised Land*; Harnecker, *Con la mirada en alto*; Chávez, *Poets and Prophets*; Todd, *Beyond Displacement*.

39. Pearce, *Promised Land*, 241.

40. "Reglamentos sobre los cuales se rigen los Poderes Populares Locales," June 8, 1983; "Acuerdos sobre las tareas del Poder Popular," May 26, 1983; and Juana Serrano, "La Primera Asamblea Regional de los Poderes Populares en el Departamento de Chalatenango," May 18, 1983; all in File 13-NEST—essays, projected workplans, Box 8, CDA Records. The attribution for these documents is not clear, but they were likely part of the informational network of the FMLN's north-central regional front (Frente Paracentral "Anastasio Aquino"), directed by the FPL. These stories were likely

announced over the FMLN's clandestine radio stations, Radio Farabundo Martí (operated by the FPL) and Radio Venceremos (operated by the People's Revolutionary Army [Ejército Revolucionario del Pueblo, ERP]). On the Local Popular Governments, see also Salazar and Cruz, *CCR*. On relations between FMLN forces and civilians, see especially Wood, *Insurgent Collective Action*; Viterna, *Women in War*; Sprenkels, *After Insurgency*; and the work of Binford, listed in the bibliography.

41. On this history, consider especially Lindo-Fuentes, *Weak Foundations*; Alvarenga, *Cultura y ética de la violencia*; W. Stanley, *Protection Racket State*; Lauria-Santiago, *Agrarian Republic*; Tilley, *Seeing Indians*; Ching, *Authoritarian*.

42. Chávez, *Poets and Prophets*, 42. Chávez notes that although the FUAR was not a guerrilla movement, its "militant resistance . . . became part of the historical memory and practical experience of the insurgent organizations created in the 1970s" (47). Like FUAR, later groups decried US intervention in El Salvador.

43. Federación de Trabajadores del Campo, "Perspectiva histórica del movimiento campesino revolucionario el El Salvador" (San Salvador: Ediciones Enero '32, August 1979), 41, 47. This is a reprint of a Federation communiqué from April 1, 1977.

44. Coordinadora Revolucionaria de Masas, Platform of the Revolutionary Democratic Government, ca. March 1980, reprinted in Gettleman et al., *El Salvador*, 203.

45. Oscar Romero to Jimmy Carter, February 1980, in author's possession.

46. Gosse, *Rethinking*, 4.

47. "Berger, Victor, 1860–1929: Symbol of Milwaukee Socialism," historical essay available on the WHS website, https://www.wisconsinhistory.org/Records/Article/CS501. See also Nichols, *The "S" Word*.

48. Carbonella, "Empire," 185.

49. In Surbrug, *Beyond Vietnam*, 114.

50. Salomon, "Peace Movement," 117.

51. Gosse, *Where the Boys Are*, 159.

52. Gosse, *Rethinking*, 59–62. The celebratory assessments of Castro's policies on race belie the truly complicated nature of race relations in Cuba. On this, consider de la Fuente, *A Nation for All*; Moore, *Pichón*; Spence Benson, *Antiracism*.

53. Levin, *Cold War University*, 91; Gosse, *Where the Boys Are*, 162–63.

54. In Levin, *Cold War University*, 90.

55. On the limited nature of Cuban solidarity, see Striffler, *Solidarity*, 93.

56. Rev. Arthur Lloyd, interview by author, March 12, 2001, Madison, WI.

57. Green, "Clerics," 109. Many conference materials have been archived at WHS.

58. NACLA, "Keeping up with Latin America," *Latin America and Empire Report* 6, no. 9 (November 1972): 28–31, in Green, *We Cannot Remain Silent*, 396n7. For more on CALA's work, see ch. 5 in Kelly, *Sovereign Emergencies*.

59. "Wisconsin, a Sanctuary for Refugees," *Washington Post*, September 21, 1986, A5.

60. Coutin, *Culture of Protest*, 3.

61. FPL founder Cayetano Carpio quoted in Pearce, *Promised Land*, 127.

62. Gosse, *Where the Boys Are*, 9.

63. Ralph Sprenkels argued that the repopulations that took place in 1986 and after "were directly linked to the [politico-military organizations of the FMLN] and did not allow for noninsurgency supporters to participate" (*After Insurgency*, 361n13).

64. "Sister City Project for the City of Arcatao," 1986; Schrading, *Movimiento*; Sibrián, *Aún luchamos*.

65. Van Gosse, personal communication, July 30, 2015; Pearce, *Promised Land*; Harnecker, *Con la mirada en alto*.

66. On Morazán, see Cagan and Cagan, *Promised Land*; Macdonald and Gatehouse, *In the Mountains*; McElhinny, "Clientelism." On Salvadoran refugees in camps in Nicaragua, Costa Rica, and Panama, see Arnaiz Quintana, *Cartas desde la esperanza*; Barba and Martínez, *Memoria*; Hayden, *Salvadorans in Costa Rica*; Quizar, *My Turn to Weep*.

67. For details on these returns, see Todd, *Beyond Displacement*.

68. Carol Hoffman and Eric Popkin to Friend, February 1, 1991, File 1991 Delegations, MASCP Records. For population sites and numbers, see File Regional Reports: Jan–Mar 92, Box 6, Arvidson Papers.

69. Activists from other countries then used these images as consciousness-raising tools at home. See, for example, Goudvis, *If the Mango Tree Could Speak*; Dale, "Disrupted Lives: Children's Drawings from Central America"; and Marier, *Of Lives Uprooted*.

70. A Call to Accompaniment from the Church and the People of El Salvador, January 20, 1987, MASCP Records.

71. On emotions and solidarity, consider Nepstad and Smith, "Social Structure."

72. Karen Heimer, Rev. Jan Sollon, Billy Feitlinger, and David Wallner to Friends of the People of Arcatao, January 21, 1987, MASCP Records.

73. "A Call to Accompaniment, ca. 1987; Mary Kay Baum and Loretta M. Grow to Friends, July 20, 1994, File Origins of WICOCA, Box 1, Records of the Wisconsin Interfaith Council on Central America (hereafter WICOCA Records), WHS.

74. Mary Kay Baum, interview by author, March 13, 2001, Madison, WI. She expressed similar sentiments in a 2015 interview.

75. Medical Aid to Central America (hereafter MACA), brochure, ca. 1983, Papers of Marc Rosenthal, MASCP Records.

76. Rosenthal, "Reflections."

77. Rocha, *Desobediencia*. See also some of the writing on the Hope Border Institute and the Border Criminologies blogs.

78. Toga party—with beer table—reported in Community Action on Latin America (hereafer CALA), Steering Committee notes, File Blue Binder, Events and Minutes, Box 1, CALA Records, WHS.

79. SHARE began providing direct aid to Salvadoran refugees and internally displaced persons in 1981, and by 1983 NEST had formed "to provide humanitarian aid to Salvadoran civilians affected by the war" (USESSC, "Background Paper," File Nat'l Mtg 1993 New York City, MASCP Records). Both organizations eventually had staff and offices in California, Washington, DC, and New York.

80. Examples of these alignments are clear in the archival record, including SHARE Foundation, 1986 Annual Report, February 1987, in possession of the author; and NEST, organizational objectives and guidelines, August 1983, File 9, Box 8, CDA Records.

81. San Antonio Los Ranchos to international solidarity, 1983, File 5, Box 8, CDA Records. See also NEST, "Sister City Project," March 20, 1983, File 9; and copy of Karen Matthews, "Scenes from Our Sister City," *Berkeley Gazette*, July 22, 1983, File 5-NEST, both in Box 8, CDA Records.

82. Council of the City of Berkeley, "Resolution Establishing a Sister City Affiliation with San Antonio Los Ranchos, El Salvador," July 19, 1983, copy in author's possession.

83. Tracey Schear to Friend, August 22, 1983, File 5-NEST, Box 8, CDA Records.

84. Matthews, "Scenes."

85. Sister City Projects, ca. 1983, File 4-NEST, Box 8, CDA Records.

86. NEST, Statement of Purpose (revised), September 1987, File 8-NEST 1988, Box 8, CDA Records.

87. Julie Cohen, "Cambridge Adopts Sister City," *Guardian*, April 8, 1987. See also Jay Weaver, "Salvadoran sister city plan gets city council approval," *Cambridge Chronicle*, March 26, 1987; and Paul Hirshson, "Council asks El Salvador town to be 'sister city,'" *Boston Globe*, March 26, 1987; all in File City Council Vote 3–1987, Papers of Susan Freireich, private collection, Cambridge, MA (hereafter Freireich Papers). On Madison's resolution, see William C. Thiesenhusen, "Sister City Lets Madison Learn About El Salvador," *Wisconsin State Journal*, April 16, 1986, Section 1, 8. The exploratory stage of these relationships is clear in proposals, meeting notes from both US committees, and folders of communications between the US and Salvadoran towns.

88. Numbers drawn from Interfaith Office on Accompaniment (hereafter IOA), National Sister City Contacts, November 1988, MASCP Records; list in File January 1991 Conference; and "Ciudades Hermanas de Los Estados Unidos," ca. 1991, File ES-"Mesa de Trabajo"-1991; both in Box 8, Arvidson Papers.

89. CORDES, Listado de hermanamientos, File CORDES, Box 3, Arvidson Papers.

90. See especially File Summit '88-Materials, Box 8, Arvidson Papers. Later summits followed similar trajectories, as evidenced by records from the March 1992 and other gatherings in Arvidson Papers, MASCP Records, and the Papers of Judith Somberg, USESSC Archive (hereafter Somberg Papers).

91. On early immigrant organizations, see the work of Perla, listed in the bibliography.

92. José Artiga Escobar, "Afflicted with Hope," interviews by Saint Stephen Evangelical Lutheran Church, New Kingstown, PA, published online between June 2015 and January 2016, http://www.embracingelsalvador.org/jose-artiga/.

93. Artiga Escobar, interviews by Saint Stephen church.

94. Going Home, Blue Ribbon Committee (Partial Listing), ca. 1988, File 23, Box 10, CDA Records.

95. Artiga Escobar, interviews by Saint Stephen church.

96. Juliana Barnard and Jon Haines to Friends, August 11, 1992, File 1992–95 Nat'l Ofc, MASCP Records. See also "Present Organization of the Sister Cities Work," n.d., File Plan de trabajo 1992, Box 6, Arvidson papers.

97. Mario Dávila, interview by author, May 29, 2017, Cambridge, MA; IOA/NEST, National Sister City Contacts, February 1990, File US–El Salvador Sister Cities–National, MASCP Records.

98. José Escobar to Friends, July 30, 1988, File US–El Salvador Sister Cities–National, MASCP Records.

99. Esther Chávez, personal communication, October 2017; and Jon Haines to Friends ca. May 1994, File US–El Salvador Sister Cities–National, MASCP Records.

100. Dávila interview.

101. Margi Clarke and Matt Nichols, interview by author, July 23, 2016, Arcatao, Chalatenango; Dávila, interview; Van Gosse, personal communication, July 30, 2015; Geoff Thale, telephone interview by author, September 15, 2015; José Artiga, interview by author, July 23, 2016, Arcatao, Chalatenango.

102. Dávila interview.

103. Dávila and Artiga interviews.

104. Gosse, personal communication.

105. Dávila interview.

106. Dávila interview; Mario Dávila and Holly Grant to Sister City Projects, February 20, 1988, File Nat'l Mtg 1988 Boston, MASCP Records.

107. Many sistering activists came out of the sanctuary movement; after participating in delegations, sanctuary supporters often moved into direct collaboration with refugee accompaniment organizations and from there to permanent accompaniment through sistering relationships.

108. A remarkable number of activists found their way to sistering through Madison. Catherine Hoffman and Beth Soltzberg, both active with MASCP in the 1980s, went on to lead sistering committees in Massachusetts (in Cambridge and Arlington, respectively). Lisa Zeilinger participated in multiple delegations coordinated by the Wisconsin Interfaith Committee on Central America (WICOCA), MASCP, and Going Home, before becoming a regional promoter for SHARE and executive director of WICOCA in 1992. In the latter capacity, Zeilinger oversaw the rapid expansion of formal sistering links between churches in Milwaukee and El Salvador. And the Seattle-based physician Susan Doederlein, who participated in MASCP-coordinated health care delegations to El Salvador in the early 1990s, contributed to the formation of a sistering relationship between Seattle's St. Joseph parish and Arcatao's San Bartolomé parish.

109. Clarke, "Town Twinning in Cold-War Britain," 174.

110. In addition to Clarke, see Campbell, "Ideals"; Vion, "Town Twinning"; Zelinsky, "Twinning."

111. Juergensmeyer, "Short History . . . People-to-People Program," 9–10.

112. These programs began in 1956 and 1960, respectively. Warner and Shuman, *Citizen Diplomats*; Zelinsky, "Twinning"; Chilsen and Rampton, *Friends in Deed*.

113. Chilsen and Rampton, *Friends in Deed*, 20.

114. In Chilsen and Rampton, *Friends in Deed*, 20. The close links with government offices are clearly visible in the Wisconsin–Nicaragua Partners of the Americas Records, WHS.

115. Chilsen and Rampton, *Friends in Deed*, 20.

116. According to some accounts, after the Somoza regime fell, Partners attempted to continue working under the new Sandinista government. Rather than intimate any support for the Nicaraguan Revolution, however, the WNPA Board of Directors formulated an explicitly nonpolitical statement of purpose. Both Nicaraguan and US officials came to view the organization with suspicion, putting a damper on its activities. See Chilsen and Rampton, *Friends in Deed*, ch. 2; and Weber, *Visions*, 38.

117. Chilsen and Rampton, *Friends in Deed*, xi. Some of WCCN's organizational files have been archived at WHS.

118. Quoted in USESSC, *Aquí estamos*, 7–8.

119. On negotiating strategies and collective identities in the broader Central America solidarity movement, consider Weber, *Visions*; Smith, *Resisting Reagan*; and the work of Gosse, listed in the bibliography. For a view of Central America solidarity within a broader context of US-based solidarity activism, see Striffler, *Solidarity*.

120. Clarke and Nichols interview.

121. Diane Greene, memorandum of phone conversation with Andy Tuch, October 30, 1984, File 21-NEST work plans, essays, Box 8, CDA Records.

122. Marc Rosenthal, interview by author, April 16, 2001, Madison, WI. See also meeting minutes in CALA Records, WHS.

123. Susan Freireich, notes from steering committee meeting, July 20, 1988, File Steering Committee 1986–89, Freireich Papers.

124. Notes, Sister City Planning Meeting, November 20, 1988, File SC Minutes, Somberg Papers. See also Notes, Sister City meeting, November 14, 1988, File SC Steering 1988–June 1989, Somberg Papers; and the meeting agenda in File Steering Committee, Freireich Papers. The meeting was called by Artiga and Solorzano.

125. Notes, Sister City Planning Meeting, November 20, 1988.

126. Susan Freireich, Notes from steering committee meeting, July 20, 1988.

127. Notes, Sister City Planning Meeting, November 20, 1988.

128. David Grosser, email communication, April 26, 2017.

129. Rosenthal, "Reflections."

130. Clarke and Nichols interview.

131. Mesa Grande Repopulation Committee to President Duarte, April 4, 1987, Papers of David Holiday, Americas Watch El Salvador, private collection, San Salvador.

132. Testimony from Arcatao #1, ca. March 1987, File 1986, MASCP Records.

133. Columbus-Copapayo Sister City Project (hereafter CCSCP), "U.S. Role in El Salvador," Newsletter, January 1991, Records of the Columbus-Copapayo Sister City Project, Center for Folklore Studies, Ohio State University (hereafter CCSCP Records).

134. NEST, Objectives, Political Lines-Guidelines, August 1983, File 13, Box 8, CDA Records.

135. "Statement of Sister City Common Goals, ca. January 1988," File Nat'l Mtg 1988 Boston, MASCP Records.

136. "Madison and Arcatao: Sisterhood in Action," in NEST Progress Report 1, 1987, 6, File 12, Box 14, CDA Records.

137. The History of the NEST Foundation, 1987, File 12, Box 14, CDA Records. Operation Phoenix, in January 1986, targeted northern Chalatenango, while Chávez Carreño, in May, targeted the Guazapa region. Various versions of this attack on Arcatao appear in oral history interviews, MASCP Records, and Lippold, *Hope*.

138. Coordinadora Nacional de Repoblamientos (hereafter CNR), Update from El Salvador, April 29, 1988, File Nat'l Mtg 1988 Boston, MASCP Records.

139. NEST, "Humanitarian Aid Denied," Press Release, June 20, 1987, File 3-New El Salvador Today (NEST), Box 8, CDA Records; Testimony from Arcatao #2, April 1986, File 1986, MASCP Records.

140. Tim Doulin, "Tiny Salvadoran Village Wants Only Peace," *Columbus Dispatch*, September 10, 1989, 4B, Box 8, CCSCP Records.

141. Pitching the Sister City, handwritten notes, n.d., Box 20g, CCSCP Records. See also Draft Case Statement, ca. 1992 in same box.

142. Grosser, email communication.

143. History of the NEST Foundation, 1987.

144. Press Statement, November 27, 1989, Box 8, CCSCP Records.

145. Erik Breilid to Michael Barnes, April 11, 1986, Rosenthal Papers, MASCP Records.

146. Cambridge El Salvador Sister City Project, Open Letter to the People of Cambridge and Senators Kerry and Kennedy, *The Tab*, December 5, 1989, 19, File US–El Salvador Sister Cities–National, MASCP Records.

147. Grosser, email communication.

148. Scott, *Domination*.

149. Grosser, email communication.

150. Michael Ring, email communication, January 26, 2020.

151. Thale, phone interview.

152. Artiga interview.

153. Diane Greene to Margarita Studemeister, September 24, [1983], File 19-NEST Sister Cities, Box 8, CDA Records.

154. Sister Cities Steering Committee, meeting notes, December 3, 1988, File Steering Committee, Freireich Papers.

155. Clarke and Nichols interview.

156. "Rojos Pretenden Usar Repatriados," *El Diario de Hoy*, August 15, 1988, 1; and "F.A. Fevela Plan Comunista Para Manipular Repatriados," *El Diario de Hoy*, August 15, 1988, 10, 50; both in File 23-El Salvador Repatriation, 1989, Box 10, CDA Records.

157. For examples, see File 1989–Human Rights Reports and Correspondence, MASCP Records, along with the CDA and CISPES Records at WHS.

158. "Berkeley Mayor Battles for Release of Salvadoran Mayor," *Bulletin of Municipal Foreign Policy* 3, no. 2 (Spring 1989): 11–12; Denver Council Lends Support to Central American Refugees, 12, Box 20a—Sister City 1980–89, CCSCP Records.

159. Christian Urgent Action Network for Emergency Support (CUANES) Alerts, February/March/April 1989, File SC Steering 1988–June 1989, Somberg Papers.

160. Miguel Mejía, interview by Mario Guevara, October 2018, San Salvador, recording and transcripts (Spanish and English translation) in author's possession.

161. "MASCP August Delegation: Meeting with the Arcatao Town Council," ca. August 1991, File 1991 Delegations, MASCP Records; Mejía interview by Guevara.

162. David Burnham, "Foes of Reagan Latin Policies Fear They're Under Surveillance," *New York Times*, April 19, 1985, B20; Rosenthal, "Reflections"; Leonard Cizewki Papers, WHS.

163. On Iran-Contra, see Kornbluh and Byrne, *Iran-Contra*; and Byrne, *Iran-Contra*. On Operation Sojourner, the sanctuary trials, and general harassment, see Coutin, *Culture of Protest*; Smith, *Resisting Reagan*; and Gelbspan, *Break-Ins*. On the Office of Public Diplomacy, see Grandin, *Empire's Workshop*.

164. Department of State, "Support Network for the FMLN/FDR," n.d., CDA, Box 8, Folder 11. Although the document itself is undated, the Department of State Virtual Reading Room website, https://foia.state.gov/, dates it to January 24, 1990. It is available there along with a seven-page explanation, "The Interlocking FMLN/FDR Support Network," January 24, 1990.

165. US Embassy San Salvador to Secretary of State, "FMLN Front Group NEST Brokers Third Sister City," telegram, June 27, 1987, Department of State Virtual Reading Room, https://foia.state.gov/.

166. Agenda for Board Meeting, ca. August 1984, File 13, Box 14, CDA Records.

167. Although NEST's counsel found that "there are no complaints against the organization" and that "the inquiry was commenced because of a mistake on the state's part," it appears that the audit went forward. John K. Van de Kamp to NEST, October 9, 1984, File 21, Box 8, CDA Records.

168. Elliot Abrams to Mr. Conyers, December 19, 1986, File 11, Box 8, CDA Records.

169. L. Francis Bouchey to IRS, January 8, 1987; and J. Michael Waller, "CIS Charges Two El Salvador Charitable Groups with Fraud: Calls on IRS to Investigate," News Bulletin, January 12, 1987, both in File 11, Box 8, CDA Records. Later that year, Waller offered US officials a 135 page tome on the FMLN's "secret support network" in the United States: "Financing Terrorism in El Salvador: The Secret Support Network for the FMLN," June 4, 1987, Department of State Virtual Reading Room, https://foia.state.gov/.

170. Excerpts from transcript of Iran-Contra hearings of June 3, 1987, in Movement Support Network, memorandum to Central American and South African Solidarity Groups, "Groups named as being in possible violation of #501(c)(3) tax-exempt status," June 16, 1987, File 12, Box 14, CDA Records.

171. Rep. Robert K. Dornan to Commissioner Lawrence Gibbs, September 3, 1987, Folder II, Box 8, CDA Records.

172. Bouchey to IRS, January 8, 1987.

173. Grandin, *Empire's Workshop*, 151.

174. Rosenthal, "Reflections."

175. El Salvador Accompaniment Project of WICOCA, "History and Context of Project," September 7, 1988, File WICOCA, MASCP Records.

176. Scigliano, "Sisterhood."

177. Quan, "Looking Glass," 276; Grandin, *Empire's Workshop*.

178. Quan, "Looking Glass," 288, 280.

Chapter 2. Re-educating Empire

1. Graduates of 2nd-level adult literacy class at Mesa Grande Refugee camp, "Este Poema," July 1983; Pedrina, "Canción," July 1983; Cristóbal, "Poema dedicado a todos los refugiados," n.d., all in *Rescate cultural*.

2. Salazar and Cruz, *CCR*, 95.

3. Salazar and Cruz, *CCR*, 100.

4. Freire, *Pedagogy*.

5. Rodriguez and Equipo de Educación Maíz, *Educación popular*, 5, 107. For more on popular education in the Salvadoran context, see especially Hammond, *Fighting to Learn*; Chávez, *Poets and Prophets*; Todd, *Beyond Displacement*, esp. 162–74; and Comunidad de Santa Marta, "Sistematización de la educación popular," unpublished manuscript, 2002, in author's possession. The United States has its own history of popular education, ranging from Myles Horton and the Highlander Folk School, to the Student Nonviolent Coordinating Committee and Freedom Schools, to the oral history work of Staughton and Alice Lynd.

6. Statement of Sister City Common Goals, National Gathering, Boston, March 6, 1988, File National Meetings and Encuentros-1988, MASCP Records.

7. Rate from C. Smith, *Resisting Reagan*, 77; quotation from Gosse, "El Salvador Is Spanish for Vietnam." On a precursor to US solidarity with Central America, see Gosse, *Where the Boys Are*.

8. C. Smith, *Resisting Reagan*, 157–58. Smith incorrectly asserts that Witness for Peace was "the only group that intentionally transported delegations to battle areas to witness the destruction, document cases of human rights abuses" and discourage attacks (159). Gosse states that by 1987 an estimated ten thousand people had traveled to Nicaragua alone ("El Salvador Is Spanish for Vietnam," 319). My own research suggests the numbers are much higher; delegations to El Salvador coordinated by just two smaller Wisconsin-based organizations, WICOCA and MASCP, involved more than one thousand people between 1986 and 1990.

9. President Carter appointed Bowdler Assistant Secretary of State for Latin America in 1979. Rogers had held the same post in the Ford and Nixon administrations. On their mission, see LeoGrande, *Our Own Backyard*, 62–63; Christopher Dickey, "U.S. Mission Arrives in El Salvador to Probe Killing of 4 Catholics," *Washington Post*,

December 7, 1980. On the El Mozote delegation, see Raymond Bonner, "Massacre of Hundreds Reported in Salvador Village," *New York Times*, January 27, 1982; and Alma Guillermoprieto, "Salvadoran Peasants Describe Mass Killing," *Washington Post*, January 27, 1982; as well as United Nations Commission on the Truth for El Salvador, *Truth Commission Report*; and Binford, *El Mozote Massacre*.

10. Perla, "Si Nicaragua Venció," 154. This also emerged in many of my interviews with both Salvadoran and US American activists.

11. Perla and Coutin, "Legacies," 10.

12. Perla and Coutin, "Legacies," 12.

13. Smith, *Resisting Reagan*, 77–78, 157–61, 77–78.

14. Gosse, "El Salvador Is Spanish for Vietnam," 319.

15. Borland, "A Brief Social History of Humanitarian Engagement," 15.

16. Grusky, "International Service Learning," 859.

17. The uptick in interest in "service learning" and "voluntourism" over the past decade has given rise to whole new subfields of scholarly inquiry, as evidenced by articles recently published in education, tourism, and international studies journals. These studies critically examine pedagogical and community-based research methodologies, and address a variety of related themes, including the personal and social development outcomes of global education and "study abroad" programs, the power asymmetries inherent in "First World" citizens' travels to "Third World" locations, and the problematics of advocacy versus neutrality in programming. See, for example, recent articles in *Journal of Sustainable Tourism* and *Journal of Experiential Education*, along with chapters in Borland and Adams, *International Volunteer Tourism*.

18. On Witness for Peace, see Griffin-Nolan, *Witness for Peace*; Williams, "Grassroots Movements." On Peace Brigades International, see Mahony and Eguren, *Unarmed Bodyguards*; Coy, "Cooperative Accompaniment"; Henderson, "Citizenship." On sanctuary, see Golden and MacConnell, *Sanctuary*; Cunningham, *God and Caesar*; Perla and Coutin, "Legacies"; Coutin, *Culture of Protest*. More recently, scholars have placed sustained attention on delegations to and accompaniment of the Colombian Peace Communities and the Zapatistas of southern Mexico. A few examples include Koopman, "Making Space"; Alther, "Colombian Peace Communities"; and Olesen, *International Zapatismo*.

19. Westerman, "Reciprocity."

20. By the early 1990s, Sister Cities affiliates had prepared an instructional manual with a planning calendar that spanned nearly two years, running from pre-trip publicity, recruitment, fund-raising, and group orientations, through in-country itinerary, to post-delegation follow-up and publicity. "How to Plan and Coordinate a Delegation," n.d., File 1990s Delegations Orientation Information, MASCP Records.

21. Gill, "Limits," 668.

22. Ilse to MACA, memorandum, February 16, 1987, Rosenthal Papers, MASCP Records; WICOCA, "History."

23. NEST, General Workplan for 1987, File 3-New El Salvador Today (NEST), Box 8, CDA Records.

24. Carol Hoffman and Eric Popkin to Friends, February 1, 1991, File 1991-Delegation, MASCP Records.

25. Steven Chrzanowski, "Speaking up for the innocent victims of war," *News Journal*, December 2, 1991, A2, File Fall Tour '91, Box 5, Arvidson Papers. On López's awards, see the many tour files in same box.

26. Joy Aruguete and Eric Popkin to Friend of MASCP, January 11, 1988, File More Accomp, Box 6, Records of the Chicago Religious Task Force on Central America, WHS (hereafter CRTFCA Records); A Call to Accompaniment from the Church and the People of El Salvador, January 20, 1987.

27. Eric Popkin to Friends January 11, 1988, File Accompaniment, Box 6, CRTFCA Records.

28. Going Home, Letter to President Arias, September 22, 1987, File 23-El Salvador Repatriation, 1989, Box 10, CDA Records; José Artiga, cited in Perla, "Transnational Public Diplomacy," 175.

29. Going Home; "4,500 Salvadoran Refugees Journey Home Accompanied by North American Religious," Press Release, October 8, 1987, File 23-El Salvador Repatriation, 1989, Box 10, CDA Records.

30. Going Home to President Arias, September 22, 1987. Government targeting of repatriated refugees was nothing new; references to such events lace archival records from the early 1980s through the 1990s, including from the United Nations High Commissioner for Refugees, CRIPDES and CNR (which distributed weekly and monthly calendars to their international contacts), sistering committees, and even the US government.

31. Stern, *Battling*, 115.

32. IOA, Proposed Agenda for National Meeting of USESSC, August 5–6, 1989, MASCP Records.

33. See File Sister City Steering 1988–June 1989, Somberg Papers.

34. NEST, "The Destruction of Rural Life in El Salvador," May 1986, File 10 Reports, Various Organizations, Box 16, CDA Records.

35. History of the NEST Foundation, 1987.

36. NEST, "The Destruction of Rural Life in El Salvador."

37. Draft Report on Delegation Trip to San José Las Flores, May 1987, File 28-ES Repopulations, Box 10, CDA Records.

38. For a primer on the culture of fear in other areas of Latin America, see especially the work of Linda Green and Michael Taussig, excerpted in Scheper-Hughes and Bourgois, *Violence in War and Peace*.

39. USESSC, Program, ca. 1986, MASCP Records. Documents from all Sister City committees contain precisely the same language.

40. USESSC, "Work Plan for Sister City Tour: Oct–Dec 1991," revised draft plan, September 2, 1991, File Tour/1991, Box 5, Arvidson Papers; "U.S.–El Salvador Sister Cities," ca. 1990, File 1992–95 National Office, MASCP Records. See also SHARE, Tours by Salvadoran Parish, Community, and Institutional Representatives to USA Parishes and Communities, ca. 1993, File SHARE/Building a New El Salvador Today, Box 1, WICOCA Records.

41. Conversation with Ruth Navidad, flier, November 19, 1991, File Fall Tour '91, Box 5, Arvidson Papers.

42. "Vision of a New El Salvador," flier, November 1, 1991, File Fall Tour '91, Box 5, Arvidson Papers.

43. USESSC, "Building an Active Grassroots Network for the '90s," September 15, 1992, File 1992–95 National Office, MASCP Records.

44. Mirtala López, borrador de carta abierta, ca. 1991, File Tour 1991-Reports, Box 4, Arvidson Papers.

45. On testimonio, consider Gugelberger and Kearney, "Voices for the Voiceless: Testimonial Literature in Latin America"; Beverley, "Margin"; and Arias, *Controversy*. For insights into testimonial truths in Chile under dictatorship, see Stern, *Battling*, esp. ch. 3.

46. For examples of heavy schedules, see File Tour 1991-Reports, Box 4, Arvidson Papers.

47. USESSC, "Notes from Julio's Testimony," handwritten notes, 1989; USESSC, "Biographical information for visa application/letters of invitation," 1989; and USESSC, "Testimony of Life Under the Bombs," 1989, all in File Tour, Box 5, Arvidson Papers.

48. "Mirtala Lopez: A Personal Experience of War," File Mirtala Packet, Box 4, Arvidson Papers.

49. Westerman, "Refugee Testimonies," 500.

50. Stern, *Battling*, 101.

51. Westerman, "Refugee Testimonies," 502.

52. Stuelke, "Reparative Politics," 768.

53. Henderson, "Citizenship," 971; Sassen, "Repositioning."

54. Henderson, "Citizenship," 971; Sassen, "Repositioning." See also Weber, *Visions*. In the words of Vincent Bulathsinghala of the Center for Conscientization, "There is no rule of law in Sri Lanka, but the government and the police respect the outsider, especially those with white skin. It is not good; it is an imperialist attitude, but is true here. So the presence of an international group . . . gave our group strength." (Cited in Coy, "Cooperative Accompaniment," 98.)

55. Grosser, email communication.

56. Center for Global Service and Education, The Pre-Trip Orientation, File Delegations to Honduras, Box 6, CRTFCA Records.

57. Margaret Topp, Application, ca. July 1995, File 1995–07 Health Care and Education Delegation, MASCP Records.

58. As one manual put it, "Talk about key people to participate and plan delegation with them in mind." ("How to Plan and Coordinate a Delegation," n.d., File 1990s Delegations Orientation Information, MASCP Records.)

59. For the police records, delegation coordinators instructed participants to "go to your local police station and ask for a police clearance letter for visa purposes. It should only take a few minutes for them to process your request." This was, of course, assuming one had no record. Oral history interviews revealed that at least a few delegates had been involved in social activism for years, if not decades, and had been arrested

in the past for civil disobedience. They worked around the police clearance letter by going to a police station in a different county or state.

60. CESES Program, Requirements for Safe-Conduct Passes to the Countryside as of February 1988, File Delegations, Box 2, CRTFCA Records.

61. Ronald Dellums and Joseph Kennedy to José Napoleón Duarte, June 10, 1987, File 3-New El Salvador Today (NEST), Box 8, CDA Records.

62. Scott, *Domination*, 2.

63. Scott, *Domination*, 2.

64. Scott, *Domination*, 4.

65. Orientation for July trip to El Salvador, June 4, 1988, File Delegations, Box 2, CRTFCA Records; "Major Events in Salvadoran History" and "Basic Facts and Background Data," n.d., both in File 1990s Delegations Orientation Information, MASCP Records.

66. *In the Name of the People*, directed by Frank Christopher (Brooklyn, NY: Icarus Films, 1985). In later years, solidarists frequently used *Romero*, directed by John Duigan (Worcester, PA: Vision Video, 2009 [1989]); and *María's Story*, directed by Pamela Cohen and Monona Wali (Oakland, CA: PM Press, 2010 [Camino Films, 1990]). Sistering committee records also contained references to and copies of documentary videos produced by the Going Home campaign, Radio Venceremos, and their own members. Among the latter are MASCP's *They Saw Their Blood Flow*, and Goudvis, *If the Mango Tree Could Speak*.

67. For example: "Bibliography More Reading on El Salvador," n.d., File 1990s Delegations Orientation Information, MASCP Records; "Recommended Reading" and "Recommended Reading (additions)," in File Reading List, Freireich Papers.

68. Other frequently listed texts included Pearce, *Under the Eagle*; Herman and Brodhead, *Demonstration Elections*; Bonner, *Weakness and Deceit*. In addition to the sources listed earlier, see "El Salvador Suggested Reading List," ca. late 1991, File 1990s Delegation Orientation Information, MASCP Records. It is worth noting that many of the materials included in the reading lists were from left-leaning presses, including the independent socialist *Monthly Review* and cooperatives and nonprofits like Zed and South End Press.

69. Companion School Delegation Orientation Session 1, September 15, 1987, File Delegations, Box 2, CRTFCA Records. The CRTFCA coordinated a sister school project and served as an incubator for the Chicago–Cinquera Sister City Project.

70. The earliest organizations to coordinate delegations to the refugee camps in Honduras and to El Salvador developed multipage security guidelines documents, which were then adapted and used by other sistering groups through the 1980s and 1990s. These organizations included the American Friends Service Committee, CRTFCA, and SHARE.

71. Security Guidelines for El Salvador Delegations, ca. 1988, File Accompaniment, Box 6, CRTFCA Records.

72. Security Guidelines for El Salvador Delegations, ca. 1988; NEST, Delegation announcement, June 1987, File 15-NEST Prog Report II Deleg, Box 14, CDA Records;

Holly Grant to Joy Aruguete, March 7, 1987, File MW & W Regional Training Sept 1990, MASCP Records; CESES, delegation orientation packet [excerpts], 1987, Folder El Salvador Orientation Trip Packet 1987, Box 3, CRTFCA Records.

73. See "Orientation for July 1991 Delegation to El Salvador," Coordinator's copy, ca. late July 1991, File 1991 Delegations, MASCP Records; Delegation announcement, June 1987.

74. "Internal security" was the first agenda point discussed by the WICOCA Executive Committee at one meeting: see Minutes, August 26, 1991, File Board Meeting Minutes, Box 1, WICOCA Records.

75. CESES, delegation orientation packet [excerpts], 1987.

76. Security Guidelines for El Salvador Delegations, ca. 1988, File Accompaniment, Box 6, CRTFCA Records.

77. CESES, delegation orientation packet [excerpts], 1987.

78. American Friends Service Committee (hereafter AFSC), "Some information for AFSC Visitors *Before* Coming to Honduras," November 1984, File 16 SHARE's Honduran Delegation 11.84, Box 17, CDA Records.

79. Security Guidelines for El Salvador Delegations, ca. 1988.

80. Security Guidelines for El Salvador, n.d.; CESES, delegation orientation packet [excerpts], 1987; Security Guidelines for El Salvador Delegations, ca. 1988; AFSC, "Some information for AFSC Visitors."

81. AFSC, "Some information for AFSC Visitors."

82. Consulado General de El Salvador, Visa Application, n.d., File 1990s Delegations Orientation, MASCP Records. As with visas, delegates' signatures on salvoconductos issued by the High Command carried legal weight; under penalty of "sanctions," they vowed to not transport military equipment (*pertrechos de guerra*) or any item not specified on the salvoconductos. Juan Orlando Zepeda H., Salvodonducto, June 18, 1987, Ivan Reynaldo Díaz, Salvoconducto, March 16, 1990, both in File 3-New El Salvador Today (NEST), Box 8, CDA Records; Juan Emilio Velasco Alfaro, Salvoconducto, July 27, 1991, File 1987–94 Delegations and Congressional Ltrs Support, MASCP Records.

83. Meeting minutes, February 2, 1989, File Meeting Minutes, MASCP Records; NEST, San José Las Flores Anniversary Delegation Report and Evaluation, ca. June 26, 1987, File 3-New El Salvador Today (NEST), Box 8, CDA Records.

84. NEST, San José Las Flores Anniversary Delegation Report and Evaluation, ca. June 26, 1987. Zepeda also warned them that "the press is trying to take advantage of the Cambridge sister city."

85. Jeannie Berwick, interview by author, April 15, 2013, Seattle, WA.

86. AFSC, "Some information for AFSC Visitors."

87. AFSC, "Some information for AFSC Visitors"; "Orientation for July 1991 Delegation to El Salvador," Coordinator's copy, ca. late July 1991.

88. Security Guidelines for El Salvador Delegations, ca. 1988.

89. Security Guidelines for El Salvador Delegations, ca. 1988.

90. In the event that an emergency call to the NEST coordinators had to be made from the field, this document noted: "Do not use your real name nor mine." Grant to Aruguete, March 7, 1987.

91. Security Guidelines for El Salvador, n.d.

92. IOA, Columbus Delegation Orientation Agenda, August 20, 1989, Box 20a, CCSCP Records.

93. Orientation for July trip to El Salvador, June 4, 1988, File Delegations, Box 2, CRTFCA Records.

94. Packing List for El Salvador Delegations, n.d., File 1990s Delegations Orientation Information, MASCP Records; AFSC, "Some information for AFSC Visitors."

95. Security Guidelines for El Salvador Delegations, ca. 1988.

96. Eric Popkin and Tim Lohrentz to Lisa [Zeilinger], October 9, 1990, File 1990 Delegations, MASCP Records.

97. Eric Popkin to Friends, January 11, 1988, File Accompaniment, Box 6, CRTFCA Records; "Itinerary, WICOCA November 13–21 Delegation," November 1991, File 1991 Delegations, MASCP Records; Health Care Delegation to El Salvador, flier, ca. April 1991, File 1991–07 Health Care Delegation WICOCA-MASCP, MASCP Records; Health-Care Delegation to El Salvador, flier, ca. June 1991, File 1991 Delegations, MASCP Records; Delegation itinerary, March 1985, Folder 14-NEST 1985 Fact-Finding Deleg, Box 14, CDA Records.

98. See Todd, *Beyond Displacement*, esp. chs. 2 and 3.

99. Leigh Anne Jones, "Newport Meets Secretly with Rebel Forces in El Salvador," *Berkeley Voice*, March 27, 1985, File 4 NEST, Box 8, CDA Records.

100. Gus Newport, itinerary and notes from March 1985 delegation to El Salvador, File 14, Box 14, CDA Records.

101. Jones, "Newport Meets Secretly with Rebel Forces."

102. "Sister City Project for the City of Arcatao," 1986, File Arcatao Projects 1986–1989, MASCP Records.

103. Delegation itinerary, March 1985, File 14-NEST 1985 Fact-Finding Deleg, Box 14, CDA Records.

104. Popkin and Lohrentz to [Zeilinger], October 9, 1990; Popkin to Friends, January 11, 1988.

105. Health-Care Delegation to El Salvador, flier, ca. April 1991; Health-Care Delegation to El Salvador, flier, ca. June 1991.

106. "How to Plan and Coordinate a Delegation," n.d., File 1990s Delegations Orientation Information, MASCP Records.

107. It is important to note that this is an essentialized narrative that covers up any internal power relations and debates. For more on this, see especially Perla, "Transnational Public Diplomacy." For insights beyond the heroic version, see Viterna, *Women in War*.

108. Ring, email communication.

109. Art and Sue Lloyd, interview by author, March 12, 2001, Madison, WI. Marc Rosenthal, also of Madison, described a huge party in 1989, with at least five hundred

guerrillas and several thousand campesinos (see Rosenthal, "Reflections.") Similar recollections, shared with more than a little pride, came from older attendees at Sister Cities national gatherings in Austin (2014), Lawrence (2015), and Cambridge (2016).

110. Leah Iraheta, interview by author, June 10, 2014, Seattle, WA.

111. Delegation itinerary, March 1985, File 14-NEST 1985 Fact-Finding Deleg, Box 14, CDA Records.

112. Jones, "Newport Meets Secretly with Rebel Forces."

113. Baum interview, 2001.

114. Tate, *Counting*; Levine, "Evolution," 46.

115. Berwick interview.

116. Baum interview, 2001.

117. Weber, *Visions*, 56–57.

118. MASCP, 25th Anniversary Celebration, Madison, WI, recording and transcript in author's possession. In a similar vein, Brazilian colleagues told Art Lloyd "don't bring your students down here—go back home and do your work at home." Lloyd interview.

119. Lloyd interview.

120. Sister City Projects, ca. 1983, File 4-NEST, Box 8, CDA Records.

121. NEST, Publicity and Education Workplan, October 19, 1983, File 9-NEST/BSCP Propaganda, Box 8, CDA Records.

122. USESSC, Program, ca. 1986; NEST, "New El Salvador Today's Community-to-Community Program," brochure, ca. 1985, File 4-NEST, Box 8, CDA Records.

123. WICOCA, meeting minutes, ca. early 1985; and WICOCA, meeting minutes, March 12, 1985; both in File "File," Box 1, WICOCA Records.

124. MASCP, meeting minutes, February 22, 1989, File Meeting Minutes, MASCP Records; NEST, "New El Salvador Today's Community-to-Community Program."

125. NEST, Publicity and Education Workplan.

126. WICOCA Delegation Statement, November 18, 1985, File "File," Box 1, WICOCA Records.

127. Jones, "Newport Meets Secretly with Rebel Forces."

128. Leigh Anne Jones, "Mayor Reflects on El Salvador Trip: Exclusive Interview," *Berkeley Voice*, March 27, 1985, File 4-NEST, Box 8, CDA Records.

129. MASCP, meeting minutes, May 3, 1989, File MASCP Meeting Minutes, MASCP Records.

130. USESSC, Program, ca. 1989. Sister Cities committee records from Cambridge, Madison, Columbus, and elsewhere provide evidence of this and similar campaigns.

131. See reports from the Hemisphere Initiatives, whose authors were closely connected to the Cambridge Sister City committee. Sister Cities committee records contain repeated references to affiliates providing testimony to local, state, and national officials.

132. "FOCUS Time Line," Papers of Dick and Diana Williams (hereafter Williams Papers), USESSC Archive.

133. Sharon Haas and Don McClain to Bettie Aldrich Eisendrath, February 10, 1985, File 1, Box 3, Bettie Aldrich Eisendrath Papers; Central America Week poster and

calendar of events, File CAC-101, Box 1, Alan and Kristin Dooley Papers, both at WHS.

134. Sister Cities, meeting minutes, April 11, 1989, File SC-Meeting Minutes, Somberg Papers.

135. Susan Freireich, slideshow script for tray #3, File Slideshow, Freireich Papers. See also NEST, "The Dawn of a New Society," slideshow script, Folder 9-NEST, BSCP Propaganda, Box 8, CDA Records.

136. Several US Americans with experience in El Salvador accompanied the caravan. Art Lloyd to all the WICOCA folk, December 20, 1986, File "File," Box 1, WICOCA Records. During the late 1980s and early 1990s, Sister Cities activists collaborated with Pastors for Peace to organize several massive caravans to deliver aid material to El Salvador. The Arvidson Papers contain details about several of these caravans.

137. Consider MASCP, meeting minutes, February 22 and 29 and March 1, 1989, File Meeting Minutes, MASCP Records; Paul Scire to Sister Communities and Sister Parishes, "An Urgent Call to Prayer, Fasting, and Action," August 19, 1991, File SHARE-Sister Parish Program, Box 1, WICOCA Records; and "A Pledge to Pray, Fast, and Act," ca. Sep. 1991, File 10-Sister Cities, Box 7, CDA Records.

138. CCR to Hrnos. Ciudades Hermanas de los Estados Unidos, August 10, 1989, File Tour, Box 5, Arvidson Papers.

139. "Responses to put-offs"; "Tour visit rap"; Margi Clarke to Sister Cities, August 30, 1989, all in File Tour, Box 5, Arvidson Papers; and IOA, Proposed Agenda for National Meeting of USESSC, Rosenthal Papers, MASCP Records.

140. USESSC, "Notes from Julio's Testimony," handwritten notes, 1989; USESSC, "Biographical information for visa application/letters of invitation," 1989; USESSC, "Testimony of Life under the Bombs," 1989.

141. Chrzanowki, "Speaking up."

142. USESSC, national meeting minutes, August 5–6, 1989, Box 20a, CCSCP Records.

143. Gira de Ciudades Hermanas, Resumen de Trabajo de Columbus, Ohio, October 12–15, 1991, File Tour 1991-Reports, Box 4, Arvidson Papers.

144. Rosenthal, "Reflections."

145. Prudence Barber, interview by author, February 18, 2015, Madison, WI.

146. Rosenthal, "Reflections" and interview.

147. On smoking, see MACA, meeting notes, September 9, 1986, spiral notebook, Rosenthal Papers, MASCP Records. Extreme tensions surfaced between Paul Davis, a Congressional aide, and Maytee Colorado, a health worker, during the June 1988 Cambridge medical delegation; see Judith Somberg, handwritten notes, June 1988; and Susan Freireich, notes from delegation debriefing, July 9, 1988; both in File SC Delegation June 1988, Somberg Papers. And warnings about the notorious fellow appear in Judith Somberg, handwritten notes, ca. April 1989, File SC-June 1989 Delegation, Somberg Papers.

148. USESSC, national meeting minutes, January 1990, File National Meetings and Encuentros, MASCP Records; Gira de Ciudades Hermanas, October 1991.

149. CRIPDES, CORDES, SHARE, USESSC, Resumen de la discusión sobre hermanamientos, February 9, 1993, File CRIPDES and Sistering, Box 7, Arvidson Papers.

150. SHARE, Tours by Salvadoran Parish, Community, and Institutional Representatives to USA, ca. 1993.

151. USESSC, Report and Conclusions from Fourth National Conference, ca. February 1993, File National Meetings and Encuentros, MASCP Records. Although Berkeley unquestioningly takes first place, Madison and Cambridge activists continue friendly sparring to this day about who takes second.

152. USESSC, *Aquí estamos*, 9.

153. Margi [Clarke] to Carol [Hoffman], August 3, 1990, File 1990–92 Arcatao Projects, MASCP Records.

154. Chalatenango directiva presidents to Tracey Schear, August 8, 1989, File Tour, Box 5, Arvidson Papers.

155. USESSC, national meeting minutes, January 1990.

156. Karen Matthews, "Scenes from our Sister City," *Berkeley Gazette*, July 22, 1983, File 5-NEST, Box 8, CDA Records.

157. Delegation announcement, June 1987, Folder 15-NEST Prog Report II Deleg, Box 14, CDA Records.

158. Letters of support and salvoconductos indicate that thirty people from the United States had originally planned on participating. See NEST files in CDA Records.

159. Open Letter to President Duarte from Community of Cambridge, MA, *El Mundo*, June 17, 1987, Folder 3-New El Salvador Today (NEST), Box 8, CDA Records. For dozens of letters of support see this file and File 28-ES Repopulations, Box 10.

160. NEST, San José Las Flores Anniversary Delegation Report and Evaluation, ca. June 26, 1987.

161. Thale, phone interview.

162. NEST, San José Las Flores Anniversary Delegation Report and Evaluation.

163. NEST, "Humanitarian Aid Denied," press release, June 20, 1987; F. Michael McFadden, statement, June 20, 1987; Delegation, statement, June 20, 1987, all in Folder 3-New El Salvador Today (NEST), Box 8, CDA Records.

164. CRIPDES, Denuncia, ca. June 25, 1987, Folder 3-New El Salvador Today (NEST), Box 8, CDA Records. See same file for many other statements issued by CRIPDES on this day. Among the individuals CRIPDES named were Colonel Gilberto Rubio Rubio and Colonel Benjamín Eladio Canjura Alvayero. Rubio was first in command in Chalatenango at the time, and Canjura second. Both have been linked to human rights abuses, including illegal detention, torture, and the 1989 assassination of six Jesuit priests and two women.

165. Radio Farabundo Martí, ca. July 31, 1987; and News Roundup from El Salvador, June 15–21, 1987, both in File 12-RFM Boletín 1987, Box 15, CDA Records; NEST, San José Las Flores Anniversary Delegation Report and Evaluation; Nancy Ryan and Cathy Hoffman, interview by author, May 30, 2017, Cambridge, MA.

166. NEST, San José Las Flores Anniversary Delegation Report and Evaluation.

167. Jim Wallace, interview by author, May 26, 2017, Cambridge, MA.

168. Ryan and Hoffman interview.

169. NEST, San José Las Flores Anniversary Delegation Report and Evaluation; Ryan and Hoffman interview.

170. NEST, San José Las Flores Anniversary Delegation Report and Evaluation.

171. "ORDENANA SALIR A 21 NORTEAMERICANOS," *El Mundo*, June 26, 1987, File 3-New El Salvador Today (NEST), Box 8, CDA Records.

172. "ORDENAN SALIR." All delegates departed the country as originally planned, without incident.

173. Thale interview.

174. NEST, San José Las Flores Anniversary Delegation Report and Evaluation.

175. Ring, email communication.

176. Brief for Julio Tobar, handwritten notes, ca. 1989, File Tour, Box 5, Arvidson papers.

177. Perla and Coutin, "Legacies," 12; Westerman, "Central American Refugee Testimonies." See also Stuelke, "Reparative Politics."

178. Ring, email communication.

179. In Draft Report on Delegation Trip to San Jose Las Flores, May 1987, File 28-ES Repopulations, Box 10, CDA Records.

180. Bassano, "Boomerang," 24.

181. Quan, "Looking Glass," 279, 286.

182. Quan, "Looking Glass," 286–87.

183. Stern, *Battling*, 101.

184. Quan, "Looking Glass," 278.

Chapter 3. New Horizons

1. "A Milestone for El Salvador," editorial, *Chicago Tribune*, March 24, 1994, 26; "Salvadoran Success," editorial, *Washington Post*, April 27, 1994, A22.

2. Cambridge committee, meeting notes, December 14, 1988, File SC Minutes [1986–89]; and Susan Freireich, Delegation Debriefing, handwritten notes, July 9, 1988, File SC Delegation June 1988, both in Somberg Papers.

3. Staff of the Arms Control and Foreign Policy Caucus, "Barriers to Reform: A Profile of El Salvador's Military Leaders," Report to the Arms Control and Foreign Policy Caucus, May 21, 1990.

4. Ring, email communication.

5. Susan Freireich, Delegation Debriefing.

6. Interview with CCR, ca. April 1989, File SC Steering 1988–June 1989, Somberg Papers.

7. Cinny Poppen to Friend, May 1, 1989, File SC Steering 1988–June 1989, Somberg Papers.

8. Poppen to Friend, May 1, 1989; and CUANES, Alerts, February/March/April 1989.

9. CRIPDES, "Resumen Informativo," August 1989, in File 1989-A, MASCP Records.

10. Poppen to Friend, May 1, 1989.

11. Ring, email communication.

12. Central American Presidents, "Procedure for the Establishment of a Firm and Lasting Peace in Central America," presented to the UN General Assembly, 42nd session, August 7, 1987, https://peacemaker.un.org/sites/peacemaker.un.org/files/CR%20 HN%20GT%20NI%20SV_870807_EsquipulasII.pdf.

13. Although the CIREFCA process took its name from the Spanish acronym for the International Conference on Central American Refugees, held in May 1989, it encompassed a series of other meetings and agreements that took place between 1988 and 1994. "International Conference on Central American Refugees (CIREFCA)," *International Journal of Refugee Law* 1, no. 4 (1989), 582–96; United Nations High Commission for Refugees-Central Evaluation Section, "Review of the CIREFCA Process" EVAL/ CIREF/14, May 1, 1989, https://www.unhcr.org/research/evalreports/3bd410804/.

14. National Agenda for Peace in El Salvador, "Introduction," Final Document of the National Debate for Peace in El Salvador (English translation), September 4, 1988, File National Debate for Peace, Somberg Papers. Quotations drawn from sections 5.1 and 5.3. According to the Cambridge sistering committee, more than one hundred groups participated in the National Agenda, representing 65 percent of the population of El Salvador. (Planning meeting notes, November 20, 1988, File SC Minutes, Somberg Papers.)

15. FMLN-General Command, Proposal to Convert the Elections to a Contribution Towards Peace, January 23, 1989, File SC Steering 1988–June 1989, Somberg Papers.

16. Interview with CCR, ca. April 1989.

17. George H. W. Bush, Address before a Joint Session of the Congress on the State of the Union, January 29, 1991, George Bush Presidential Records, Public Papers, George H. W. Bush Presidential Library, https://bush41library.tamu.edu/archives/ public-papers/2656.

18. "Summary of Accomplishments of Previous Accords," ca. late 1991, File National Conference Packet—Originals, Arvidson Papers.

19. Tim Lohrentz, "Growth in CRIPDES: January 1990–June 1991," ca. June 1991, File ES Mesa de Trabajo 1991, Box 8, Arvidson Papers.

20. CORDES, "Nos estamos preparando ante la posibilidad de que estalle la paz," *Horizontes Nuevos*, no. 6 (July 1991): 4–5, File Nuestra Tierra, Box 7, Arvidson Papers. I discuss the New Initiative in detail in chap. 4.

21. Meeting minutes, February 8, 1989, File SC minutes, Somberg Papers.

22. Representatives of Salvadoran Sister Cities in the United States and Canada, "Appeal to President José Napoleón Duarte and the Salvadoran Armed Forces," February 9, 1989, File MASCP Meeting Minutes 1989, MASCP Records.

23. USESSC, Newsletter, April 1991, File 1988–94 National Office, MASCP Records.

24. Lohrentz, "Growth in CRIPDES."

25. Informe sobre viaje, ca. August 1991, File ES Mesa de Trabajo 1991, Box 8, Arvidson Papers.

26. Jack Mills, Report on visit to Guancorita, March 21, 1990, File Delegation Reports, Box 4, CCSCP Records.

27. "Ron Meyers—March 1989 Journal," File Delegation Reports, Box 4, CCSCP Records.

28. Inocente de Jesús Orellana y Moises Calles to Sister Cities (English translation), July 13, 1988, File Summit '88-Materials, Box 8, Arvidson Papers.

29. See for example, Mayor F. Joseph Sensenbrenner Jr., Resolution, May 5, 1988, File Summit '88-Materials, Box 8, Arvidson Papers.

30. Open Letter to the Government of President José Napoleón Duarte and the Armed Forces of the Republic of El Salvador, August 30, 1988, File Summit '88-Materials, Box 8, Arvidson Papers.

31. Carol [Hoffman] and Eric [Popkin], "Congressional strategy," in USESSC national meeting minutes, August 5–6, 1989, File Sister City 1980–89, Box 20a, CCSCP Records.

32. Rosenthal, "Reflections."

33. USESSC, national meeting minutes, August 5–6, 1989.

34. Eric Popkin and Tim Lohrentz to Lisa [Zeilinger], October 9, 1990.

35. Kathryn Wysockey to supporter, ca. March 1991, File MASCP 1987–94 Delegations and Congressional Ltrs Support, MASCP Records.

36. "Third Sister Cities Summit with El Salvador 'Joint Declaration,'" March 23, 1991, File National Meetings and Encuentros, MASCP Records.

37. "Third Sister Cities Summit with El Salvador 'Joint Declaration.'"

38. The IOA promised to lead at least ten delegations to El Salvador between June 1991 and June 1992 alone. (IOA, "Appropriate Technology for Human Development," June Delegation 1991, File 1991–2007 Health Care Delegation, MASCP Records.)

39. Nancy M. Ryan to Ambassador Edwin G. Corr, July 22, 1988, File Exclusion from El Salvador, Box 1, Somberg Papers.

40. Ross Gelbspan, "US Is Linked to Intimidation of Activists in Latin America," *Boston Globe*, November 24, 1988, A2, 6–7, File Exclusion from El Salvador, Box 1, Somberg Papers.

41. Wallace interview.

42. David B. Dlouhy to Nancy Ryan, August 17, 1988, File Exclusion from El Salvador, Box 1, Somberg Papers.

43. Wallace interview.

44. Judy Somberg, handwritten notes, February 15, 1989, File Exclusion from El Salvador, Box 1, Somberg Papers.

45. Somberg, handwritten notes, February 15, 1989.

46. Wallace interview.

47. James Wallace to David Dlouhy, February 13, 1989, File Emerg. Deleg, Papers of James Wallace (hereafter Wallace Papers), Cambridge, MA, private collection. The one exception was Rep. Kennedy's aide, Paul Davis. Officials claimed that the delegation had provided supplies to the FMLN, a charge vehemently challenged by Sister Cities activists. Images captured by professional photographer Van Hardy documented

that the medical supplies they brought to their sister city "were given military clearance and used by [the] San José Las Flores clinic for civilians (especially children)." Sister Cities, meeting minutes, April 11, 1989, File SC-Meeting Minutes, Somberg Papers.

48. Wallace interview. See also James E. Wallace to Sen. Edward Kennedy, Request to Salvadoran Authorities for Reinstatement of Medical Delegation, April 11, 1989, Wallace Papers.

49. Wallace interview.

50. Meeting minutes, April 11, 1989.

51. Nancy Ryan, Report on exclusion from El Salvador, ca. October 1988, File Exclusion from El Salvador, Box 1, Somberg Papers.

52. Gelbspan, "US Is Linked to Intimidation," and *Break-Ins.*

53. Meeting minutes, April 11, 1989.

54. Jim Wallace to Nancy Soderberg, April 12, 1989, File Exclusion from El Salvador, Box 1, Somberg Papers.

55. Wallace to Soderberg, April 12, 1989.

56. Rosenthal, "Reflections."

57. Julie [Derwinski], "July Health Care Delegation to Arcatao," report, July 1991, File 1988–94 Health Care and Women's Organizing, Rosenthal Papers, MASCP Records.

58. Rosenthal, "Reflections."

59. Rosenthal, "Reflections."

60. Gilberto Rubio R. to Jim Moody, July 10, 1991, File 1987–94 Delegations and Congressional Ltrs Support, MASCP Records.

61. "Orientation for July 1991 Delegation to El Salvador," ca. late July 1991, File 1991 Delegations, MASCP Records.

62. WICOCA, News Release, ca. July 23, 1991, File 1987–94 Delegations and Congressional Ltrs Support, MASCP Records.

63. Rosenthal, "Reflections." A press release put it much more diplomatically: "Moody's office negotiating with Salvadoran military and government officials and US Embassy personnel to secure a pass, ensure safety." WICOCA, News Release, ca. July 23, 1991.

64. Rosenthal, "Reflections."

65. WICOCA, "Congressman Moody Secures Release of Medical Supplies," press release, ca. July 27, 1991, File 1987–94 Delegations and Congressional Ltrs Support, MASCP Records.

66. Juan Emilio Velasco Alfaro, Salvoconducto, July 27, 1991, File 1987–94 Delegations and Congressional Ltrs Support, MASCP Records.

67. Report on Exit from Chalatenango, August 2, 1991, File 1988–94 Health Care and Women's Organizing, Rosenthal Papers, MASCP Records.

68. Rosenthal, "Reflections."

69. Meeting notes, ca. 1991, steno notebook, File ES Mesa de Trabajo 1991, Box 8, Arvidson Papers.

70. Lisa Robinson, "Peasant Organizing in Rural El Salvador," ca. 1987, Papers of Mary Kay Baum (hereafter Baum Papers), MASCP Records.

71. Comisión Nacional de Hermanamientos, meeting minutes, January 11, 1993, File Sistering Commission/Tim, Box 6, Arvidson Papers.

72. Tomasa Ruíz, "Toward a Rural Communal Movement," in USESSC, Report on Visit to El Salvador, July 1992, File 1992–95 National Office, MASCP Records.

73. "Chalatenango Regional Report," April 14, 1992, File Regional Reports: Jan–Mar '92, Box 6, Arvidson Papers.

74. Ruíz, "Toward a Rural Communal Movement."

75. "Chalatenango Regional Report," April 14, 1992.

76. CRIPDES Sistering Commission, Regional Update for Chalatenango, April 6, 1993, File Regional Reports 93, Box 6, Arvidson Papers.

77. For a grassroots perspective, consider Salazar and Cruz, *CCR*.

78. On the sense of abandonment in the wake of the peace accords, see especially Silber, *Everyday Revolutionaries*; and Peterson, "Consuming Histories."

79. [Julie Derwinsky,] Dec. Delegation, handwritten notes, December 1993, File 1993 Delegations, MASCP Records.

80. [Derwinsky], Dec. Delegation notes.

81. CRIPDES Sistering Commission, Regional Update for Chalatenango, April 6, 1993; Rosa Rivas to Sister Cities National Center, handwritten memo, March 30, 1993, File Sistering Commission/Tim, Box 6, Arvidson Papers.

82. CRIPDES Sistering Commission, Regional Update for Chalatenango, April 6, 1993.

83. [Derwinski], Dec. Delegation, notes. A critical function of the mayors after returning to their posts was establishing and maintaining civil registries and issuing birth and death certificates and identity documents required for voter registration.

84. [Tim Lohrentz], handwritten notes, April 17, 1993, File Sistering Commission/Tim, Box 6, Arvidson Papers.

85. [Derwinski], Dec. Delegation, notes.

86. [Derwinski], Dec. Delegation, notes.

87. [Tim Lohrentz], handwritten notes, April 17, 1993.

88. CRIPDES Sistering Commission, Regional Update for Chalatenango, April 6, 1993.

89. [Derwinsky], Dec. Delegation, notes.

90. Rivas to Sister Cities National Center, March 30, 1993.

91. Spence and Vickers, *Toward a Level Playing Field*; O'Donnel, Spence, and Vickers, *Elections 1994*.

92. Spence and Vickers, *Toward a Level Playing Field*, 17. The code went into effect eight months later than the accords had stipulated; and the Tribunal delayed approving regulations to put the code into practice. (O'Donnel, Spence, and Vickers, *Elections 1994*, 1.)

93. Some exiled leftists returned to El Salvador in 1987 and participated in the 1989 elections, with some gains, illustrating that "political space had widened" since 1980. Yet the 1994 election was the first in which all parties of the opposition agreed to participate. See Spence and Vickers, *Toward a Level Playing Field*.

94. William M. LeoGrande, Op-Ed, *New York Times*, May 29, 1993, in File Elections-Campaigns and Materials, Box 6, Arvidson Papers.

95. Juan José Dalton, "El Salvador: FMLN Leader Villalobos Arrested," Inter-Press Service, October 19, 1994, File Sister Cities 1994, Somberg Papers.

96. Sister Cities to Friends, June 9, 1994, File 1988–94 National Office, MASCP Records.

97. Margaret Gruenke to Jan Meyers, March 4, 1991, File 1987–94 Delegations and Congressional Ltrs Support, MASCP Records.

98. Sister Cities to Friends, June 9, 1994.

99. Spence and Vickers, *Toward a Level Playing Field*, 15.

100. USESSC, "Action Alert," October 26, 1993, MASCP Records.

101. Spence and Vickers, *Toward a Level Playing Field*, 21.

102. Sister Cities to Friends, June 9, 1994; O'Donnel, Spence, and Vickers, *Elections 1994*, 3.

103. O'Donnel, Spence, and Vickers, *Elections 1994*; Gruenke to Meyers, March 4, 1991.

104. O'Donnel, Spence, and Vickers, *Elections 1994*, 12; "Continúa preocupación por posible fraude electoral," *Diario Latino*, April 20, 1993, 3.

105. Iniciativa Social Para la Democracia (hereafter ISD), Boletín #1, File Elections-Background Info, Box 6, Arvidson Papers.

106. "Continúa preocupación."

107. "Continúa preocupación."

108. ISD, Goals and Objectives (English translation), ca. March 1993, File Elections-Background Info, Box 5, Arvidson Papers.

109. ISD, "Proyecto de Emergencia," March 1993, File Elections-Background Info, Box 6, Arvidson Papers; ISD, Goals and Objectives.

110. ISD, "Proyecto," ca. March 1993, File Elections-Background Info, Box 6, Arvidson Papers.

111. ISD, "Propuesta de Estrategia de la Solidaridad," File Elections-Campaigns and Materials, Box 6, Arvidson Papers.

112. ISD, "Ideas for the role of solidarity in the 1994 El Salvador Elections," File Elections-Campaigns and Materials, Box 6, Arvidson Papers.

113. USESSC, Campaign for Democracy, ca. mid-1993, and other materials in File Elections-Campaigns and Materials, Box 6, Arvidson Papers.

114. David Grosser to Ann S., draft letter, July 1, 1993, File Elections-Campaigns and Materials, Box 6, Arvidson Papers.

115. "Transition to Democracy," in Lisa Zeilinger to Friends, December 14, 1993, Baum Papers, MASCP Records.

116. USESSC, "Action Alert"; Denis Johnston to Rep. Robert Menendez, October 26, 1993, File 1993 Misc, MASCP Records; Jon Haines, Program-Political Pressure and Visibility, handwritten notes, ca. mid-1993, File Elections-Campaigns and Materials, Box 6, Arvidson Papers.

117. USESSC, "Campaign for Democracy"; MASCP, "Madisonian to Release El Salvador Video," press release, July 28, 1993; and MASCP, "Proposal for Fall Action Campaign," ca. July 1993, all in File Elections-Campaigns and Materials, Box 6, Arvidson Papers.

118. USESSC, "Campaign for Democracy."

119. Cambridge–San José Las Flores Sister City Project, "Cambridge Sister City Group Joins National Effort," press release, June 24, 1993; CISPES, "Building Democracy in El Salvador," flier, spring 1993; and Petition to President Clinton, 1993, all in File Elections-Campaigns and Materials, Box 6, Arvidson Papers. Other cosponsors of the campaign included SHARE and CISPES. More than two hundred organizations signed on as supporters.

120. Flynn and Prokosch, "Accompanying the Salvadoran movement in the 1993–94 elections," draft proposal, July 1993, File Elections-Campaigns and Materials, Box 6, Arvidson Papers. See also Lisa Zeilinger to Friends, November 22, 1993, File 1994 Election Observation Delegation, Baum Papers, MASCP Records.

121. Jenny Utech to Sister City supporter, June 30, 1994, File Sister Cities 1994, Somberg Papers. Delegations accompanied both the March general elections and the April run-off elections.

122. Sister Cities to Friends, June 9, 1994.

123. Natasha Kassulke, "Madison's Salvadoran Sister City Left Out of Upcoming Elections," *Wisconsin State Journal*, March 13, 1994, File Polling Place Denial 3/14/94, MASCP Records.

124. Handwritten notes, ca. March 1994, File Polling Place Denial 3/14/1994, MASCP records.

125. Kassulke, "Madison's Salvadoran Sister City Left Out."

126. Mary Kay Baum to MASCP staff, fax, March 17, 1994, File Polling Place Denial, MASCP Records.

127. Anne Woehrle to Supreme Electoral Tribunal, fax, March 13, 1994; Anne Woehrle to US Embassy in El Salvador, fax, March 13, 1994, File Polling Place Denial, MASCP Records.

128. MASCP, press release, March 18, 1994, File Polling Place Denial, MASCP Records.

129. Abel Escalante López, José Gervasio Ayala, José Reynaldo Alas, and Eduardo Gadamez, Denunciation (English translation), March 18, 1994; MASCP, "Ante el pueblo salvadoreño," open letter, *Diario Co-Latino*, March 17, 1994, both in File Polling Place Denial, MASCP Records.

130. Kassulke, "Madison's Salvadoran Sister City Left Out."

131. Mary Kay Baum, interview by author, February 13, 2015, Middleton, WI.

132. Sister Cities to Friends, June 9, 1994.

133. Quoted in Sister Cities to Friends, June 9, 1994.

134. Utech to Sister City supporter, June 30, 1994.

135. Sister Cities to Friends, June 9, 1994.

136. Stahler-Sholk, Vanden, and Becker, "Introduction," 8.

137. The WICOCA Sister Community Project, n.d., File SHARE—Sister Parish Program, Box 1, WICOCA Records.

138. Quoted in Lippold, *Hope.*

139. WICOCA Sister Community Project.

140. USESSC, "Background Paper," ca. December 1992, File 1992–95 National Office, MASCP Records.

141. SHARE, "Building a New El Salvador Today," ca. June 1992, File NEST, Box 1, WICOCA Records. Weber notes that both Witness for Peace and the Wisconsin Coordinating Council on Nicaragua also "took care to avoid the reproduction of imperialist and racist relationships with Nicaraguans. The very notion of Solidarity was about undoing the North to South history of domination." (Weber, *Visions,* 56–57.)

142. WICOCA Sister Community Project. It is worth noting here that multiple WICOCA and MASCP members have lived in intentional communities, much like their southern neighbors did during the first years of the repopulation movement.

143. Ilse to MACA, February 16, 1987. Internal documents from both Community Action on Latin America and MACA reveal that such discussions began in May 1984 and continued through MACA's existence. At heart in the debate was the extent to which each group and its affiliates wanted to "be political" or "endorse particular political parties."

144. MACA History, ca. 1988, Rosenthal Papers, MASCP Records; WICOCA Board of Directors, meeting minutes, April 21, 1992, and August 27, 1992, both in File Board Meeting Minutes; and WICOCA, meeting minutes, September 10, 1985, File "File," all in Box 1, WICOCA Records.

145. Art Lloyd, handwritten notes, July 15, 1986; and Eunice Wagner, WICOCA meeting minutes, July 15, 1986, both in File "File," Box 1, WICOCA Records. According to the minutes, it was Leonard Cizewski, as co-coordinator for Wisconsin Witness for Peace, who raised the scholarship idea at the meeting.

146. These themes are especially clear in the files relating to NEST in the CDA Records.

147. Central American Solidarity Alliance and Community Action on Latin America, proposal to the CISPES national convention, May 1985, File 1985 Nat'l Con, Box 1, CISPES Records, WHS.

148. National Agenda for Peace in El Salvador, "Join in the National Advocacy Day for El Salvador, September 20, 1993," ca. August 1993, File Elections-Campaigns and Materials, Box 6, Arvidson Papers. This advocacy day was part of a national campaign, co-sponsored by Sister Cities, SHARE, and other groups, known as "Journey to Justice."

149. Sister Cities to Friends, June 9, 1994.

150. Enrique García to Brothers, Sisters and Friends (English translation), ca. January 21, 1992, File Nat'l Conference Packet—Originals (1992), Arvidson Papers.

Chapter 4. This Promised Land

1. Nancy Nusser, "Former Foes in El Salvador Cheer Signing of Peace Accord," *Atlanta Journal and Constitution,* January 17, 1992, A6; Tim Golden, "The Salvadorans

Make Peace in a 'Negotiated Revolution,'" *New York Times*, January 5, 1992, Sec. 4, 3; Douglas Grant Mine, "Rival Block Parties Celebrate Peace in El Salvador," Associated Press, January 16, 1992.

2. In addition to the other sources listed in this chapter, see van der Borgh, "Decision-Making," 51–52; and Stanley, "State-Building," 109.

3. Gobierno de El Salvador y el Frente Farabundo Martí para la Liberación Nacional, *Acuerdos de El Salvador: En el camino de la paz* (hereafter *Acuerdos de paz*), 80.

4. *Acuerdos de paz*, 87–88.

5. *Acuerdos de paz*, 85.

6. See de Bremond, "Politics"; and Chávez, "How Did War End."

7. Chávez, "How Did War End," 1788, 1796.

8. Stern, *Reckoning*, 367.

9. CRIPDES-CNR, "Programa Global 1992–1993," July 1991, 19, File CRIPDES Global Prjt, Box 6, Arvidson Papers.

10. "Final Document of the National Debate for Peace in El Salvador," English Translation, September 4, 1988, Sections 2.1.1, 2.1.2, 2.2.3, and 1.2.3, File National Debate for Peace, Somberg Papers.

11. Department of Social Sciences, "Analysis," 428; CRIPDES-CNR, "Programa Global," July 1991.

12. Villacorta Zuluaga, "Transición," 70.

13. De Soto and del Castillo, "Obstacles Revisited," 210.

14. Regional Project for Sister Relationships in the Chalatenango Region (draft translation), ca. January 1992, Baum Papers, MASCP Records.

15. Salvador Orellana, "The Struggle for an Economic and Political Alternative," in USESSC, Report on Visit to El Salvador, July 1992, File 1992–95 National Office, MASCP Records.

16. CRIPDES-CNR, "Programa Global 1992–1993," July 1991, File "CRIPDES Global Prjt," Box 6, Arvidson papers.

17. USESSC, handwritten planning notes, August 27, 1990, File SC Training—Boston 1990, Arvidson Papers.

18. CORDES, Redefinición Institucional Fundación CORDES, February 1993, File CORDES, Box 3, Arvidson Papers.

19. CORDES, "Repobladores y desplazados: nuestra razón de existir," editorial, *Horizontes Nuevos*, no. 6 (July 1991): 2, File Nuestra Tierra, Box 7, Arvidson Papers.

20. CORDES, "Repobladores y desplazados."

21. "Memoria del IV Cumbre de hermanamientos, ca. March 23, 1992, File Regional Reports: Jan–Mar 92, Box 6, Arvidson Papers.

22. Holly Grant and Barbara Burch to Friends, December 1990, WICOCA Files, MASCP Records.

23. CRIPDES-CNR, "Programa Global," 22.

24. *Acuerdos de paz*, 43.

25. National NGO Association, Position on National Reconstruction, draft translation, 4, January 31, 1992, File Reconstruction, Box 4, Arvidson Papers.

26. *Acuerdos de paz*, 53.

27. Wood, "Los Acuerdos de Paz," 116.

28. Rosa and Foley, "El Salvador," 138.

29. "Memoria del IV Cumbre de hermanamientos."

30. National NGO Association, Position on National Reconstruction, 4. The breakdown of the draft budget included the following allocations: electric energy (50 percent), basic infrastructure (14 percent), road rehabilitation (7 percent), purchase of land (.05 percent), health (2.26 percent), education (1.76 percent), community development (.07 percent). See also Wood, "Los Acuerdos de Paz"; and Ibisate, "Plan de reconstrucción," 184.

31. Orellana, "The Struggle."

32. Final Document of the National Debate for Peace in El Salvador, Sections 1.2.3, 2.1, and 2.2.3. Percentages of participants voting in favor of these three explanations were 98 percent, 93 percent, and 95 percent, respectively.

33. Orellana, "The Struggle."

34. Orellana, "The Struggle." See also Argüello Romero and Granillo Funes, "Plan de reconstrucción nacional." Grandin details the connections between US domestic politics and economic restructuring and warmongering abroad in *End of the Myth*.

35. CRIPDES, "Los anhelos de paz del pueblo salvadoreño," in "Resumen informativo," ca. September 1989, File 1989 Human Rights Reports and Correspondence, MASCP Records.

36. CRIPDES-CNR, "Programa Global," 18.

37. CRIPDES-CNR, "Programa Global," 18.

38. Regional Project for Sister Relationships in Chalatenango, ca. January 1992.

39. CRIPDES-CNR, "Programa Global," 8.

40. Orellana, "The Struggle."

41. National NGO Association, Position on National Reconstruction, 4.

42. CORDES, "Nos estamos preparando ante la posibilidad de que estalle la paz," *Horizontes Nuevos* 6, July 1991, 5, File Nuestra Tierra, Box 7, Arvidson Papers.

43. "Memoria del IV Cumbre de hermanamientos, ca. March 23, 1992. Initially established by CORDES and a few other organizations, by March 1992 the New Initiative involved thirteen nongovernmental groups.

44. CORDES, "Nos estamos preparando," 5.

45. "Memoria del IV Cumbre de hermanamientos."

46. Orellana, "The Struggle."

47. Orellana, "The Struggle."

48. CORDES, "Nos estamos preparando," 5.

49. Ruíz, "Toward a Rural Communal Movement."

50. CORDES, "Nos estamos preparando," 5.

51. "Memoria del IV Cumbre de hermanamientos."

52. *Acuerdos de paz*, 80. A land reform program initiated in 1980 by the Salvadoran government did not move very far in the context of war. See also McReynolds, "Land Reform."

53. Ruiz, "Toward a Rural Communal Movement."

54. De Bremond, "Politics," 1544.

55. Nancy G. Walker to CNR and Members of the Repopulated Communities, May 10, 1988, File Summit '88-Materials, Box 8, Arvidson Papers.

56. "Land situacion [*sic*] update," ca. late 1993 or early 1994, File Land Campaigns, Box 1, Arvidson Papers.

57. "Land situacion [*sic*] update."

58. McReynolds, "Land Reform," 142.

59. United Nations Peacekeeping, "El Salvador-ONUSAL Background," https://peacekeeping.un.org/mission/past/onusalbackgr2.html.

60. FMLN/FPL Comisión de Tierras, "Balance del estado actual del programa de transferencia de tierras," December 1994, File Land Campaigns, Box 1, Arvidson Papers. Originally scheduled to close on March 31, 1995, the UN, FMLN, and Salvadoran government agreed to extend the program multiple times. See McReynolds, "Land Reform."

61. "Land situacion [*sic*] update."

62. Nancy Ryan, "Opinion Piece," ca. January 1995, File SC delegation 1995, Box 2, Somberg Papers.

63. Mike Hoffman, "Evaluation of Land Transference," January 16, 1995, File Land Campaigns, Box 1, Arvidson Papers.

64. Mike Hoffman, Summary of Meeting with CCR on Question of Land Transference, January 19, 1995, 3, File 1995–56 Land Transfer, MASCP Records.

65. Mike Hoffman, Summary of Meeting with CCR.

66. "Land situacion [*sic*] update."

67. "Land situacion [*sic*] update." Although this report does not carry Hoffman's name, he is likely the author; the typeface and style parallel the other reports attributed to Hoffman during this period.

68. Mike Hoffman, "Update on Land," November 9, 1994, File Land Campaigns, Box 1, Arvidson Papers.

69. Hoffman, "Update on Land," "Evaluation of Land Transference," and Summary of Meeting with CCR. For more on tensions arising from different levels of beneficiary status, see Silber, *Everyday Revolutionaries*, 62–65.

70. National NGO Association, Position on National Reconstruction, 4.

71. Hoffman, "Update on Land."

72. "Land situacion [*sic*] update."

73. Hoffman, "Evaluation of Land Transference."

74. "Land situacion [*sic*] update."

75. Hoffman, "Evaluation of Land Transference."

76. Chicago–Cinquera Sister City Project, delegation report, August 1995, MASCP Records.

77. Michael Shimkin to Steven Meinbath, December 4, 1995, File Sistering Commission/Tim, Box 6, Arvidson Papers.

78. CRIPDES Sistering Commission, Regional Update for Chalatenango, February 22, 1993.

79. Chicago–Cinquera Sister City Project, delegation report, August 1995.

80. CRIPDES Sistering Commission, Regional Update for Chalatenango, February 22, 1993.

81. Shimkin to Meinbath, December 4, 1995.

82. "Land situacion [*sic*] update."

83. Hoffman, Summary of Meeting with CCR; "A Peace Denied," November 1994, File SC Delegation 1995, Box 2, Somberg Papers.

84. Hoffman, "Evaluation of Land Transference."

85. Hoffman, Summary of Meeting with CCR; Spence, Vickers, and Dye, *Progress Report*.

86. Martínez Peñate, "ARENA," 6–7.

87. Hoffman, "Evaluation of Land Transference." On divisions within ARENA, see also Spence, Vickers, and Dye, *Progress Report*, 24–25; Martínez Peñate, "ARENA."

88. Hoffman, "Evaluation of Land Transference."

89. "Land situacion [*sic*] update."

90. "Update on Peace Accords and Land Transfer Program," March 1995, File Land Campaigns, Box 1, Arvidson Papers.

91. "A Peace Denied," 17–18.

92. "Land situacion [*sic*] update"; Jennifer Utech to family and friends, April 10, 1995, in File SC delegation 1995, Box 2, Somberg Papers; "A Peace Denied"; and Ryan "Opinion Piece."

93. "Land situacion [*sic*] update."

94. "Land situacion [*sic*] update."

95. Hoffman, Summary of Meeting with CCR, 4; Ryan, "Opinion Piece"; and "Propuesta para una peregrinacion," ca. late 1994, File Land Campaigns, Box 1, Arvidson Papers. According to the archival records, this appears to be one of the few events where Chalatenango-based activists openly and directly collaborated with activists in Morazán.

96. Utech to family and friends, April 20, 1995; Lisa Zeilinger to President Alfredo Cristiani, in "Governmentgram," May 24, 1993, File Emergency Response Network late '80s early '90s, MASCP Records; Draft advocacy letter, January 26, 1995, File Land Campaigns, Box 1, Arvidson Papers.

97. Hoffman, Summary of Meeting with CCR; "Update #4: Pilgrimage for Land," December 16, 1994, Untitled File, Box 7, Arvidson Papers; Hoffman, "Update on Land."

98. Campaign Land for El Salvador, ca. late 1994, File Land Campaigns, Box 1, Arvidson Papers. See also Cambridge committee, El Salvador Land Campaign, event flier, ca. April 1995; and Amy Miler, "Struggle for Land Grips El Salvador Sister City," ca. 1995, both in Freireich Papers.

99. Esther Chávez, notes from USESSC conference call, December 7, 1995, File 1992–95 National Office, MASCP Records; Esther Chávez, USESSC conference call, meeting minutes, December 7, 1995, Untitled File, Box 7; and Land Advocacy Tracking Report, January 12, 1995, File Land Campaigns, Box 1, both in Arvidson Papers.

100. See especially File Land Campaigns, Box 1, Arvidson Papers.

101. SHARE, "Strategy" and "Land Transfer Advocacy Talking Points," ca. January 1995, File 1995 Land Transfer, MASCP Records.

102. Utech to family and friends, April 10, 1995.

103. Ryan, "Opinion Piece"; Draft advocacy letter, January 26, 1995.

104. "Campaign Land for El Salvador," ca. late 1994; SHARE, "Strategy" and "Land Transfer Advocacy Talking Points." Ryan ("Opinion Piece") cites a study by USAID that identified fifty interdependent steps required to complete one legal land transfer—assuming everything went smoothly the first time.

105. Hoffman, "Update on Land."

106. Hoffman, "Update on Land"; Ken Ward to Joy Olson, New Salvadoran government plan for Land Transfer Program, fax, November 18, 1995, File SC Delegation 1995, Box 2, Somberg Papers.

107. Hoffman, "Update on Land."

108. Utech to family and friends, April 10, 1995. See also "Piden agilizar transferencia," *El Mundo*, March 24, 1995, 3; "Piden a GOES cumplir con acuerdos," *Latinoticias*, March 23, 1995, 24; all in same file.

109. Cambridge–El Salvador Sister City Project, Land Action Call in Day, flier, April 1995, File SC General 1995, Box 2, Somberg Papers.

110. CCR, CORDES, and SHARE, Regional Sistering Project for Chalatenango, ca. November 1994, File SC Delegation 1994, Box 2, Somberg Papers.

111. "A Peace Denied," 22.

112. Hoffman, Summary of Meeting with CCR.

113. Hoffman, Summary of Meeting with CCR. See also CCR et al., Regional Sistering Project for Chalatenango, ca. November 1994.

114. "A Peace Denied," 14, 22.

115. MASCP Steering Committee, meeting notes, April 13, 1997, File 1997 MASCP Minutes and Nat'l Gathering, MASCP Records.

116. "A Peace Denied," 22.

117. Hoffman, Summary of Meeting with CCR.

118. Chicago–Cinquera Sister City Project, delegation report, August 1995.

119. Hoffman, Summary of Meeting with CCR.

120. "Land situacion [*sic*] update."

121. Hoffman, Summary of Meeting with CCR; "A Peace Denied," 20.

122. "Land situacion [*sic*] update."

123. MASCP Steering Committee, meeting notes, April 13, 1997.

124. Significantly, residents named the neighborhood Colonia Jesús Rojas after a Nicaraguan revolutionary who assisted the FMLN through the war. Rojas, whose given name was Antonio Cardenal, was a member of the Political Diplomatic Commission of the FMLN and a participant on the FMLN's negotiating team when, in April 1991, he and thirteen others were executed in a government ambush in northeastern Chalatenango.

125. "Chicago–Cinquera Sister Cities: A History," ca. 1994, File 1995 Health Care and Education Delegation, MASCP Records.

126. "Friends of Las Anonas '94," campaign announcement in Romero Inter-faith Center, *Waging Peace*, newsletter, January 1994, File Philad. Newsletters 1992–1996, Arvidson Papers.

127. Sally Milbury-Steen, "History of Copapayo-Delaware," ca. February 2018, in author's possession.

128. "A Peace Denied," 22, 25; CCR et al., Regional Sistering Project for Chala-tenango, ca. November 1994.

129. "Chalatenango Regional Report," June 30, 1992, File Regional Reports: April–June '92; and "Informe Regional de PROGRESO, Cuscatlán, Cabañas," April 2, 1992, File Regional Reports: Jan–Mar 92, both in Box 6, Arvidson Papers.

130. "Informe Regional de PROGRESO," April 2, 1992; "Chalatenango Regional Report," June 30, 1992; "Chalatenango Regional Report," April 14, 1992.

131. "Chalatenango Regional Report," June 30, 1992; "Chalatenango Regional Report," April 14, 1992. In the postwar period, CORDES reorganized and developed an expertise in such a way that it became a powerhouse in El Salvador's nongovern-mental economic development sphere. Sister Cities records trace this process through the early 1990s. For more on CORDES and the parallel "NGO-ization" of the CCR, see Silber, *Everyday Revolutionaries*.

132. "Informe Regional de PROGRESO," April 2, 1992.

133. Dirigentes del CRIPDES, meeting minutes, November 28, 1992, File Sister-ing Commission/Tim, Arvidson Papers.

134. The many regional reports contain details about specific projects relating to centers for orphans and children, assistance to widows, and programs for women and girls. Sistering summit materials, CRIPDES "global program" and human rights train-ing materials, and documents from health-related delegations during the mid-1990s offer insights into the issue of women's rights. For an example of sources referencing housing lottery systems, see Chicago–Cinquera Sister City Project, delegation report, August 1995.

135. McReynolds, "Land Reform," 150. Elizabeth Wood points out that although land tenure remained unequal, it was "significantly less so than before the war." Between 1971 and 1998, she noted, the fraction of the adult population with land increased nearly 9 percent and that with no land decreased by nearly 11 percent. Wood, "Agrarian Reform," 170. After coming to power in 1979, the Sandinistas of Nicaragua carried out the greatest land reform of the region.

136. Rosa and Foley, "El Salvador," 138.

137. Segovia, "Macroeconomic Performance," 52.

138. Foley, Vickers, and Thale, *Tierra*, 5.

139. Segovia, "Macroeconomic Performance," 51.

140. Foley, Vickers, and Thale, *Tierra*, 13. This plan had grown out of years of work formulating a new agrarian policy, marked by a series of laws designed to promote the parcelization of cooperatively held land, phase out agrarian reform agencies, and restruc-ture debt. Kowalchuk, "Competition to Cooperation," 48; World Bank, *Rural Develop-ment*, 185–86.

141. Kowalchuk, "Competition to Cooperation," 46; Foley, Vickers, and Thale, *Tierra*, 13. The precise amount of agrarian debt shouldered during this period is difficult to pin down; numbers range from $120 million on the low end to near $650 million.

142. Hoffman, "Update on Land."

143. MASCP, delegation report, August 1995, File August 1995 Health Care and Education Delegation, MASCP Records.

144. CISPES, "Victory for farmers and cooperatives!" *El Salvador Watch*, no. 64 (November 1997), http://www.hartford-hwp.com/archives/47/191.html.

145. "A Peace Denied." Unlike most international donations that had to work through the bureaucracies of aid organizations as well as the US and Salvadoran governments, remittances and funds from solidarity groups flowed horizontally, making more money available at the grassroots level, more quickly, and with fewer strings attached. Salvadoran government sources reported that citizens abroad remitted nearly US$1 billion in 1993 and 1994, which analysts at the Hemisphere Initiative noted was "three times the amount earned in coffee exports." Spence, Vickers, and Dye, *Progress Report*, 22, 21. Several authors discuss the role of remittances during the transition period in Boyce, *Economic Policy*.

146. "A Peace Denied."

147. McReynolds, "Land Reform," 140, 145.

148. McReynolds, "Land Reform," 146.

149. McReynolds, "Land Reform," 146.

150. See, for example, Foro Nacional Para la Defensa y Recuperación del Sector Agropecuario (hereafter Foro Agropecuario) to Álvaro de Soto, September 18, 1996; and Pedro Juan Hernández Romero, "La ley de la tierra," ca. May 1996, both in File CRIPDES and Sistering, Box 7, Arvidson Papers.

151. Hernández Romero, "La ley de la tierra." Hernández denounced Decree 719 in particular as "the *coup de grâce* for agrarian reform."

152. Rosa and Foley, "El Salvador," 117. Agricultural sector growth was 0.9; the GDP average rate was 4.6.

153. Kowalchuk, "Competition to Cooperation"; Kowalchuk, "Peasant Mobilization"; Foley, Vickers, and Thale, *Tierra*; Foro Agropecuario, *Estrategia*, in File SC April 1998 Delegation, Box 1, Somberg Papers.

154. Foro Agropecuario, *Estrategia*, 11, 12.

155. Foro Agropecuario to de Soto.

156. Foro Agropecuario to de Soto.

157. Kowalchuk, "Peasant Mobilization," 31–33. Kowalchuk notes that middle-class intellectuals were the spokespersons for the Foro; they helped to get peasants' perspectives into the public realm, even if peasants themselves were not asked to be spokespersons.

158. Kowalchuk, "Peasant Mobilization," 19; Kowalchuk, "Competition to Cooperation," 56–57; Wood, "Agrarian Reform."

159. Cambridge–El Salvador Sister City Project, delegation invitation flier, ca. March 1998, File SC 1998, Box 1, Somberg Papers.

160. Sister Cities and CISPES, draft letter to President William Clinton, in Michael Ring to Sister Cities and Friends, "Advocacy Alert," email, January 31, 1999, File 1998–99 Agro Issues, MASCP Records.

161. Michael Ring to US–ES Sister Cities, email, February 26, 1999, File 1998–99 Agro Issues, MASCP records.

162. CISPES, "Victory." See also World Bank, *Rural Development*, esp. Annex 6; and Kowalchuk, "Competition to Cooperation," 58. Debt relief programs were not without their critics, of course. After noting that the United States had agreed to forgive 75 percent of the $615 million in debt that El Salvador owed to US aid agencies, David Clark Scott of the *Christian Science Monitor* explained that such a "debt pardon is consistent with the Bush administration's Enterprise for the Americas Initiative, which advocates debt forgiveness to encourage free-trade and market-oriented reforms in Latin America." ("Debt Relief Gift from US Marks Salvador's New Peace," *Christian Science Monitor*, December 18, 1992.)

163. Ring to Sister Cities, email, February 26, 1999.

164. Barbara Alvarado to President Armando Calderón Sol, February 1999, MASCP Records; Michael Ring to Sister Cities, "URGENT: FAX CALDERON SOL," email, February 26, 1999, both in File 1998–99 Agro Issues, MASCP Records.

165. Cambridge–El Salvador Sister City Project, delegation invitation flier, ca. March 1998.

166. USESSC, October national meeting minutes, email, November 16, 1998, File SC 1998, Box 1, Somberg Papers.

167. Central American Solidarity Organizations to Brian Atwood, organizational sign on letter, in Michael Ring to USESSC Contacts, December 9, 1998, File SC 1998, Box 1, Somberg Papers.

168. Ring to USESSC Contacts, December 9, 1998.

169. Michael Ring to All Sister City Committees and Friends, email, January 20, 1997, Papers of Barbara Moser Schaible (hereafter Schaible papers), private collection, Lawrence, KS.

170. Kowalchuk, "Peasant Mobilization," 35.

171. Michael Ring to Committee leaders of USESSC, "Sample Fundraising Letter," email, December 9, 1998, File SC 1998, Box 1, Somberg Papers.

172. See, for example, Ring to All, January 20, 1997; and Michael Ring to USESSC, "Mitch advocacy input requested," email, December 22, 1998, also in Schaibel Papers.

173. On this "NGO-ization," consider Silber, *Everyday Revolutionaries*; and Beck, *How Development Projects Persist*.

174. Women and People of El Salvador to the US government, "Peace and Human Rights," October 15, 1986, File 1986, MASCP Records.

175. Quoted in Salazar and Cruz, *CCR*, 43–44.

176. See Rosenthal Papers, MASCP Records.

177. "Community Health Assessment of a 'Repopulated' Village in El Salvador," June 1988, 9, 10, 12, File 1988 Cambridge Health Delegation Report, MASCP Records.

178. "Community Health Assessment," June 1988. Delegates also found it "striking" that residents of Las Flores attributed 91 percent of household deaths directly to the Armed Forces (p. 10).

179. Todd, *Beyond Displacement*; Hammond, *Fighting to Learn*; Binford, "Grassroots Development"; Cagan and Cagan, *Promised Land*.

180. Support for Popular Education (SUPE), "Popular Education in El Salvador," delegation report, ca. November 1994, File 1995 Education, MASCP Records.

181. For example: "San José Las Flores suma a municipios sin analfabetismo," *La Prensa Gráfica*, January 29, 2013, https://www.laprensagrafica.com/elsalvador/San-Jose-Las-Flores-suma-a-municipios-sin-analfabetismo-20130129-0104.html.

182. Smith-Nonini, "'Popular' Health," 637. See also Smith-Nonini, *Healing*, esp. 181–83.

183. Smith-Nonini, *Healing*, 201.

184. CRIPDES-CNR, "Programa Global," July 1991; "Chalatenango Regional Report," June 30, 1992; Salazar and Cruz, *CCR*, 82–87.

185. CRIPDES-CNR, "Centro Médico de atención para la salúd, 1991–1993," report, April 8, 1991, File CRIPDES Clinic, Box 6, Arvidson Papers.

186. CRIPDES-CNR, "Centro Médico," 39.

187. CRIPDES-CNR, "Centro Médico," 39, 5.

188. Smith-Nonini, "'Popular' Health," 635.

189. CRIPDES-CNR, "Centro Médico," 15.

190. CRIPDES-CNR, "Centro Médico," 41, 40.

191. CRIPDES-CNR, "Centro Médico," 5.

192. MASCP, delegation report, ca. August 1995.

193. Smith-Nonini, *Healing*, 201.

194. CRIPDES-CNR, "Centro Médico"; Kathleen Krchnavek, "After the War: The Popular Health Care Promoters of Arcatao, Chalatenango–El Salvador," unpublished paper, May 1994, File 1994, MASCP Records.

195. Many Sister Cities committee records document the local and national health care and education working groups, delegations, workshops, and trainings.

196. Smith-Nonini, "'Popular' Health," 639–41; Almeida, *Waves*; Almeida, "Social Movement Unionism"; Schuld, "Hospitals"; Krchnavek, "After the War."

197. Smith-Nonini, *Healing*, 261.

198. Schuld, "Hospitals," 42.

199. Smith-Nonini, *Healing*, 261.

200. Schuld, "Hospitals," 42.

201. CRIPDES Sistering Commission, Regional Update for Northern San Salvador and La Libertad—UCRES, February 22, 1993, File 11: Regional Reports 93, Box 6, Arvidson papers. The EDUCO and SILOs programs of the Ministries of Education and Health, respectively, were especially contentious.

Conclusion

1. MASCP, 25th Anniversary Celebration, October 2011.

2. Trinkl, "Struggles," 61; MASCP, Fact Sheet, ca. 1987, File SHARE-Sister Relations Conf 92, MASCP Records.

3. Field notes, International Sistering Exchange, July 2016, in possession of author. All unattributed quotations in this chapter are from my field notes and recordings from this event. In a few cases, I reconstruct quotations from my notes; I use quotation marks for these as well as the fully transcribed quotations in order to avoid confusion.

4. Field notes, Arcatao Popular Consultation Delegation, November 2015, in possession of the author. On mining and opposition in El Salvador, see Erzinger, González, and Ibarra, *Lado oscuro*; and Spalding, "El Salvador's Anti-Mining Movement" and "From Streets to Chamber." The murder of environmental and anti-mining activists gained international attention in late 2009; consider Lisa Skeen, "Salvadoran Anti-Mining Activists Risk Their Lives by Taking On 'Free Trade,'" North American Council on Latin America, February 1, 2010, https://nacla.org/news/salvadoran-anti-min ing-activists-risk-their-lives-taking-%E2%80%98free-trade%E2%80%99; and Edgardo Ayala, "El Salvador: Activists Link Mining Co. to Murders." Inter Press Service News Agency, January 27, 2010.

5. Human Rights Watch, *Deported to Danger*.

6. On the US Fugue State, see Anastario, *Parcels*.

7. Orantes et al., "Epidemiology." According to this study, conducted by researchers with the Salvadoran National Institute of Health, renal failure was the leading cause of hospital deaths for men in 2011 and the fifth cause for women. See also Mejía et al., "Pesticide-Handling Practices"; Scammell et al., "Exposures in Kidney Disease."

8. SHARE, "Building a New El Salvador Today," ca. June 1992.

9. Hoffman, Summary of Meeting with CCR, January 19, 1995.

10. Memoria del IV Cumbre de hermanamientos, ca. March 23, 1992. Participants at the 2016 summit reiterated this point.

11. Krchnavek, "After the War," 17.

12. Krchnavek, "After the War," 17.

13. Smith-Nonini, *Healing*, 260.

14. CRIPDES, "Historic Framework and Present Situation of the Sister Cities," October 1995, File 1992–95 National Office, MASCP Records.

15. "Fomlenio: ¿misión cumplida?," *Noticias UCA*, September 21, 2012, https:// noticias.uca.edu.sv/editoriales/fomilenio-mision-cumplida.

16. This situation is not peculiarly Salvadoran; on roads and highway systems as tools to eradicate "blight" (and perpetuate racial divisions and poverty) in the United States, consider Alana Semuels, "The Role of Highways in American Poverty: They Seemed Like Such a Good Idea in the 1950s," *Atlantic*, March 18, 2016; Emily Badger and Darla Cameron, "How Railroads, Highways and Other Man-Made Lines Racially

Divide America's Cities," *Washington Post*, July 16, 2015; and DiMento and Ellis, *Changing Lanes*.

17. Spalding, "Civil Society," 103–4.

18. Keck and Sikkink, *Activists*, 11.

19. Beck, *How Development Projects Persist*, esp. ch. 2.

20. Keck and Sikkink, *Activists*, 13.

21. Keck and Sikkink, *Activists*, 12. For an extension of this theory, consider the "spiral model" developed in Risse and Sikkink, "Socialization." For an overview of these and other models, see Sikkink, "Patterns."

22. Coordinating Committee, "Discussion on Political Projection of Sistering," meeting notes, June 28, 1991, File ES-Mesa de Trabajo-1991, Box 8, Arvidson Papers.

23. Citing John Holloway in Stahler-Sholk, Vanden, and Becker, "Introduction," 8.

24. Olesen, "Globalising the Zapatistas," 256. See also Olesen, *International Zapatismo*.

25. For additional context, see Silber, *Everyday Revolutionaries*; Ching, *Stories*; and Peterson, "Consuming Histories."

26. CRIPDES, "Historic Framework."

27. Almeida, "Neoliberal Forms of Capital," 20–21.

28. Kowalchuk, "Peasant Mobilization," 35.

29. SHARE, "Building a New El Salvador Today."

30. MASCP, 25th Anniversary Celebration, October 2011.

31. CRIPDES, "Historic Framework."

32. SHARE, "Building a New El Salvador Today."

33. MASCP, 25th Anniversary Celebration, October 2011.

Bibliography

Adams, Jaqueline. "What Is Solidarity Art?" In *The Art of Solidarity: Visual and Performative Politics in Cold War Latin America*, edited by Jessica Stites Mor and Carmen Suescun Pozas, 241–57. Austin: University of Texas Press, 2018.

Agamben, Giorgio. *Homo Sacer: Sovereign Power and Bare Life*. Translated by Daniel Heller-Roazen. Stanford: Stanford University Press, 1998.

Allcock, Thomas Tunstall. "The First Alliance for Progress? Reshaping the Eisenhower Administration's Policy Toward Latin America." *Journal of Cold War Studies* 16, no. 1 (Winter 2014): 85–110.

Almeida, Paul D. "Neoliberal Forms of Capital and the Rise of Social Movement Partyism in Central America." *Journal of World-Systems Research* 21, no. 1: 8–24.

Almeida, Paul D. "Social Movement Unionism, Social Movement Partyism, and Policy Outcomes: Health Care Privatization in El Salvador." In *Latin American Social Movements: Globalization, Democratization, and Transnational Networks*, edited by Hank Johnston and Paul Almeida, 57–73. Lanham, MD: Rowman & Littlefield, 2006.

Almeida, Paul D. *Waves of Protest: Popular Struggle in El Salvador, 1925–2005*. Minneapolis: University of Minnesota Press, 2008.

Alther, Gretchen. "Colombian Peace Communities: The Role of NGOs in Supporting Resistance to Violence and Oppression." *Development in Practice* 16, nos. 3/4 (June 2006): 278–91.

Alvarenga, Ana Patricia. *Cultura y ética de la violencia: El Salvador, 1880–1932*. San José: Editorial Universitaria Centroamericana, 1996.

Americas Watch. "Draining the Sea: Sixth Supplement to the Report on Human Rights in El Salvador." New York: Americas Watch Committee, 1985.

Anastario, Mike. *Parcels: Memories of Salvadoran Migration*. New Brunswick, NJ: Rutgers University Press, 2019.

Arévalo, Juan José. *Fábula del tiburón y las sardinas*. Mexico City: Editorial América Nueva, 1956.

Argüello Romero, Aida Celia, and Ricardo Miguel Granillo Funes. "Plan de reconstrucción nacional, su impacto en la economía nacional 1992–1993." *Revista Realidad* 5, no. 36 (November–December 1993): 605–35.

Arias, Arturo, ed. *The Rigoberta Menchú Controversy.* Minneapolis: University of Minnesota Press, 2001.

Arnaiz Quintana, Angel. *Cartas desde la esperanza: Testimonio de la comunidad de Nueva Esperanza (El Salvador).* Barcelona: Associació d'Agermanament Igualada, 2001.

Arnson, Cynthia. *Crossroads: Congress, the Reagan Administration, and Central America.* New York: Pantheon, 1989.

Bakker, Janel Kragt. *Sister Churches: American Congregations and Their Partners Abroad.* Oxford: Oxford University Press, 2014.

Barba, Maribel, and Concha Martínez. *De la memoria nace la esperanza.* Barcelona: Fundació Pau i Solidaritat, 1996.

Barnett, Michael. *Empire of Humanity: A History of Humanitarianism.* Ithaca, NY: Cornell University Press, 2011.

Barnett, Michael. "Humanitarianism, Paternalism, and the UNHCR." In *Refugees in International Relations,* edited by Alexander Betts and Gil Loescher, 105–32. New York: Oxford University Press, 2010.

Barnett, Michael, and Thomas G. Weiss, eds. *Humanitarianism in Question: Politics, Power, Ethics.* Ithaca, NY: Cornell University Press, 2008.

Bassano, David. "The Boomerang Pattern: Verification and Modification." *Peace & Change* 39, no. 1 (January 2014): 23–48.

Beck, Erin. *How Development Projects Persist: Everyday Negotiation with Guatemalan NGOs.* Durham, NC: Duke University Press, 2017.

Beverley, John. "The Margin at the Center: On Testimonio (Testimonial Narrative)." In *The Real Thing: Testimonial Discourse and Latin America,* edited by George M. Gugelberger, 23–41. Durham, NC: Duke University Press, 1996.

Binford, Leigh. *The El Mozote Massacre: Human Rights and Global Implications.* Revised and expanded ed. Tucson: University of Arizona Press, 2016.

Binford, Leigh. "Grassroots Development in Conflict Zones of Northeastern El Salvador." *Latin American Perspectives* 24, no. 2 (March 1997): 56–79.

Binford, Leigh. "Reply: Solidarity." *Dialectical Anthropology* 32, no. 3 (2008): 177–82.

Bollier, David, and Silke Helfrich, eds. *The Wealth of the Commons: A World beyond Market and State.* Amherst, MA: Levellers Press, 2012.

Bonner, Raymond. *Weakness and Deceit: U.S. Policy and El Salvador.* New York: Times Books, 1984.

Borland, Katherine. "A Brief Social History of Humanitarian Engagement." In *International Volunteer Tourism: Critical Reflections on Good Works in Central America,* edited by Katherine Borland and Abigail E. Adams, 7–21. New York: Palgrave Macmillan, 2013.

Borland, Katherine, and Abigail E. Adams, eds. *International Volunteer Tourism: Critical Reflections on Good Works in Central America.* New York: Palgrave Macmillan, 2013.

Boyce, James K., ed. *Economic Policy for Building Peace: The Lessons of El Salvador.* Boulder, CO: Lynne Rienner, 1996.

Bradley, Mark Philip. *The World Reimagined: Americans and Human Rights in the Twentieth Century.* New York: Cambridge University Press, 2016.

Brands, Hal. *Latin America's Cold War.* Cambridge, MA: Harvard University Press, 2012.

Browning, David. *El Salvador: Landscape and Society.* Oxford: Clarendon Press, 1971.

Bruey, Alison. *Bread, Justice, and Liberty: Grassroots Activism in Pinochet's Chile.* Madison: University of Wisconsin Press, 2018.

Bush, Daniel Alan. "Seattle's Cold War[m] Policy, 1957–1990: Citizen Diplomats and Grass Roots Diplomacy, Sister Cities and International Exchange." PhD diss., University of Washington, 1998.

Byrne, Malcolm. *Iran-Contra: Reagan's Scandal and the Unchecked Abuse of Presidential Power.* Lawrence: University Press of Kansas, 2014.

Cagan, Beth, and Steve Cagan. *This Promised Land, El Salvador.* New Brunswick, NJ: Rutgers University Press, 1991.

Campbell, Edwina. "The Ideals and Origins of the Franco-German Sister Cities Movement, 1945–70." *History of European Ideas* 8, no. 1 (1987): 77–95.

Carbonella, August. "Empire and Solidarity: Some Preliminary Thoughts on a Relationship." *Dialectical Anthropology* 32 (2008): 183–9.

Catholic Institute for International Relations. *Right to Survive: Human Rights in Nicaragua.* London: Catholic Institute for International Relations, 1987.

Central American Refugee Center. *The Repopulation of Rural El Salvador.* Washington, DC: Central American Refugee Center, 1989.

Chávez, Joaquín M. "How Did the Civil War in El Salvador End?" *American Historical Review* (2015): 1784–97.

Chávez, Joaquín M. *Poets and Prophets of the Resistance: Intellectuals and the Origins of El Salvador's Civil War.* New York: Oxford University Press, 2017.

Chilsen, Liz, and Sheldon Rampton. *Friends in Deed: The Story of U.S.–Nicaragua Sister Cities.* Madison: Wisconsin Coordinating Council on Nicaragua, 1988.

Ching, Erik. *Authoritarian El Salvador: Politics and the Origins of the Military Regimes, 1880–1940.* Notre Dame, IN: University of Notre Dame Press, 2014.

Ching, Erik. *Stories of Civil War in El Salvador: A Battle Over Memory.* Chapel Hill: University of North Carolina Press, 2016.

Chomsky, Noam. *Turning the Tide: U.S. Intervention in Central America and the Struggle for Peace.* Boston: South End Press, 1985.

Clarke, Nick. "In What Sense 'Spaces of Neoliberalism'? The New Localism, the New Politics of Scale, and Town-Twinning." *Political Geography* 28 (2009): 496–507.

Clarke, Nick. "Town Twinning in Cold-War Britain: (Dis)Continuities in Twentieth-Century Municipal Internationalism." *Contemporary British History* 24, no. 10 (June 2010): 173–91.

Clements, Charles. *Witness to War: An American Doctor in El Salvador.* Toronto: Bantam Books, 1984.

Comisión para el Esclarecimiento Histórico. "Guatemala, Memoria del Silencio." Informe de la Comisión para el Esclarecimiento Histórico. Guatemala City: UNOPS, 1999.

Compher, Vic, and Betsy Morgan. *Going Home: Building Peace in El Salvador, The Story of Repatriation.* New York: Apex Press, 1991.

Corrigan, Ralph L. *El Salvador at a Crossroads.* Fairfield, CT: Sacred Heart University Press, 2014.

Cortina Orero, Eudald. "Discurso en (r)evolución: Lucha ideológica y captación de solidaridad en el movimiento revolucionario salvadoreño." *Naveg@mérica: Revista electrónica editada por la Asociación Española de Americanistas,* no. 17 (2016): 1–22.

Cortina Orero, Eudald. "Redes militates y solidaridad con El Salvador: Una aproximación desde la comunicación insurgente." *Nuevo Mundo/Mundos Nuevos,* October 10, 2016.

Coutin, Susan Bibler. *The Culture of Protest: Religious Activism and the U.S. Sanctuary Movement.* Boulder, CO: Westview Press, 1993.

Coy, Patrick. "Cooperative Accompaniment and Peace Brigades International in Sri Lanka." In *Transnational Social Movements and Global Politics: Solidarity beyond the State,* edited by Jackie Smith, Charles Chatfield, and Ron Pagnucco, 81–100. Syracuse, NY: Syracuse University Press, 1997.

Cremer, Rolf D., Anne de Bruin, and Ann Dupuis. "International Sister-Cities: Bridging the Global-Local Divide." *American Journal of Economics and Sociology* 60, no. 1 (January 2001): 377–401.

Cunningham, Hillary. *God and Caesar at the Rio Grande: Sanctuary and the Politics of Religion.* Minneapolis: University of Minnesota Press, 1995.

Dale, Linda, curator. "Disrupted Lives: Children's Drawings from Central America." Touring exhibition, Canada, 1986–87.

de Bremond, Ariane. "The Politics of Peace and Resettlement Through El Salvador's Land Transfer Programme: Caught between the State and the Market." *Third World Quarterly* 28, no. 8 (2007): 1537–56.

de la Fuente, Alejandro. *A Nation for All: Race, Inequality, and Politics in Twentieth-Century Cuba.* Chapel Hill: University of North Carolina Press, 2001.

Department of Social Sciences, Universidad de El Salvador. "An Analysis of the Correlation of Forces in El Salvador." *Latin American Perspectives* 14, no. 4 (Fall 1987): 426–52.

de Soto, Álvaro, and Graciana del Castillo. "Obstacles to Peacebuilding Revisited." *Global Governance* 22 (2016): 209–27.

De Witte, Michaël. *Diario Sebastián.* Amberes, Belgium: EPO and Michaël De Witte Foundation, 1989.

DiMento, Joseph F. C., and Cliff Ellis. *Changing Lanes: Visions and Histories of Urban Freeways.* Cambridge, MA: MIT Press, 2012.

Dinges, John. *The Condor Years: How Pinochet and His Allies Brought Terrorism to Three Continents.* New York: New Press, 2004.

Dirección General de Estadística y Censos de El Salvador. *Primer Censo Agropecuario.* San Salvador: Dirección General de Estadística y Censos, October 1954.

Diskin, Martin, ed. *Trouble in Our Backyard: Central America and the United States in the Eighties.* New York: Pantheon Books, 1983.

Duffy, Richard, director. *El pasado no es historia: Memorias de guerra y revolución en Chalatenango, El Salvador.* El Museo de la Memoria Histórica de Arcatao, 2015.

Dussel, Enrique. "From Fraternity to Solidarity: Toward a *Politics of Liberation.*" *Journal of Social Philosophy* 38, no. 1 (Spring 2007): 73–92.

Eckel, Jan, and Samuel Moyn, eds. *The Breakthrough: Human Rights in the 1970s.* Philadelphia: University of Pennsylvania Press, 2013.

Erzinger, Florian, Luis González, and Angel M. Ibarra. *El lado oscuro del oro: Impactos de la minería metálica en El Salvador.* San Salvador: ICONO Publicidad, 2008.

Los escuadrones de la muerte en El Salvador. San Salvador: Editorial Jaraguá, 1994.

Faulk, Karen Ann. *In the Wake of Neoliberalism: Citizenship and Human Rights in Argentina.* Stanford: Stanford University Press, 2013.

Federici, Silvia. *Re-Enchanting the World: Feminism and the Politics of the Commons.* Oakland, CA: PM Press, 2019.

Finch, Eleanor. "People to People." *American Journal of International Law* 52, no. 4 (October 1958): 766.

Foley, Michael W., George R. Vickers, and Geoff Thale. *Tierra, paz y participación: El desarrollo de una política agraria de posguerra en El Salvador y el papel del Banco Mundial.* Washington, DC: Washington Office on Latin America, 1997.

Forché, Carolyn. *What You Have Heard Is True: A Memoir of Witness and Resistance.* London: Penguin Press, 2019.

Foro Agropecuario. *Estrategia para el desarrollo agropecuario y rural de El Salvador.* San Salvador: Foro Agropecuario, 1998.

Freire, Paulo. *Pedagogy of the Oppressed.* Translated by Myra Bergman Ramos. New York: Continuum, 1997.

Galeano, Eduardo. *Open Veins of Latin America: Five Centuries of the Pillage of a Continent.* New York: Monthly Review Press, 1973.

García Canclini, Néstor. *Culturas híbridas: Estrategias para entrar y salir de la modernidad.* Mexico City: Editorial Grijalbo, 1990.

Gelbspan, Ross. *Break-Ins, Death Threats and the FBI: The Covert War Against the Central America Movement.* Cambridge, MA: South End Press, 1991.

Gettleman, Marvin, Patrick Lacefield, Louis Menashe, and David Mermelstein, eds. *El Salvador: Central America in the New Cold War.* New York: Grove Weidenfeld, 1986.

Gill, Lesley. "The Limits of Solidarity: Labor and Transnational Organizing Against Coca-Cola." *American Ethnologist* 36, no. 4 (November 2009): 667–80.

Gill, Lesley. *The School of the Americas: Military Training and Political Violence in the Americas.* Durham, NC: Duke University Press, 2004.

Giugni, Marco, and Florence Passy, eds. *Political Altruism? Solidarity Movements in International Perspective.* Lanham, MD: Rowman & Littlefield, 2001.

Gobierno de El Salvador y el Frente Farabundo Martí para la Liberación Nacional. *Acuerdos de El Salvador: En el camino de la paz.* San Salvador: Editorial Arcoiris, 1992.

Golden, Renny, and Michael MacConnell. *Sanctuary: The New Underground Railroad.* Maryknoll, NY: Orbis Books, 1986.

Gosse, Van. "'El Salvador Is Spanish for Vietnam': A New Immigrant Left and the Politics of Solidarity." In *The Immigrant Left in the United States,* edited by Paul Buhle and Dan Georgakas, 302–29. Albany: State University of New York Press, 1996.

Gosse, Van. "'The North American Front': Central American Solidarity in the Reagan Era." In *Reshaping the U.S. Left: Popular Struggles in the 1980s,* edited by Mike Davis and Michael Sprinker, 11–50. London: Verso, 1988.

Gosse, Van. *Rethinking the New Left: An Interpretative History.* New York: Palgrave Macmillan, 2005.

Gosse, Van. *Where the Boys Are: Cuba, Cold War America and the Making of a New Left.* London: Verso, 1993.

Goudvis, Patricia, director. *If the Mango Tree Could Speak.* New Day Films, 1992.

Grabill, Joseph L. *What Happens When Sisters Embrace? A History of the Vladimir/ Canterbury Sister City Association of Bloomington/Normal: 1986–1996.* Bloomington/ Normal, IL: Vladimir/Canterbury Sister City Association, 1996.

Grandin, Greg. *Empire's Workshop: Latin America, the United States, and the Rise of the New Imperialism.* New York: Metropolitan Books, 2006.

Grandin, Greg. *The End of the Myth: From the Frontier to the Border Wall in the Mind of America.* New York: Metropolitan Books, 2019.

Green, James. "Clerics, Exiles, and Academics: Opposition to the Brazilian Military Dictatorship in the United States, 1969–1974." *Latin American Politics and Society* 45, no. 1 (Spring 2003): 87–117.

Green, James. "(Homo)Sexuality, Human Rights, and Revolution in Latin America." In *Human Rights and Revolutions,* edited by Jeffrey N. Wasserstrom, Greg Grandin, Lynn Hunt, and Marilyn B. Young, 139–53. Lanham, MD: Rowman & Littlefield, 2007.

Green, James. *We Cannot Remain Silent: Opposition to the Brazilian Military Dictatorship in the United States.* Durham, NC: Duke University Press, 2010.

Greenhill, Kelly. *Weapons of Mass Migration: Forced Displacement, Coercion, and Foreign Policy.* Ithaca, NY: Cornell University Press, 2010.

Grenier, Yvon. "The Rise and Fall of Revolutionary Passions in El Salvador: Some Lessons for the Study of Radical Political Movements." *Journal of Human Rights* 3, no. 3 (September 2004): 313–29.

Griffin-Nolan, ed. *Witness for Peace: A Story of Resistance.* Louisville, KY: Westminster John Knox Press, 1991.

Grossman, Richard. "Solidarity with Sandino: The Anti-Intervention and Solidarity Movements in the United States, 1927–1933." *Latin American Perspectives* 36, no. 67 (November 2009): 67–79.

Grusky, Sara. "International Service Learning: A Critical Guide from an Impassioned Advocate." *American Behavioral Scientist* 43, no. 5 (February 2000): 858–67.

Gugelberger, George M., and Michael Kearney. "Voices for the Voiceless: Testimonial Literature in Latin America." *Latin American Perspectives* 18, no. 3 (Summer 1991): 3–14.

Guidry, John A., and Mark Q. Sawyer. "Contentious Pluralism: The Public Sphere and Democracy." *Perspectives on Politics* 1, no. 2 (June 2003): 273–89.

Hammond, John. *Fighting to Learn: Popular Education and Guerrilla War in El Salvador.* New Brunswick, NJ: Rutgers University Press, 1998.

Hardt, Michael, and Antonio Negri. *Commonwealth.* Cambridge, MA: Belknap Press of Harvard University Press, 2009.

Harnecker, Marta. *Con la mirada en alto: Historia de las FPL Farabundo Martí a través de sus dirigentes.* San Salvador: UCA Editores, 1993.

Hayden, Bridget A. *Salvadorans in Costa Rica: Displaced Lives.* Tucson: University of Arizona Press, 2003.

Hellman, Judith Adler. "Real and Virtual Chiapas: Magic Realism and the Left." In *Socialist Register 2000,* edited by Leo Panitch and Colin Leys, 156–80. London: Merlin Press, 1999.

Henderson, Victoria L. "Citizenship in the Line of Fire: Protective Accompaniment, Proxy Citizenship, and Pathways for Transnational Solidarity in Guatemala." *Annals of the Association of American Geographers* 99, no. 5 (2009): 969–76.

Henríquez Consalvi, Carlos ("Santiago"). *La terquedad del izote: la historia de Radio Venceremos.* San Salvador: Museo de la Palabra y la Imagen, 2005.

Herman, Edward, and Frank Brodhead. *Demonstration Elections: U.S.-Staged Elections in the Dominican Republic, Vietnam, and El Salvador.* Boston: South End Press, 1984.

Herman, Edward, and Noam Chomsky. *Manufacturing Consent: The Political Economy of the Mass Media.* New York: Pantheon, 1988.

Hinman, George Wheeler, Jr. "The Colossus of the North." *North American Review* 226, no. 3 (September 1928): 273–80.

Huggins, Martha K. *Political Policing: The United States and Latin America.* Durham, NC: Duke University Press, 1998.

Human Rights Watch. *Deported to Danger: United States Deportation Policies Expose Salvadorans to Death and Abuse.* New York: Human Rights Watch, 2020.

Hunt, Lynn. *Inventing Human Rights: A History.* New York: W. W. Norton, 2007.

Hutchinson, Bill. *When the Dog Ate Candles: A Time in El Salvador.* Denver: University Press of Colorado, 1998.

Ibarra Chávez, Héctor. *El Salvador por la senda de la esperanza.* Valencia, Spain: Centro de Investigaciones Históricas de los Movimientos Armados, A. C., ca. 1993.

Ibisate, Francisco Javier. "El plan de reconstrucción nacional son tres: ¿Cuál es el principal??" *Revista Realidad* 5, no. 32 (March–April 1993): 153–85.

Juergensmeyer, John E. *The President, the Foundations, and the People-to-People Program.* Indianapolis: Inter-University Case Program & Bobbs-Merrill, 1965.

Juergensmeyer, John E. "A Short History of the People-to-People Program." PhD diss., Princeton University, 1958.

Keck, Margaret E., and Kathryn Sikkink. *Activists beyond Borders: Advocacy Networks in International Politics.* Ithaca, NY: Cornell University Press, 1998.

Kelly, Patrick William. *Sovereign Emergencies: Latin America and the Making of Global Human Rights Politics.* Cambridge: Cambridge University Press, 2018.

Kelly, Patrick William. "The 1973 Chilean Coup and the Origins of Transnational Human Rights Activism." *Journal of Global History* 8, no. 1 (2013): 165–86.

Keys, Barbara. *Reclaiming American Virtue: The Human Rights Revolution of the 1970s.* Cambridge, MA: Harvard University Press, 2014.

Knight, Alan. "U.S. Imperialism/Hegemony and Latin American Resistance." In *Empire and Dissent: The United States and Latin America,* edited by Fred Rosen, 23–52. Durham, NC: Duke University Press, 2008.

Koopman, Sara. "The Imperialism Within: Can the Master's Tools Bring Down Empire?" *ACME: An International E-Journal for Critical Geographies* 7, no. 2 (2008): 283–307.

Koopman, Sara. "Making Space for Peace: International Protective Accompaniment in Colombia." In *Geographies of Peace: New Approaches to Boundaries, Diplomacy and Conflict,* edited by Fiona McConnell, Nick Megoran, and Philippa Williams, 109–30. London: I. B. Tauris, 2014.

Kornbluh, Peter, and Malcolm Byrne. *The Iran-Contra Scandal: The Declassified History.* New York: New Press, 1993.

Kowalchuk, Lisa. "From Competition to Cooperation: Threats, Opportunities, and Organizational Survival in the Salvadorean Peasant Movement." *Revista Europea de Estudios Latinoamericanos y del Caribe* 74 (April 2003): 43–63.

Kowalchuk, Lisa. "Peasant Mobilization, Political Opportunities, and the Unfinished Agrarian Reform in El Salvador." Unpublished paper, n.d.

Kozel, Andrés, Florencia Grossi, and Delfina Moroni, eds. *El imaginario antiimperialista en América latina.* Buenos Aires: CLACSO, 2015.

LaFeber, Walter. *Inevitable Revolutions: The United States in Central America.* 2nd ed. New York: W. W. Norton, 1993.

Lauria-Santiago, Aldo A. *An Agrarian Republic: Commercial Agriculture and the Politics of Peasant Communities in El Salvador, 1823–1914.* Pittsburgh: University of Pittsburgh Press, 1999.

LeoGrande, William M. *Our Own Backyard: The United States in Central America, 1977–1992.* Chapel Hill: University of North Carolina Press, 1998.

Leppert, Glenn Wesley. "Dwight D. Eisenhower and People-to-People as an Experiment in Personal Diplomacy: A Missing Element for Understanding Eisenhower's Second Term as President." PhD diss., Kansas State University, 2003.

Levin, Matthew. *Cold War University: Madison and the New Left in the Sixties.* Madison: University of Wisconsin Press, 2013.

Levine, Daniel. "The Evolution of the Theory and Practice of Rights in Latin American Catholicism." In *Religious Responses to Violence: Human Rights in Latin America, Past and Present,* edited by Alexander Wilde, 27–61. Notre Dame, IN: University of Notre Dame Press, 2016.

Lindo-Fuentes, Héctor. *Weak Foundations: The Economy of El Salvador in the Nineteenth Century, 1821–1898.* Berkeley: University of California Press, 1990.

Lindo-Fuentes, Héctor, and Erik Ching. *Modernizing Minds in El Salvador: Education Reform and the Cold War, 1960–1980.* Albuquerque: University of New Mexico Press, 2012.

Linebaugh, Peter. *Stop, Thief! The Commons, Enclosures, and Resistance.* Oakland, CA: PM Press, 2014.

Lippold, Lu. *Hope, Faith and Revolution: The US-El Salvador Sister Cities.* Lu Lippold Video, 2000.

Lischer, Sarah Kenyon. *Dangerous Sanctuaries: Refugee Camps, Civil War and the Dilemmas of Humanitarian Aid.* Ithaca, NY: Cornell University Press, 2005.

Lofland, John. "Consensus Movements: City Twinning and Derailed Dissent in the American Eighties." *Research in Social Movements, Conflict and Change* 11 (1989): 163–96.

Macdonald, Mandy, and Mike Gatehouse. *In the Mountains of Morazán: Portrait of a Returned Refugee Community in El Salvador.* London: Latin American Bureau, 1995.

Mahony, Liam, and Luis Enrique Eguren. *Unarmed Bodyguards: International Accompaniment for the Protection of Human Rights.* West Hartford, CT: Kumarian Press, 1997.

Marier, Pierre. *Of Lives Uprooted.* Short film based on *Disrupted Lives* exhibit. National Film Board of Canada, 1988. https://www.nfb.ca/film/of_lives_uprooted/.

Markarian, Vania. *Left in Transformation: Uruguayan Exiles and the Latin American Human Rights Networks, 1967–1984.* New York: Taylor and Francis, 2005.

Martí, José. "Nuestra América." *El Partido Liberal* (Mexico City), January 20, 1891.

Martínez Peñate, Oscar. "ARENA: Divisiones y protagonismo político." Unpublished essay, 1999.

Martínez Peñate, Oscar. "La diplomacia paralela en el conflicto armado salvadoreño." In *Historia y debates sobre el conflicto armado salvadoreño y sus secuelas*, edited by Jorge Juárez Ávila, 189–201. San Salvador: Instituto de Estudios Históricos, Antropológicos y Arqueológicos, Universidad de El Salvador, 2014.

Martínez Peñate, Oscar. *El Salvador: Del conflicto armado a la negociación, 1979–1989.* San Salvador: Editorial Nuevo Enfoque, 1997.

McClintock, Cynthia. *Revolutionary Movements in Latin America: El Salvador's FMLN and Peru's Shining Path.* Washington, DC: US Institute of Peace Press, 1998.

McClintock, Michael. *The American Connection: State Terror and Popular Resistance in El Salvador.* London: Zed Books, 1985.

McElhinny, Vincent J. "Between Clientelism and Radical Democracy: The Case of Ciudad Segundo Montes." In *Landscapes of Struggle: Politics, Society, and Community in El Salvador*, edited by Aldo Lauria-Santiago and Leigh Binford, 147–65. Pittsburgh: University of Pittsburgh Press, 2004.

McPherson, Alan. *Intimate Ties, Bitter Struggles: The United States and Latin America since 1945.* Dulles, VA: Potomac Books, 2006.

McPherson, Alan. *A Short History of U.S. Interventions in Latin America and the Caribbean.* Chichester, West Sussex: John Wiley & Sons, 2016.

McReynolds, Samuel A. "Land Reform in El Salvador and the Chapultepec Peace Accord." *Journal of Peasant Studies* 30, no. 1 (October 2002): 135–69.

McSherry, J. Patrice. *Predatory States: Operation Condor and Covert War in Latin America.* Lanham, MD: Rowman & Littlefield, 2005.

Mejía, Roberto, Edgar Quinteros, Alejandro López, Alexandre Ribó, Humberto Cedillos, Carlos M. Orantes, Eliette Valladares, and Dina L. López. "Pesticide-Handling Practices in Agriculture in El Salvador: An Example from 42 Patient Farmers with Chronic Kidney Disease in the Bajo Lempa Region." *Occupational Diseases and Environmental Medicine* 2, no. 3 (2014): 56–70.

Menjívar, Cecilia, and Néstor Rodríguez, eds. *When States Kill: Latin America, the U.S., and Technologies of Terror.* Austin: University of Texas Press, 2005.

Metzi, Francisco. *The People's Remedy: The Struggle for Health Care in El Salvador's War of Liberation.* New York: Monthly Review Press, 1988.

Montgomery, Tommie Sue. *Revolution in El Salvador: From Civil Strife to Civil Peace.* 2nd ed. Boulder, CO: Westview Press, 1995.

Moodie, Ellen. "Inequality and Intimacy between Sister Communities in El Salvador and the United States." *Missiology: An International Review* 41, no. 2 (2013): 146–62.

Moodie, Ellen. "Untellable Stories and the Limits of Solidarity in a Sister-Community Relationship." In *International Volunteer Tourism: Critical Reflections on Good Works in Central America,* edited by Katherine Borland and Abigail E. Adams, 53–65. New York: Palgrave Macmillan, 2013.

Moore, Carlos. *Pichón: Race and Revolution in Castro's Cuba; A Memoir.* Chicago: Chicago Review Press, 2008.

Moyn, Samuel. *The Last Utopia: Human Rights in History.* Cambridge, MA: Harvard University Press, 2010.

Moyn, Samuel. *Not Enough: Human Rights in an Unequal World.* Cambridge, MA: Harvard University Press, 2018.

Munkres, Susan. "Being 'Sisters' to Salvadoran Peasants: Deep Identification and Its Limitations." In *Identity Work in Social Movements,* edited by Jo Reger, Daniel J. Myers, and Rachel L. Einwohner, 189–212. Minneapolis: University of Minnesota Press, 2008.

Naciones Unidas—Comisión de la verdad para El Salvador. *De la locura a la esperanza: La guerra de 12 años en El Salvador.* San Salvador and New York: Naciones Unidas, 1993.

National Commissioner for the Protection of Human Rights in Honduras. *Honduras: The Facts Speak for Themselves.* New York: Human Rights Watch, 1994.

Nelson, Diane M. *Reckoning: The Ends of War in Guatemala.* Durham, NC: Duke University Press, 2009.

Nepstad, Sharon Erickson. *Convictions of the Soul: Religion, Culture, and Agency in the Central America Solidarity Movement.* New York: Oxford University Press, 2004.

Nepstad, Sharon Erickson, and Christian Smith. "The Social Structure of Moral Outrage in Recruitment to the U.S. Central American Peace Movement." In *Passionate Politics: Emotions and Social Movements,* edited by Jeff Goodwin, James M. Jasper, and Francesca Polletta, 158–74. Chicago: University of Chicago Press, 2001.

Nichols, John. *The "S" Word: A Short History of an American Tradition . . . Socialism.* London: Verso, 2011.

Nyers, Peter. *Rethinking Refugees: Beyond States of Emergency.* New York: Routledge, 2006.

O'Donnel, Madalene, Jack Spence, and George Vickers. *El Salvador Elections 1994: The Voter Registration Triangle*. Cambridge, MA: Hemisphere Initiatives, 1993.

Olesen, Thomas. "Globalising the Zapatistas: From Third World Solidarity to Global Solidarity?" *Third World Quarterly* 25, no. 1 (2004): 255–64.

Olesen, Thomas. *International Zapatismo: The Construction of Solidarity in the Age of Globalization*. London: Zed Books, 2004.

Oñate-Madrazo, Andrea. "Insurgent Diplomacy: El Salvador's Transnational Revolution." PhD diss., Princeton University, 2016.

Orantes, Carlos M., et al. "Epidemiology of Chronic Kidney Disease in Adults of Salvadoran Agricultural Communities." *MEDICC Rev.* 16, no. 2 (April 2014): 23–30.

Osgood, Kenneth. *Total Cold War: Eisenhower's Secret Propaganda Battle at Home and Abroad*. Lawrence: University Press of Kansas, 2006.

Pearce, Jenny. *Promised Land: Peasant Rebellion in Chalatenango, El Salvador*. London: Latin America Bureau, 1986.

Pearce, Jenny. *Under the Eagle: U.S. Intervention in Central America and the Caribbean*. Boston: South End Press, 1981.

Perla, Héctor, Jr. "Si Nicaragua Venció, El Salvador Vencerá: Central American Agency in the Creation of the U.S.–Central American Peace and Solidarity Movement." *Latin American Research Review* 43, no. 2 (2008): 136–58.

Perla, Héctor, Jr. "Transnational Public Diplomacy: Assessing Salvadoran Revolutionary Efforts to Build U.S. Public Opposition to Reagan's Central America Policy." In *The United States and Public Diplomacy: New Directions in Cultural and International History*, edited by Kenneth A. Osgood and Brian C. Etheridge, 166–91. Leiden, The Netherlands: Koninkliijke Brill NV, 2010.

Perla, Héctor, Jr., and Susan Bibler Coutin. "Legacies and Origins of the 1980s US–Central American Sanctuary Movement." *Refuge* 26, no. 1 (2009): 7–19.

Peterson, Brandt Gustav. "Consuming Histories: The Return of the Indian in Neoliberal El Salvador." *Cultural Dynamics* 18, no. 2 (2006): 163–88.

Plewes, Betty, and Rieky Stuart. "The Pornography of Poverty: A Cautionary Fundraising Tale." In *Ethics in Action: The Ethical Challenges of International Human Rights Nongovernmental Organizations*, edited by Daniel A. Bell and Jean-Marc Coicaud, 23–37. New York: Cambridge University Press, 2007.

Polman, Linda. *The Crisis Caravan: What's Wrong with Humanitarian Aid?* London: Picador, 2011.

Pratt, Mary Louise. "Arts of the Contact Zone." *Profession* (1991): 33–40.

Pratt, Mary Louise. *Imperial Eyes: Travel Writing and Transculturation*. London: Routledge, 1992.

Quan, Adán. "Through the Looking Glass: U.S. Aid to El Salvador and the Politics of National Identity." *American Ethnologist* 32, no. 2 (2005): 276–93.

Quizar, Robin Ormes. *My Turn to Weep: Salvadoran Refugee Women in Costa Rica*. Westport, CT: Bergin & Garvey, 1998.

Rabe, Stephen. *The Killing Zone: The United States Wages Cold War in Latin America*. New York: Oxford University Press, 2012.

Recovery of Historical Memory Project. *Guatemala: Never Again! The Official Report of the Human Rights Office of the Archdiocese of Guatemala.* Translated by Gretta Tovar Siebentritt. Maryknoll, NY: Orbis Books, 1999.

Risse, Thomas, and Kathryn Sikkink. "The Socialization of International Human Rights Norms into Domestic Practices: Introduction." In *The Power of Human Rights: International Norms and Domestic Change,* edited by Thomas Risse, Stephen C. Ropp, and Kathryn Sikkink, 1–38. Cambridge: Cambridge University Press, 1999.

Rocha, José Luis. *La desobediencia de las masas: La migración no autorizada de centroamericanos a Estados Unidos como desobediencia civil.* San Salvador: UCA Editores, 2017.

Rodriguez, Mirthele, and Equipo de Educación Maíz. *Educación popular: Una metodología.* Panama City: Instituto Cooperativo Interamericano, 1997.

Rollemberg, Denise. "The Brazilian Exile Experience: Remaking Identities." *Latin American Perspectives* 34, no. 4 (July 2007): 198–212.

Roniger, Luis, James N. Green, and Pablo Yankelevich, eds. *Exile and the Politics of Exclusion in the Americas.* East Sussex: Sussex Academic Press, 2012.

Rosa, Herman, and Michael Foley. "El Salvador." In *Good Intentions: Pledges of Aid for Postconflict Recovery,* edited by Shepard Forman and Stewart Patrick, 113–57. Boulder, CO: Lynne Rienner, 2000.

Rosen, Fred. "Introduction." In *Empire and Dissent: The United States and Latin America,* edited by Fred Rosen, 1–19. Durham, NC: Duke University Press, 2008.

Rubin, Jeffrey W. "Meanings and Mobilizations: A Cultural Politics Approach to Social Movements and States." *Latin American Research Review* 39, no. 3 (October 2004): 106–42.

Salazar, Armando, and María del Carmen Cruz. *CCR: Organización y lucha popular en Chalatenango.* San Salvador: Asociación de Comunidades para el Desarrollo de Chalatenango, 2012.

Saldívar, José David. *Trans-Americanity: Subaltern Modernities, Global Coloniality, and the Cultures of Greater Mexico.* Durham, NC: Duke University Press, 2012.

Salomon, Kim. "The Peace Movement—An Anti-Establishment Movement." *Journal of Peace Research* 23, no. 2 (1986): 115–27.

Sassen, Saskia. "The Repositioning of Citizenship: Emergent Subjects and Spaces for Politics." *Berkeley Journal of Sociology* 46 (2002): 4–26.

Sattamini, Lina Penna, and James N. Green, eds. *A Mother's Cry: A Memoir of Politics, Prison, and Torture under the Brazilian Military Dictatorship.* Durham, NC: Duke University Press, 2010.

Scammell, Madeleine K., Caryn M. Sennett, Zoe E. Petropoulos, Jeanne Kamal, and James S. Kaufman. "Environmental and Occupational Exposures in Kidney Disease." *Seminars in Nephrology* 39, no. 3 (May 2019): 230–43.

Scheper-Hughes, Nancy, and Philippe Bourgois, eds. *Violence in War and Peace.* West Sussex: Blackwell, 2009.

Schmidli, William Michael. *The State of Freedom Elsewhere: Human Rights and U.S. Cold War Policy toward Argentina.* Ithaca, NY: Cornell University Press, 2013.

Scholz, Sally J. *Political Solidarity*. University Park: Pennsylvania State University Press, 2008.

Schrading, Roger. *El movimiento de repoblación en El Salvador*. San José: Instituto Interamericano de Derechos Humanos, 1991.

Schuld, Leslie. "El Salvador: Who Will Have the Hospitals?" *NACLA Report on the Americas* 36, no. 4 (January/February 2003): 42–45.

Scigliano, Eric. "Sisterhood." *New Republic* 207 (1992): 12–13.

Scott, James C. *Domination and the Arts of Resistance: Hidden Transcripts*. New Haven, CT: Yale University Press, 1990.

Seagle, Charles Hanford. "Is This What We Wanted to Support? Figured Worlds of Local Politics, Development, and Sister Community Relations of Nicaraguans and Americans." PhD diss., University of North Carolina, 2003.

Segovia, Alexander. "Macroeconomic Performance and Policies Since 1989." In *Economic Policy for Building Peace: The Lessons of El Salvador*, edited by James K. Boyce, 51–72. Boulder, CO: Lynne Rienner, 1996.

Servicio Jesuita para el Desarrollo "Pedro Arrupe." *Tiempo de recordar y tiempo de contar: Testimonios de comunidades repatriadas y reubicadas de El Salvador*. San Salvador: SJDPA, 1994.

Shaffer, Deborah, director. *Witness to War: Dr. Charlie Clements*. Skylight Pictures, 1985.

Shuman, Michael H. "Dateline Main Street: Local Foreign Policies." *Foreign Policy* 65 (Winter 1986–87): 154–74.

Sibrián, Keny, ed. *Aún luchamos: La historia del pueblo de Arcatao, su organización y su lucha durante el conflicto armado salvadoreño*. San Salvador: Instituto de Derechos Humanos, Universidad Centroamericana "José Simeón Cañas," 2016.

Sikkink, Kathryn. *The Justice Cascade: How Human Rights Prosecutions Are Changing World Politics*. New York: W. W. Norton, 2012.

Sikkink, Kathryn. "Patterns of Dynamic Multilevel Governance and the Insider-Outsider Coalition." In *Transnational Protest and Global Activism*, edited by Donatella della Porta and Sidney Tarrow, 151–73. Lanham, MD: Rowman & Littlefield, 2005.

Silber, Irina Carlota. *Everyday Revolutionaries: Gender, Violence and Disillusionment in Post-War El Salvador*. New Brunswick, NJ: Rutgers University Press, 2004.

Skinner, Rob, and Alan Lester. "Humanitarianism and Empire: New Research Agendas." *Journal of Imperial and Commonwealth History* 40, no. 5 (December 2012): 729–47.

Smith, Christian. *Resisting Reagan: The U.S. Central America Peace Movement*. Chicago: University of Chicago Press, 1996.

Smith, Jackie, Charles Chatfield, and Ron Pagnucco, eds. *Transnational Social Movements and Global Politics: Solidarity beyond the State*. Syracuse, NY: Syracuse University Press, 1997.

Smith-Nonini, Sandy. *Healing the Body Politic: El Salvador's Popular Struggle for Health Rights from Civil War to Neoliberal Peace*. New Brunswick, NJ: Rutgers University Press, 2010.

Smith-Nonini, Sandy. "'Popular' Health and the State: Dialectics of the Peace Process in El Salvador." *Social Science Medicine* 44, no. 5 (1997): 635–45.

Spalding, Rose J. "Civil Society Engagement in Trade Negotiations: CAFTA Opposition Movements in El Salvador." *Latin American Politics and Society* 49, no. 4 (Winter 2007): 85–114.

Spalding, Rose J. "From the Streets to the Chamber: Social Movements and the Mining Ban in El Salvador." *European Review of Latin American and Caribbean Studies* 106 (July–December 2018): 47–74.

Spalding, Rose J. "Transnational Networks and National Action: El Salvador's Anti-Mining Movement." In *Transnational Activism and National Movements in Latin America: Bridging the Divide*, edited by Eduardo Silva, 23–55. New York: Routledge, 2013.

Spence, Jack, and George Vickers. *Toward a Level Playing Field? A Report on the Post-War Salvadoran Electoral Process*. Cambridge, MA: Hemisphere Initiatives, 1994.

Spence, Jack, George Vickers, and David Dye. *The Salvadoran Peace Accords and Democratization: A Three-Year Progress Report and Recommendations*. Cambridge, MA: Hemisphere Initiatives, 1995.

Spence Benson, Devyn. *Antiracism in Cuba: The Unfinished Revolution*. Chapel Hill: University of North Carolina Press, 2016.

Sprenkels, Ralph. *After Insurgency: Revolution and Electoral Politics*. Notre Dame, IN: University of Notre Dame Press, 2018.

Stahler-Sholk, Richard, Harry E. Vanden, and Marc Becker. "Introduction: New Directions in Latin American Social Movements." In *Rethinking Latin American Social Movements: Radical Action from Below*, edited by Richard Stahler-Sholk, Harry E. Vanden, and Marc Becker, 1–18. Lanham, MD: Rowman & Littlefield, 2014.

Stahler-Sholk, Richard, Harry E. Vanden, and Marc Becker, eds. *Rethinking Latin American Social Movements: Radical Action from Below*. Lanham, MD: Rowman & Littlefield, 2014.

Stanley, William Deane. "El Salvador: State-Building before and after Democratization, 1980–95." *Third World Quarterly* 27, no. 1 (2006): 101–14.

Stanley, William Deane. *The Protection Racket State: Elite Politics, Military Extortion, and Civil War in El Salvador*. Philadelphia: Temple University Press, 1996.

Stedman, Stephen John, and Fred Tanner. "Refugees as Resources in War." In *Refugee Manipulation: War, Politics, and the Abuse of Human Suffering*, edited by Stephen John Stedman and Fred Tanner, 1–16. Washington, DC: Brookings Institution, 2003.

Stern, Steve J. *Battling for Hearts and Minds: Memory Struggles in Pinochet's Chile, 1973–1988*. Durham, NC: Duke University Press, 2006.

Stern, Steve J. *Reckoning with Pinochet: The Memory Question in Democratic Chile, 1989–2006*. Durham, NC: Duke University Press, 2010.

Stern, Steve J., and Scott Straus, eds. *The Human Rights Paradox: Universality and Its Discontents*. Madison: University of Wisconsin Press, 2014.

Stites Mor, Jessica, ed. *Human Rights and Transnational Solidarity in Cold War Latin America*. Madison: University of Wisconsin Press, 2013.

Stites Mor, Jessica. "Introduction: Situating Transnational Solidarity within Critical Human Rights Studies of Cold War Latin America." In *Human Rights and*

Transnational Solidarity in Cold War Latin America, edited by Jessica Stites Mor, 3–18. Madison: University of Wisconsin Press, 2013.

Stites Mor, Jessica, and Carmen Suescun Pozas, eds. *The Art of Solidarity: Visual and Performative Politics in Cold War Latin America*. Austin: University of Texas Press, 2018.

Stjernø, Steinar. *Solidarity in Europe: The History of an Idea*. New York: Cambridge University Press, 2004.

Stoltz Chinchilla, Norma, Nora Hamilton, and James Loucky. "The Sanctuary Movement and Central American Activism in Los Angeles." *Latin American Perspectives* 36, no. 6 (November 2009): 101–13.

Striffler, Steve. *Solidarity: Latin America and the US Left in the Era of Human Rights*. London: Pluto Press, 2019.

Stuelke, Patricia. "The Reparative Politics of Central America Solidarity Movement Culture." *American Quarterly* 66, no. 3 (September 2014): 767–90.

Surbrug, Robert, Jr. *Beyond Vietnam: The Politics of Protest in Massachusetts, 1974–1990*. Amherst: University of Massachusetts Press, 2009.

Sznajder, Mario, and Luis Roniger. *The Politics of Exile in Latin America*. New York: Cambridge University Press, 2009.

Tarrow, Sidney, and Doug McAdam. "Scale Shift in Transnational Contention." In *Transnational Protest and Global Activism*, edited by Donatella della Porta and Sidney Tarrow, 121–47. Lanham, MD: Rowman & Littlefield, 2005.

Tate, Winifred. *Counting the Dead: The Culture and Politics of Human Rights Activism in Colombia*. Berkeley: University of California Press, 2007.

Terry, Fiona. *Condemned to Repeat? The Paradox of Humanitarian Action*. Ithaca, NY: Cornell University Press, 2002.

Tilley, Virginia Q. *Seeing Indians: A Study of Race, Nation, and Power in El Salvador*. Albuquerque: University of New Mexico Press, 2005.

Todd, Molly. *Beyond Displacement: Campesinos, Refugees, and Citizen Action in the Salvadoran Civil War*. Madison: University of Wisconsin Press, 2010.

Todd, Molly. "The Paradox of Transamerican Solidarity: Gender, Race, and Representation in the Guatemalan Refugee Camps of Mexico, 1980–1990." *Journal of Cold War Studies* 19, no. 4 (Spring/Summer 2017): 74–112.

Todd, Molly. "The Politics of Refuge: Salvadoran Refugees and International Aid in Honduras." In *Human Rights and Transnational Solidarity in Cold War Latin America*, edited by Jessica Stites Mor, 209–38. Madison: University of Wisconsin Press, 2014.

Todd, Molly. "'We Were Part of the Revolutionary Movement There': Wisconsin Peace Progressives and Solidarity with El Salvador in the Reagan Era." *Journal of Civil and Human Rights* 3, no. 1 (Fall 2017): 1–56.

Trinkl, John. "Struggles for Disarmament in the USA." In *Reshaping the US Left: Popular Struggles in the 1980s*, edited by Mike Davis and Michael Sprinker, 51–62. London: Verso, 1988.

Tsing, Anna. *The Mushroom at the End of the World: On the Possibility of Life in Capitalist Ruins*. Princeton, NJ: Princeton University Press, 2015.

Tula, María Teresa. *Este es mi testimonio*. San Salvador: Editorial Sombrero Azul, 1994.

United Nations Commission on the Truth for El Salvador. *From Madness to Hope: The 12-Year War in El Salvador*. San Salvador and New York: United Nations, 1993.

US–El Salvador Sister Cities. *Aquí estamos*. San Salvador: US–El Salvador Sister Cities, 2011.

U.S. Senate–Select Committee to Study Governmental Operations (Church Committee). "Alleged Assassination Plots Involving Foreign Leaders: An Interim Report." November 20, 1975.

Valencia, Ricardo J. "The Making of the White Middle-Class Radical: A Discourse Analysis of the Public Relations of the Committee in Solidarity with the People of El Salvador between 1980 and 1990." PhD diss., University of Oregon, 2018.

van der Borgh, Chris. "Decision-Making and Participation in Poverty Alleviation Programmes in Post-War Chalatenango, El Salvador." *Foro Internacional* 37, no. 1 (January–March 1997): 49–66.

Villacorta Zuluaga, Carmen Elena. "Transición a la democracia electoral y neoliberalismo en El Salvador." In *Historia y debates sobre el conflicto armado salvadoreño y sus secuelas*, edited by Jorge Juárez Ávila, 63–71. San Salvador: Instituto de Estudios Históricos, Antropológicos y Arqueológicos, 2014.

Vion, Antoine. "Europe from the Bottom Up: Town Twinning in France during the Cold War." *Contemporary European History* 11, no. 4 (2002): 623–40.

Viterna, Jocelyn. *Women in War: The Micro-Processes of Mobilization in El Salvador*. New York: Oxford University Press, 2013.

Warner, Michael, and Michael Shuman. *Citizen Diplomats: Pathfinders in Soviet-American Relations—And How You Can Join Them*. New York: Continuum, 1987.

Weber, Clare. *Visions of Solidarity: U.S. Peace Activists in Nicaragua from War to Women's Activism and Globalization*. Lanham, MD: Lexington Books, 2006.

Weiss, Thomas G. *Humanitarian Business*. Cambridge, UK: Polity, 2013.

Weiss, Thomas G. "Principles, Politics, and Humanitarian Action." *Ethics and International Affairs* 13, no. 1 (March 1999): 1–22.

Westerman, William. "Central American Refugee Testimonies and Performed Life Histories in the Sanctuary Movement." In *The International Yearbook of Oral History and Life Stories III: Migration and Identity*, edited by Rina Benmayor and Andor Skotnes, 167–81. Oxford: Oxford University Press, 1994.

Westerman, William. "Central American Refugee Testimonies and Performed Life Histories in the Sanctuary Movement." In *The Oral History Reader*, edited by Robert Perks and Alistair Thomson, 495–505. London: Routledge, 1998.

Westerman, William. "Reciprocity and the Fabric of Solidarity: Central Americans, Refugees, and Delegations in the 1980s." In *International Volunteer Tourism: Critical Reflections on Good Works in Central America*, edited by Katherine Borland and Abigail E. Adams, 39–51. New York: Palgrave Macmillan, 2013.

White, Richard Alan. *The Morass: U.S. Intervention in Central America*. New York: Harper & Row, 1984.

Williams, Virginia S. "Grassroots Movements and Witnesses for Peace: Challenging U.S. Policies in Latin America in the Post-Cold War Era." *Peace and Change* 29, nos. 3/4 (July 2004): 419–30.

Wood, Elisabeth Jean. "Agrarian Reform, Land Occupation, and the Transition to Democracy in El Salvador." In *Distributive Justice in Transitions*, edited by Morten Bergsmo, César Rodríguez-Garavito, Pablo Kalmanovitz, and Maria Paula Saffon, 141–75. Oslo: Torkel Opsahl Academic EPublisher and Peace Research Institute, 2010.

Wood, Elisabeth Jean. "Los Acuerdos de Paz y la reconstrucción de posguerra." In *Ajuste hacia la paz: La política económica y la reconstrucción de posguerra en El Salvador*, edited by James K. Boyce et al., 103–40. Mexico City: Programa de las Naciones Unidas para el Desarrollo and Plaza y Valdés, 1999.

Wood, Elisabeth Jean. *Insurgent Collective Action and Civil War in El Salvador*. New York: Cambridge University Press, 2003.

World Bank. *El Salvador: Rural Development Study*. Washington, DC: Latin America and the Caribbean Regional Office, World Bank, 1998.

Wright, Thomas C., and Rody Oñate. *Flight from Chile: Voices of Exile*. Albuquerque: University of New Mexico Press, 1998.

Zelinsky, Wilbur. "The Twinning of the World: Sister Cities in Geographic and Historical Perspective." *Annals of the Association of American Geographers* 81, no. 1 (1991): 1–31.

Zolberg, Aristide, Astri Suhrke, and Sergio Aguayo. *Escape from Violence: Conflict and the Refugee Crisis in the Developing World*. New York: Oxford University Press, 1989.

Index

abductions, 109. *See also* disappearances

abortion, 137

Abrams, Elliot, 62

accompaniment: delegations and, 71–72; imperialism and, 18; military blockades and, 116; privilege and, 78; repopulation movements and, 41; rights and, 26; sistering and, 5, 8, 39–51, 135. *See also* witnessing

activism. *See* solidarity activism

Activists beyond Borders (Keck and Sikkink), 190

aesthetics, 77–78

affective networks, 14. *See also* fictive kinship

African Americans, xi, 37, 183. *See also* Black people

Agenda for Peace in El Salvador, 112, 131

Agrarian Reform Law, 161

Agrarian Sector Reactivation Law, 163

Agricultural Development Bank, 148–54

Agricultural Sector Reform and Investment Project, 160

agriculture: collectives and, 31–34, 86, 124, 168; land transfer and, 139, 145–69; neoliberalism and, 140–46, 159–66, 182; solidarity activism and, 50, 107–8, 141, 184–87. *See also* land reform

agro-export economics, 140–46

Alfaro, Marta Cerna, 155

Alliance for Progress, 8, 30–31, 35, 50

Alternative Financial System, 157–58

Alvarado, Barbara, 166

Álvarez, Antonio, 154

The American Connection: State Terror and Popular Resistance in El Salvador (McClintock), 82

American Friends Service Committee, 47, 53

Americas Watch Committee, 68, 190

Amnesty International, 14, 72, 190

apartheid, 10

Araniva, René García, 102

Arcatao. *See* Madison-Arcatao Sister City Project

ARENA party: agriculture and the, 165–66, 169, 189; land transfer and the, 151, 156; military blockades and, 117; Salvadoran revolution and the, 138–39, 143; and the transition to peace, 108–11; voting rights and, 133

Arévalo, Juan José, 31

Arlington=Teosinte sistering relationship, 48, 156

Armed Forces of Liberation, 40

arms spending, 36–37, 63, 93

arrests, 26, 32, 60–61, 72–73, 118

Artiga Escobar, José, 45–49, 53, 58
Aruguete, Joy, 49
Asociación para el Desarrollo de El
  Salvador. *See* CRIPDES
assassinations, 26, 30, 82, 109
Association for the Development of El
  Salvador. *See* CRIPDES
Association of Communities for the
  Development of Chalatengo. *See* CCR
Atwood, Brian, 167
authoritarianism, 10, 32–33, 73, 86–87,
  108, 123–24
Avelar, José Alberto, 180
Ayala, Juan Francisco Durán, 182

Bach, Leo, 98
Bangor-Carasque sistering relationship,
  75, 184
Barber, Prudence, 96
Barnard, Juliana, 7
Barnes, Michael, 57
Barnett, Michael, 17
Batista, Fulgecio, 35
Baum, Dawn, 134
Baum, Mary Kay, 3–4, 42, 56–57, 73,
  88–90, 132, 194
Beck, Erin, 188–90
Becker, Marc, 190
Belmont–El Higueral sistering
  relationship, 48, 97
Berkeley Gazette, 43
Berkeley–San Antonio Los Ranchos
  Sister City, 43, 58–60, 71–72, 86, 92,
  98
Berkeley Voice, 86, 92
Berwick, Jeannie, 89–90
BFA. *See* Agricultural Development
  Bank
blacklisting, 115, 119–20
Black people, 10, 36, 136. *See also* African
  Americans
blockades. *See* military blockades
Bloque Popular Revolucionario, 32

Bollier, David, 13
bombings, 72
Bonner, Raymond, 68
Boston Coalition to Support the Peace
  Accords, 131
Boston Globe, 119–20
Boston Globe Magazine, 120
Bouchey, L. Francis, 63
Boutros-Ghali, Boutros, 125, 128
Bowdler, William, 68
boycotts, 132–33
Breilid, Erik, 57
Brown, Robert McAfee, 5
Bush, George H. W., xii, 93, 111

Cáceres, Jesús, 73
CAFTA. *See* Central American Free
  Trade Agreement
CALA, 37–38, 52, 136
Calderón Sol, Armando, 165
Cambridge–Las Flores Sister Cities
  Project, 44, 48, 53–54, 58, 72–73, 83,
  99–100, 109–20, 165–66
campesinos, 65, 148–49, 154, 159, 161–63.
  See also rural people
Canclini, Néstor García, 12, 106
capitalism, 32, 39, 42, 140, 143, 186
Carasque. *See* Bangor-Carasque sistering
  relationship
caravans, 93, 99–100, 152, 179. *See also*
  migrant caravans; tours
CARECEN, 47, 131
Cartagena, Manuel, 59, 72, 110
Carter, Jimmy, 28, 30–31, 35, 68, 216n9
Casa El Salvador, 45–46, 49
Castro, Fidel, 35, 37
the Catholic Church, 33–35, 39–40, 123
CCR, 66, 109, 126, 128, 155, 168
Center for Democracy in the Americas,
  131
Central American Free Trade Agreement,
  182, 188
Central American Peace Plan, 110

constitutional reforms, 111, 127
consumer safety, 36
contact zones, 16
Contadora Group, 110
Conyers, John, 62
cooperation, 4, 32, 146
cooperatives, 123–24, 126, 161
Coordinator of Communities and
Repopulations of Chalatenango. *See*
CCR
Copapayo. *See* Columbus-Copapayo
Sister City Project
CORDES, 135–37, 140–45, 153–55, 158,
162–64, 168
corporations, 36. *See also* multinational
corporations
Council for Inter-American Security,
62–63
Council for World Freedom, 63
counterinsurgency, 30
coups, 37, 182. *See also* military coups
Coutin, Susan Bibler, 38
CRIPDES: agriculture and, 162–65,
167–68; delegations and, 72–74, 85;
health care and, 173–77; land transfer
and, 152–53, 158; military blockades
and, 113–14, 117, 120; politics of sistering and, 55, 59–61; repopulation
movements and, 39–41, 44–45, 50,
76–77; Salvadoran revolution and,
139, 143–46; solidarity activism and,
xiii, xvi, 20, 97–103, 180–87, 193–95;
and the transition to peace, 109–12;
voting rights and, 124–25, 128–31
CRIPDES-CNR. *See* CNR; CRIPDES
Cristiani, Alfredo, xii, 109, 111, 131, 143, 151
Cruz, Miguel Antonio, 60
the Cuban Revolution, 10, 37
customs. *See* immigration

D'Aubuisson Group, 151
Dávila, Mario, 47–49, 53, 59
Davis, Paul, 115–19

Death Squad Group, 151
death squads, 82, 104, 109, 127–28
debt economics, 12, 145, 154, 159–61,
163–64, 167–68. *See also* structural
adjustment programs
decentralization, 12
del Castillo, Graciana, 140
delegations: imperialism and, 90–96;
land transfer and, 153; and the
limits of solidarity, 96–104; military
blockades and, 114–23; politics and,
52, 56–60; privilege and, 78–90;
public education and, 67–78; sistering
and, 43–49; solidarity activism and,
xiii, xiv, 104–6, 136, 191; voting rights
and, 132. *See also* tours; travel
DeLoughy, David, 100
demilitarization, 108, 116, 123. *See also*
disarmament
democracy: delegations and, 79, 86, 89,
91; education and, 77; imperialism
and, 20; military blockades and, 113;
repopulation movements and, 39,
42; rights and, 25–29; Salvadoran
revolution and, 145; sistering and,
6–7, 11, 23, 50, 90; and the transition
to peace, 107–12; US imperialism
and, 10, 30, 34, 36; voting rights and,
123–34
Democratic Campesino Alliance, 163
democratic socialism, 10
Democrats, 36
depopulation, 7, 25, 39, 57. *See also*
repopulation movements
deportation, 38, 60, 115, 118, 183–84
de Soto, Álvaro, 138, 140, 163
detention, 38, 85, 109. *See also*
imprisonment; incarceration
development: collective, 86; land transfer
and, 147, 155, 157–58; Salvadoran
revolution and, 139–42, 145–46;
self-government and, 112; sistering
and, 8, 44, 50, 64, 98, 185; US

imperialism and, 31; voting rights and, 129, 131
de Witte, Michaël, 116
dictatorships, xi, 10, 14, 25, 35, 37, 109
diplomacy, 4, 15, 29, 119–20, 135, 190
direct action, 53–54
directivas. *See* community councils
dirty wars, 5
disappearances: delegations and, 73, 85, 91; repopulation and, 26; Salvadoran government and, 109; sistering and, 4–5, 10
disarmament, 110
disease, 114, 172, 184
Diskin, Martin, 82
displacement: agriculture and, 161; delegations and, 73; depopulation and, 39, 72; land transfer and, 147–48; military blockades and, 113; repopulation movements and, 42, 46; rights and, 24–25, 29; Salvadoran revolution and, 144; sistering and, 4–5, 14, 61, 63; and the transition to peace, 110; voting rights and, 124. *See also* exiles; refugees
documentation, 38, 80, 85, 113–14, 119, 126, 129–30
Duarte, José Napoleón: delegations and, 73, 91; military blockades and, 114; politics of sistering and, 55–57; repopulation movements and, 39; sistering and, 4; solidarity activism and, 99; and the transition to peace, 108, 112
Duffy, Richard, xv

Earle, Anthony S., 38
economic aid, 5, 43, 98, 106, 131, 160. *See also* international aid; military aid
economic rights, 39, 107, 140. *See also* rights
education: agriculture and, 161, 169; delegations and, 71–74; military

blockades and, 114; popular, 65–66, 216n5; privilege and, 78–90; repopulation movements and, 42; Salvadoran revolution and, 141–43, 145; sistering and, 3–5, 14, 50; solidarity activism and, 67–70, 96–106, 171, 174–77, 185, 187; tours and, 74–78; and the transition to peace, 107, 110; in the US, xi–xii; US imperialism and, 31–32, 37, 90–96, 217n17; voting rights and, 129–31
Educational Consultative Group of El Salvador, 171–72
egalitarianism, 158
Eisenhower, Dwight D., 49
the elderly, 56, 116
elections, 7, 30–32, 36, 64, 107, 123–34, 139, 185
electricity, 31, 142–43, 150
El Higueral. *See* Belmont–El Higueral sistering relationship
Ellacuría, Ignacio, 32–33
El Mozote massacre, 68
El Mundo, 4, 99, 102
El Rescate, 51
El Salvador government: agriculture and the, 161, 163; delegations and the, 73, 77–85, 100; land transfer and the, 147–48, 154; military blockades and the, 113–23; negotiated revolution and, 138; politics of sistering and the, 56–62; repopulation and the, 26, 45, 96; revolution and the, 138–42, 145; rights and the, 25–26; sistering and the, 54, 64, 90; solidarity activism and the, 104; and the transition to peace, 107, 110, 113; US imperialism and the, 33; violence and the, 76; voting rights and the, 123–34
empathy, 17, 68–69, 78–79, 81
empire. *See* United States imperialism
employment, 37, 139, 143
the environment, 145, 184, 190

Equipo Maíz, 66
Esquipulas Process, 110, 114–15
ethnicity, 19
exclusion, 39, 64, 117, 119–20, 180
exiles, 16, 45–47, 63, 124, 150, 191. *See also* displacement; refugees
export markets, 31

Fair Play for Cuba Committee, 37
faith-based organizing: education and, 65; military blockades and, 114–17, 121, 123; politics of sistering and, 54; repopulation movements and, 42, 46; sanctuary movements and, 14; sistering and, 51; solidarity activism and, 43; US imperialism and, 37–38. *See also* Christian base communities
Farabundo Martí National Liberation Front. *See* FMLN
Farabundo Youth group, 131
farmers, 161. *See also* agriculture; campesinos
Farm Labor, 36
Fast for Life, 95
Fast for Peace, 95
Federación de Trabajadores del Campo. *See* Federation of Rural Workers
Federal Bureau of Investigation, 60
Federation of Rural Workers, 35
Federici, Silvia, 12
Fellowship of Reconciliation, 8–9
fictive kinship, 13, 16, 105, 135, 191
Fife, John, 62
Fischer, John, 115, 121–23
Flynn, Shelagh, 131
FMLN: agriculture and the, 160–63; delegations and the, 81, 83, 86–87, 92; health care and the, 170–74; imperialism and the, 21; land transfer and the, 147, 149–50, 154, 156; military blockades and the, 115–16, 120–21; politics of sistering and the, 51–55, 58–59, 62; public education and the,

66–68, 77; repopulation movements and the, 39–40, 73; rights and the, 25, 28; Salvadoran revolution and the, 138–39, 142; sistering and the, 3–4, 6–7, 15; solidarity activism and the, 98, 180–85, 192–93; and the transition to peace, 107–8, 111–13; US imperialism and the, 33–34, 36; voting rights and the, 124–28, 131, 133
food aid, 41, 73, 114–16, 141, 143, 145
Foundation for Cooperation and Communal Development of El Salvador. *See* CORDES
Foundation for Cooperation with Salvadoran Repopulators and Displaced. *See* CORDES
FPL: delegations and the, 87, 89, 92; education and the, 68; imperialism and the, 22; politics of sistering and the, 51–52, 58–59; repopulation movements and the, 40, 45–47; sistering and the, 14–15, 63; solidarity activism and the, 43, 47–48; US imperialism and, 32–34; voting rights and the, 124–25
free speech, 36
free trade, 182
Freire, Paulo, 66
Freireich, Susan, 73, 117, 119
Frente Unido de Acción Revolucionaria. *See* FUAR
FUAR, 34–35
Fuerzas Populares de Liberación Nacional. *See* FPL
fund-raising, 42–44, 47–48, 62, 95–96. *See also* charity
Funes, Mauricio, 180

Galeano, Eduardo, 82
gang violence, 183
Gárate, Gorka, 142
García, Enrique, 137
Gelbspan, Ross, 120

human rights (*continued*)
  movements and, 26, 45, 50–51;
  Salvadoran revolution and, 140–41;
  sistering and, 4–11, 14, 43, 46, 64;
  solidarity activism and, 104–5; testimony and, 74, 77; and the transition
  to peace, 107, 109; transnational
  solidarity and, 48; US imperialism
  and, xii, 35
Human Rights Accord, 111, 120
Human Rights Commission of El
  Salvador, 85
Human Rights Watch, 184
The Hundredth Monkey (Keyes), xii
hunger strikes, 95, 118–19
Hurricane Mitch, 167

identity, 19
Immediate Reaction Infantry Battalions,
  xii
immigration, 36, 38, 60, 118–19, 122
Imperial Eyes (Pratt), 16
imperialism. *See* United States
  imperialism
imprisonment, 71–72, 76. *See also*
  detention; incarceration; political
  prisoners
incarceration, xi. *See also* detention;
  imprisonment; political prisoners
Indians, 136
indigenous people, 190
individualism, 10–11, 146
infrastructure, 141–43, 145, 147–48, 150,
  169
Inter-American Affairs, 62, 153, 155
Inter-American Development Bank, 167
Interfaith Office for Accompaniment,
  45–49, 53, 67
Interinstitutional Coordinating
  Committee, 112, 145
Internal Revenue Service. *See* IRS
international aid: military blockades
  and, 113–23; repopulation and, 40;

Salvadoran revolution and, 142, 146;
  sistering and, 64, 112; US imperialism
  and, 29–30, 82, 93–95. *See also*
  humanitarian aid; military aid
International Association of Machinists,
  36
International Center for Settlement of
  Investment Disputes, 182
International Conference on Central
  American Refugees, 110
international finance institutions,
  143, 159–60. *See also* International
  Monetary Fund; World Bank
internationalism, 49
international law, 55, 57, 114
International Monetary Fund, 12, 140,
  167. *See also* international finance
  institutions
international solidarity. *See* solidarity
  activism
interventionism. *See* United States
  imperialism
In the Name of the People (documentary),
  81
IOA. *See* Interfaith Office for
  Accompaniment
Iraheta, Leah, 87
Iran-Contra scandal, 60–63
irrigation, 158
IRS, 60, 63

Jim Crow, 37
Johnston, Catie, 192
journalism, 92. *See also* media

Keck, Margaret, 188
Kelly, Patrick William, 9–10, 17
Kennedy, John F., 30, 49–50
Kennedy, Joseph P. III, 115, 117–18, 120
Kennedy, Ted, 57
Kerry, John, 57, 118
killings, xii, 4–5, 73, 91, 109, 182. *See also*
  massacres

MASCP. *See* Madison-Arcatao Sister
City Project
massacres: delegations and, 68, 86;
refugees and, 24; Salvadoran
government and, 109, 111; the
Salvadoran government and, 33;
sistering and, 5, 64; US imperialism
and, xii. *See also* killings
mass returns, 72, 114, 141. *See also*
repopulation movements
Matthews, Karen, 43
McClintock, Michael, 82
McClure, James, 62–63
McCormick, Thomas, xii
McCoy, Al, xii
McCullom, William, 62–63
McFadden, Michael, 100, 102
Médecins sans Frontières, 17
media, 77, 91–92, 119–20, 132, 163; and
journalism, 92
medical aid, 38, 42, 73, 114–16, 121–22,
170–77
Medical Aid to Central America, 136,
170
Medical Aid to El Salvador, 62
Meiselas, Susan, 68
Mejía, José Antonio, 170
Mejía, Miguel, 60–61
Mélida Anaya Montes women's
organization, 131
Menjívar, Agustín, 6
mental health, 86
Merio, Jairo, 151
Merkt, Stacy, 62
Mesa Grande refugee camp, 24–28, 40,
55, 65, 72, 102, 114, 170–71
Metzi, Francisco, 81
Mexican Americans, 182
Mexico Accord, 111
Meyers, Jan, 128
migrant caravans, 26, 42, 183
migration, 183–84
militant organizations, 33

militarization, 63, 86
military aid: public education and, 95;
sistering and, 5, 51, 53; US imperialism
and, xi, xii, 31, 35, 43, 106. *See also*
international aid
military blockades, 113–23, 171
military coups, 30
military dictatorships. *See* dictatorships
military embargoes, 114
Mills, Jack, 114
minimum wage, 32
mining, xiii, xiv, 182, 189, 194
Moakley, Joseph, 118
Molina, Arturo, 32
Monge, Milton, 4, 184–85
Monroe, James, 29
Monroe Doctrine, 30
Monsanto, 182
Montalvo, Rafael, 153
Moody, Jim, 115, 120–22
morality, 54–55, 89
Morgan, Ron, 49
Moyne, Samuel, 10
multinational corporations, xiv
Municipalities in Action, 143
mutual-aid societies, 32
Myers, Ron, 114

NAFTA. *See* North American Free Trade
Agreement
National Advocacy Day, 131
National Center for US–El Salvador
Sister Cities, 44, 131, 133, 152–53
National Consultation of Aid
Institutions and Organizations of
Refugee . . . , 112
National Coordination of Repopulations.
See CNR
National Debate for Peace in El Salvador,
110–12, 139–40, 143
National Development Plan, 142
National Forum for the Defense and
Recovery of the Agrarian Sector, 162

nationalism, 16
National Reconstruction Plan, 141–43,
    145–46, 149, 153, 160, 163
National Republican Alliance party. *See*
    ARENA party
nation-states, 106
Navidad, Ruth, 74–75, 95
negotiation, 138–41
neoliberalism, 17, 21, 127, 140–44, 147,
    159–69, 183–86, 192–94
Neoliberalism for Beginners (CRIPDES),
    144
NEST: delegations and, 72–73, 86;
    military blockades and, 115; politics
    of sistering and, 51–55, 58–59, 62–63;
    public education and, 67, 96;
    repopulation movements and, 46,
    49–50; sistering and, 4, 43–44;
    solidarity activism and, 97–99,
    102–3, 136; and the transition to
    peace, 112
New El Salvador Today Foundation.
    See NEST
New Initiative for Popular Self-
    Development, 112, 145–46, 157, 169
New Jersey–Los Amates Sister City
    Project, 47
Newport, Eugene "Gus," 86–88, 92
New York Times, 127, 138
Nicaraguan Contras, 63. *See also*
    Iran-Contra scandal
Nicaraguan Revolution, 111
Nichols, Matt, 58–59
Nixon, Richard, 30–31
No More Deaths, 42
nongovernmental organizations, 17,
    39–40, 66, 131, 145, 188–90
nonviolence, 7, 59, 63
North American Congress on Latin
    America, 38
North American Free Trade Agreement,
    182, 191
Northern Longitudinal Highway, 187

not-for-profit organizations, 38
nuclear war, xi–xii, 37
"Nuestra América" (Martí), 12

occupations, 32–33, 36, 109, 163
Oceana Gold, xiv, 182
Olesen, Thomas, 191
oligarchies, 25, 32–35
Oñate-Madrazo, Andrea, 15
Open Veins of Latin America (Galeano),
    82
Operation Sojourner, 60–61
Orellana, Inocente, 60–61
Orellana, Salvador, 140–45
Orero, Eudald Cortina, 15
Organization of American States, 14
Ortega, Esperanza, 6
"Our America" (Martí), 12

Pacific Rim, xiv
Pan American Health Organization, 173
paramilitary organizations, 30, 72, 82
Partners of the Americas, 7–8, 49–50
The Past Is Not History (film), xv
peace accords, xii, 21, 44, 107–33, 138–42,
    146, 150–51, 155–61
Peace Brigades International, 8–9, 67, 69
Pearce, Jenny, xv, 81
peasant federations, 85
pedagogy, 78–90, 217n17
Pedagogy of the Oppressed (Freire), 66
Peñate, Oscar Martínez, 15, 151
The People's Remedy (Metzi), 81
People's Revolutionary Army, 40
people-to-people exchanges, 69, 95–96,
    104, 191, 195
People-to-People Program, 7, 49
Peronism, 10
Philadelphia–Las Anonas sistering
    relationship, 49, 181
Phoenix operation, 56, 73
phone tapping, 60, 83–84. *See also*
    harassment

and, 97–103; voting rights and, 124, 126, 130–33. *See also* depopulation
Report on Human Rights in El Salvador (Americas Watch Committee), 68
revolutionary movements, 10, 20, 54, 58, 138–41, 177–78
Revolutionary Party of Central American Workers, 40
Reynolds, John, 50
Ricciuti, Nick, 119
the Right, 108, 131–32. *See also* ARENA party
rights: education and, 77; land transfer and, 152; repopulation movements and, 46; Salvadoran revolution and, 140–41; sistering and, 7, 55; and the transition to peace, 107. *See also* civil rights; economic rights; human rights; voting rights
Ring, Michael, 20, 58, 87, 104, 110, 167–68
Rivas-Gallont, Ernesto, 119
Rivera, Guillermo, 153
Rivera, Marcelo, 182
Rivera, Rosa, xiii–xv, 22
Rivera y Damas, Arturo, 110, 121
Rogers, William, 68
Rojas, Jesús, 87
Romero, Óscar, 35, 82
Roosevelt, Theodore, 30
Rosenthal, Marc, 29, 42, 52–54, 60, 96, 115, 120–23, 185, 192–93
Rothko Chapel, 71
Rousseff, Dilma, 182
Rubio, Gilberto, 121
Ruíz, Tomasa, 124, 145, 147
rural activism: agriculture and, 167–68; imperialism and, 20; land transfer and, 151–53, 156, 158; rights and, 169–70; Salvadoran revolution and, 139, 141, 146; and the transition to peace, 107; US imperialism and, 34, 86. *See also* repopulation movements

rural people, 112, 138–58. *See also* campesinos; rural activism
Russell, Daniel, 117, 192–93
Ryan, Nancy, 100, 116–19, 154

Saldívar, José David, 12
Salvadoran Communist Party, 33
Salvadoran Humanitarian Aid, Research and Education Foundation. *See* SHARE
Salvadoran Human Rights Commission, 91
Salvadoran military: blockades and the, 113–24; depopulation and the, 25; politics of sistering and the, 55–57; sistering and the, 3, 54; and the transition to peace, 108, 112
Salvadorans for Peace with Justice Caravan, 95
San Antonio Los Ranchos. *See* Berkeley–San Antonio Los Ranchos Sister City
sanctuary movements: politics and, 60–62; refugees and, 68; repopulation and, 42; sistering and, 97, 212n107; solidarity movements and, 8–9, 14, 38, 45–46, 103
Sandinista National Liberation Front, 6, 10, 28, 35, 50, 191, 213n116
Sandino, Augusto, 31
San José Las Flores. *See* Cambridge–Las Flores Sister Cities Project
Santa María Madre de los Pobres Medical Center, 173
Santos, Pepe, 156
Sassen, Saskia, 78, 106
Schaibel, Barbara, 49
Schear, Tracey, 4, 43, 49, 98
schools. *See* education
Schultz, Gustav, 46, 49, 71
Scondras, David, 114
scorched-earth operations, xv, 24, 39, 64, 71, 88–89
Scott, James, 80

St. Francis House Episcopal Church, 38
"Stop the Invasion of Our Sister Cities"
  campaign, 72
strikes, 32, 36
structural adjustment programs, 12, 139,
  159–60, 167. *See also* debt economics
student activists, 33, 36–38, 42
study-abroad programs, 69. *See also*
  service-learning programs; travel
Stuelke, Patricia, 77–78
summits, 44, 142, 181
Supreme Electoral Tribunal, 127–29,
  132–34
surveillance, 26, 32, 60
Surviving Historic Memory Committee,
  xv, xvi
sustainable development. *See*
  development

Tate, Winifred, 89
tax audits, 63
technology, 50, 146
tenedores, 147–50
Teosinte. *See* Arlington–Teosinte
  sistering relationship
terrorism, 26, 29–30, 53, 62–64, 77, 88,
  118–22, 128–32
Terry, Fiona, 17
testimony, 74–78, 88–89
Thale, Geoff, 102
Tobar, Julio, 76–77, 95, 103, 153
Tobar, Milagro, 153
Topp, Margaret, 79
torture: education and, 76; imperialism
  and, 19; politics of sistering and,
  55, 59–61; repopulation and, 26;
  Salvadoran government and, 109;
  sistering and, 10, 71; US imperialism
  and, 5
tourism, 162. *See also* travel; voluntourism
tours, 68, 71, 74–78, 90, 153, 191. *See also*
  delegations; travel
trade, 159

trade unions, 85. *See also* unions
Trans-Americanity, 12
Transition to Democracy Campaign, 131
transnational solidarity. *See* solidarity
  activism
travel, 9, 68–69, 80–82, 95, 115–22.
  See also delegations; service-learning
  programs; study-abroad programs;
  tourism; tours; voluntourism
Trouble in Our Backyard (Diskin), 82
Trump, Donald, 184, 193
26th of July Movement, 35

unemployment. *See* employment
Union of Rural Workers, 33–34
unions, 32, 66, 68, 85. *See also* labor
  movements; trade unions
United Nations: agriculture and the,
  163; imperialism and the, 17; land
  transfer and the, 147–48, 152–53;
  negotiated revolution and the, 138;
  repopulation movements and the, 46;
  rights and the, 26; sistering and the,
  59; solidarity activism and the, 14;
  and the transition to peace, 107, 111;
  voting rights and the, 125–28, 131, 133
United Revolutionary Action Front. *See*
  FUAR
United States government, 119–23. *See
  also* specific presidents
United States imperialism: delegations
  and, 79, 81–82, 88–89; dissent and,
  29–39; politics of sistering and, 56–59,
  63; privilege and, 105, 123; public
  education and, 65, 69, 131; repopulation movements and, 45–46, 96;
  Salvador revolution and, 140, 143;
  sistering and, 5–9, 11, 43, 50–51, 64,
  90; solidarity activism and, 99–100,
  103–6, 137, 179–95; and the transition
  to peace, 111–12; the transition to
  peace and, 107
United States military, 36–37

Urioste, Monsignor Ricardo, 53
US Agency for International Development. *See* USAID
USAID, 105–6, 143, 153–54, 160, 167–68
US–Central America solidarity. *See* solidarity activism
US Congressional Arms Control and Foreign Policy Caucus, 108
USESSC. *See* Sister Cities
US immigration, 38
US–Nicaragua Friendship Conference, 50
Utech, Jennifer, 154

Vanden, Harry, 190
Vernier, Alice, 157
Vicaría de la Solidaridad, 14
victimhood, 19, 21, 28, 55, 78, 104–5
Vietnam War, xi, 36–38
violence: delegations and, 79, 85, 89; imperialism and, 18; land transfer and, 158; military aid and, 35; Salvadoran revolution and, 140; sistering and, 5, 14, 57; state-sponsored, 76–77, 87, 95, 108–10; US imperialism and, 28; voting rights and, 127–28, 131, 133
visibility, 18
Voices on the Border, 67
voluntourism, 69, 217n17. *See also* tourism; travel
voting rights, 123–34

Walker, William, 119
Wallace, Jim, 100, 102, 117–20
Wallace, Julia, 118
War on Drugs, xi
water, 31, 169, 184
Watson, Alexander, 153, 155
Weakland, Rembert, 115, 121

wealth distribution, xvii, 31, 98, 139–42, 147–50, 156, 173
Westerman, William, 69, 77
Western Hemisphere Subcommittee, 57
whiteness, 17–18, 38, 136
WICOCA. *See* Wisconsin Coordinating Committee on Central America
Williams, Dick, 93
Winpisinger, William, 36
Wisconsin Coordinating Committee on Central America, 46, 49, 60, 122
Wisconsin Coordinating Council on Nicaragua, 50
Wisconsin Council of Churches, 115
Wisconsin Interfaith Committee on Central America, 50, 67
Wisconsin–Nicaragua Partners of the Americas, 50
Wisconsin State Journal, 92
Wisconsin Witness for Peace, 136
Witness for Peace, 8–9, 67, 69, 216n8
witnessing, 5. *See also* accompaniment; testimony
Witness to War (Clements), 15
women, 36, 41–42, 56, 76, 85, 116, 131, 137, 158, 190
Women's Association of El Salvador, 85
women's rights, 68
Wood, Elizabeth, 31, 142
workers, 32, 76, 85, 137
World Bank, 12, 159–60, 166–68, 182, 185–86. *See also* international finance institutions
World Social Forum, 23
Wysockey, Kathryn, 116

Zapatistas, 19, 191
Zepeda, Juan Orlando, 83

Critical Human Rights

From War to Genocide: Criminal Politics in Rwanda, 1990–1994
ANDRÉ GUICHAOUA; translated by DON E. WEBSTER

Innocence and Victimhood: Gender, Nation, and Women's Activism in Postwar Bosnia-Herzegovina
ELISSA HELMS

Inside Rwanda's "Gacaca" Courts: Seeking Justice after Genocide
BERT INGELAERE

Amending the Past: Europe's Holocaust Commissions and the Right to History
ALEXANDER KARN

Civil Obedience: Complicity and Complacency in Chile since Pinochet
MICHAEL J. LAZZARA

Torture and Impunity
ALFRED W. MCCOY

Elusive Justice: Women, Land Rights, and Colombia's Transition to Peace
DONNY MEERTENS

Conflicted Memory: Military Cultural Interventions and the Human Rights Era in Peru
CYNTHIA E. MILTON

Historical Justice and Memory
Edited by KLAUS NEUMANN and JANNA THOMPSON

The Wars inside Chile's Barracks: Remembering Military Service under Pinochet
LEITH PASSMORE

Buried Histories: The Anti-Communist Massacres of 1965–1966 in Indonesia
JOHN ROOSA

The Human Rights Paradox: Universality and Its Discontents
Edited by STEVE J. STERN and SCOTT STRAUS

Human Rights and Transnational Solidarity in Cold War Latin America
Edited by JESSICA STITES MOR

Remaking Rwanda: State Building and Human Rights after Mass Violence
Edited by SCOTT STRAUS and LARS WALDORF

Long Journey to Justice: El Salvador, the United States, and Struggles against Empire
MOLLY TODD

Beyond Displacement: Campesinos, Refugees, and Collective Action in the Salvadoran Civil War
MOLLY TODD

The Social Origins of Human Rights: Protesting Political Violence in Colombia's Oil Capital, 1919–2010
LUIS VAN ISSCHOT

The Soviet Union and the Gutting of the UN Genocide Convention
ANTON WEISS-WENDT

The Politics of Necessity: Community Organizing and Democracy in South Africa
ELKE ZUERN